POLYNEERING

A PRACADEMIC LIFELONG LEARNING WORKBOOK

(pioneers, entrepreneurs, designers, engineers, pollinators)

M.D. Wilson & Dr. Dale Deardorff

The self is not something ready-made, but something in continuous formation through choice of action.

-John Dewey

create.mheducation.com

ISBN-13: 9781265664855

ISBN-10: 1265664854

Contents

Contents

Chronology of Entrepreneurship Education

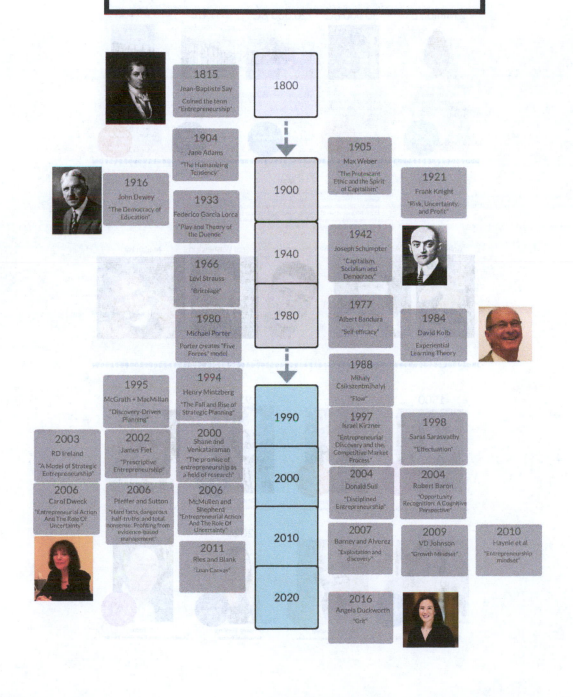

1800

1815 Jean-Baptiste Say — Coined the term "Entrepreneurship"

1904 Jane Adams — "The Humanizing Tendency"

1905 Max Weber — "The Protestant Ethic and the Spirit of Capitalism"

1916 John Dewey — "The Democracy of Education"

1921 Frank Knight — "Risk, Uncertainty, and Profit"

1933 Federico García Lorca — "Play and Theory of the Duende"

1900

1942 Joseph Schumpter — "Capitalism, Socialism and Democracy"

1940

1966 Levi Strauss — "Bricolage"

1977 Albert Bandura — "Self-efficacy"

1984 David Kolb — Experiential Learning Theory

1980

1980 Michael Porter — Porter creates "Five Forces" model

1988 Mihaly Csikszentmihalyi — "Flow"

1994 Henry Mintzberg — "The Fall and Rise of Strategic Planning"

1995 McGrath + MacMillan — "Discovery-Driven Planning"

1990

1997 Israel Kirzner — "Entrepreneurial Discovery and the Competitive Market Process"

1998 Saras Sarasvathy — "Effectuation"

2000 Shane and Venkataraman — "The promise of entrepreneurship as a field of research"

2002 James Fiet — "Prescriptive Entrepreneurship"

2003 RD Ireland — "A Model of Strategic Entrepreneurship"

2000

2004 Donald Sull — "Disciplined Entrepreneurship"

2004 Robert Baron — "Opportunity Recognition: A Cognitive Perspective"

2006 Carol Dweck — "Entrepreneurial Action And The Role Of Uncertainty"

2006 Pfeffer and Sutton — "Hard facts, dangerous half-truths and total nonsense: Profiting from evidence-based management"

2006 McMullen and Shepherd — "Entrepreneurial Action And The Role Of Uncertainty"

2010

2007 Barney and Alverez — "Exploitation and discovery"

2009 VD Johnson — "Growth Mindset"

2010 Haynie et al — "Entrepreneurship mindset"

2011 Ries and Blank — "Lean Canvas"

2020

2016 Angela Duckworth — "Grit"

A BRIEF HISTORY OF POLYNEERING

The 5 Archetypes of Polyneering

Polyneering's pillars are visible from the dawn of humanity.

2 Million B.C	50,000 BC	20,000 BC	312 BC	30 BC

The first stone tools are crafted. The birth of the *Engineering toolset*.

Engineering toolset

Cave paintings are appearing all over the world. The *pollination* of ideas is at work.

Pollinating

Hunters follow the Woolly Mammoth to North America. *Pioneering* is innately human.

Pioneering

Rome no longer has water stores to sustain population growth. The aqueducts are the result of *design thinking*.

Design Thinking

Entrepreneurship thrives as The Silk Road connects China, Southeast Asia, India, the Middle East, Africa, and Europe.

Entrepreneurial mindset

SPIRIT

A pioneer – a person frustrated, unnerved, goaded, cajoled, or otherwise fueled into taking on the unknown, at all cost – sets off into unchartered territory. The spirit comes from the gut or other jarring or harrowing corners. Either because of nature or nurture or a mad combo of both, the go-getter takes on an impending challenge or impossible problem head-on. No human legend; fictional or real, exists without the spirit.

Achilles	Amelia Earhart	Muhamamd Ali	George Washington	Madan Lal

1500	1875	1920	1920

Leonardo Da Vinci
Artist, Sculptor, Inventor and Architect

POLYNEER

Johaness Brahms
Musician, Composer, Polyphonic Thinker

Entrepreneurial mindset

JOHN DEWEY
Pragmatist, "The Democracy of Education"

Pioneering

Freeman Dyson
Nuclear physicist and Polymath

Engineering toolset

1940	1994	2020	2020

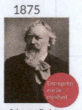
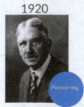

Rachel Carson
Conservationist, "The Silent Spring"

Pioneering

Nelson Mandela
Freedom Fighter, President of South Africa

Pollinating

Melanie Perkins
Entrepreneur, Designer

Design Thinking

Jeff Bezos
Computer Scientist, Entrepreneur, Futurist

POLYNEER

Introduction:

The year 2020 signifies a timestamp for a humankind transmutation – a race against nature, including femtotechnology on the micro-cellular scope, virtual computing on the macro-spatial sphere, and man-machine fusion on the galactic scale. Such a transhuman evolution for spurring advancement requires well-informed *polyneers* (pioneers, entrepreneurs, designers, engineers, and pollinators).

Polyneering is a practical strategy to ignite a *pioneering spirit by combining an entrepreneurial mindset, a design-thinking skill-set, and an engineering toolset through a pollinating process*. Lifelong learning does not refer to a managerial, one-model mold or universal, solve-all plugin, but to a way of life in adapting context or conditions for a pioneering person using entrepreneurial mindsets, design-thinking modes, and engineering methods by cross-pollinating ideas or things.

Like the '*Pracademic,*' with the heart of a philosopher, the hand of a practitioner, and the head of an academic, this pracademic workbook blends theory with application for purposeful results. Use this guide as an active handbook to take notes, doodle concepts, jot down ideas; for calculations, shorthand code, names or places, to catapult your lot in life by doing.

Guidebook Overview:

The Polyneering life book outlines five core and nine complimentary chapters by balancing three primary elements: Money (resources), Management (people), and Minutes (timing). A sub-theme of polyneering consists of an abiding appreciation for processing math, music, and many languages.

Core Chapters:

1. Wild Imaginations (innovating by adapting)
2. Spontaneous Expectations (resolving amidst ambiguity)
3. Anticipatory Modeling (predicting with focus)
4. Generative Learning (designing decision-making)
5. Radical Collaboration (dynamic diversity)

Polyneering is not a philosophy so much as a movement, a way for stakeholders to embrace ambiguity and face unpredictable circumstances by providing apprentice-like, evidence-based outcomes indeed "to touch the head, hand, and heart" (Pilotte et al, 2012).

> *"It is not in the nature of (wo)man – nor any living entity, to start out by giving up."*
> *-Ayn Rand*

I.   Spirit:

The *polyneer* encompasses five elements through a palindrome and acronym "PEDEP" model:
1. **P**ioneering, 2. **E**ntrepreneuring, 3. **D**esigning, 4. **E**ngineering, and 5. **P**ollinating. The model collectively creates a transdisciplinary schema. A polyneer is part pioneer, entrepreneur, designer, engineer, and pollinator. Polyneering infuses art, skills, and disciplines of people, processes, and projects with program management and leadership practices.

A pioneer – a person frustrated, unnerved, goaded, cajoled, or otherwise fueled into taking on the unknown, at all cost – sets off into unchartered territory. The spirit comes from the gut or other jarring or harrowing corners. Either because of nature or nurture or a mad combo of both, the go-getter takes on an impending challenge or impossible problem head on.

Today, professor-driven theory must go beyond taxonomy, topology, and technology to unite education with practice because entrepreneurship is a societal force, like an extension of democracy, to unearth human potential. Immigrants, tinkerers, professionals, experts, misfits, all alike, all different, become modes and models for scholarly debate to uncover how venture creation weaves through the tapestry of our lives.

And, what is transdisciplinary?

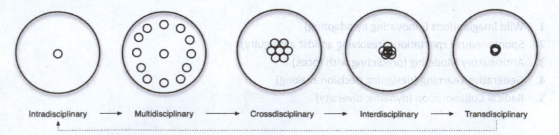

The basic illustration above accentuates the differences pictographically of what each discipline means contextually. *Intradisciplinary* occurs within the scope of scholarly disciplines, integrating reading, writing, and orating in language arts as an example. *Multidisciplinary* refers to problem solving within established or similar boundaries. For example, when studying math, history, reading, or science, teams use similar assumptions, restrictions, perspectives, and philosophies. *Crossdisciplinary* then integrates aspects from multiple academic disciplines to address problems arising from narrow concentrations or specialized fields. And yet with *interdisciplinary*, an overlap or harmony of discipline boundaries occurs, forming sub disciplines and a blending of common assumptions, restrictions, and solutions drawing on established fields of studies. *Transdisciplinary* happens when one with new knowledge and theoretical solutions draws on non-traditional ideas to cross-pollinate contradictory assumptions, restrictions, and philosophies. Thus, transdisciplinary work moves beyond bridging with academia and engages directly with the production and use of knowledge outside of the academy. The catalyst exists in forming an outcropping, a forging of the new polyneering scaffold that draws from the polyglot, polyrhythms, polymaths, using polytropes.

1.1   Historical Context

The notion of a polyneer and in practicing polyneering finds its beginnings in the Latin word *humanitas* used to describe the formation of someone educated in the virtues of character suited for an active life of public service. Insofar as humanitas, as the Greek go-to definition, echoes the description by Cicero (a wealthy Roman politician, lawyer, and consul) as "the capacity to win the affections of lesser folk without impinging on greater" (61-112 A.D.), the concept translated in the Italian renaissance as *humanisti.* Petrarch (scholar and poet) cultivated and converted the concept into the "humanities," in which grammar, rhetoric, poetry, history, and morality defined the letters as the "light of literature" or *lumen litteraruma* with a sketch and a companion candle. Thus, began the crusade of humanism, which brought about and institutionalized the new form of education. Humanistic studies included Latin but also principles in living a moral, responsible, and successful life. The studies formed and trained students in law, medicine, philosophy, and theology.

With the invention of movable type, the oral and rhetorical traditions burgeoned when Johannes Gutenberg (a German blacksmith, goldsmith, printer, publisher, and inventor) enabled the production and dissemination of books. By the 1500s, intellectual and religious life blossomed through the rise of printing presses throughout Europe. Paolo Galluzzi (an Italian historian of science) describes the multidisciplinary work of Leonardo DaVinci and other renaissance contributors as having "universal" experiences especially within the high arts of painting, sculpture, architecture, music, and poetry, with performing arts acknowledging both theatre and dance. The renaissance period renewed an interest in technical knowledge, which Galluzzi refers to as "artificers" – people skilled in "art-science" promoting the professional artist-engineer-architect-author hybrid combinations of the many artist-scientists of the day. The polyneer is quite similar, but far different in carrying amended amalgams of the mindset, skill-set, toolset, and handset of the new age.

Polyneering Precepts and Polytropes:

Interdependence – Members responsible for own and each other's learning.

Performance – Focus is on both group and individual accountability for high quality work.

Experience – Deliberate groups distributing knowledge / expertise.

Reliance – Promoting, helping, supporting, rotating mutual efforts.

Transference – Experts and Novices working together emphasizing exponential improvement.

Polyneering Education "PEDEP" Model:

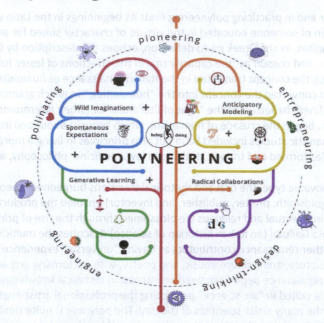

The PEDEP Polyneering Model is a pictographic and holistic perspective drawing from five *artefacts* observed through five effects within three distinct disciplines and two catalysts. Quite symmetrically, the separation occurs between the left side of the brain (analytical) and the right side of the brain (intuitive) and drawing from both creates the polyphonic mind of creators such as pianist and composer phenom Johannes Brahms. The model here draws from the theory of constructivism, which refers to a kind of learning in which people make their own knowledge determined by their own constructs (Papert 1991). Lev Vygotsky (1978) theorized that cognitive development stems from interactions with a zone of proximal development as children and their parents co-construct knowledge. Polyneering also weaves in experiential learning drawing on Kolb's (1984) learning styles of concrete experience and abstract concepts processed as active experimentation and reflective observation.

Artefact: An artificial product or effect observed in a natural system, especially one introduced by the technology used in scientific investigation or by experimental error. An **artefact** can also be any object made or modified by human culture that shows signs of human modification, such as fire cracked rocks from a hearth or plant material used for food. As you can see, the same word can have multiple meanings relevant to the movement of a theory, mindset, or discussion.

PEDEP as an acronym and also a palindrome – a word that reads the same forward and backward, derived from Greek meaning "running back" – makes the new language memorable: **P.**ioneering, **E.**ntrepreneurial, **D.**esign-thinking, **E.**ngineering, **P.**ollinating processes. Language, after all, makes the world and ehtnosphere go 'round states the polyneering Ethnobotanist and National Geographic Explorer Wade Davis. The flow is such that the polyneer can jump into any point of the five elements for the necessary polyneering affect or attribute. The PEDEP Model serves like a gyroscope, in which the axis of rotation is free to assume any orientation by itself regardless of angular velocity. Similarly, creativity augments or affects the "white matter" of the brain, with two hemispheres (right / left), at the atomic and quantum levels. As the protons, or what we call *polytropes* (i.e. tropes), are the forces that move the wing of a starling bird, driving the flock, just as the creative "wing" of the Polyneer soars to new heights of brain and muscle combinations, which in turn activate a myriad of biological, chemical, and even physical outcomes.

Similar to the Kolb learning cycle, which involves listening, looking, leaping, and learning, a polyneer uses past experience to interpret, reinterpret, or even imagine a completely new experience. Congruent with processing or creating new information to solve challenges, invent new solutions, or create original offerings, the polyneer applies various affects, whether tacit or abstract, to produce an outcome. The constant loop of envisioning, experimenting, performing, reflecting, and adjusting forms a flow similar to Kolb's four phase diverging, assimilating, converging, and accommodating attributes (Kolb 1984), but different in that the polyneering process can start or stop at any of the Polyicon levels and layers of mindsets, skill-sets, toolsets, or handsets, including processes from various domains that are fused to form wholly new combinations of resources. Polyneering is often of the moment and dynamic to constantly changing situations.

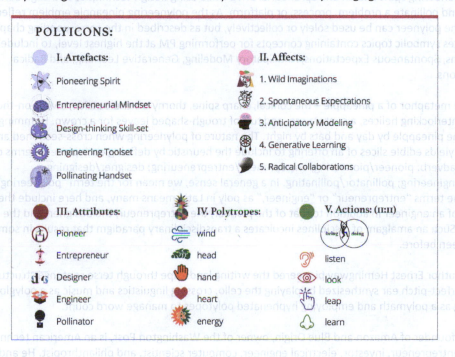

POLYICONS:

I. Artefacts:
- Pioneering Spirit
- Entrepreneurial Mindset
- Design-thinking Skill-set
- Engineering Toolset
- Pollinating Handset

II. Affects:
1. Wild Imaginations
2. Spontaneous Expectations
3. Anticipatory Modeling
4. Generative Learning
5. Radical Collaborations

III. Attributes:
- Pioneer
- Entrepreneur
- Designer
- Engineer
- Pollinator

IV. Polytropes:
- wind
- head
- hand
- heart
- energy

V. Actions: (II:II)
- listen
- look
- leap
- learn

Pioneer
A high-wire walker performs with spirit and for/with conviction to achieve.

Entrepreneur
An apple battery - uses available resources to junksculpt a new offering.

Designer
Iterating solutions by using a measurement system that is palatable and precise.

Engineer
An open box with an infinity symbol is emblematic of solving unsolvable problems.

Pollinator
A circle melting into a rectangle represents a new type of matter which is solid and liquid at the same time or non-Newtonian.

Wild Imaginations
A cubism portrait in Picasso's style, why not!

Spontaneous Expectations
Drawing a heart with a single pen stroke under instant life-and-death stress.

Anticipatory Modeling
Water flow in the mind to resolve a problem before it materializes or advances.

Generative Learning
An atom symbol in a dreamcatcher, for catching new unheard-of ideas.

Radical Collaborations
A flock of flying starlings controlled at the proton and neutron level of a single wing flap.

1.2   Pineapples as Polyneers

Polyneering provides a way of approaching Project Management (PM). The polyneer, wittingly or unwittingly, applies a pioneering spirit and an entrepreneurial drive while using design techniques and engineering tactics to iterate and pollinate a problem, process, or platform. As the polyneering pineapple emblem reflects, each wedge of the polyneer can be used solely or collectively, but as described in the corresponding chapters, each denotes symbolic topics containing concepts for performing PM at the highest level, to include: Wild Imaginations, Spontaneous Expectations, Anticipatory Modeling, Generative Learning, and Radical Collaborations.

We use the metaphor of a pineapple – the conical, sharp spine, thorny-on-the-outside, sweet-on-the-inside fruit with interlocking helices, a center core, and tuft of trough-shaped leaves for a crown. Hummingbirds pollinate the pineapple by day and bats by night. The nature of polyneering when cross-sectioned and quartered, yields edible slices of an offering to include the heuristic by defining each piece in terms of the respective adverb: pioneer/pioneering; entrepreneur/entrepreneuring; designer/designing; engineer/engineering; pollinator/pollinating. In a general sense, we mean for the term "polyneering" to supplant the terms "entrepreneur" or "engineer," as poly in Latin means many, and here include the attributes of an engineer in addition to that of the pioneer, the entrepreneur, the designer, and the pollinator. Such an amalgam of disciplines inculcates a transdisciplinary paradigm that results in something new, not seen before.

Erstwhile author Ernest Hemingway pioneered the writing landscape through terse sentence structure, using his near perfect-pitch ear synthesized by playing the cello, crossing linguistics and music as a polyglot while performing as a polymath and employing hyphenated polytopes to manage word count.

Jeff Bezos, founder of Amazon and Blue Origin, owner of the Washington Post, is an American technology and retail entrepreneur, investor, electrical engineer, computer scientist, and philanthropist. He and or his entities will likely surpass the trillion-dollar threshold in 2020. From the polyneer litmus test framework, Bezos pioneered online selling at Amazon first with books, and then with all kinds of products in a multitude of categories. He has started, invested, founded, and operated several businesses, qualifying him as an entrepreneur. Having majored in electrical engineering and computer science, and by combining skill-sets and methods, he derived a better way to sell products over the internet and is as well looking to colonize Mars through his space-travel entity. He aptly applied design-thinking precepts in constructing and architecting the backbone to Amazon both logistically and in the cloud; as well as cross-pollinated by acquiring Whole Foods to adopt the grocery chain into the Amazon distribution network. In addition, he recently created a way for shoppers to physically visit Amazon Go whereby RFID technology bypasses the need for a human cashier all-together; and is investigating the potential to deliver any product from Amazon, perishable and non-perishable items alike, by way of syncopated drones for negating any human interaction whatsoever. Bezos is a polyneer.

1.3   Tables and Visual Rubrics

Tautology: $(1X)^5$ is a logic where the 1 before the X is understood and the 5th power is exponential i.e. an added bonus.

Polyneer versus Engineer: Tinker-Thinker Theoretical Model

Polyneer – High Tinker	Bridge Builder – High Theory
– High Theory	– Low Tinker
– High Practice	– Low Practice
Mechanci – Low Theory	Sub-Commander – High Theory
– High Tinker	– Low Tinker
– High Practice	– High Practice

The Pracademic Pendulum:

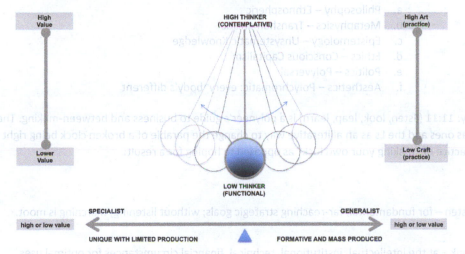

(Created with Michael Gray at Yuiwe Lab)

Topology as a pictographic continuum changing / improving the morphology of the polyneer:

Chronological Polyneering pictograph: Gypsy > Pot & Pan Mender > Hoop > Tinkerer >Bricoleur>Pioneer> Inventor > Machinist> Entrepreneur > Designer > Engineer > Thinker > Gamer>Collaborator>Pollinator

Taxonomy – a quasi-way of classifying kinds of entrepreneurs with modern examples:

1. Innovative Entrepreneur; role creator (Elon Musk)
2. Immigrant Entrepreneur; survival (George Soros)
3. Replicative Entrepreneur; reforming (Fred Smith)
4. Hypomanic Entrepreneur; spontaneous (Steve Jobs)
5. Intrapreneurial Entrepreneur; inside out (Jack Welch)
6. Social Entrepreneur; profit not just dollars (Anita Roddick)
7. Serial Entrepreneur; multiple plays (Jack Dorsey)

Entrepreneurship education heuristics (approaches) with methods and modalities:

1. Effectuation – using a means over expectations to the best of one's ability.
2. Bricolage – an action over engagement, combining resources by "making do."
3. Discovery-driven – testing assumptions even in the midst of uncertainty.
4. Disciplined-driven – a systematic approach but ever ready to adjust or modify.
5. Evidence-driven – using facts over gut-feelings.
6. Prescriptive – searching by uncovering opportunities and potential.
7. Lean/Product-driven – constant and continued feedback for product-market fit.
8. Design-thinking – an iterative process based on user research.

Ethnosphere and the epistemologies (scope) of entrepreneurship:

Ethnosphere - the sum of all thoughts and intuitions, myths, beliefs, ideas, and inspirations brought into being by the human imagination since the dawn of consciousness.

a. Philosophy – Ethnospheric
b. Metaphysics – Transhumanistic
c. Epistemology – Unsystematic Knowledge
d. Ethics – Conscious Capitalism
e. Politics – Polyversal
f. Aesthetics – Polychromatic: every~body's different

Pedagogy: 11:11 {listen, look, leap, learn} is a polyneer's guide to business and between-making. The elevens (I I) dub as ones and the Ls as an alliterative way to change the parable of a broken clock being right twice a day; a practice of "making your own luck" as opposed to hoping for a result:

listen – for fundamental, far-reaching strategic goals; without listening, marching is moot.

look – at the intellectual, institutional, technical, financial circumstances for optimal uses.

leap – do not wait. Build and deploy. The purpose of a project or company is prosperity.

learn – from the actions taken and modify for improvement; Rollout and Debug. Now.

SPACE-MAKER   RISK-TAKER

1.4   <u>Pioneering Spirit</u>

The pioneer within a polyneer sees potential long before the concept or idea becomes validated or comes to fruition. A pioneer is an innovator willing to try new things by pushing boundaries to advance a cause, break a record, break a plate, or disrupt the also-rans. Men and women alike experience success in a myriad of fields and most typically by overcoming great challenges through a pioneering spirit.

There are scores of examples of pioneers both in settling new terrain physically and in creating new fields altogether, as with flight or space programs. Pioneers probe, inquire, enterprise, and profess new methods, new roads; they forge entrenchments, make encampments, and even create new occupations, from ecology to astronomy and anything in between. This drive requires the ability and skill-set to challenge mindsets and create new revolutionary paradigms.

When the pioneering way is ignited by raw, unbridled spirit, the world becomes effused with a thrill-to-awe experience, a rarity in time when the hair raises on the nape of the neck. Jaw-dropping, as when Phillip Petit high wire walked between the twin towers in Manhattan on a brisk morning; or when Amelia Earhart attempted to circumnavigate the world chock-full of esprit to the nth degree. It is the free solo climb of Yosemite's El Capitan mountain's face by bare-handed climber Alex Honnold, or the recent ascent and descent of K2, the Savage Mountain, by adventurer Andrezej Bargiel without an oxygen mask, climbing up and skiing down and just because. It is an unrehearsed solo by jazz saxophonist Sonny Rollins on an unremarkable Tuesday evening in a smoky club on the southside of Chicago. Spirit forms the lifeblood of being, and a pioneering spirit is the derivative, an exponential multiplier of doing.

"The gravel in ya' guts and the spit in ya' eye"
-Shel Silverstein

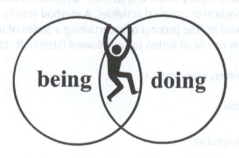

1.5   Entrepreneurial Mindset

"The ability to sense, act, and mobilize under certain conditions" is the academic best choice definition of an entrepreneurial mindset by Barringer and Ireland (2003). But where does "thinking about thinking" stem from and is the cognitive ability innate, learned, borrowed, hatched, or birthed through osmosis? We just don't know. Edward de Bono popularized the term in his 6-Thinking Hat's material in which he used a "Blue Hat" metaphor to identify the need to think about the thinking. The CoRT program established the roadmap and interconnected ability to identify different thinking skills such as Parallel Thinking, Lateral Thinking, Vertical Thinking, Abstract Thinking, and Direct Attention Thinking.

Since the early 1900s, business scholars like Knight and Schumpeter suggest that the entrepreneur stands as the primary agent of "creative destruction," which loosely means that the manifestation of all ideas or processes might be a dispositional trait adopted through a learning state. Entrepreneurship is at a crossroads for determining the cognitive puzzle. An example could be the nonsensical idea of "Loading mercury with a pitchfork" (R. Brautigan), and yet the entrepreneurial mindset finds a way. Polyneering and life is about learning to walk a fish.

For the purposes of this guidebook and practical workbook, the mindset of a polyneer is adept at being what I call "resourcefully resourceful" (Wilson, 2020). Professor Sarasvathy of the University of Virginia uses "effectuation" to describe the approach of making decisions and performing actions by assessing resources available. Whereas Professor Stevenson of Harvard University posits a working definition as "the pursuit of opportunity beyond resources controlled," indicating relentless focus on novel ideas or solutions. And still, Professor Fiet of the University of Louisville prefers 'prescribing' what entrepreneurs ought to do rather than studying, post-hoc, what the entrepreneur did. Actual entrepreneurs just pay themselves.

Delineating between a method and process casts a wide net to include terms like heuristics, guidelines, approaches, frameworks, scaffolding, principles, practices, procedures, models and the venerable scientific rigorous research methodologies. A method is defined as "a way of thinking and acting, built on a set of assumptions using a portfolio of techniques to create guidance for action" (Neck and Green 2011; Mansoori, 2015). The mode of thinking entails inquiry under a systematic direction to understand entrepreneurship as a set of ideas applying either theoretical or practical activities. A method should not be confused merely with business planning, which is defined as "the process of ascertaining a series of potential courses to be taken by the firm and selecting the best course of action to be followed (Steinhoff, 1970).

There are six steps used in a business plan process:

1. Define the business and mission
2. Set goals and objectives
3. Create a strategy to perform objectives
4. Identify resources
5. Implement and execute strategies
6. Evaluate performances

Latching on to what Stanford Professor Carol Dweck determines in her research of "growth" versus "fixed" mindsets, an entrepreneurship mindset is simply a choice for anyone to understand and enact a method to improve ability by embracing any challenge. To be sure, and as often documented, an entrepreneur unconsciously chooses a direction or path fraught in resistance or against conventional academic discourse, thankfully, to break barriers and trailblaze a path not recommended, seen, supported, or researched. Herein, an inverse of what we are taught in our formative years just might be the starting point for understanding innovation. Entrepreneurship is about creating, whereas leadership is about influencing, and management is about facilitating. When we triangulate disciplines, the polyneer's "felt self" emerges to foster new realms or paradigms not thought remotely possible.

Entrepreneur

An apple battery - uses available resources to junksculpt a new offering.

1.6   <u>Design-Thinking Skill-Set</u>

Decades of literature exist on the validation of design-thinking as an iterative process that operates around value creation (Dorst, 2006). As Kees Dorst, professor of transdisciplinary innovation at the University of Technology, elucidates, problem solving for designers and engineers means to create a solution that operates with working precepts on a daily basis. The "open" and "abduction" reasoning process is associated with conceptual design:

thing ?   +   working principle !   leads to = VALUE

Such designerly ways of thinking do not come without scores of tensions between academics, practitioners, critics, and companies, as suggested in the table below on applying actual design:

IDEO	Inspiration, Ideation, Implementation
Stanford Design School	Empathy, Define, Ideate, Prototype, Test
IBM	Explore, Prototype, Evaluate
Bell Laboratories	Back, Middle, Front for an "Idealized Design"*

The polyneer sees sensibility in a quad or four legs of a table of design-thinking skill-sets by identifying user needs, determining what is technically possible by generating strategic value, and designing from the end rather than from the front.

*Footnote: Idealized Design (2006) R. Ackoff, *Wharton School Publishing*

Designer
Iterating solutions by using a measurement
system that is palatable and precise.

1.7   Engineering Toolset

As a concept, engineering itself seems hard to define because there exists no guaranteed outcome, no hint of the absolute, no deterministic truth. For theoretical problem sets, we solve for X. However, real engineering in the yard, the community, the cockpit, or the field always reeks of the uncertain. Finding a provisional solution is ad hoc and greatly on par with the plot of an entrepreneur. The two methods, engineering and entrepreneurship, are inextricably linked. Professor Billy Vaughn Koen from the University of Texas at Austin suggests that engineering is a rule-of-thumb strategy method "for causing the best change in a poorly understood situation with the available resources" – as almost an echo or inverse mirror for the definition of an entrepreneur being resourcefully resourceful.

An engineering toolset, then, incorporates trade-offs in utility according to the challenge or circumstance at hand. The engineer toolset is a metaphor for an ability to achieve a solution by manipulating a perceived reality regardless of a choice between efficiency or thoroughness, since there is not merely one right answer to a problem. The engineer and the toolset afforded or available become optimized at the boundary of failure.

Engineer
An open box with an infinity symbol is
emblematic of solving unsolvable problems.

1.8   Cross Pollinating Handset

Dynamic disciplines open opportunities and avenues not typically assimilated in same-discipline collaborations. However, the measure of pollination might not be as potent, say, on recording patent output as on the realm of including and forging new capacities. New strains, mixtures, feeds, formulas, recipes – regardless of failure or success – form the ridgepole to sharing and showing. Degrees of talent, racial divides, economic stratums, or any other quantifiable metric simply cannot measure the crossing of a shrike with a locomotive. And make no mistake, pollination serves as an elixir for change, not an algorithm for faster, better, cheaper. The ethnosphere is a fabric like none other, not to be reduced but rather perpetuated, augmented, and randomized against any bias.

Thrivability through nature and culture and artificial intelligence hinges on pollination. Frans Johannson coined the term "Medici effect" after the Medici dynasty in the 14th century known for investing in painters, poets, philanthropists, and philosophers, as much as in architecture, science, and music or math prodigies. Innovation is a consequence of diverse disciplines that when intersected, yield ideas from one field and reimagine possibilities for another.

Pollinator
A circle melting into a rectangle represents
a new type of matter which is solid and
liquid at the same time or non-Newtonian.

II.   Wild Imaginations:

Imagine trying to load mercury with a pitchfork – yes, a nonsensical view of a person with a pitchfork trying to lift a liquid metal with an impossible tool, and yet somehow it happens. Walking a fish might be next! Whether you envision an adaption of having the forks of the pitchfork shaped like spoons or putting a leash on a fish within a foot of rainwater, both of these mental images require using your imagination.

> *So, what the hell is imagination?*

Well, imagination is a nonexistent complex mental image assembled from the input of our senses.

> *Okay, where is imagination located?*

Well, we don't perfectly know exactly where imagination is located.

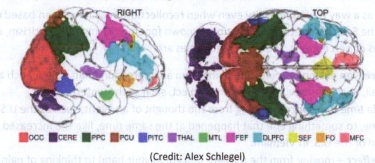

(Credit: Alex Schlegel)

But we do know that types of imagination are broken into *Positive* and *Negative* imaginations:

Negative imaginations –

- *Nightmares*
- *Hallucinations*
- *Schizophrenia*
- *Delusions*
- *Complexes*

A negative imagination creates a feeling of insecurity, anxiety, or fear of bad things happening, leading to unstable negative mental emotions. The basic premise holds that imagining the "worst" or catastrophic thinking can lead to mental suffering. This validation of discouragement can be envisioned as dark energies that drain us unconsciously. We have all had a nightmare that either scared us or made us wake up.

There are also positive imaginations –

- *Dreams*
- *Daydreaming*
- *Visual Imagery* (Mind's Eye)

A positive imagination creates a feeling of euphoria, happiness, optimism, and a positive mental attitude. This type of imagination can create a mental belief that something from fantasy is possible and that unique elements can be reassembled into something new and feasible.

2.1   The Gang of Three History: (Philosophers, Poets, Pickpockets)

Aristotle was a student of Plato, philosophers, who lived from 384 BC-322 BC. Aristotle invented the three Laws of Association and a Law of Frequency that are considered by many to be the epicenter of behavioral learning theories, from which purposeful imagination spawned.

The laws are as follows:

- *Law of Similarity* – the experience or recall of one object will elicit the recall of things similar to that object.
- *Law of Contrast* – the experience or recall of one object will elicit the recall of opposite things.
- *Law of Contiguity* – the experience or recall of one object will elicit the recall of things that were originally experienced along with that object.
- *Law of Frequency* – the more frequently two things are experienced together, the more likely it will be that the experience or recall of one will stimulate the recall of the second.

The laws were used as a way to define reality even when recollections may have been based on untruths. Next, David Hume, the Scottish poet and essayist best known for empiricism and skepticism, claimed that there are three types of perceptions. The three regularities are:

- *Resemblance* – an example would be moving from an impression of an object, such as a picture of a waterfall, to the thought of the pictured object, such as the waterfall itself.
- *Contiguity in time and space* – moving from the thought of an event, such as the U.S. NASA moon landing, to something else that happened at the same time, like the increased participation of the U.S. in Vietnam.
- *Cause and effect* – moving from the thought of a cut in your hand to thinking of pain.

Lastly, Walt Disney, a pickpocket of a magician, used imagination to trick our senses allowing us to see or visualize things that are not true. He created illusions and mental images that propose that the impossible is possible. Thus, the three byproducts of imagination are:

- *Curiosity* – Your imagination makes you consider the impossible; you can ponder the "what if" possibilities of anything.
- *Exploration* – Your imagination allows you to travel anywhere in the universe and experience the possibilities of being anyone.
- *Disruption* – Your imagination allows you to construct any reality you desire at any moment to tell a fictitious story.

The Disney "Secret Sauce" about imagination has never been fully explained or divulged to the general public. The closest we can get is a creative description of a strategy to tell stories based on three mental trigger areas called the Dreamer, Realist, and Spoiler or Critic.

The Dreamer – Strategy to let team's imagination run free and dream of the ultimate picture they would like to have. In the *Dreamer* state, you can develop visions by asking questions like:

- What would we love to put on the screen? What excites and inspires us about it?

The Realist – Strategy to take the ideas of the *Dreamer* and turn them into something that could work. This would mean a step-by-step plan using logic, reason, and pragmatism.

The Spoiler or Critic – Strategy used at key stages of the creative process in group meetings, using vivid imagination and keen business sense to bridge the gap between imagination and reality. In the *Critic* state, you can identify constraints and limits by asking questions like:

- Is this the best we can do? Are we missing something here? Is the voice, right? Is the music appropriate? Can we improve the color and detail?

Walt Disney's strategy was highlighted and modeled later in 1994 by NLP (Neural Linguistic Programming) expert Robert Dilts. Both men explored and experimented and codified "Imagineering" – the blending of creative imagination with technical know-how.

> *"If you can dream it, you can do it."*
> *– Walt Disney*

By integrating historical perspectives of imagination from all of the resources available, we can consolidate the previous concepts into five unique categories that are referred to as Wild Imaginations:

- Abstract
- Replication
- Surrogate
- Prophesy
- Ingenious

Wild Imaginations describe a person's purposeful ability to think and dream about anything with intensely vivid and colorful thoughts or ideas. If we review the previously described historical information on Imagination, we can create a toolset of different imaginations that can be used to develop new and unique ideas in any realm desired. We must break away from the mindset that imaginations are truths or untruths and focus more on strategies based on the possibilities of what seems impossible.

A 'wicked problem' is difficult or impossible to solve because of incomplete, contradictory, and changing scenarios. If your imagination is applied in a focused and directed way, it acts as an incredible cognitive asset for positive creative thinking. The five new wild imagination strategies or unique focus directions help create ideas and concepts in the face of challenge.

The **Abstract Imagination** strategy is based on imagining something that is not initially real or possible. The process of abstraction refers to the act of considering something as its generic quality or characteristics separated from concreate realities, specific objects, or actual instances.

- Abstract Imagination – Picture a nonexistent mountain in Florida. Not having a physical or concrete existence.

The **Replication Imagination** strategy is based on imagining something that is repeated, reproduced, or duplicated from a previous experience or situation, similar to using a mental recipe to create a new meal based on previous knowledge.

- Replication Imagination – Bring back a mental scene from the past.

The **Surrogate Imagination** strategy is based on imagining something that is liberated from our personal self and embraced from substitution of a new or unique image.

- Surrogate Imagination – Allows us to be someone else.

The ***Prophesy Imagination*** strategy is based on imagining something that is liberated from a declaration or foretold from a divine inspiration. It is developed from predation and foretelling imaginations. These are sometimes seen as spiritual or based on what is needed by humankind.

- Prophecy Imagination – Make us foresee the best, while preparing for the worst.

The ***Ingenious Imagination*** strategy is based on imagining something that is clever, original, resourceful, or intelligent. It appears to be a new idea established from a novel genius that is clearly inventive. You may see this as visions that are bright, gifted, or adroit.

- Ingenious Imagination – Combine known elements in order to produce the unknown.

Using any one of the five imagination strategies will liberate mental capacity and focus predetermined crafty ideas. The ability to position your mental thinking from a starting point to using an imagination strategy becomes enhanced with the use of an imagination process.

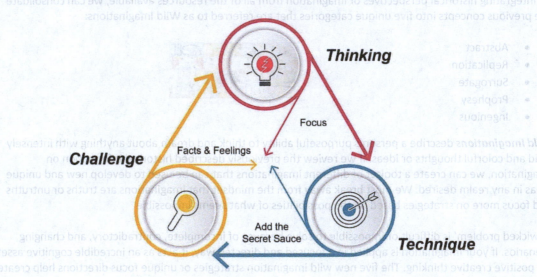

2.2   <u>Imagination Process</u>

A process should show how to accomplish an objective or task and the flow of steps to follow for success. The imagination process has three steps:

     A.   *Challenge* – The first process step is to develop the Challenge for thinking. This step requires a complete understanding of the space, problem, or opportunity you want to think about. You must understand the background information available as completely as possible.

     B.   *Thinking* – The second process step is to establish the Thinking space. To accomplish this step, you create a Challenge Statement. Sometimes these are referred to as scope, purpose, or problem statements.

     C.   *Technique* – The third process step is to propose the imagination Technique to use. There are five separate imagination types which can be selected, allowing you to open the thinking space.

By using this imagination process, you can purposely allow your imagination to explore any subject you want with guaranteed results.

Recent research makes clear that we can only roughly measure imagination, typically mapped against creative thinking. Everyone has the ability to imagine, daydream, visualize and ponder moments of what-if possibilities.

*"Every invention or human construct—whether a spaceship, an architectural wonder, or an iPhone—
once existed as a mere idea, imagined in someone's mind"*

- Raya Bidsharari

We have heard the old English idiom that "a picture is worth a thousand words," but Wild Imaginations are worth a thousand possibilities.

III.   Spontaneous Expectations:

Spontaneous expectations refer to a philosophy of a sudden inner impulse or inclination without premeditation to achieve something positive; an immediate recognition that something really good or great is available that was not expected previously. Spontaneous expectations could occur in a situation in which a thing or circumstance was not available, but because of one's situational awareness, the opportunity to capture or explore something new becomes available.

We have all been in situations in which our expectations were disappointingly unmet or misled. There is uniformity in nature and in our ability to recognize the actions, events, and possibilities that fall into this general truth. A polyneer, therefore, is open to the ability to recognize and embrace the phenomenon of spontaneous expectations. Polyneering spontaneous expectations require pushback on paradigm paralysis, a clear understanding of predictive behavior, decision logic, and contradictions that exist in one's current mental models.

A practical example of the philosophy of spontaneous expectation: You're having dinner at your favorite restaurant. As you check in at the front desk, you're told that a special table is available due to a cancellation. You quickly say yes to this table and then find out that the chef has a friend, who is another great chef, offering her special desert tonight only, and at no cost. You say yes to the special desert and you ultimately have the most incredible culinary experience you have ever had. This practical example of a polyneering spontaneous expectation demonstrates a clear focus on the cognitive areas of paradigm paralysis and a clear understanding of predictive behavior, decision logic, and contradictions that exist in your current mental models. These cognitive areas will be discussed in the following sections.

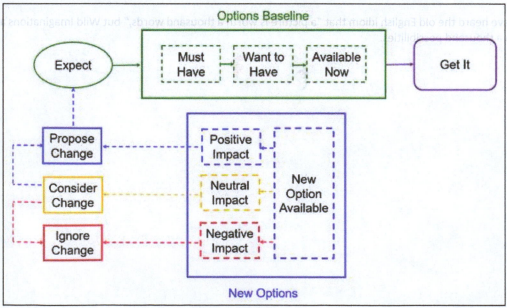

3.1 Paradigm Paralysis

Imagine yourself walking down a railroad track and you decide to cross the tracks. As soon as you get on the tracks, you hear the train whistle and can see a train coming towards you. Do you go forward and cross or do you back up to where you were?

What can also happen is that you freeze at that position and don't get out of the way of the train. The fictitious scenario shows how powerful it can be to stay frozen into a specific perception. The clear definition for *paradigm paralysis* refers to the refusal or inability to think or see outside or beyond the current framework or way of thinking and perceiving things. Paradigm paralysis can also indicate a general lack of cognitive flexibility and adaptability.

A polyneer exercises a natural flexibility of thinking, which allows for adjustment in thinking from one situation to another. Flexibility gives the ability to overcome responses or thinking that may have become habitual. It permits adaptation naturally, openly, and freely to new situations.

A paradigm is a mental model or thinking pattern based on a shared set of assumptions about the world we perceive. We create and develop expectations, sometimes referred to as truths, based on these assumptions. When this happens, we see or experience data that strongly reinforces these mental models and patterns. This occurrence can also be called psychological inertia, or reluctance to do something in a different way due to our resistance to change our actions. We are then drawn to behave or think in a specific way. But as a polyneer, we are willing to listen and review information and data from different theories.

Indeed, new theories provide insights as identified by Gordon Cameron (Trizics: Teach yourself Triz), listing eight potential causes of psychological inertia:

- Having a fixed vision (model) of the solution or the root cause.
- False assumptions (trusting the data).
- Specific terminology in a language that is a strong carrier of psychological inertia.
- Experience, expertise, and reliance upon previous results.
- Limited knowledge, hidden resources, or mechanisms.
- Inflexibility (model worship), trying to prove a specific theory, stubbornness.
- Reusing the same strategy.
- Rushing to a solution, incomplete thinking.

Any or all of these can limit our capacity to think clearly or completely. The ability to recognize these potential causes and human programming provides us with the ability to understand predictive behaviors.

3.2   <u>Predictive Behavior</u>

Behavior refers to the way in which one acts or conducts oneself in response to a particular situation or stimulus (e.g., you drive the same way home every day). Behavior can also be based on the natural phenomenon or functionality of a machine or mechanical object (your car won't start). Predictive behavior is the ability to anticipate a specific act or action based on some level of data analysis. Many organizations engage in data modeling for predictive behavior hypothesis and testing. These firms research on the front line of deep neural analysis of the future behavior of people. Active investigations are based on algorithms and algorithmic models (neural networks) that map and describe previous behaviors and the assumptions underlying them. The importance of this deep learning methodology rests on the need to understand current or future potential customers. Every time you go grocery shopping, for example, you create a digital footprint that describes you. The day you go shopping, the coupons that you use, the products that you purchase, the amount of time that you spend there, the type of payment you use, and your basic descriptions for age, sex, education level, ethnic background, marital status, and income level all form part of a data set that is a model of "YOU."

This data and information offer an ability to predict possibilities and actions by others. A polyneer does that type of analytical prediction intuitively. These actions are evaluated by both logical and intuitive understanding for positive openings (opportunities) and negative risks (problems). Each time a decision is made, it is based on a personal model of probability. If someone behaves in a specific way in the past, a likelihood exists that they will repeat that behavior, creating a pattern of sequential behavior. Ultimately, one can develop the ability to understand and accurately predict "what comes next." This action is not a guess, but a capacity to think clearly with an unbiased focus on the facts balanced by intuition and lessons learned for making the best decisions possible.

3.3 Decision Logic

To arrive at the best decision, one needs to include a balance of evidence, arguments, and intuition. For example, when you get up in the morning, you make decisions such as what to wear. For some people, choosing what to wear comes easy; for others, it is a challenge of logical decision making. A polyneer intuitively uses all three elements of evidence, arguments, and intuition balanced together to make the decision at the moment of getting dressed.

Additionally, logical decision making encompasses one's emotions and insights, which occur unconsciously. Current publications propose that, "People need to feel in order to decide" (Susan Weinschenk). This notion means that decisions are not automatically processed in our brains. They are broken down into either a goal-based or habit-based decision, but not both at the same time. The school of thought proposes that if you are given a lot of information, you will switch from habit to directed goal. Further, if you give people too many choices, they may not be able to make a decision. Information and data overload happen when we are given more than 3 or 4 options. As described above, the polyneering process for decision making purposely uses a balanced review of the following elements:

- *Evidence* – decision making about a program, policy or practice that is grounded in the best available research evidence and informed by experiential evidence from the field of relevant contextual evidence.

- *Arguments* – decision making based on a selection from multiple alternatives that explore both the pros and cons of various strengths. This approach gives a balance of distinguishing between pessimistic and optimistic attitudes.

- *Intuition* – decision making based on a gut broad evaluation that does not include a subset of additional decisions. The aptitude can be established due to in-depth knowledge of the subject or domain expertise.

The polyneering decision-making process is both logical and practical. It encompasses the blending of logical, rational, informed judgements interpreted through rules, consideration of facts, and careful reasoning. Also, the process contains our belief systems, cognitive biases, and assumptions. The hardest decision to make may be one that has no right answer. Here, the challenge becomes choosing the best of a no-win scenario. Sometimes these types of no-win decisions arise because of contradictions.

3.4   Contradiction

A contradiction is widely described as two situations, events, or statements that are used in combination, but one statement makes the other impossible. It refers to something that is "X" and "non-X" at the same time. Hence, decision making based on a contradiction proves challenging. Take the example of a juror listening to testimony. A court witness's second statement changes the details of their first statement regarding what they saw during a crime (e.g., "I never saw a gun in the defendant's hand;" "The defendant then put the gun in his pocket and walked away"). These two truths, not based on a purposeful lie, stand in opposition to each other. In a technical environment, a contradiction could occur when something needs to be hot and cold at the same time.

Many times, problems can be formulated in the format of a contradiction to illustrate the technical challenges. Take a situation in which you are designing a new engine for a car that needs increased speed capacity. This new design requires a larger engine to create higher horsepower, but the larger engine's extra weight would signify a decrease in the mileage of the car. The contradiction clearly compels a tradeoff between speed and weight. Our current mindset does not allow both to happen at the same time. Using the notion of "contrariety," the scenario becomes an example of a static contradiction (black and white or an echo of black versus nonblack).

Harold Walsby proposes three types of contradictions:

- *Static Contradiction* – when two things mutually exclude each other while joining in a complemental relation.
- *Dynamic Contradiction* – when action and reaction are equal and opposite in duality.
- *Self-Contradiction* – when separate identities of the two begin to break up and merge together, making it difficult to define the boundary between them.

These three types of contradictions could also be referred to as a paradox. A paradox is a logical self-contradictory statement that runs contrary to your expectation. Decision making using this type of logic can become cognitively confusing and nonsensical. The statement that someone is a "wise fool" serves as an example of a paradox. If both words in the statements are true, then they both negate each other. In situations of contradicting data or information like in this example, one should use a polyneering process for decision making, based on factual evidence, clear arguments, and intuition, ignoring and dismissing logical contradictions and paradoxes.

IV. Anticipatory Modeling:

Anticipatory Modeling refers to a new field based on the contention that past data can be used to predict future behavior. The idea of predicting, or releasing a statement about a future event, does not require superintelligence. A prediction often, but not always, occurs based upon experience or knowledge, and can also occur based on instinct and gut feeling. So, Anticipatory Customer Solutions (ACS) models result using water logic and flowscapes.

Imagine if you could approach your customers with the product, process, or service before they needed it?

4.1   <u>Water Logic</u>

Let's examine a couple of these new areas to make sure we understand the ACS method. Water logic is an Edward de Bono philosophy centered on "flow," establishing that, in a system of connectedness, everything moves to something and somewhere, similar to a river.

The two philosophies lead us into two very different paths:

- *Rock Logic* – The traditional thinking metaphor alludes to the physical characteristics of a rock – hard, unchanging and unyielding. This form of thinking is the basis of our judgement and our certainty and serves us well even though it can lead to what De Bono calls "brutal arrogance."

- *Water Logic* – Water, conversely, is seen as gentle, soft, and yielding. If you attack water, it offers no resistance, but then surrounds you. With water, you can lose some from the glass and still keep some in the glass – it does not have to be either/or.

The underlying understanding between these two philosophies establishes rock logic as based on what "is" and water logic as based on "to" – what does this flow to? What does this lead to? And what does this add up to? Water logic allows variability, adaptability, the ability to change your perception or understanding of the truth.

When a polyneer engages in anticipatory modeling, they use water logic as a frame of reference, allowing "openness" to new ideas and truths. Water logic allows the mind to explore new opportunities that are closed off to others because they use rock logic to think automatically.

The addition of a flowscape method illustrates the water logic flow to bring visual clarity about simplified systems and representations that we have made about our inner and external world views, people, and the environment based on our past experiences, memories, knowledge, and perceptions.

Flowscapes

A flowscape is a visual method of illustrating a provisional way of looking at the shape of a perception. If you stood on a hillside and looked across into a lower valley, you may only see a small portion of the landscape. If you then took a small plane or helicopter and looked down at the topology of everything, you would see a very different view.

The ACS Flowscape Model:

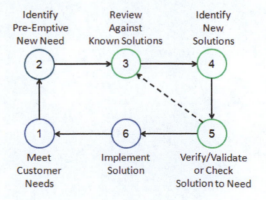

4.2   Anticipatory Customer Solutions Model

The model illustrates a series of six thinking steps which start at step 1 and flow in a repeating connected loop. The solid arrows provide the direction and connections for the thinking. Notice the dashed arrow between steps 5 and 3, indicating a possible loop from step 5 back to step 3. Additionally, notice that the circles in steps 3, 4, and 5 are green, indicating a divergent thinking mode.

To use the ACS process:

1) **Meet Customer Needs** – Note that this is not a problem-solving process, but rather an exercise designed to create new opportunities. You need to identify a starting point, describing a product or service that currently meets the customer's needs. For example, a "car" used for transportation to and from work.

2) **Identify Pre-Emptive New Need** – Identify a new need, such as a "new car" to replace the old one.

3) **Review Against Known Solutions** – Understand the customer's current needs for a car, perhaps standard transportation with good gas mileage.

4) **Identify New Solutions** – Say the price of gas is going to increase about 50 cents a gallon this year, which makes the customer's current car too expensive to drive every day to and from work. You identify a new hybrid car that allows the customer to drive in the carpool lane, increasing the speed of daily transportation and requiring less gas.

5) **Verify/Validate or Check Solution to Need** – Use logic to create checks against perceptions of the possible new needs and characteristics of the new solution.

6) **Implement Solution** – Offer the new solution, a hybrid car model describing the positive features.

Exceptional service comes from recognizing the possible opportunities in a customer interaction and anticipating the needs of your customers. Organizations that recognize the importance of their customers and provide possible options for them to embrace will build solid, long-term relationships. Proactive, anticipatory service creates a bond and emotional connection with the customer, which leads to trust and faith in your performance.

Yo, what is Intelligence?

A widely accepted notion posits that there are many different types of "Intelligence" – analytic, linguistic, and emotional – and that these are connected to each other. Argument occurs, however, around the notion of a single, general, all-encompassing intelligence called "G". In other words, one can possess strong emotional intelligence without being gifted analytically or linguistically.

Popular theorist Robert Sternberg believes that types of intelligence can be broken down into three subsets: analytic, creative, and practical. To embrace all three of these types of intelligence only requires that you take a positive step forward in that direction.

חיים
精神　協力
جميلة

4.3 <u>No FOBFO</u>

The language of a Polyneer is based on many unique perspectives, including verbal, visual, intuitive, pictographic, computer, sign, jargon, lingo, Swahili, and slang, to name a few. Today, roughly 6,500 known spoken languages exist in the world. Anticipatory modeling constitutes a language used to blend a combination of these languages together, creating a vastly rich and deep dialect used by polyneers. This type of language is meant to be more honest, clearer, and focused on communicating a clear message based on multiple perspectives and points of view.

- *Polyneer Lingo* – This term vaguely refers to the speech of a particular community or group and is therefore loosely synonymous with many of the other words in the polyneer vocabulary. An example would be a "THINKINAUT" – anyone focused on becoming a cognitive astronaut specializing in imagination.

- *Polyneer Slang* – Slang refers to a vocabulary of terms (at least initially) employed in a specific subculture. Slang terms, either invented words or those whose meanings are adapted to new senses, develop out of a need to clarify communication. For example, "No FOBFO" is a phrase borrowed from a small manufacturing company in North America which means *no freaking out before finding out*.

- *Polyneer Colloquial* – Anything not employed in formal writing or conversation, including terms that might be a positive reference. *Colloquial* terms may be perceived as pejorative, but they merely refer to informal terminology. An example would be "Idea Ninjas" who are specific people with an exceptional skillset for ideation.

The polyneering model contains references to things that may seem unconventional and at times nonsensical as, say, when a pitchfork pracademic picks your pocket. Ha!

Finally, the phrase "it's too wet to plow and you can't tap dance" is an idiom that sounds like a country western song. It is actually a phrase used in the Midwest, meaning you may as well do something because you can't or don't have the opportunity to do anything else.

Vocabulary and language provide clarity to anticipatory modeling, though not apparent unless one is immersed inside a unique culture. Polyneers provide translations and language clarity based on symbols, phrases, pictographs, flowscapes, and positive messages.

V.   Generative Learning:

Perhaps most distinct from a design mindset is the theory around a generative learning process, based on adding new data to long term memory. This active construct suggests that preexisting mental schema becomes integrated with new ideas. Unsurprisingly, self-regulation and motivation, along with advents in machine-learning, lead to generative learning and design uniting for an unprecedented automaticity in learning.

> **Recall** – using and repeating factual or conceptual information until fully grasped.
>
> **Integration** – altering and integrating new information by paraphrasing or analogizing content.
>
> **Organization** – linking knowledge through main point or strategic list ranking.
>
> **Elaboration** – connecting new concepts in creative ways by imagining into daily faculties.

As humans, what we imagine, design, and create is subconsciously linked to our experiences and perceptions. The future of making and living tethers design, engineering, and marketing, all stitched cohesively within co-developed projects through digitally generated solutions and human curation. Learning communities will change knowledge and concept inventories by connecting data and mentors seamlessly and tirelessly. Simultaneous collaboration affords permutations not ever thought possible. Cognitive and psychometric measures of knowledge, abilities, attitudes, and personality are primarily concerned with the study of differences between individuals. Generative learning envisions being able to draw from past, present, and future data in order to assess a student's progress and possibilities, not just for aptitude but also for ability to process.

The process of learning for a polyneer is based on trial and error. Learning from mistakes and adapting is a natural reflex, referred to as a "pivot." This pivot includes a progression of experiences practiced over and over until mastered. The logic required reflects the ability to re-learn by un-learning. If you do not un-learn the old action or behavior, you are doomed to continue to make the same mistakes over and over again.

By 2120, or certainly by 2525, many of the current worldviews on learning and the debate over the inviolable falsifications over truth in science versus the postmodernists of today will have been completely upended, morphed, and obliterated, for the nature of progress and potential mandates change – it is unavoidable unless time stops. But even in liminality, the course of humankind moves in a forward transspecies trajectory.

Learning paradigms will be inseparable from a person's being or conscious mind: Syndicated information forms the sinewy bloodstream for productivity regardless of variability and when you modify as in an *Ikara* polyneer, who naturally incorporates the arts, skills, and disciplines of people, process, and project management including program leadership.

Ikara is an aboriginal word defined as either a meeting place or throwing stick (boomerang). The image above is an icon for meeting place (concentric circles) and journey path (lines). The boomerang represents double and triple loop learning interconnections.

When translating the icon for a project or within a program management concentration, a mental lens can be interpreted as a series of integrated skills on many levels represented by the concentric circles as: Skills inside skills, inside skills. Comprising the nature of a polyneering philosophy with the integration of business, engineering, and design skills is complimented by the pioneering, entrepreneurial, and design thinking mindsets as a holistic process.

The lines in the icon represent your connection to the outside world through interactions of data, information, opinion, philosophy, and lifelong learning (i.e., your journey).

VI.   Radical Collaborations:

Take a murmuration of starlings as the epitome of radical collaboration. The starlings (birds) flying in unison, almost wingtip to wingtip, create turn-on-a-dime holistic formations in which one move at the neuron level moves the entire complex flock. Radical collaboration requires the ability to think differently and work together by behaving together even if not initially intuitive.

Breaking down "radical collaborations" into its individual terms, we have "radical," meaning something significantly different from the usual or traditional; and "collaborations," referring to opportunities to work jointly with others especially in an intellectual endeavor. Radical collaboration, therefore, stands as "an unusual or non-traditional opportunity to work jointly with others or together especially in an intellectual or creative endeavor resulting in a total effect greater than the sum of the individual effects" (Deardorff, 2018).

Thinking together paves the way towards exponential relationships targeted to challenge impossible opportunities. These relationships also require a polyneer's ability to create a metamorphous or positive shape shift in skills, beliefs, and actions.

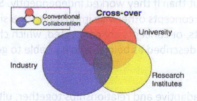

Radical collaborations enable transformations based on people from any mindset, background, location, or position coming together and creating an emotional or cognitive connection as well as inter-relations for a symbiotic mutually beneficial balance. This process keeps us constantly moving forward in a positive direction, no matter how many steps one takes in any direction. The first step in this journey allows us the ability to create adaptive relationships.

6.1   Adaptive Relationships

Without any psychobabble or mumble jumble, we need to understand an adaptive relationship and the results it can produce. An adaptive relationship is a relationship based on an expected behavior. This kind of association may require a new behavior that does not come naturally, since we are suggesting that certain actions are expected or even anticipated.

Such actions are ultimately based on developing synergy, collaboration, which creates a strong sense of togetherness sometime described as, "We are all bozos on this bus." Said another way, we are all unique experiments that make mistakes, say wrong things, think insanely stupid thoughts, and at times model poor behavior. We wake up in the middle of the night and worry about everything from what other people think of us to what the future holds. We have the opportunity to create and imagine the most spectacular events or in the reverse to do nothing with our lives.

Synergy is where the creation of a whole is greater than the simple sum of its parts, such as when two people begin functioning together at a new level because of the support and collaboration that they share with each other.

Collaboration – C. S. Lewis stated that "two heads are better than one, not because either is infallible, but because they are unlikely to go wrong in the same direction."

When people work together, they consume the fewest resources possible to get a job done, while achieving a higher quantity and quality output than if they worked independently. Synergy can help create new ideas, solve problems and develop new concepts otherwise impossible for a single person. A relationship is created when two or more people, objects, or concepts are connected, which changes the regard or way they behave. Being adaptive could be described as being flexible or able to get along with your environment by being synchronized.

When we blend the concepts of adaptive and relationships together, ultimately, we create a new personal operational definition in which an adaptive relationship creates a desire to work in a collaborative environment that fosters relationships that explore impossible opportunities.

6.2 Impossible Opportunities

Impossible opportunities are balanced on the edge of chaos with a flavor of inspiration. They are around us every day but often we fail to recognize them because of blind spots. Blinders can be called paradigms, mindsets, or biases that prevent us from even considering the possibility of an arresting opportunity.

The Apollo Moon Landing was considered an impossible opportunity. President John F. Kennedy's challenge was accomplished on the Apollo 11 mission when astronauts Neil Armstrong and Buzz Aldrin landed their lunar module on July 20, 1969. They walked on the lunar surface, while Michael Collins remained in lunar orbit in the Command/Service Module. All three landed safely back on Earth on July 24, 1969. Once this actually happened, the impossible became possible. Kennedy's provocative announcement and speech on May 25, 1961 described a plan to put a man on the moon before the decade was over. What may have seemed crazy became realized, but not without overcoming Wicked Problems & Contradictions. A positive provocation is a statement used to inspire or cognitively challenge people to achieve something that may seem impossible.

Similarly, finding a cure for cancer by 2025 may seem, to some people, impossible; to others, it seems a challenge to the current mindset and achievable. Like a runner breaking the 4-minute mile, as Sir Roger Banister did in 1954, the possibilities of human capability are many times constrained only by an impossible opportunity.

Today's impossible opportunities are filled with wicked problems. A *wicked problem* refers to a social or cultural problem that is difficult or impossible to solve for as many as four reasons: incomplete or contradictory knowledge, the number of people and opinions involved, the large economic burden, and the interconnected nature of these problems with other problems. The universal problems of poverty, sustainability, equality, and health and wellness are all within solving with the right people focused on creating impossible opportunities. The concept of contradictions prevails because the resulting solutions to a wicked problem can only be described as good or bad, true or false. The solution will improve the situation but not necessarily completely solve the problem.

An environmentalist that does not recycle or saying that one never breaks the law but has multiple speeding tickets form examples of contradictions. The contradictions associated with today's impossible opportunities mask potential solutions because they prevent us from even thinking solutions are possible. Our belief systems prevent us from believing that spending the time or effort required may be of any value. We spend our energy solving simple, easy-to-see problems. Without realizing, we have become lazy due to the abundance of what we have, rather than the recognition of what we don't have.

- Every day almost 7,500 people die in the U.S.; 105 people die each minute, but a new baby is born every 8 seconds.
- Over 553,742 people in the U.S. are experiencing homelessness but we build approximately 1,257,000 housing completions per year.
- One in 6 people in the U.S. face hunger but it is estimated that we waste 30-40% of our food supply.

(Figures are from a simple Google search)

Impossible opportunities require a desire to make a change that would seem unachievable. We must learn how to work and think together to embrace impossible opportunities.

6.3   Working & Thinking Together

Working together presents an easy solution to creating a culture in which we use the diversity of practice as a community to perform at a higher level.

Working together as a proposed solution does not describe the need to think together. Many times, failures occur as situations in which people just could not work together. Working together can be as simple as five people doing the same job in an assembly line – all independently thinking for themselves and forming a positive situation as long as they achieve a quota. We even describe this scenario as a battle rhythm for efficiency, similar to having a series of independent machines working together. When one stops working or compromises efficiency, it is simply replaced with a new machine. But this perspective does not give a system thinking approach and does not manage people as biological living things with complexity and independent thinking.

The systems thinking perspective addresses the complexity in radical collaborations by viewing people as connected and interconnected in a network that experiences chaos, complexity, and the dynamic nature of life. This view opens the need to look for a model of working together by thinking together. Though there are many solutions to achieve this goal, the best lies in parallel thinking – a thinking process in which focus is split in specific directions. When collaboratively done in a group, this kind of thinking effectively avoids the consequences of the adversarial thinking approach. In adversarial thinking, the output is debated, and the objective is to prove or disprove statements put forward by different people. With parallel thinking, the objective lies in unifying discussion or dialog along a specific direction or metaphoric theme, since, even when we think we are concentrating on one area, we may be unable to focus specifically enough to be productive.

When we think together, we share the same objective, focus, and direction of thinking, but we also experience a diversity of thinking. We can create a collaborative thinking environment where everyone's input is valuable and important. Too often, we create homogeneous thinking environments, comfortable and with little or no conflict. A same-style thinking mode prevents asking hard questions and exploring uncomfortable issues, leading to a passive thinking approach based on the knowledge of groupthink or like-minded individuals. Parallel thinking allows you to explore a heterogeneous mindset based on true diversity of thinking.

Under parallel thinking, people work together by thinking together especially when focused on moving forward in a positive direction. Sometimes moving forward requires fighting against the mindset of procrastination in thinking. There is never a perfect moment to start thinking about the challenges we face today, but establishing forward momentum establishes velocity. This behavior of velocity leads to the positive action of thinking together, sometimes referred to as polyneer shape shifting.

Thinking

Complexity

Identity

Connecting

Tinkering

Reasoning

Excite

Inquire

Incite

Explaining

6.4 Shape Shifting

The octopus is a soft bodied, eight-armed mollusk that can instantly change its color and body surface texture. This shape-shifting ability also allows it to mimic an object, such as a coconut shell bouncing along the ocean bottom, a floating piece of driftwood, or a piece of algae drifting in the current. This purposeful behavior helps confuse other animals or disguise itself, even though the octopus is color blind and sometimes huge in size – the pacific octopus can grow to 30 feet across and weigh more than 600 pounds.

Many stories tell of both men and women with the ability to change their form. In mythology, folklore, and speculative fiction, shapeshifting occurs in a being or creature that completely transforms its physical form or shape, either through the mythological creature's inherent ability, divine intervention, or the use of magic. A polyneer has the mental ability to become a shape shifter.

Shape shifters embrace the mindset of a merchant supplier by looking for areas that can be mutually beneficial using collaboration and opportunity to move forward in a positive direction. Your competitor can become your partner, your business product can become a piece of something different, and your problems, issues, and concerns can become possibilities. The transformation from one state or thing into another occurs naturally and effortlessly if it is embraced as a positive strategy.

To accomplish this shape shift, a polyneer can simply imagine themselves as someone or something different. They are not afraid of organizational transformations – they embrace these as opportunities to try or become something new. This exciting personal transformation opens up new mindsets and breaks paradigms.

```
          Meet the Problem
                 |
                 v
          List Known Facts  <---
             |        |         \
             v        v          \
     Research      List Unknowns  /
     Unknowns  <----------------
                 |
                 v
      Generate Possible Solutions
                 |
                 v
       Choose Most Viable Solution
                 |
                 v
           Report Solution
```

Paradigm paralysis is one of the greatest barriers to a paradigm shift. Paradigms are referred to as a standard perspective or set of ideas that automatically guide your way of thinking or looking at something. The word has been overused and its meaning diffused. Thomas Kuhn described a paradigm shift in his book, The Structures of Scientific Revolutions, in a much narrower way as a fundamental change in the basic concepts and practices of a scientific discipline. Joel Barker popularized the term by visually describing examples of paradigm paralysis. His story of a pig is one example. Here, a driver comes around a turn and sees a car in his lane. He swerves out of the way while the other driver screams "pig" at him. He yells back "cow" and feels content because he was able to get back at the other driver. He then speeds off around a hairpin turn and proceeds to hit a pig.

The story illustrates a couple of key themes, the first being that what people scream out may need deeper understanding instead of being instinctively dismissed. The other theme points to our refusal or inability to think beyond our current framework or way of thinking, seeing, or perceiving things. This inability causes us to act, behave, and interact with others based upon our pre-conceived perceptions and mindsets.

Our natural thinking process toggles from fact to decision or action based on the information we have available and the images we see around us. We make assumptions and conclusions from our interpreted and selected reality. If the information and data we have available is incorrect, we can be led into an inaccurate belief structure. This paradigm paralysis can prevent us from trusting, sharing, believing, and interpreting opportunities accurately. Balancing our mental mindsets requires learning the difference between reality and chaos.

6.5   <u>Synchronicity</u>

Synchronicity is the simultaneous occurrence of events that appear significantly related but have no discernable causal connection – two or more events happen in a meaningful manner. Events are bound by meaning, a meaning that relates to what happens, with the goal that the right people were at exactly the right place at exactly the right times to do exactly the right things. Synchronicity hence stands as an example of finding order in chaos, such as in the butterfly effect, in which a single positive act can result in a profound transformational change that Carl Jung noted as events with meaningful coincidences.

A coincidence is when two events strangely or remarkably happen at the same time, but without any apparent reason or causal connection. Some people believe that their world is based on nothing more than a series of coincidences, that they have no actual power to make changes to a fatalistic, predetermined life plan. Others may believe that there is a supernatural or paranormal effect in place that causes things to happen due to another entity's interactions.

From a statistical perspective, a coincidence is nothing more than an inevitable event that appears random. For example, the probability of two people having the same birthday exceeds 50% in a group of only 23 people. When we look for the unexplainable, we usually find it. There are connections and interconnections happening around us all the time. Our ability to recognize them is a skill that can be improved, enhanced, and used to create radical collaborations.

Radical collaborations also require a polyneer to embrace many different thinking mindsets and new partner relationships based on moving forward in a positive direction. Your gut instinct becomes as valuable as the tacit knowledge that you bring as part of your "self-journey." Instinct is not always right, and intuition must balance conscious reasoning and knowledge.

Additionally, you are constantly adapting, learning, experimenting, conceptually pondering and playing as part of a transformation process. The description and philosophy of a Renaissance man or woman fits because you emulate polymath, an enlightened person whose expertise spans a significant number of various fields or subject areas. This profound knowledge is openly shared with others as you strive to reach your full potential of competence in all complimentary areas of the world around you.

Penultimately, creating radical collaborations is based on a plan of moving forward using skills that may be natural and easy, or that must be learned and practiced to become useable. You can start to create radical collaborations by simply introducing yourself to a possible new associate.

The Future of the Polyneer and Polyneering:

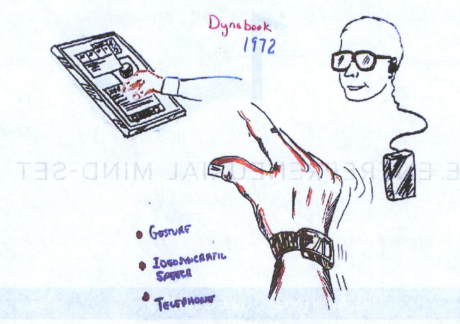

Dynabook
1972

● Gesture

● Idiosyncratic Speech

● Telephone

(Artwork provided by Alan Kay)

Every decade has a futurist that marvels the status quo. Alan Kay conceived the Dynabook beginning in 1968 to triangulate the phone with space and gesture long before Steve Jobs perfected the tablet. Buckminster Fuller conceived terms such as "Spaceship Earth" and designs known as geodesic domes. Stephen Hawking promoted and explained "Hawking Radiation" debating and challenging and betting on the future. And not all ideas or inventions are always a success. Take Nikola Tesla's thought camera from 1893 to take a picture of human thought; Tesla created some 270 patents including a wireless energy transmission tower as well as supersonic airships. And currently in 2020 there are firms and teams creating and curating a new kind of "metaverse" where digital objects are present in physical spaces creating unchartered multiprong, multigadget bi-directional communication. By 2050 spatial computing offers an always-on virtual experience blended seamlessly with trillions of interactions from people, places, and pixels. A new frictionless, voice-activated, eye-controlled extended reality morphing from a 2-D fixed-screen environment to a graphical user interface that is 3-D, invisible, and ubiquitous of past, present, future activities.

New occupations, new titles, new dimensions supersede and transform a static world for dynamicism. The polyneer becomes immersed in a transspecies world by accepting the transdisciplinary attributes and not through stagnation but with openness to change, to cross-overs once thought impossible. The Polyverse then comprises a new language and a new coda that enables communication and problem-solving to be as fitting as progress is fast.

1

THE ENTREPRENEURIAL MIND-SET

1

To introduce the concept of entrepreneurship and explain the process of entrepreneurial action.

2

To describe how structural similarities enable entrepreneurs to make creative mental leaps.

3

To highlight bricolage as a source of entrepreneurs' resourcefulness.

4

To introduce effectuation as a way expert entrepreneurs sometimes think.

5

To develop the notion that entrepreneurs cognitively adapt.

6

To introduce sustainable entrepreneurship as a means of sustaining the natural environment and communities and developing gains for others.

OPENING PROFILE

EWING MARION KAUFFMAN

Born on a farm in Garden City, Missouri, Ewing Marion Kauffman moved to Kansas City with his family when he was eight years old. A critical event in his life occurred several years later when Kauffman was diagnosed with a leakage of the heart. His prescription was one year of complete bed rest; he was not even allowed to sit up. Kauffman's mother, a college graduate, came up with a solution to keep the active 11-year-old boy lying in bed—reading. According to Kauffman, he "sure read! Because nothing else would do, I read as many as 40 to 50 books every month. When you read that much, you read anything. So I read the biographies of all the presidents, the frontiersmen, and I read the Bible twice and that's pretty rough reading."

olympics.powerbar.com

Another important early childhood experience centered on door-to-door sales. Since his family did not have a lot of money, Kauffman sold 36 dozen eggs collected from the farm or fish he and his father had caught, cleaned, and dressed. His mother was very encouraging during these formative school years, telling young Ewing each day, "There may be some who have more money in their pockets, but Ewing, there is nobody better than you."

During his youth, Kauffman worked as a laundry delivery person and was a Boy Scout. In addition to passing all the requirements to become an Eagle Scout and a Sea Scout, he sold twice as many tickets to the Boy Scout Roundup as anyone else in Kansas City, an accomplishment that enabled him to attend, for free, a two-week scout summer camp that his parents would not otherwise have been able to afford. According to Kauffman, "This experience gave me some of the sales techniques which came into play when subsequently I went into the pharmaceutical business."

Kauffman went to junior college from 8 to 12 in the morning and then walked two miles to the laundry where he worked until 7 p.m. Upon graduation, he went to work at the laundry full time for Mr. R. A. Long, who eventually became one of his role models. His job as route foreman involved managing 18 to 20 route drivers, where he would set up sales contests, such as challenging the other drivers to get more customers on a particular route than he could obtain. Kauffman says, "I got practice in selling and that proved to be beneficial later in life." R. A. Long made money not only at the laundry business but also on patents, one of which was a form fit for the collar of a shirt that would hold the shape of the shirt. He showed his young protégé that one could make money with brains as well as brawn. Kauffman commented, "He was quite a man and had quite an influence on my life."

Kauffman's sales ability was also useful during his stint in the Navy, which he joined shortly after Pearl Harbor on January 11, 1942. When designated as an apprentice seaman, a position that paid $21 per month, he responded, "I'm better than an apprentice seaman, because I have been a Sea Scout. I've sailed ships and I've ridden in whale boats." His selling ability convinced the Navy that he should instead start as a seaman first class, with a $54 monthly salary. Kauffman was assigned to the admiral's staff, where he became an outstanding signalman (a seaman who transmitted messages from ship to ship), in part because he was able to read messages better than anyone else due to his previous intensive reading. With his admiral's encouragement, Kauffman took a correspondence navigator's course and was given a deck commission and made a navigation officer.

After the war was over in 1947, Ewing Kauffman began his career as a pharmaceutical salesperson after performing better on an aptitude test than 50 other applicants. The job involved selling supplies of vitamin and liver shots to doctors. Working on straight commission, without expenses or benefits, he was earning pay higher than the president's salary by the end of the second year; the president promptly cut the commission. Eventually, when Kauffman was made Midwest sales manager, he made 3 percent of everything his salespeople sold and continued to make more money than the president. When his territory was cut, he eventually quit and in 1950 started his own company—Marion Laboratories. (Marion is his middle name.)

When reflecting on founding the new company, Ewing Kauffman commented, "It was easier than it sounds because I had doctors whom I had been selling office supplies to for several years. Before I made the break, I went to three of them and said, 'I'm thinking of starting my own company. May I count on you to give me your orders if I can give you the same quality and service?' These three were my biggest accounts and each one of them agreed because they liked me and were happy to do business with me."

Marion Laboratories started by marketing injectable products that were manufactured by another company under Marion's label. The company expanded to other accounts and other products and then developed its first prescription item, Vicam, a vitamin product. The second pharmaceutical product it developed, oyster shell calcium, also sold well.

To expand the company, Kauffman borrowed $5,000 from the Commerce Trust Company. He repaid the loan, and the company continued to grow. After several years, outside investors could buy $1,000 worth of common stock if they loaned the company $1,000 to be paid back in five years at $1,250, without any intermittent interest. This initial $1,000 investment, if held until 1993, would have been worth $21 million.

Marion Laboratories continued to grow and reached over $1 billion per year in sales, due primarily to the relationship between Ewing Kauffman and the people in the company, who were called associates, not employees. "They are all stockholders, they build this company, and they mean so much to us," said Kauffman. The concept of associates was also a part of the two basic philosophies of the company: Those who produce should share in the results or profits and treat others as you would like to be treated.

The company went public through Smith Barney on August 16, 1965, at $21 per share. The stock jumped to $28 per share immediately and has never dropped below that level, sometimes selling at a 50 to 60 price/earnings multiple. The associates of the company were offered a profit-sharing plan, where each could own stock in the company. In 1968, Kauffman brought Major League Baseball back to Kansas City by purchasing the Kansas City Royals. This boosted the city's economic base, community profile, and civic pride. When Marion Laboratories merged with Merrill Dow in 1989, there were 3,400 associates, 300 of whom became millionaires as a result of the merger. The new company, Marion Merrill Dow, Inc., grew to 9,000 associates and sales of $4 billion in 1998 when it was acquired by Hoechst, a European pharmaceutical company. Hoechst Marion Roussel became a world leader in pharmaceutical-based health care involved in the discovery, development, manufacture, and sale of pharmaceutical products. In late 1999, the company was again merged with Aventis Pharma, a global pharmaceutical company focusing on human medicines (prescription pharmaceuticals and vaccines) and animal health. In 2002, Aventis's sales reached $16.634 billion, an increase of 11.6 percent from 2001, while earnings per share grew 27 percent from the previous year.

Ewing Marion Kauffman was an entrepreneur, a Major League Baseball team owner, and a philanthropist who believed his success was a direct result of one fundamental philosophy: Treat others as you would like to be treated. "It is the happiest principle by which to live and the most intelligent principle by which to do business and make money," he said.

Ewing Marion Kauffman's philosophies of associates, rewarding those who produce, and allowing decision making throughout the organization are the fundamental concepts underlying what is now called *corporate entrepreneurship* in a company. He went even further and illustrated his belief in entrepreneurship and the spirit of giving back when he established the Kauffman Foundation, which supports programs in two areas: youth development and entrepreneurship. Truly a remarkable entrepreneur, Mr. K, as he was affectionately called by his employees, will now produce many more successful "associate entrepreneurs."

Like Ewing Marion Kauffman, many other entrepreneurs and future entrepreneurs frequently ask themselves, "Am I really an entrepreneur? Do I have what it takes to be a success? Do I have sufficient background and experience to start and manage a new venture?" As enticing as the thought of starting and owning a business may be, the problems and pitfalls inherent to the process are as legendary as the success stories. The fact remains that more new business ventures fail than succeed. To be one of the few successful entrepreneurs requires more than just hard work and luck. It requires the ability to think in an environment of high uncertainty, be flexible, and learn from one's failures.

entrepreneurial opportunities Those situations in which new goods, services, raw materials, and organizing methods can be introduced and sold at greater than their cost of production

THE NATURE OF ENTREPRENEURSHIP

Entrepreneurship plays an important role in the creation and growth of businesses, as well as in the growth and prosperity of regions and nations. These large-scale outcomes can have quite humble beginnings; entrepreneurial actions begin at the nexus of a lucrative opportunity and an enterprising individual.[1] *Entrepreneurial opportunities* are "those situations in which new goods, services, raw materials, and organizing methods can be introduced and sold at greater than their cost of production."[2] For example, an entrepreneurial opportunity could stem from introducing an existing technological product used in one market to create a new market. Alternatively, an entrepreneurial opportunity could be creating a new technological product for an existing market or creating both a new product/service and a new market. The recurring theme is that an entrepreneurial opportunity represents something new. However, such possibilities require an enterprising individual or a group of enterprising individuals to recognize, evaluate, and exploit these situations as possible opportunities. Therefore, entrepreneurship requires action—*entrepreneurial action* through the creation of new products/processes and/or the entry into new markets, which may occur through a newly created organization or within an established organization.

entrepreneurial action
Action through the creation of new products/processes and/or the entry into new markets, which may occur through a newly created organization or within an established organization

Entrepreneurs act on what they believe is an opportunity. Because opportunities exist in (or create and/or generate) high uncertainty, entrepreneurs must use their judgment about whether or not to act. However, doubt can undermine entrepreneurial action. Therefore, a key to understanding entrepreneurial action is being able to assess the amount of uncertainty perceived to surround a potential opportunity and the individual's willingness to bear that uncertainty. The individual's prior knowledge can decrease the amount of uncertainty, and his or her motivation indicates a willingness to bear uncertainty.

As illustrated in Figure 1.1, the McMullen-Shepherd model explains how knowledge and motivation influence two stages of entrepreneurial action. Signals of changes in the environment that represent possible opportunities will be noticed by some individuals but not others. Individuals with knowledge of markets and/or technology are more capable of detecting changes in the external environment, and if they are also motivated, they will allocate further attention to processing this information. Others, however, will remain ignorant of the possibility. The result of Stage 1 is an individual's realization that an opportunity exists for someone. The individual then needs to determine whether it represents an opportunity for him or her (Stage 2). This involves assessing whether it is feasible to successfully exploit the opportunity given one's knowledge and whether it is desirable given one's motivation. In other words, does this opportunity for someone (third-person opportunity belief) represent an opportunity for me (first-person opportunity belief)? If the individual overcomes enough doubt to form (1) the belief that the situation represents an opportunity for someone in general, and then (2) the belief that the opportunity for someone is an opportunity for himself or herself personally, this individual may act.

FIGURE 1.1   Entrepreneurial Action

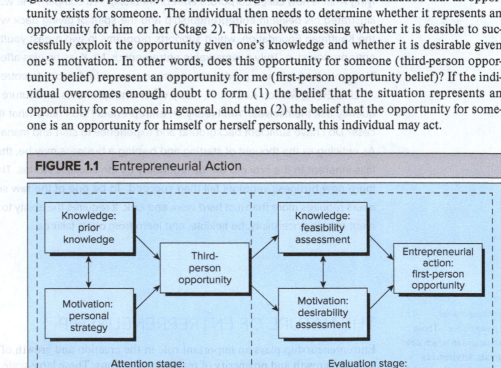

Source: McMullen, J., Shepherd, D. A., "Entrepreneurial Action and the Role of Uncertainty in the Theory of the Entrepreneur," *Academy of Management Review*, vol. 31, 2006, 132–142.

Therefore, to be an entrepreneur is to act on the possibility that one has identified an opportunity worth pursuing.[3] It involves *entrepreneurial thinking*—individuals' mental processes of overcoming ignorance to decide whether a signal represents an opportunity for someone and/or reducing doubt as to whether an opportunity for someone is also an opportunity for them specifically, and/or processing feedback from action steps taken. To explain these processes more fully, we now turn to different forms of entrepreneurial thinking.

HOW ENTREPRENEURS THINK

Entrepreneurs think differently from nonentrepreneurs. Moreover, an entrepreneur in a particular situation may think differently from when faced with some other task or decision environment. Entrepreneurs must often make decisions in highly uncertain environments where the stakes are high, time pressures are immense, and there is considerable emotional investment. We all think differently in these strained environments than we do when the nature of a problem is well understood and we have time and rational procedures at hand to solve it. Given the nature of an entrepreneur's decision-making environment, he or she must sometimes (1) think structurally, (2) engage in bricolage, (3) effectuate, and (4) cognitively adapt.

Think Structurally

Forming opportunity beliefs often requires creative mental leaps. These creative mental leaps are launched from a source—one's existing knowledge. In the case of entrepreneurial opportunities, an example of a creative mental leap is from knowledge about existing markets to a new technology that could lead to products/services that satisfy that market. Alternatively, the creative mental leap could be from knowledge about a technology to a new market that could benefit from its introduction. Making these connections between a new product (or new service, new business model, or new technology) and a target market where it can be introduced is aided by the superficial and structural similarities between the source (e.g., the market) and the destination (e.g., technology). *Superficial similarities* exist when the basic (relatively easy to observe) elements of the technology resemble (match) the basic (relatively easy to observe) elements of the market. In contrast, *structural similarities* exist when the underlying mechanisms of the technology (i.e., such as the capability of such a technology to perform a specific function) resemble (or match) the underlying mechanisms of the market (i.e., the latent demands of a large, potential group of customers). The entrepreneurial challenge often lies in making creative mental leaps based on *structural* similarities. This is best illustrated with an example based on a real case that Denis Grégoire from Syracuse University and me (Dean Shepherd from University of Notre Dame) used as part of a study of entrepreneurial thinking.[4]

The example is a technology developed by space and computer engineers at NASA's Langley Research Center. It involves big and bulky flight simulators used by space shuttle pilots. As such, the technology's superficial elements are very similar to a market for airline pilots training in flight simulators. In contrast, it has little superficial similarity with a target market of K–12 school children and their parents. The technology underlying the superficial situations includes attaching sensors to individuals' forefingers to monitor the electric conductivity of their skin to send signals to computer processors in another machine with which the individual interacts. Ultimately, these one-to-one relationships (skin to sensor and sensor to computer) culminate into a network of higher-order relationships that reflect the overall capabilities of the technology, its aims, and/or its uses. Therefore, the technology is capable of helping shuttle pilots (or airline pilots or teenage drivers) improve their abilities to focus, pay attention, and concentrate for an extended period. Looked at in a new light, however, the technology shares high levels of structural similarities with the target market of parents who

entrepreneurial thinking   Individuals' mental processes of overcoming ignorance to decide whether a signal represents an opportunity for someone and/or reducing doubt as to whether an opportunity for someone is also an opportunity for them specifically, and/or processing feedback from action steps taken

superficial similarities Exist when the basic (relatively easy to observe) elements of the technology resemble (match) the basic (relatively easy to observe) elements of the market

structural similarities Exist when the underlying mechanisms of the technology resemble (or match) the underlying mechanisms of the market

AS SEEN IN *BUSINESS NEWS*

DO ENTREPRENEURS BENEFIT FROM PARANOIA?

Some believe that paranoia is a psychological condition that causes dysfunction. But, at least in terms of business, Andrew Grove, president and CEO of Intel Corp., believes that "Only the Paranoid Survive." By placing yourself in a state of paranoia, you become highly concerned about, and sensitive to, threats to your company and you are motivated to take action to alleviate or eliminate those threats.

PRINCIPLES OF ACTING PARANOIA

Underlying paranoia is a recognition that others want to achieve success and are willing to take it away from you. They are watching your business and how you respond to changes in the competitive environment. Therefore, Andrew Grove worries about product defects, releasing products too early, factories not performing efficiently, having too much (or too little) capacity, and so on. The principles of paranoia are the following:

1. **Paranoia Means Not Resting on Your Laurels.** This simply means that even given your past successes there are still threats out there; you must be vigilant to notice and then respond to these threats. Andrew Grove calls this a *guardian attitude*—the attitude that

is required to protect the firm from potential competitor moves or other environmental threats.

2. **Paranoia Means Being Detail Orientated.** This means attending to even the smallest details because this is a major line of defense against threats. This means attending both to the details internal to running the business and to those external including catering to the demands of your customers.

Paranoia is particularly important when the business environment is characterized in terms of high levels of competition and high number of opportunities.

THE DOWNSIDE OF PARANOIA

There may be such thing as too much paranoia—too much time and effort invested in noticing and responding to threats. One entrepreneur uses the examples of using $500 worth of accounting time to find a $5 error (which does not make sense unless there is information of a more systematic problem that led to the $5 error). Worrying "obsessively" could also be a warning sign, one that requires a remedy. Although entrepreneurs are known to often be thinking about their business, an inability to "turn it off," at least for short periods, can

seek nonpharmaceutical alternatives to treat attention deficit (ADHD). This opportunity to apply the technology to the market of parents seeking nonpharmaceutical alternatives to treat ADHD was not obvious to individuals who were distracted from the deeper structural similarities by the superficial mismatch between the technology and the new market.

Thus, individuals who can see or create structural matches between a technology and a target market, especially in the presence of superficial mismatches, are more likely to identify entrepreneurial opportunities. Knowledge specific to a technology and/or a market can facilitate this ability,[5] and the good news is that this skill can also be enhanced through practice and training.

Bricolage

bricolage Entrepreneurs making do by applying combinations of the resources at hand to new problems and opportunities

Entrepreneurs often lack resources. As a result, they either seek resources from others to provide the "slack" necessary to experiment and generate entrepreneurial opportunities or they engage in bricolage. By *bricolage* we mean that some entrepreneurs make "do by applying combinations of the resources at hand to new problems and opportunities."[6] This involves taking existing resources (those at hand) and experimenting, tinkering, repackaging, and/or reframing them so they can be used in a way for which they were not originally cause psychological and physical problems. That is, having some work life balance can be beneficial to the individual both as an entrepreneur and as a human being.

Paranoia can also lead to fear, such as fear of failure. Fear of failure can constrict thinking and lead to inaction and inaction can make the entrepreneur's firm more vulnerable. One entrepreneur noted that if he was fearful then his business would never have got off the ground. Indeed, perhaps entrepreneurs are already so paranoid that any more paranoia may push them over the edge of what is healthy. They may be so paranoid about the business that their words and actions begin to discourage employees and customers. That is, paranoia that your employees or customers are out to get you may lead to them leaving and creating an actual (rather than an imagined) threat to the business. Indeed, for the entrepreneur's business to grow and achieve success, he or she may need to put some faith in the organization's employees and customers.

"CRITICAL EVALUATION" RATHER THAN PARANOIA

Perhaps the term *paranoia* is too loaded, and therefore care must be taken in advising entrepreneurs that they need to become more paranoid. But Andrew Grove's point is well taken. It might be better to talk about critical evaluation or critical analysis, which means to look at everything (suggests Stephen Markoitz, director of governmental and political relations of a small business association). He suggests that if the entrepreneur is paranoid then he or she is unable to look at everything. That is, the entrepreneur may be particularly good at noticing threats but miss opportunities. (But is it ever possible to see and evaluate everything?)

Whatever it is called, the point is that entrepreneurs are likely to keep worrying about their business, keep trying to attend to both threats and opportunities, and think constantly about how to enable their business to succeed.

ADVICE TO AN ENTREPRENEUR

A friend who has just become an entrepreneur has read the above article and comes to you for advice:

1. I worry about my business; does that mean I am paranoid?
2. What are the benefits of paranoia and what are the costs?
3. How do I know I have the right level of paranoia to effectively run the business and not put me in the hospital with a stomach ulcer?
4. Won't forcing myself to be more paranoid take the fun out of being an entrepreneur?

Source: Mark Henricks, "How Smart Entrepreneurs Harness the Power of Paranoia," *Entrepreneur magazine, March 1997,* www.entrepreneur.com.

designed or conceived.[7] From this process of "making do," entrepreneurs can create opportunities. Baker and Nelson (2005: 341–42) offer the following example of bricolage.

Tim Grayson was a farmer whose land was crisscrossed by abandoned coal mines. He knew that the tunnels—a nuisance to farmers because of their tendency to collapse, causing mammoth sinkholes in fields—also contained large quantities of methane. Methane is another nuisance, a toxic greenhouse gas that poisons miners and persists in abandoned mines for generations. Grayson and a partner drilled a hole from Grayson's property to an abandoned mine shaft, then acquired a used diesel generator from a local factory and crudely retrofitted it to burn methane. During the conversion process, Grayson was repeatedly blown off his feet when the odorless, colorless gas exploded. His bricolage produced electricity, most of which he sold to the local utility company using scavenged switchgear. Because Grayson's generator also produced considerable waste heat, he built a greenhouse for hydroponic tomatoes, which he heated with water from the generator's cooling system. He also used electricity generated during off-peak hours to power special lamps to speed plant growth. With the availability of a greenhouse full of trenches of nutrient-rich water that were heated "for free," Grayson realized he might be able to raise tilapia, a tropical delicacy increasingly popular in the United States. He introduced the fish to the waters that bathed the tomato roots and used the fish waste as fertilizer. Finally, with abundant methane still at hand, Grayson began selling excess methane to a natural gas company. As you can see from this example, bricolage is a resourceful way of thinking and behaving that represents an important source of entrepreneurial opportunities.

Effectuation

As potential business leaders, you are trained to think rationally and perhaps admonished if you do not. This admonishment might be appropriate given the nature of the task, but it appears that there is an alternate way of thinking that entrepreneurs sometimes use, especially when thinking about opportunities. Professor Saras Sarasvathy (from Darden, University of Virginia) has found that entrepreneurs do not always think through a problem in a way that starts with a desired outcome and focuses on the means to generate that outcome. Such a process is referred to as a *causal process*. But, entrepreneurs sometimes use an *effectuation process*, which means they take what they have (who they are, what they know, and whom they know) and select among possible outcomes. Think about cooking dinner tonight. You could select a dinner that you would like, find a recipe that lists the ingredients and the order of the tasks required to cook the meal, and then go shopping for the ingredients (assuming you know what is in the pantry at home). This way of thinking about the problem of fixing dinner involves the process of causation. Another way to approach the problem of fixing dinner is to go home, see what food is in the pantry (and the pots and pans and equipment in the cupboards), and imagine all the dinners that are possible using some combination of these ingredients, select one, and start cooking. This way of cooking is consistent with the effectuation logic. That is, effectuation starts with what is available and thinking about the many possible alternatives that can be generated.

To continue with the cooking example, but applying it to entrepreneurship, Professor Sarasvathy offered a thought experiment to illustrate the distinction between causation and effectuation.[i] The thought experiment starts with an imaginary Indian restaurant called "Curry-in-a-Hurry". Following a causation process, the entrepreneur could follow the textbook. The classic textbook is *Marketing Management* by Philip Kotler (1991), which details the 11 necessary sequence of steps to be followed to bring a new product or service to market. In short, this process involves the stages of segmenting, targeting, and positioning. What does this mean to the entrepreneur of Curry-in-a-Hurry? She can begin the process by thinking about the universe of potential customers in her city. She can then segment the market based on demographics (e.g., age and gender), socioeconomic status of neighborhoods, family income, and dining patterns. The entrepreneur can then survey a random sample of people in the different segments and use that information to select a target market, for example, families in a wealthy neighborhood who eat at restaurants twice a week. Having selected the target market, she can then make decisions about the location and décor of the restaurant, the food and the price for the menu, and other operational issues. As you can imagine, this process would take considerable time and some financial resources; and this is before she is able to sell anything.

However, let's continue the thought experiment but this time use the effectuation process. Rather than assume that there is an existing market and she has the resources to invest in finding out what would be the ideal restaurant for that market (as done through causation), the entrepreneur would start by taking stock of what resources she has available (i.e., who she is, what she knows, and who she knows) and think about the possible things she could do with different combinations of those resources. She could try and secure a partnership with an established restaurateur or she would approach a local Indian restaurant and

causal process A process that starts with a desired outcome and focuses on the means to generate that outcome

effectuation process A process that starts with what one has (who they are, what they know, and whom they know) and selects among possible outcomes

---

[i] S. Sarasvathy, "Causation and Effectuation: Toward a Theoretical Shift from Economic Inevitability to Entrepreneurial Contingency," *Academy of Management Review* vol. 26 (2001), p. 245.

ask them if she could set up a stand to sell her Indian specialties—perhaps specialties that complement the restaurant's existing menu. Deciding what is offered might be made "on the fly" as information becomes available. Because the costs are low she can experiment with different foods and different approaches. This experimentation provides information about what the market wants and is willing to pay for (and what the market does not want) and brings in some money while doing so.

Another option might be for the entrepreneur to take stock of who she knows and, as a result, take food to a friend's office so his colleagues can try the assortment of items. This action, and feedback, may lead the entrepreneur to start a food deliver business. As the delivery business grows, the entrepreneur learns about people's tastes and hones her menu, and more and more people learn about Curry-in-a-Hurry. The entrepreneur now has the knowledge and the customer base (and the cash flow) to open up a restaurant. After opening the restaurant, the entrepreneur continues to learn and the world continues to change, and both may present opportunities to change the nature of the business and/or create a new business. Professor Sarasvathy offers a number of possibilities including: (1) Curry Favors—a catering and party planning business, (2) School of Curry—a school that teaches about Indian cooking, culture, and music, and (3) Curryland Travels—a business offering themed tours of India and the Far-East. Okay, these examples are a bit fanciful. But fanciful is okay. Fanciful engages uncertainty and involves creativity, play, and experimentation; all of which are elements important to entrepreneurship.

We are not suggesting that effectuation is a superior thought process to causation; rather, it represents a way that entrepreneurs sometimes think. Effectuation . . . helps entrepreneurs think in an environment of high uncertainty. Indeed organizations today operate in complex and dynamic environments that are increasingly characterized by rapid, substantial, and discontinuous change.[11] Given the nature of this type of environment, most managers of firms need to take on an *entrepreneurial mind-set* so that their firms can successfully adapt to environmental changes.[12] This *entrepreneurial mind-set* involves the ability to rapidly sense, act, and mobilize, even under uncertain conditions.[13] In developing an entrepreneurial mind-set, individuals must attempt to make sense of opportunities in the context of changing goals, constantly questioning the "dominant logic" in the context of a changing environment and revisiting "deceptively simple questions" about what is thought to be true about markets and the firm. For example, effective entrepreneurs are thought to continuously "rethink current strategic actions, organization structure, communications systems, corporate culture, asset deployment, investment strategies, in short every aspect of a firm's operation and long-term health."[14]

entrepreneurial mind-set
Involves the ability to rapidly sense, act, and mobilize, even under uncertain conditions

cognitive adaptability
Describes the extent to which entrepreneurs are dynamic, flexible, self-regulating, and engaged in the process of generating multiple decision frameworks focused on sensing and processing changes in their environments and then acting on them

To be good at these tasks, individuals must develop a *cognitive adaptability*. Mike Haynie, a retired major of the U.S. Air Force and now professor at Syracuse University, and me (Dean Shepherd from Indiana University) have developed a number of models of cognitive adaptability and a survey for capturing it, to which we now turn.[15]

Cognitive Adaptability

Cognitive adaptability describes the extent to which entrepreneurs are dynamic, flexible, self-regulating, and engaged in the process of generating multiple decision frameworks focused on sensing and processing changes in their environments and then acting on them. Decision frameworks are organized on knowledge about people and situations that are used to help someone make sense of what is going on.[16] Cognitive adaptability is reflected in an entrepreneur's metacognitive awareness, that is, the ability to reflect upon, understand, and control one's thinking and learning.[17] Specifically, metacognition describes a higher-order cognitive process that serves to organize what individuals know and recognize about themselves, tasks, situations, and their environments to promote effective and *adaptable* cognitive functioning in the face of feedback from complex and dynamic environments.[18]

How cognitively adaptable are you? Try the survey in Table 1.1 and compare yourself to some of your classmates. A higher score means that you are more metacognitively aware, and this in turn helps provide cognitive adaptability. Regardless of your score, the good news is that you can learn to be more cognitively adaptable. This ability will serve you well in most

---

TABLE 1.1   Mike Haynie's "Measure of Adaptive Cognition"

How Cognitively Flexible Are You? On a scale of 1 to 10, where 1 is "not very much like me" and 10 is "very much like me," how do you rate yourself on the following statements?

Goal Orientation

I often define goals for myself.	Not very much—1 2 3 4 5 6 7 8 9 10—Very much like me like me
I understand how accomplishment of a task relates to my goals.	Not very much—1 2 3 4 5 6 7 8 9 10—Very much like me like me
I set specific goals before I begin a task.	Not very much—1 2 3 4 5 6 7 8 9 10—Very much like me like me
I ask myself how well I've accomplished my goals once I've finished.	Not very much—1 2 3 4 5 6 7 8 9 10—Very much like me like me
When performing a task, I frequently assess my progress against my objectives.	Not very much—1 2 3 4 5 6 7 8 9 10—Very much like me like me

Metacognitive Knowledge

I think of several ways to solve a problem and choose the best one.	Not very much—1 2 3 4 5 6 7 8 9 10—Very much like me like me
I challenge my own assumptions about a task before I begin.	Not very much—1 2 3 4 5 6 7 8 9 10—Very much like me like me
I think about how others may react to my actions.	Not very much—1 2 3 4 5 6 7 8 9 10—Very much like me like me
I find myself automatically employing strategies that have worked in the past.	Not very much—1 2 3 4 5 6 7 8 9 10—Very much like me like me
I perform best when I already have knowledge of the task.	Not very much—1 2 3 4 5 6 7 8 9 10—Very much like me like me
I create my own examples to make information more meaningful.	Not very much—1 2 3 4 5 6 7 8 9 10—Very much like me like me
I try to use strategies that have worked in the past.	Not very much—1 2 3 4 5 6 7 8 9 10—Very much like me like me
I ask myself questions about the task before I begin.	Not very much—1 2 3 4 5 6 7 8 9 10—Very much like me like me
I try to translate new information into my own words.	Not very much—1 2 3 4 5 6 7 8 9 10—Very much like me like me
I try to break problems down into smaller components.	Not very much—1 2 3 4 5 6 7 8 9 10—Very much like me like me
I focus on the meaning and significance of new information.	Not very much—1 2 3 4 5 6 7 8 9 10—Very much like me like me

Metacognitive Experience

I think about what I really need to accomplish before I begin a task.	**Not very much—1 2 3 4 5 6 7 8 9 10—Very much like me** **like me**
I use different strategies depending on the situation.	**Not very much—1 2 3 4 5 6 7 8 9 10—Very much like me** **like me**
I organize my time to best accomplish my goals.	**Not very much—1 2 3 4 5 6 7 8 9 10—Very much like me** **like me**
I am good at organizing information.	**Not very much—1 2 3 4 5 6 7 8 9 10—Very much like me** **like me**
I know what kind of information is most important to consider when faced with a problem.	**Not very much—1 2 3 4 5 6 7 8 9 10—Very much like me** **like me**
I consciously focus my attention on important information.	**Not very much—1 2 3 4 5 6 7 8 9 10—Very much like me** **like me**
My "gut" tells me when a given strategy I use will be most effective.	**Not very much—1 2 3 4 5 6 7 8 9 10—Very much like me** **like me**
I depend on my intuition to help me formulate strategies.	**Not very much—1 2 3 4 5 6 7 8 9 10—Very much like me** **like me**

Metacognitive Choice

I ask myself if I have considered all the options when solving a problem.	**Not very much—1 2 3 4 5 6 7 8 9 10—Very much like me** **like me**
I ask myself if there was an easier way to do things after I finish a task.	**Not very much—1 2 3 4 5 6 7 8 9 10—Very much like me** **like me**
I ask myself if I have considered all the options after I solve a problem.	**Not very much—1 2 3 4 5 6 7 8 9 10—Very much like me** **like me**
I re-evaluate my assumptions when I get confused.	**Not very much—1 2 3 4 5 6 7 8 9 10—Very much like me** **like me**
I ask myself if I have learned as much as I could have after I finish the task.	**Not very much—1 2 3 4 5 6 7 8 9 10—Very much like me** **like me**

Monitoring

I periodically review to help me understand important relationships.	**Not very much—1 2 3 4 5 6 7 8 9 10—Very much like me** **like me**
I stop and go back over information that is not clear.	**Not very much—1 2 3 4 5 6 7 8 9 10—Very much like me** **like me**
I am aware of what strategies I use when engaged in a given task.	**Not very much—1 2 3 4 5 6 7 8 9 10—Very much like me** **like me**
I find myself analyzing the usefulness of a given strategy while engaged in a given task.	**Not very much—1 2 3 4 5 6 7 8 9 10—Very much like me** **like me**
I find myself pausing regularly to check my comprehension of the problem or situation at hand.	**Not very much—1 2 3 4 5 6 7 8 9 10—Very much like me** **like me**
I ask myself questions about how well I am doing while I am performing a novel task. I stop and re-read when I get confused.	**Not very much—1 2 3 4 5 6 7 8 9 10—Very much like me** **like me**

Result—A higher score means that you are more aware of the way that you think about how you make decisions and are therefore more likely to be cognitively flexible.

Source: M. Haynie and D. Shepherd, "A Measure of Adaptive Cognition for Entrepreneurship Research," *Entrepreneurship, Theory and Practice*, vol. 33, no. 3, 2009, 695–714.

new tasks, but particularly when pursuing a new entry and managing a firm in an uncertain environment. Put simply, it requires us to "think about thinking which requires, and helps provide, knowledge and control over our thinking and learning activities—it requires us to be self-aware, think aloud, reflect, be strategic, plan, have a plan in mind, know what to know, and self-monitor.[19] We can achieve this by asking ourselves a series of questions that relate to (1) comprehension, (2) connection, (3) strategy, and (4) reflection.[20]

comprehension questions Questions designed to increase entrepreneurs' understanding of the nature of the environment

1. *Comprehension questions* are designed to increase entrepreneurs' understanding of the nature of the environment before they begin to address an entrepreneurial challenge, whether it be a change in the environment or the assessment of a potential opportunity. Understanding arises from recognition that a problem or opportunity exists, the nature of that situation, and its implications. In general, the questions that stimulate individuals to think about comprehension include: What is the problem all about? What is the question? What are the meanings of the key concepts? Specific to entrepreneurs, the questions are more likely to include: What is this market all about? What is this technology all about? What do we want to achieve by creating this new firm? What are the key elements to effectively pursuing this opportunity?

connection tasks Tasks designed to stimulate entrepreneurs to think about the current situation in terms of similarities to and differences from situations previously faced and solved

2. *Connection tasks* are designed to stimulate entrepreneurs to think about the current situation in terms of similarities to and differences from situations previously faced and solved. In other words, these tasks prompt the entrepreneur to tap into his or her knowledge and experience without overgeneralizing. Generally, connection tasks focus on questions like: How is this problem similar to problems I have already solved? Why? How is this problem different from what I have already solved? Why? Specific to entrepreneurs, the questions are more likely to include: How is this new environment similar to others in which I have operated? How is it different? How is this new organization similar to the established organizations I have managed? How is it different?

strategic tasks Tasks designed to stimulate entrepreneurs to think about which strategies are appropriate for solving the problem (and why) or pursuing the opportunity (and how)

3. *Strategic tasks* are designed to stimulate entrepreneurs to think about which strategies are appropriate for solving the problem (and why) or pursuing the opportunity (and how). These tasks prompt them to think about the what, why, and how of their approach to the situation. Generally, these questions include: What strategy/tactic/ principle can I use to solve this problem? Why is this strategy/tactic/principle the most appropriate one? How can I organize the information to solve the problem? How can I implement the plan? Specific to entrepreneurs, the questions are likely to include: What changes to strategic position, organizational structure, and culture will help us manage our newness? How can the implementation of this strategy be made feasible?

reflection tasks Tasks designed to stimulate entrepreneurs to think about their understanding and feelings as they progress through the entrepreneurial process

4. *Reflection tasks* are designed to stimulate entrepreneurs to think about their understanding and feelings as they progress through the entrepreneurial process. These tasks prompt entrepreneurs to generate their own feedback (create a feedback loop in their solution process) to provide the opportunity to change. Generally, reflection questions include: What am I doing? Does it make sense? What difficulties am I facing? How do I feel? How can I verify the solution? Can I use another approach for solving the task? Specific to the entrepreneurial context, entrepreneurs might ask: What difficulties will we have in convincing our stakeholders? Is there a better way to implement our strategy? How will we know success if we see it?

Entrepreneurs who are able to increase cognitive adaptability have an improved ability to (1) adapt to new situations—that is, it provides a basis by which a person's prior experience and knowledge affect learning or problem solving in a new situation; (2) be creative—that is, it can lead to original and adaptive ideas, solutions, or insights; and

(3) communicate one's reasoning behind a particular response.[21] We hope that this section of the book has provided you not only a deeper understanding of how entrepreneurs can think and act with great flexibility but also an awareness of some techniques for incorporating cognitive adaptability in your life.

We have discussed how entrepreneurs make decisions in uncertain environments and how one might develop an ability to be more cognitively flexible. It is important to note that entrepreneurs not only think but they also intend to act.

THE INTENTION TO ACT ENTREPRENEURIALLY

Entrepreneurial action is most often intentional. Entrepreneurs intend to pursue certain opportunities, enter new markets, and offer new products—and this is rarely the process of unintentional behavior. Intentions capture the motivational factors that influence a behavior; they are indications of how hard people are willing to try and how much of an effort they are planning to exert to perform the behavior. As a general rule, the stronger the intention to engage in a behavior, the more likely should be its performance.[22] Individuals have stronger intentions to act when taking action is perceived to be *feasible* and *desirable*. Entrepreneurial *intentions* can be explained in the same way.

entrepreneurial intentions The motivational factors that influence individuals to pursue entrepreneurial outcomes

The perception of feasibility has much to do with an entrepreneurial self-efficacy. *Entrepreneur's self-efficacy* refers to the conviction that one can successfully execute the behavior required; people who believe they have the capacity to perform (high self-efficacy) tend to perform well. Thus, it reflects the perception of a personal capability to do a particular job or set of tasks. High self-efficacy leads to increased initiative and persistence and thus improved performance; low self-efficacy reduces effort and thus performance. Indeed, people with high self-efficacy think differently and behave differently than people with low self-efficacy.[23] Self-efficacy affects the person's choice of action and the amount of effort exerted. Entrepreneurship scholars have found that self-efficacy is positively associated with the creation of a new independent organization.[24]

entrepreneurial self-efficacy The conviction that one can successfully execute the entrepreneurial process

Not only must an individual perceive entrepreneurial action as feasible for entrepreneurial intention to be high, the individual must also perceive this course of action as desirable. *Perceived desirability* refers to an individual's attitude toward entrepreneurial action—the degree to which he or she has a favorable or unfavorable evaluation of the potential entrepreneurial outcomes.[25] For example, creative actions are not likely to emerge unless they produce personal rewards that are perceived as relatively more desirable than more familiar behaviors.[26]

perceived desirability The degree to which an individual has a favorable or unfavorable evaluation of the potential entrepreneurial outcomes

Therefore, the higher the perceived desirability and feasibility, the stronger the intention to act entrepreneurially. We next investigate the background characteristics of entrepreneurs to understand why some individuals are more likely to engage in entrepreneurship than other individuals. That is, we examine how background characteristics provide an indication of whether certain individuals are more or less likely to perceive entrepreneurial action as feasible and/or desirable and therefore whether they are more or less likely to intend to be entrepreneurs.

ENTREPRENEUR BACKGROUND AND CHARACTERISTICS
Education

Although some may feel that entrepreneurs are less educated than the general population, research findings indicate that this is clearly not the case. Education is important in the upbringing of the entrepreneur. Its importance is reflected not only in the level of education obtained but also in the fact that it continues to play a major role in helping entrepreneurs cope with the problems they confront. Although a formal education is not necessary for starting a new business—as is reflected in the success of such high school dropouts as Andrew Carnegie, William Durant, Henry Ford, and William Lear—it does provide a good background, particularly when it is related to the field of the venture. For example, entrepreneurs have cited an educational need in the areas of finance, strategic planning, marketing (particularly distribution), and management. The ability to communicate clearly with both the written and the spoken word is also important in any entrepreneurial activity.

Even general education is valuable because it facilitates the integration and accumulation of new knowledge, providing individuals with a larger opportunity set (i.e., a broader base of knowledge casts a wider net for the discovery or generation of potential opportunities), and assists entrepreneurs in adapting to new situations.[27] The general education (and experiences) of an entrepreneur can provide knowledge, skills, and problem-solving abilities that are transferable across many different situations. Indeed, it has been found that while education has a positive influence on the chance that a person will discover new opportunities, it does not necessarily determine whether he will create a new business to exploit the discovered opportunity.[28] To the extent that individuals believe that their education has made entrepreneurial action more feasible, they are more likely to become entrepreneurs.

Age

The relationship of age to the entrepreneurial career process also has been carefully researched.[29] In evaluating these results, it is important to differentiate between entrepreneurial age (the age of the entrepreneur reflected in his or her experience) and chronological age (years since birth). As discussed in the next section, entrepreneurial experience is one of the best predictors of success, particularly when the new venture is in the same field as the previous business experience.

In terms of chronological age, most entrepreneurs initiate their entrepreneurial careers between the ages of 22 and 45. A career can be initiated before or after these ages, as long as the entrepreneur has the necessary experience and financial support, and the high energy level needed to launch and manage a new venture successfully. Also, there are milestone ages every five years (25, 30, 35, 40, and 45) when an individual is more inclined to start an entrepreneurial career. As one entrepreneur succinctly stated, "I felt it was now or never in terms of starting a new venture when I approached 30." Generally, male entrepreneurs tend to start their first significant venture in their early 30s, while women entrepreneurs tend to do so in their middle 30s. However, an entrepreneurial career is quite popular later in life when the children have left home, there are fewer financial concerns, and individuals start to think about what they would really like to do with the rest of their lives.[30]

Work History

work history The past work experience of an individual

Work history can influence the decision to launch a new entrepreneurial venture, but it also plays a role in the growth and eventual success of the new venture. While dissatisfaction with various aspects of one's job—such as a lack of challenge or promotional opportunities, as well as frustration and boredom—often motivates the launching of a new venture, previous technical and industry experience is important once the decision to launch has been made. Experience in the following areas is particularly important: financing, product or service development, manufacturing, and the development of distribution channels.

As the venture becomes established and starts growing, managerial experience and skills become increasingly important. Although most ventures start with few (if any) employees, as the number of employees increases, the entrepreneur's managerial skills come more and more into play. In addition, entrepreneurial experiences, such as the startup process, making decisions under high levels of uncertainty, building a culture from "scratch," raising venture capital, and managing high growth, are also important. Most entrepreneurs indicate that their most significant venture was not their first one. Throughout their entrepreneurial careers, they are exposed to many new venture opportunities and gather ideas for many more new ventures.

Finally, previous startup experience can provide entrepreneurs with expertise in running an independent business as well as benchmarks for judging the relevance of information, which can lead to an understanding of the "real" value of new entry opportunities, speed up the business creation process, and enhance performance.[31] Previous startup experience is a relatively good predictor of starting subsequent businesses.[32] To the extent that startup experience provides entrepreneurs with a greater belief in their ability to successfully achieve entrepreneurial outcomes, this increased perceived feasibility will strengthen entrepreneurial intentions.

ROLE MODELS AND SUPPORT SYSTEMS

One of the most important factors influencing entrepreneurs in their career path is their choice of a *role model*.[33] Role models can be parents, brothers or sisters, other relatives, or other entrepreneurs. Successful entrepreneurs frequently are viewed as catalysts by potential entrepreneurs. As one entrepreneur succinctly stated, "After evaluating Ted and his success as an entrepreneur, I knew I was much smarter and could do a better job. So I started my own business." In this way, role models can provide important signals that entrepreneurship is feasible for them.

role models Individuals whose example an entrepreneur can aspire to and copy

Role models can also serve in a supportive capacity as mentors during and after the launch of a new venture. An entrepreneur needs a strong support and advisory system in every phase of the new venture. This support system is perhaps most crucial during the startup phase, as it provides information, advice, and guidance on such matters as organizational structure, obtaining needed financial resources, and marketing. Since entrepreneurship is a social role embedded in a social context, it is important that an entrepreneur establish connections and eventually networks early in the new venture formation process.

As initial contacts and connections expand, they form a network with similar properties prevalent in a social network—density (the extensiveness of ties between the two individuals) and centrality (the total distance of the entrepreneur to all other individuals and the total number of individuals in the network). The strength of the ties between the entrepreneur and any individual in the network is dependent upon the frequency, level, and reciprocity of the relationship. The more frequent, in-depth, and mutually beneficial a relationship, the stronger and more durable the network between the entrepreneur and the individual.[34] Although most networks are not formally organized, an informal network for moral and professional support still greatly benefits the entrepreneur.

Moral-Support Network

moral-support network Individuals who give psychological support to an entrepreneur

It is important for each entrepreneur to establish a *moral-support network* of family and friends—a cheering squad. This cheering squad plays a critical role during the many difficult and lonely times that occur throughout the entrepreneurial process. Most entrepreneurs indicate that their spouses are their biggest supporters and allow them to devote the excessive amounts of time necessary to the new venture.

Friends also play key roles in a moral-support network. Not only can friends provide advice that is often more honest than that received from other sources, but they also provide encouragement, understanding, and even assistance. Entrepreneurs can confide in friends without fear of criticism. Finally, relatives (children, parents, grandparents, aunts, and uncles) also can be strong sources of moral support, particularly if they are also entrepreneurs. As one entrepreneur stated, "The total family support I received was the key to my success. Having an understanding cheering squad giving me encouragement allowed me to persist through the many difficulties and problems."

Professional-Support Network

In addition to encouragement, the entrepreneur needs advice and counsel throughout the establishment of the new venture. This advice can be obtained from a mentor, business associates, trade associations, or personal affiliations—all members of a *professional-support network*.

professional-support network Individuals who help the entrepreneur in business activities

Most entrepreneurs indicate that they have mentors. How does one find a mentor? This task sounds much more difficult than it really is. Since a mentor is a coach, a sounding board, and an advocate—someone with whom the entrepreneur can share both problems and successes—the individual selected needs to be an expert in the field. An entrepreneur can start the "mentor-finding process" by preparing a list of experts in various fields—such as in the fundamental business activities of finance, marketing, accounting, law, or management—who can provide the practical "how-to" advice needed. From this list, an individual who can offer the most assistance should be identified and contacted. If the selected individual is willing to act as a mentor, he or she should be periodically apprised of the progress of the business so that a relationship can gradually develop.

Another good source of advice can be cultivated by establishing a network of business associates. This group can be composed of self-employed individuals who have experienced starting a business; clients or buyers of the venture's product or service; experts such as consultants, lawyers, or accountants; and the venture's suppliers. Clients or buyers are a particularly important group to cultivate. This group represents the source of revenue to the venture and is the best provider of word-of-mouth advertising. There is nothing better than word-of-mouth advertising from satisfied customers to help establish a winning business reputation and promote goodwill.

Suppliers are another important component in a professional-support network. A new venture needs to establish a solid track record with suppliers to build a good relationship and to ensure the adequate availability of materials and other supplies. Suppliers also can provide good information on the nature of trends, as well as competition, in the industry.

In addition to mentors and business associates, trade associations can offer an excellent professional-support network. Trade association members can help keep the new venture competitive. Trade associations keep up with new developments and can provide overall industry data.

Finally, personal affiliations of the entrepreneur also can be a valuable part of a professional-support network. Affiliations developed with individuals through shared hobbies, participation in sporting events, clubs, civic involvements, and school alumni groups are excellent potential sources of referrals, advice, and information. Each entrepreneur needs to establish both moral and professional-support networks. These contacts provide confidence, support, advice, and information. As one entrepreneur stated, "In your own business, you are all alone. There is a definite need to establish support groups to share problems with and to obtain information and overall support for the new venture."

Therefore, it is important to recognize that entrepreneurial activity is embedded in networks of interpersonal relationships. These networks are defined by a set of actors (individuals and organizations) and a set of linkages between them, and they provide individuals access to a variety of resources necessary for entrepreneurial outcomes.[35] These resources may assist in efforts to discover and exploit opportunities, as well as in the creation of new independent organizations.[36] The trust embedded in some of these networks provides potential entrepreneurs the opportunity to access highly valuable resources. For example, business networks are composed of independent firms linked by common interests, friendship, and trust and are particularly important in facilitating the transfer of difficult-to-codify, knowledge-intensive skills that are expensive to obtain in other ways.[37] These networks also create opportunities for exchanging goods and services that are difficult to enforce through contractual arrangements, which facilitates the pursuit of opportunities.[38] To the extent that a network provides an individual greater belief in his or her ability to access resources critical to the successful achievement of entrepreneurial outcomes, this increased perceived feasibility will strengthen entrepreneurial intentions. This can include intentions for sustainable entrepreneurship.

SUSTAINABLE ENTREPRENEURSHIP

Sustainable development is perhaps the most important issue of our time, and entrepreneurship can have a positive impact on this issue. That is, entrepreneurial action can help us both sustain and develop. Specifically, *sustainable entrepreneurship* is focused on preserving nature, life support, and community (sustainability) in the pursuit of perceived opportunities to bring future products, processes, and services into existence for gain (entrepreneurial action) where gain is broadly construed to include economic and noneconomic benefits to individuals, the economy, and society (development).[39]

Based on the McMullen-Shepherd model, we know that entrepreneurial action is driven by knowledge and motivation. Those with greater knowledge of the natural environment—the physical world, including the earth, biodiversity, and ecosystems[40]—are more likely to notice changes in that environment that form opportunity beliefs than those with less knowledge. However, we cannot underestimate the role of entrepreneurial knowledge of markets, technologies, and/or opportunity exploitation; without entrepreneurial knowledge, opportunities for sustainable development are unlikely to become a reality.

For entrepreneurial actions that preserve nature to be considered sustainable entrepreneurship, they must also develop gains for the entrepreneur, others, and/or society. It has long been accepted that entrepreneurs can generate economic wealth for themselves, but their impact on development can be far greater. They can generate gains for others that are economic, environmental, and social, including employment opportunities, improved access to quality/valuable goods, and revenues for the government(s). The environmental gain generated for others could be reduced air pollution, improved air quality, improved drinking-water quality, and other enhanced living conditions. The social gains include improved child survival rates, longer life expectancy, superior education, equal opportunity, and so on. For example, individuals who were knowledgeable about cooking practices in developing countries were able to recognize opportunities for hybrid stoves that substantially reduced particle pollutants in households but were consistent with traditional recipes.[41] It is not just the natural environment that can be sustained, though; communities also need to be preserved. Indeed, knowledge of indigenous groups' cultures has led to the pursuit of opportunities that serve to sustain these cultures.

sustainable entrepreneurship Entrepreneurship focused on preserving nature, life support, and community (sustainability) in the pursuit of perceived opportunities to bring future products, processes, and services into existence for gain (entrepreneurial action) where gain is broadly construed to include economic and noneconomic benefits to individuals, the economy, and society (development)

 E T H I C S

AN ORGANIZATION'S CODE OF ETHICS

There has been a litany of financial scandals, which have led to increased action by governments in an attempt to regulate against such actions. But companies themselves are placing higher priority on ethical behavior, and that goes for the organization's employees. One way that they have done this is to create a code of ethics for all employees (indeed, many schools in universities have created a student code of ethics).

There are some distinct advantages from creating and implementing an employee code of ethics. The first is that the code makes everyone within the organization aware of what represents ethical behavior (and, through deduction, what is unethical behavior). To the extent that employees understand what ethical behavior is, they are more likely to ensure that their behavior remains consistent with that expectation. But it should be noted that a code of ethics is not solely a formal statement delineating ethical from nonethical behavior but also an important positive statement about the beliefs and values of the organization. The code is part of a broader system, such as the following:

Leaders Are the "Walking Talking" Embodiment of the Ethical Values of the Organization: Having something in writing is good but not sufficient to encourage ethical behavior. Employees often take their cues from the organization's leaders. That is, they model the behaviors of their leaders, whether that behavior is ethical or unethical. Therefore, everyone within the organization needs to abide by the code of ethics, especially its managers. For example, even a simple transgression of the code by a manager can have a substantially negative impact on the code's effectiveness with the rest of those within the organization—they see a distinction between what is said should be done and the way things are really done within the organization. Of course, this completely undermines the code of ethics. Therefore, if managers do not always follow the code of ethics, they should not be surprised if the employees do not follow the code either.

Ethics Is One of the Organization's Core Values: Organizations known for the ethical actions of their managers and employees have ethics as one of its core values—it is part of the organization's identity and reflected in the organizational culture. Being

at the core of the organization's values, members of the organization realize that *ethical behavior* is "what we do around here." Indeed, this is reflected in hiring practices—organizations want to hire managers and employees who already share their core values including ethics. In one study (reported in this news article), 58 percent of managers indicated that what impressed them the most were candidates who displayed honesty and integrity.

Creating a Safe Environment for Employees to Voice Concerns: Part of creating an ethical climate within the organization involves creating a culture where employees feel psychologically safe to voice concerns about potentially unethical behavior. If they feel that they can voice concerns, then the management is able to become aware of ethical transgressions and fix them before the event blows out of control and/or before the ethical culture of the organization is destroyed. Both have a considerable negative impact on the organization. The key for managers is to notice and respond early to ethical issues, and one critical way for managers to notice these transgressions is to encourage employees to voice their concerns. Employees have to feel that in voicing their concerns they are not going to be penalized.

Once aware of ethical transgressions, no matter how small, managers must act. Action reinforces the code of ethics; inaction undermines it.

One way to ensure that organizational members understand and "buy into the code" is to involve them in the process of creating the code.

By implementing a code of ethics, having it reflected in the organization's core values, and reinforcing the code through words and actions, the organization can ensure ethical behavior, which is a critical basis of an entrepreneurial firm.

Source: Max Messmer, "Does Your Company Have a Code of Ethics?" *Strategic Finance*, April 2003.

We recognize that our explanation of sustainable entrepreneurship could be considered highly idealistic. However, it is consistent with thinking of entrepreneurial action as a tool (e.g., a hammer) that can be used for good (e.g., to build a community center) or for bad (e.g., as a weapon for harming others). Indeed, in a study of 83 entrepreneurs, the researchers found that while most entrepreneurs had positive attitudes toward the natural environment, under some conditions, they disengaged these values to decide to exploit an opportunity that caused harm to the natural environment.[42] We do believe, however, that there are many people in the world today who are motivated to use the tool of entrepreneurial action to sustain the natural environment and communities and develop gains for others. Perhaps you are one of these people.

IN REVIEW

SUMMARY

Entrepreneurship involves action. Before action, individuals use their knowledge and motivation to overcome ignorance to form a belief that there exists an opportunity for someone. They then need to determine if this opportunity for someone matches their knowledge and motivation—is it an opportunity for them? Individuals engaging in the entrepreneurial task think differently from those engaged in other tasks, such as managerial tasks. The process requires that the individual and the firm have an entrepreneurial mind-set. We started our discussion of this mind-set with the concepts of thinking structurally and effectually, which challenges traditional notions of the way that entrepreneurs think about their tasks.

By thinking structurally and not being distracted by superficial features, entrepreneurs are able to identify opportunities by making connections between a technology and a market that may not be obvious. Furthermore, although entrepreneurs think about some tasks in a causal way, they also are likely to think about some tasks effectually (and some entrepreneurs more so than other entrepreneurs). Rather than starting with the desired outcome in mind and then focusing on the means to achieving that outcome, entrepreneurs sometimes approach tasks by looking at what they have—their means—and selecting among possible outcomes. Who is to say whether the "causal chef" who starts with a menu or the "effectual chef" who starts with what is in the cupboard produces the best meal? But we can say that some expert entrepreneurs think effectually about opportunities. Thinking effectually helps entrepreneurs make decisions in uncertain environments. Entrepreneurs are often situated in resource-scarce environments but are able to make do with (and recombine) the resources they have at hand to create opportunities.

The external environment can also have an impact on performance and therefore the entrepreneur needs to be able to adapt to changes in the environment. In this chapter, we introduced the notion of cognitive flexibility and emphasized that it is something that can be measured and learned. By asking questions related to comprehension, connection, strategy, and reflection, entrepreneurs can maintain an awareness of their thought process and in doing so develop greater cognitive adaptability.

Individuals become entrepreneurs because they intend to do so. The stronger the intention to be an entrepreneur, the more likely it is that it will happen. Intentions become stronger as individuals perceive an entrepreneurial career as feasible and desirable. These perceptions of feasibility and desirability are influenced by one's background and characteristics, such as education, personal values, age and work history, role models and support systems, and networks.

22   PART 1   THE ENTREPRENEURIAL PERSPECTIVE

The outcome of entrepreneurial action can be economic gain for the entrepreneur and his or her family. But this may not be the only motivation for the intention to be an entrepreneur. Some individuals exploit opportunities that sustain (the natural environment and/or communities) and generate gains for others. We call this process sustainable entrepreneurship.

RESEARCH TASKS

1. Speak to people from five different countries and ask what entrepreneurship means to them and how their national culture helps and/or hinders entrepreneurship.

2. Ask an entrepreneur about his or her business today and ask him or her to describe the decisions and series of events that led the business from startup to its current form. Would you classify this process as causal, effectual, or both?

3. Ask two entrepreneurs and five students (not in this class) to fill out the Haynie-Shepherd "Measure of Adaptive Cognition" (see Table 1.1). How do you rate relative to the entrepreneurs? Relative to your fellow students?

4. When conducting a homework exercise for another class (especially a case analysis), ask yourself comprehension questions, connection questions, strategy questions, and reflection questions. What impact did this have on the outcome of the task?

5. What impact does entrepreneurship have on your natural environment? What impact does it have on sustaining local communities? Use data to back up your arguments.

CLASS DISCUSSION

1. List the content that you believe is necessary for an entrepreneurship course. Be prepared to justify your answer.

2. Do you really think that entrepreneurs think effectually? What about yourself—do you sometimes think effectually? In what ways is it good? Then why are we taught in business classes to always think causally? Are there particular problems or tasks in which thinking causally is likely to be superior to effectuation? When might effectuation be superior to causal thinking?

3. To be cognitively flexible seems to require that the entrepreneur continually question himself or herself. Doesn't that create doubt that can be seen by employees and financiers such that success actually becomes more difficult to achieve? Besides, although flexibility is a good thing, if the firm keeps changing based on minor changes in the environment, the buyers are going to become confused about the nature of the firm. Is adaptation always a good thing?

4. Do you believe that sustainable development should be part of an entrepreneurship course, or did the textbook authors just include a section on it to be "politically correct"?

5. Provide some examples of the mental leaps that entrepreneurs have taken.

6. What excites you about being an entrepreneur? What are your major concerns?

SELECTED READINGS

An, Wenwen; Xinglu Zhao; Zhi Cao; Jianqi Zhang; and Heng Liu. (2018). How Bricolage Drives Corporate Entrepreneurship: The Roles of Opportunity Identification and Learning Orientation. *Journal of Product Innovation Management,* vol. 35, no. 1, pp. 49–65.

While most studies have viewed bricolage as a tool to overcome resource constraints in the context of new ventures, few of them have directly investigated the effects of brico-lage to identify new entrepreneurial opportunities in the context of incumbent firms. Drawing upon a subjectivist view of entrepreneurship, [the authors] ... examine the rela-tionship between bricolage and corporate entrepreneurship as well as the mediating role of opportunity identification. Moreover, as bricolage activities depend on interactive social contexts rather than individual efforts, the firm's learning orientation is proposed as a moderator that influences the positive effects of bricolage on opportunity identifica-tion. (abstract from authors and shortened)

Baker, Ted; and Reed Nelson. (2005). Something from Nothing: Resource Construction through Entrepreneurial Bricolage. *Administrative Science Quarterly,* vol. 50, no. 3, pp. 329–66.

In this article, the authors studied 29 firms and demonstrated that entrepreneurs differ in their responses to severe resource constraints. Some entrepreneurs were able to render unique services by recombining elements at hand for new purposes that chal-lenged institutional definitions and limits. They introduce the concept of bricolage to explain many of these behaviors of creating something from nothing by exploiting physical, social, or institutional inputs that other firms rejected or ignored. Central to the study's contribution is the notion that companies engaging in bricolage refuse to enact the limitations imposed by dominant definitions of resource environments; rather, they create their opportunities. (from journal's abstract)

Baron, Robert. (1998). Cognitive Mechanisms in Entrepreneurship: Why and When Entre-preneurs Think Differently Than Other People. *Journal of Business Venturing,* vol. 13, no. 4, pp. 275–95.

In this conceptual article, the author presents information on a study that examined the possible differences in the thinking of entrepreneurs and other people. This article offers a number of implications of a cognitive perspective for entrepreneurship research.

Davidsson, Per; and Benson Honig. (2003). The Role of Social and Human Capital among Nascent Entrepreneurs. *Journal of Business Venturing,* vol. 18, pp. 301–31.

This study examines nascent entrepreneurship by comparing individuals engaged in nascent activities with a control group and finds that social capital is a robust predictor for nascent entrepreneurs, as well as for advancing through the startup process. With regard to outcomes like first sale or showing a profit, only one aspect of social capital, viz., being a member of a business network, had a statistically significant positive effect. The study supports human capital in predicting entry into nascent entrepreneurship, but only weakly for carrying the startup process toward successful completion.

Grégoire, Denis A.; Andrew C. Corbett; and Jeffery S. McMullen. (2011). The Cognitive Perspective in Entrepreneurship: An Agenda for Future Research. *Journal of Management Studies,* vol. 48, no. 6, pp. 1443–77.

Despite its many achievements, scholarship at the intersection of entrepreneurship and cognition has focused primarily on the consequences of what happens when an entre-preneur benefits from various cognitive characteristics, resources, or other dispositions. As such, cognitive research in entrepreneurship continues to suffer from narrow theoreti-cal articulations and weak conceptual foundations that lessen its contribution to the managerial sciences. To address these issues, we draw from extant work on the nature and practice of cognitive research to develop a systematic approach to study entrepre-neurship cognition. (abstract from authors and shortened)

Grégoire, Denis; and Dean A. Shepherd. (2012). Technology Market Combinations and the Identification of Entrepreneurial Opportunities. *Academy of Management Journal,* vol. 55, no. 4, pp. 753–85.

Integrating theoretical work on the nature of entrepreneurial opportunities with cognitive science research on the use of similarity comparisons in making creative mental leaps, the authors develop a model of opportunity identification that examines the independent effects of an opportunity idea's similarity characteristics and the interaction of these characteristics with an individual's knowledge and motivation. They test this model with an experiment where they asked entrepreneurs to form beliefs about opportunity ideas for technology transfer. They found that the superficial and structural similarities of technology-market combinations impact the formation of opportunity beliefs, and that individual differences in prior knowledge and entrepreneurial intent moderate these relationships. (from journal's abstract)

Haynie, J. Michael; Dean A. Shepherd; Elaine Mosakowski; and Christopher Earley. (2010). A Situated Metacognitive Model of the Entrepreneurial Mindset. *Journal of Business Venturing*, vol. 25, no. 2, pp. 217–29.

The authors develop a framework to investigate the foundations of an "entrepreneurial mindset"—described by scholars as the ability to sense, act, and mobilize under uncertain conditions. They focus on metacognitive processes that enable the entrepreneur to think beyond or reorganize existing knowledge structures and heuristics, promoting adaptable cognitions in the face of novel and uncertain decision contexts. They integrate disparate streams of literature from social and cognitive psychology toward a model that specifies entrepreneurial metacognition as situated in the entrepreneurial environment. They posit that foundations of an entrepreneurial mindset are metacognitive in nature, and subsequently detail how, and with what consequence, entrepreneurs formulate and inform "higher-order" cognitive strategies in the pursuit of entrepreneurial ends. (from journal's abstract)

Haynie, J. Michael; and Dean A. Shepherd. (2011). Toward a Theory of Discontinuous Career Transition: Investigating Career Transitions Necessitated by Traumatic Life-Events. *Journal of Applied Psychology*, vol. 96, pp. 501–24.

Career researchers have focused on the mechanisms related to career progression. Although less studied, situations in which traumatic life events necessitate a discontinuous career transition are becoming increasingly prevalent. Employing a multiple case study method, the authors offer a deeper understanding of such transitions by studying an extreme case: soldiers and Marines disabled by wartime combat. Their study highlights obstacles to future employment that are counterintuitive and stem from the discontinuous and traumatic nature of job loss. Effective management of this type of transitioning appears to stem from efforts positioned to formulate a coherent narrative of the traumatic experience and thus reconstruct foundational assumptions about the world, humanity, and self. These foundational assumptions form the basis for enacting future-oriented career strategies, such that progress toward establishing a new career path is greatest for those who can orientate themselves away from the past (trauma), away from the present (obstacles to a new career), and toward an envisioned future career positioned to confer meaning and purpose through work. (from journal's abstract)

Hitt, Michael; Barbara Keats; and Samuel DeMarie. (1998). Navigating in the New Competitive Landscape: Building Strategic Flexibility and Competitive Advantage in the 21st Century. *Academy of Management Executive*, vol. 12, pp. 22–43.

The article cites the importance of building strategic flexibility and a competitive advantage for organizations to survive in the face of emerging technical revolution and increasing globalization. The nature of the forces in the new competitive landscape requires a continuous rethinking of current strategic actions, organization structure, communication systems, corporate culture, asset deployment, and investment strategies—in short, every aspect of a firm's operation and long-term health.

Hmieleski, Keith; and Andrew Corbett. (2006). Proclivity for Improvisation as a Predictor of Entrepreneurial Intentions. *Journal of Small Business Management*, vol. 44, pp. 45–63.

This study examines the relationship between improvisation and entrepreneurial intentions and finds that entrepreneurial intentions are associated with measures of personality, motivation, cognitive style, social models, and improvisation. The strongest relationship is found between entrepreneurial intentions and improvisation.

Keh, Hean; Maw Der Foo; and Boon Chong Lim. (2002). Opportunity Evaluation under Risky Conditions: The Cognitive Processes of Entrepreneurs. *Entrepreneurship: Theory and Practice*, vol. 27, pp. 125–48.

This study uses a cognitive approach to examine opportunity evaluation, as the perception of opportunity is essentially a cognitive phenomenon. The authors present a model that consists of four independent variables (overconfidence, belief in the law of small numbers, planning fallacy, and illusion of control), a mediating variable (risk perception), two control variables (demographics and risk propensity), and the dependent variable (opportunity evaluation). They find that illusion of control and belief in the law of small numbers are related to how entrepreneurs evaluate opportunities. Their results also indicate that risk perception mediates opportunity evaluation.

Krueger, Norris. (2000). The Cognitive Infrastructure of Opportunity Emergence. *Entrepreneurship: Theory and Practice*, vol. 24, pp. 5–23.

In this article, the author argues that seeing a prospective course of action as a credible opportunity reflects an intentions-driven process driven by known critical antecedents. On the basis of well-developed theory and robust empirical evidence, he proposes an intentions-based model of the cognitive infrastructure that supports or inhibits how individuals perceive opportunities. The author also shows the practical diagnostic power this model offers to managers.

Kuemmerle, Walter. (May 2002). A Test for the Fainthearted. *Harvard Business Review*, pp. 122–27.

Starting a business is rarely a dignified affair. The article discusses what really makes an entrepreneur; what characteristics set successful entrepreneurs apart, enabling them to start ventures against all odds and keep them alive even in the worst of times; and finally, whether, if you don't possess those characteristics, they can be developed.

McGrath, Rita; and Ian MacMillan. (2000). *The Entrepreneurial Mindset: Strategies for Continuously Creating Opportunity in an Age of Uncertainty.* Cambridge, MA: Harvard Business School Press.

In this book, the authors provide tips on how to achieve an entrepreneurial mindset. For example, they discuss the need to focus beyond incremental improvements to entrepreneurial actions, assess a business's current performance to establish the entrepreneurial framework, and formulate challenging goals by using the components of the entrepreneurial framework.

McMullen, Jeffery S.; and Dean Shepherd. (2006). Entrepreneurial Action and the Role of Uncertainty in the Theory of the Entrepreneur. *Academy of Management Review*, vol. 31, pp. 132–52.

By considering the amount of uncertainty perceived and the willingness to bear uncertainty concomitantly, the authors provide a conceptual model of entrepreneurial action that allows for examination of entrepreneurial action at the individual level of analysis while remaining consistent with a rich legacy of system-level theories of the entrepreneur. This model not only exposes limitations of existing theories of entrepreneurial action but also contributes to a deeper understanding of important conceptual issues, such as the nature of opportunity and the potential for philosophical reconciliation among entrepreneurship scholars.

Sarasvathy, Saras. (2006). *Effectuation: Elements of Entrepreneurial Expertise.* Cheltenham, UK: Edward Elgar Publishers.

This book gives the history of the development of effectuation and provides provocative new applications and future research directions.

Sarasvathy, Saras. www.effectuation.org.

This website provides an up-to-date collection of works on effectuation.

Shepherd, Dean A.; and Holger Patzelt. (2011). Sustainable Entrepreneurship: Entrepreneurial Action Linking "What Is to Be Sustained" with "What Is to Be Developed." *Entrepreneurship: Theory and Practice*, vol. 1, pp. 137–63.

Informed by the sustainable development and entrepreneurship literatures, the authors offer the following definition: Sustainable entrepreneurship is focused on the preservation of nature, life support, and community in the pursuit of perceived opportunities to bring into existence future products, processes, and services for gain, where gain is broadly construed to include economic and noneconomic gains to individuals, the economy, and society. (from journal's abstract)

Shepherd, Dean A.; and Holger Patzelt. (2015). Harsh Evaluations of Entrepreneurs Who Fail: The Role of Sexual Orientation, Use of Environmentally Friendly Technologies, and Observers' Perspective Taking. *Journal of Management Studies*, vol. 52, pp. 253–84.

Although there is a pervasive anti-failure bias in society, we investigate why some entrepreneurs who fail are evaluated more harshly than others. Building on attribution theory and the literatures on prejudice, pro-social intentions, and perspective taking, we offer an evaluation model of entrepreneurial failure and test this model on 6,784 assessments made by 212 observers. We find that variance in the harshness of failure evaluations depends on both the attributes of the entrepreneur and the attributes of the observer, and the interaction between the two. Specifically, entrepreneurs who are homosexual are evaluated more harshly by some observers and entrepreneurs who use environmentally friendly technology are evaluated less harshly. Moreover, observers high in perspective taking are more "lenient" in their failure evaluations of those who use environmentally friendly technology than those low in perspective taking. (from journal's abstract)

Shepherd, Dean A.; and Holger Patzelt. (2018). *Entrepreneurial Cognition: Exploring the Mindset of Entrepreneurs.* Palgrave Macmillan.

This book is open access—it is free—and can be downloaded from:

https://www.palgrave.com/us/book/9783319717814

Shepherd, Dean A.; Trenton A. Williams; and Holger Patzelt. (2015). Thinking about Entrepreneurial Decision Making Review and Research Agenda. *Journal of Management*, vol. 41, no. 1, pp. 11–46.

Judgment and decision-making research has a long tradition in management and represents a substantial stream of research in entrepreneurship. Despite numerous reviews of this topic in the organizational behavior, psychology, and marketing fields, this is the first review in the field of entrepreneurship. In this review, the authors inductively categorize the articles into decision-making topics arranged along the primary activities associated with entrepreneurship—opportunity assessment decisions, entrepreneurial entry decisions, decisions about exploiting opportunities, entrepreneurial exit decisions, heuristics and biases in the decision-making context, characteristics of the entrepreneurial decision maker, and environment as decision context. (from journal's abstract)

Tang, Jintong; K. Michele (Micki) Kacmar; and Lowell Busenitz (2012). Entrepreneurial alertness in the pursuit of new opportunities. *Journal of Business Venturing*, vol. 27, no. 1, pp. 77–94.

The recognition and development of new opportunities are at the heart of entrepreneurship. Building from Kirzner's (1973, 1999) work, cognition theory, and McMullen and Shepherd's (2006) recent development, we offer a model involving three distinct elements of alertness: scanning and search, association and connection, and evaluation and judgment. We then conduct multiple studies to develop and validate a 13-item alertness scale that captures these three dimensions. Results demonstrate appropriate dimensionality, strong reliability, and content, convergent, discriminant, and nomological validity. The resultant instrument provides researchers with a valuable tool for probing the entrepreneurial opportunity development process including antecedents and outcomes. (abstract by authors)

Welter, Chris; and Sungho Kim. (2018). Effectuation under risk and uncertainty: A simulation model. *Journal of Business Venturing*, vol. 33, no. 1, pp. 100–16.

Effectuation was first proposed as an expert entrepreneur's decision-making framework under uncertainty, but the applications of effectuation beyond the condition of uncertainty have seen less attention. Using an agent-based simulation model, this paper investigates the effectiveness of effectuation relative to causation in uncertain and risky contexts. The simulation overcomes the shortcomings of think aloud protocols typically used in effectuation research. The results suggest that effectuation outperforms causation in both risky and uncertain contexts until the entrepreneur can predict the future correctly > 75% of the time. This suggests expanding the boundary of effectuation from uncertainty to whenever predicting the future is challenging. (abstract by authors)

Wood, Matthew S.; David W. Williams; and Will Drover. (2017). Past as Prologue: Entrepreneurial Inaction Decisions and Subsequent Action Judgments. *Journal of Business Venturing*, vol. 32, no. 1, pp. 107–27.

We add richness and depth to entrepreneurial action theory by investigating the role of entrepreneurial inaction decisions—deliberate decisions not to pursue a perceived opportunity—in influencing entrepreneurs' paths both away from and toward action judgments on subsequent opportunities. Doing so, we utilize a sequential decision-judgment perspective to uniquely theorize that entrepreneurs' mental representations qualified by doubt carry over from initial entrepreneurial inaction decisions to consequentially impact assessments of opportunities that follow. ... we find that initial inaction decisions negatively affect entrepreneurs' likelihood of subsequent action judgments. However, this effect is mitigated when entrepreneurs perceive subsequent opportunities as dissimilar, rather than similar. (abstract by authors but shortened)

END NOTES

1. S. Venkataraman, "The Distinctive Domain of Entrepreneurship Research: An Editor's Perspective," in J. Katz and R. Brockhaus (eds.), *Advances in Entrepreneurship, Firm Emergence, and Growth* 3 (1997), pp. 119–38 (Greenwich, CT: JAI Press).
2. Scott Shane and S. Venkataraman, "The Promise of Entrepreneurship as a Field of Research," *The Academy of Management Review* 25, no. 1 (January 2000), pp. 217–26.
3. J. S. McMullen and D. A. Shepherd, "Entrepreneurial Action and the Role of Uncertainty in the Theory of the Entrepreneur," *The Academy of Management Review* 31, no. 1 (2006), pp. 132–52.
4. Denis Grégoire and Dean A. Shepherd, "Technology Market Combinations and the Identification of Entrepreneurial Opportunities," *Academy of Management Journal* 55, no. 4 (2012), pp. 753–85.
5. D. A. Grégoire, P. S. Barr, and D. A. Shepherd, "Cognitive Processes of Opportunity Recognition: The Role of Structural Alignment," *Organization Science* 21, no. 2 (2010), pp. 413–31.
6. T. Baker and R. E. Nelson, "Creating Something from Nothing: Resource Construction through Entrepreneurial Bricolage," *Administrative Science Quarterly* 50, no. 3 (2005), p. 329.
7. J. M. Senyard, T. Baker, and P. R. Steffens, "Entrepreneurial Bricolage and Firm Performance: Moderating Effects of Firm Change and Innovativeness," Presentation at 2010 Annual Meeting of the Academy of Management, Montreal, Canada (2010).
8. S. Sarasvathy, "Causation and Effectuation: Toward a Theoretical Shift from Economic Inevitability to Entrepreneurial Contingency," *Academy of Management Review* 26 (2001), p. 245.
9. H. A. Simon, "Theories of Decision Making in Economics and Behavioral Science," *American Economic Review* 49 (1959), pp. 253–83.
10. Sarasvathy, "Causation and Effectuation," pp. 245–47.
11. M. A. Hitt, "The New Frontier: Transformation of Management for the New Millennium," *Organizational Dynamics* 28, no. 3 (2000), pp. 7–17.

12. R. D. Ireland, M. A. Hitt, and D. G. Sirmon, "A Model of Strategic Entrepreneurship: The Construct and Its Dimensions," *Journal of Management* 29 (2003), pp. 963–90; and Rita McGrath and Ian MacMillan, *The Entrepreneurial Mindset: Strategies for Continuously Creating Opportunity in an Age of Uncertainty* (Cambridge, MA: Harvard Business School Press, 2000).

13. Ireland, Hitt, and Sirmon, "A Model of Strategic Entrepreneurship."

14. M. A. Hitt, B. W. Keats, and S. M. DeMarie, "Navigating in the New Competitive Landscape: Building Strategic Flexibility and Competitive Advantage in the 21st Century," *Academy of Management Executive* 12 (1998), pp. 22–43 (from page 26).

15. M. Haynie, D. A. Shepherd, E. Mosakowski, and C. Earley, "A Situated Metacognitive Model of the Entrepreneurial Mindset," *Journal of Business Venturing* 25, no. 2 (2010), pp. 217–29; and M. Haynie and D. A. Shepherd, "A Measure of Adaptive Cognition for Entrepreneurship Research," *Entrepreneurship: Theory and Practice* 33, no. 3 (2009), pp. 695–714.

16. Haynie and Shepherd, "A Measure of Adaptive Cognition for Entrepreneurship Research."

17. G. Schraw and R. Dennison, "Assessing Metacognitive Awareness," *Contemporary Educational Psychology* 19 (1994), pp. 460–75.

18. A. Brown, "Metacognition and Other Mechanisms," in F. E. Weinert and R. H. Kluwe (eds.), *Metacognition, Motivation, and Understanding* (Hillsdale, NJ: Lawrence Erlbaum Associates, 1987).

19. E. Guterman, "Toward a Dynamic Assessment of Reading: Applying Metacognitive Awareness Guiding to Reading Assessment Tasks," *Journal of Research in Reading* 25, no. 3 (2002), pp. 283–98.

20. Z. R. Mevarech and B. Kramarski, "The Effects of Metacognitive Training versus Worked-out Examples on Students' Mathematical Reasoning," *British Journal of Educational Psychology* 73, no. 4 (2003), pp. 449–71; and D. Shepherd, M. Haynie, and J. McMullen (working paper), "Teaching Management Students Metacognitive Awareness: Enhancing Inductive Teaching Methods and Developing Cognitive Adaptability."

21. Mevarech and Kramarski, "The Effects of Metacognitive Training."

22. J. Ajzen, "The Theory of Planned Behavior," *Organizational Behavior and Human Decision Processes* 50 (1991), pp. 179–211.

23. A. Bandura, *Self-Efficacy: The Exercise of Control* (New York: W. H. Freeman, 1997); and D. A. Shepherd and N. Krueger, "An Intentions-Based Model of Entrepreneurial Teams' Social Cognition," Special Issue on Cognition and Information Processing, *Entrepreneurship: Theory and Practice* 27 (2002), pp. 167–85.

24. N. F. J. Krueger and D. V. Brazael, "Entrepreneurial Potential and Potential Entrepreneurs," *Entrepreneurship: Theory and Practice* 18 (1994), pp. 91–104.

25. Shepherd and Krueger, "An Intentions-Based Model."

26. C. M. Ford and D. A. Gioia, *Creativity in Organizations: Ivory Tower Visions and Real World Voices* (Newbury Park, CA: Sage, 1995).

27. See J. Gimeno, T. Folta, A. Cooper, and C. Woo, "Survival of the Fittest? Entrepreneurial Human Capital and the Persistence of Underperforming Firms," *Administrative Science Quarterly* 42 (1997), pp. 750–83.

28. P. Davidsson and B. Honig, "The Role of Social and Human Capital among Nascent Entrepreneurs," *Journal of Business Venturing* 18 (2003), pp. 301–31. D. R. DeTienne, D. A. Shepherd, and J. O. De Castro, "The Fallacy of 'Only the Strong Survive': The Effects of Extrinsic Motivation on the Persistence Decisions for Under-Performing Firms," *Journal of Business Venturing* 23 (2008), pp. 528–46.

29. Much of this information is based on research findings in Robert C. Ronstadt, "Initial Venture Goals, Age, and the Decision to Start an Entrepreneurial Career," *Proceedings of the 43rd Annual Meeting of the Academy of Management*, August 1983, p. 472; and Robert C. Ronstadt, "The Decision Not to Become an Entrepreneur," *Proceedings, 1983 Conference on Entrepreneurship*, April 1983, pp. 192–212. See also M. Lévesque, D. A. Shepherd, and E. J. Douglas, "Employment or Self-Employment: A Dynamic Utility-Maximizing Model," *Journal of Business Venturing* 17 (2002), pp. 189–210.

30. See also Lévesque, Shepherd, and Douglas, "Employment or Self-Employment."

31. A. C. Cooper, T. B. Folta, and C. Woo, "Entrepreneurial Information Search," *Journal of Business Venturing* 10 (1995), pp. 107–20; and M. Wright, K. Robbie, and C. Ennew, "Venture Capitalists and Serial Entrepreneurs," *Journal of Business Venturing* 12, no. 3 (1997), pp. 227–49.

32. Davidsson and Honig, "The Role of Social and Human Capital."

33. The influence of role models on career choice is discussed in E. Almquist and S. Angrist, "Role Model Influences on College Women's Career Aspirations," *Merrill-Palmer Quarterly* 17 (July 1971), pp. 263–97; J. Strake and C. Granger, "Same-Sex and Opposite-Sex Teacher Model Influences on Science Career Commitment among High School Students," *Journal of Educational Psychology* 70 (April 1978), pp. 180–86; Alan L. Carsrud, Connie Marie Gaglio, and Kenneth W. Olm, "Entrepreneurs-Mentors, Networks, and Successful New Venture Development: An Exploratory Study," *Proceedings, 1986 Conference on Entrepreneurship*, April 1986, pp. 29–35; and Howard Aldrich, Ben Rosen, and William Woodward, "The Impact of Social Networks on Business Foundings and Profit: A Longitudinal Study," *Proceedings, 1987 Conference on Entrepreneurship*, April 1987, pp. 154–68.

34. A thoughtful development of the network concept can be found in Howard Aldrich and Catherine Zimmer, "Entrepreneurship through Social Networks," in *The Art and Science of Entrepreneurship* (Cambridge, MA: Ballinger, 1986), pp. 3–24.

35. H. Hoang and B. Antoncic, "Network-Based Research in Entrepreneurship: A Critical Review," *Journal of Business Venturing* 18 (2003), pp. 165–88.

36. S. Birley, "The Role of Networks in the Entrepreneurial Process," *Journal of Business Venturing* 1 (1985), pp. 107–17; A. Cooper and W. Dunkelberg, "Entrepreneurship and Paths to Business Ownership," *Strategic Management Journal* 7 (1986), pp. 53–68; and B. Johannisson, "Networking and Entrepreneurial Growth," in D. Sexton and H. Landström (eds.), *The Blackwell Handbook of Entrepreneurship* (Oxford, MA: Blackwell, 2000), pp. 26–44.

37. A. Larson, "Network Dyads in Entrepreneurial Settings: A Study of the Governance of Exchange Relationships," *Administrative Science Quarterly* 37 (1992), pp. 76–104; W. Powell, "Neither Market nor Hierarchy: Network Forms of Organization," in B. Staw and L. Cummings (eds.), *Research in Organizational Behavior* (Greenwich, CT: JAI Press, 1990); and B. Uzzi, "The Sources and Consequences of Embeddedness for the Economic Performance of Organizations: The Network Effect," *American Sociological Review* 61 (1996), pp. 674–98.

38. Uzzi, "The Sources and Consequences of Embeddedness."

39. Dean A. Shepherd and Holger Patzelt, "Sustainable Entrepreneurship: Entrepreneurial Action Linking 'What Is to Be Sustained' with 'What Is to Be Developed,'" *Entrepreneurship: Theory and Practice* 1 (2011), pp. 137–63.

40. T. M. Parris and R. W. Kates, "Characterizing and Measuring Sustainable Development," *Annual Review of Environment and Resources* 28, no. 1 (2003), pp. 559–86.

41. C. K. Prahalad, *The Fortune at the Bottom of the Pyramid: Eradicating Poverty through Profits* (Wharton, 2010).

42. D. Shepherd, H. Patzelt, and R. Baron, "'I Care about Nature, but...': Disengaging Values in Assessing Opportunities that Cause Harm," *Academy of Management Journal* 56, no. 5 (2013), pp. 1251–73.

CHAPTER 2

Opportunities

> *It is not often that a man can make opportunities for himself. But he can put himself*
> *in such shape that when or if the opportunities come he is ready.*
> **Theodore Roosevelt**

How can an entrepreneur identify and select a valuable opportunity?

The identification and evaluation of opportunities is one of the entrepreneur's most important tasks. Good opportunities address important market needs. Examining social, technological, and economic trends can lead to the identification of emerging needs. Entrepreneurs seek to build new ventures and to act on a good opportunity when it matches their capabilities and interests, exists in a favorable context, exhibits the potential for sustainable long-term growth, and facilitates the acquisition of required resources. Such opportunities offer a reasonable chance of success and require the entrepreneur to make a difficult decision to act or not act. The choice of an opportunity and the decision to act is a critical juncture in the life of an entrepreneur. Table 2.8 outlines a five-step process for evaluating opportunities. ■

2.1 Types of Opportunities

The first role of the entrepreneur—an individual or a group of people—is to discover or create and select an appropriate opportunity. An opportunity is a timely and favorable set of circumstances that enables the creation of a new product, service, business, or experience that meets a need [Sarasvathy et al., 2003]. Effective entrepreneurs often find that opportunity identification is a creative process that relates a need to the methods, means, or services that address or solve it—all within a reasonable period of time.

Opportunities can develop from market demand or from new technological possibilities. These opportunities are "demand pull" and "technology push" respectively [Di Stefano et al., 2012]. With demand-pull opportunities, an entrepreneur begins by assessing a need or problem that cries out for a solution. An example is the fight for an effective cancer treatment. The founders of new industries capitalize on demand pull to create disruptive innovations that lead to new products that satisfy the demand.

As Vinod Khosla, the cofounder of Sun Microsystems and a well-known venture capitalist, is fond of saying, "Every problem is an opportunity." In turn, great opportunities are often disguised as difficult problems.

An effective tactic for identifying these problems is to focus on situations where a potential customer experiences significant "pain," which represents the extent of need for the solution to a problem: a customer who feels significant pain of need seeks a high-value solution. For example, when Jessica Alba gave birth to her first child in 2008, she was intimidated by her own history of childhood illness and by news that ingredients in prevalent baby products included petrochemicals and synthetic fragrances. After a product recommendation from her mother caused her baby to break out in welts, she became inspired to start her own venture. The Honest Company aims to promote ethical consumerism by offering nontoxic household products.

Sam Goldman, the founder of d.light, also began with a painful problem. Goldman grew up in Mauritania, Pakistan, Peru, India, and Rwanda before becoming a Peace Corps volunteer in Benin. He then moved on to study biology and environmental studies in Canada before receiving his MBA from Stanford. While Goldman was living in Benin, his neighbor's son was badly burned by a kerosene lamp. This inspired him to create a new source of light, which could match kerosene lamps on price but be safe for use around small children. d.light now creates extremely efficient LED lights that are 8 to 10 times brighter than a kerosene lamp and 50 percent more efficient than fluorescent lights.

Problem-driven opportunities can be identified through a five-step process called "pain-storming." In the first step, the entrepreneur identifies a particular customer or type of person. In the second step, she describes something that the customer does, and what the customer is trying to accomplish. In the third step, the entrepreneur identifies the various pain points and emotions that accompany this activity. In the fourth step, she selects the biggest pain point and the root cause of the customer's problem. Finally, in the fifth step, she identifies the

Demand Pull at ResMed

Obstructive sleep apnea (OSA) was a widespread but underdiagnosed problem during the 1980s and early 1990s. OSA occurs when tissue at the back of the throat collapses during sleep, blocking the airway and preventing breathing. Oxygen levels drop in the bloodstream, causing sharp fluctuations in heart rate and blood pressure. OSA is strongly correlated with other severe conditions—nearly half of all heart failure patients and 60 percent of type 2 diabetes patients suffer from OSA. It was estimated that 2 percent of the U.S. population suffered from OSA in some form. It was clearly a massive problem waiting for a solution.

ResMed was founded in Australia to combat this problem. The company created a novel device that pressurized the airway during sleep to prevent the airway from blocking. The device was fantastically successful, and as recognition of OSA expanded during the early 1990s, ResMed took off. ResMed correctly identified a huge unsolved problem and provided a solution that fit into both the patient's life and the health insurers' plans. As a result, the company has been incredibly successful. It is now public on the New York Stock Exchange with revenues of more than $1.8 billion in 2016.

assumptions behind this root cause [Furr and Dyer, 2014]. For example, Uber started when its founders focused on people who use taxis and what they were trying to accomplish—getting from one location to another quickly, reliably, and cheaply. They then listed out all of the problems or pain points that someone encountered when trying to get a taxi, from finding the taxi in the first place to the uncertainty of payment. They then developed a solution that reduced these pains.

As the Uber example highlights, once an entrepreneur has identified a problem, he works to develop a solution. For example, Scott Cook, who founded Intuit, saw a problem experienced by people who wanted to easily and reliably keep their own home budget records, do their taxes, and pay the bills. Cook thought this problem could be solved through financial software that was so intuitive that most people could use it without resorting to the manual—thus, the name of the firm: Intuit (www.intuit.com). Entrepreneurs like Cook develop a solution by first asking, "How would an unconstrained person solve the problem?" Starting without constraints such as price and physical limits opens up many possibilities. Then, once a good unconstrained solution appears attractive, it can often be rearranged to accommodate reasonable constraints. Cook solved a big problem with an easy-to-use solution.

Technology-push opportunities might be said to begin with a solution rather than a problem. The development of a new technology, such as stem cells in biotechnology or carbon nanotubes in nanotechnology, leads entrepreneurs to search for ways to apply it. For example, Sandra Lerner and Leonard Bosack formed Cisco Systems in 1984 to exploit the capabilities of a router to transmit and translate data to and from disparate computers. By 2017, Cisco had revenues of nearly $50 billion.

Demand pull | Technology push

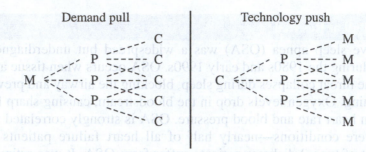

M = Market need; P = Product (or service); C = Technological capability

FIGURE 2.1 Demand Pull and Technology Push Opportunities
Source: Barr, S. H., T. Baker, S. K. Markham, and A. L. Kingon. "Bridging the valley of death: lessons learned from 14 years of commercialization of technology education." *IEEE Engineering Management Review*, March 2014, 13–24.

The power of *serendipity*—making useful discoveries by accident—can also lead to good opportunities. Working in a microwave lab, Percy Spencer observed a chocolate bar melting by microwave power—thus, leading to the microwave oven. Clarence Birdseye was a fur trader in Canada when he noticed a phenomenon while ice fishing. At 50 degrees below zero, fish froze rock-hard almost instantly, yet when thawed, they were fresh and tender. After some experimentation, he learned that the key was the speed at which foods were frozen. That observation led to the flash freezing process that created a multibillion-dollar industry and made Birdseye a success.

Would-be entrepreneurs need to be careful, however, not to mistake a new technology for a solution in itself. Ultimately, customers want a need filled or a problem solved. Usually, they do not care what technology is employed toward this goal. Thus, entrepreneurship is not about having a great technological idea, but rather about delivering a product or service that solves a problem.

Figure 2.1 summarizes and illustrates demand-pull and technology-push opportunities. In the demand-pull case, the entrepreneur begins with a market need. That need may be filled with several potential products, which may (or may not) have special technological capabilities. In the technology-push case, the entrepreneur begins with a technological capability, which is often a new technology or a new application of an existing technology. This capability needs to be combined with other capabilities to make a cohesive product (and, often, the capability can be applied to multiple products). In turn, the selected product may be applied to various market and customer needs. Sometimes, too, problems and solutions can emerge together [von Hippel and von Krogh, 2016]. In any case, however, the ultimate task of the entrepreneur is to match an important need with a good solution.

Table 2.1 further dissects different opportunities into nine categories, which we use to describe additional ways of identifying opportunities. The first category, and perhaps most common, is to increase the value of the product or service.

TABLE 2.1 Nine categories of opportunity.

1. Increasing the value of a product or service
2. New applications of existing means or technologies
3. Creating mass markets
4. Customization for individuals
5. Increasing reach
6. Managing the supply chain
7. Convergence of industries
8. Process innovation
9. Increasing the scale of the firm

This increased value can include improved performance, better quality or experience, and improved accessibility or other values unique to the product. For example, CreditKarma is a financial technology company that offers a dashboard view of a user's financial accounts, complete with tax and credit card information. The company does not provide its own credit scores or banking, but rather a consolidation of other financial services. The increased accessibility adds value.

The second category seeks new applications of existing means or technologies. Credit cards with magnetic stripes were available in the 1960s, but a thoughtful innovator recognized the application of this technology to hotel door cards and created a wholly new application and industry.

The third category concentrates on creating mass markets for existing products. A good example is VMWare's development. Initially, VMWare focused on a product that enabled software testers to check the quality of code using virtual environments. Thus, VMWare enabled a single machine to operate like multiple machines. VMWare recognized that with modest enhancements, the company could expand its product offering to run critical systems called operation workloads. The market for these operational application environments is at least an order of magnitude larger than that for quality assurance and test environments. As a result, VMWare expanded its product to a $10 billion market from an initial market of several hundred million dollars.

Customization of products for individuals, category 4, affords a new opportunity for an existing product or technology. Examples of customization can be found in the streaming music business. Spotify lets users play songs from their own libraries as well as from Spotify's collection of millions of tracks. Users can access music via a desktop app, tablet, or smartphone. Spotify also integrates with social network sites, including Facebook.

Expanding geographic reach or online reach, category 5, allows a new venture to increase its number of customers. Founded in Scotland, Optos developed a novel eye exam technology and innovative pay-per-use business model. Backed by angel investors for many years, it carefully expanded its operations into the United States and Germany. It is now a viable public company listed on the London Stock Exchange.

Managing the supply chain, category 6, is a powerful force for improvement. Wal-Mart integrated inventory-information systems in each store with its broader distribution system to reap economic benefits from improved inventory management.

Convergence of industries, category 7, affords new opportunities by creating novel combinations of markets and technologies. For example, genetic engineering is the convergence of electron microscopy, micromanipulation, and supercomputing.

Business and manufacturing process innovations, category 8, are another source of opportunity. For example, FedEx and other airborne shipping systems changed the way in which individuals and organizations ship goods to one another. Asana aims to change how teams collaborate with one another.

Finally, the ninth category of opportunity is the increasing scale or consolidation of industry. Historically, the railroad industry provides a powerful example of consolidation in the United States. Consolidation of the railroads began by the turn of the twentieth century. Today, there are five major railroad companies, down from the thousands of companies in the late 1890s. More recent consolidation examples include the automobile manufacturing industry, cable and satellite TV broadcasters, and telecommunications carriers. Through mergers and acquisitions, an industry can be consolidated with attendant cost savings and value for the customer.

Any specific business opportunity may be portrayed in the three-dimensional cube of Figure 2.2. The entrepreneur identifies the customer, the required technology, and the application of this technology to create a solution. Different opportunities typically leverage different combinations of technologies, applications, and customers.

The entrepreneur's personal background is key to the process of opportunity identification. In fact, since prior knowledge, experience, and motivation play a major role in opportunity identification, different people may not recognize or perceive the same opportunity [Gregoire and Shepherd, 2012]. The people whom an entrepreneur knows, the activities she pursues, the technical information she possesses, and the needs to which she is exposed all shape opportunity evaluation and entrepreneurial action [Autio et al., 2013]. Ironically, industry insiders often are unable to identify new opportunities since their deep experience blinds them to alternative approaches [Nelson and Irwin, 2014].

Good opportunities can also vary from person to person since it is the entrepreneur who adds value to the opportunity by creating a response. The opportunity, and even a general response to it, is not unique—many people may recognize it. Few of them, however, will possess the relevant passion and capabilities to solve the problem. For example, many people propose to exploit the new science of nanotechnology to solve various problems, but few of them will act. The true entrepreneur finds the best opportunity that matches his or her interests, skills, and knowledge—and acts to get it done. Thus, it is passion and capabilities that distinguish an entrepreneurial team.

Frank Slootman is a good example of an entrepreneur who found an opportunity that matched his interests, capabilities, and passion. Slootman joined Data Domain, a company with 20 employees, no customers, and no revenue. He felt

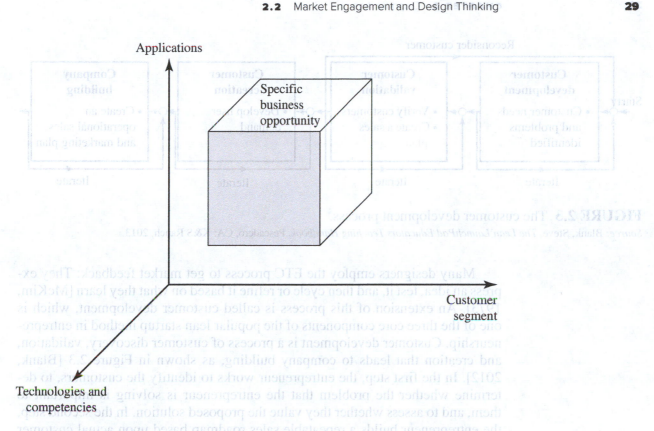

FIGURE 2.2 Finding a specific business opportunity with a combination of customer segment, technology and competencies, and applications.

he could make a meaningful difference to an organization that was pursuing a large market and if successful, under his guidance, it could become a highly valuable company. Slootman said that the problem Data Domain was solving—enabling disk economies for backup/recovery storage—"spoke to him." He also felt going in that he could provide leadership to a group of very talented technical engineers. During the next six years he led the company to become the undisputed leader in its field, taking it public and through an eventual acquisition by EMC for $2.4 billion in 2009.

2.2 Market Engagement and Design Thinking

Entrepreneurs must engage with the market on a continual basis in order to identify and validate opportunities. Market research is the process of gathering information that can be used to refine an opportunity and to plot and execute upon a strategy. This information is critical to the new venture team; without it, a new venture may launch a product only to find out that the customer does not value it. For example, Dean Kamen failed to get adequate customer feedback on the Segway, his two-wheeled self-balancing transporter. Although the Segway was highly hyped, customers failed to value its utility and did not purchase it [Grant, 2016].

30   **CHAPTER 2** Opportunities

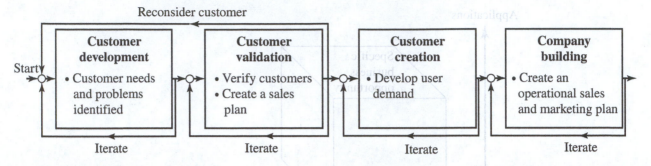

FIGURE 2.3 The customer development process.
Source: Blank, Steve. *The Lean LaunchPad Educators Teaching Handbook.* Pescadero, CA: K&S Ranch, 2013.

Many designers employ the ETC process to get market feedback: They express an idea, test it, and then cycle or refine it based on what they learn [McKim, 1973]. An extension of this process is called customer development, which is one of the three core components of the popular lean startup method in entrepreneurship. Customer development is a process of customer discovery, validation, and creation that leads to company building, as shown in Figure 2.3 [Blank, 2012]. In the first step, the entrepreneur works to identify the customers, to determine whether the problem that the entrepreneur is solving is important to them, and to assess whether they value the proposed solution. In the second step, the entrepreneur builds a repeatable sales roadmap based upon actual customer commitments. Iteration—the reconsideration and adjustment of the problem, product, and customer hypotheses—is especially common in these first two steps as the entrepreneur works to refine an idea. In the third step, customer creation, the entrepreneur works to build upon initial sales by creating end-user demand. Finally, the startup transitions from an informal learning and discovery organization into one with formal sales, marketing and business-development departments that build on the startup's success [Blank, 2013].

Primary data—that is, data collected for your specific proposed venture—are particularly important to the customer development process; there is no substitute for engaging with actual customers. As Bill Aulet, managing director of the Martin Trust Center for MIT Entrepreneurship, argues, "If there is already a market research report out there with all the information you need, it is probably too late for your new venture. You have missed the window of opportunity" [Aulet, 2013]. Instead, timely opportunities require entrepreneurs to gather their own data.

One popular form of primary research uses the focus group, which is a small group of people from the target market. These people are brought together in a room to have a discussion about the problem or proposed product. This discussion can be led by someone from the venture team or by a professional moderator who may elicit more honest feedback due to her detachment from the venture. Table 2.2 outlines the general process for convening and running a focus group. The overall goal is to obtain honest feedback from a group that is representative of your intended market.

TABLE 2.2 Steps to conduct a focus group.

1. Determine the purpose and goal of the focus group.

2. Identify and attract the appropriate people to participate, based on the purpose, goal, and target market.

3. Prepare opening questions to get the conversation started and key questions that are central to the purpose and goal of the meeting.

4. Use simple, open-ended questions.

5. Encourage critical feedback.

6. Analyze the results by determining general patterns and looking for interesting outliers.

Source: Krueger, Richard and Mary Anne Casey. *Focus Groups: A Practical Guide for Applied Research*. Thousand Oaks, CA: SAGE Publications, Inc. 2008.

Entrepreneurs can also collect data from surveys and from customer interviews. One advantage of interviews over focus groups is that individual interviewees can avoid "groupthink" that leads participants to converge toward the same responses. Typically, an entrepreneur also can entice individuals to a one-on-one interview who may not participate in a broad focus group.

Table 2.3 offers several tips for conducting customer interviews. As with focus groups, effective interviews employ open-ended questions and encourage honest feedback. It is important for entrepreneurs to use customer engagement to elicit new insights and to challenge preconceptions—not simply to seek information that confirms current assumptions [Sanchez et al., 2011].

When using customer interviews or focus groups to obtain feedback on a proposed solution, it also can be effective to use the "a day in your life" format. This format takes customers through their day before and after the new product

TABLE 2.3 Tips for customer interviews.

1. Know your goals and questions ahead of time.

2. Identify and attract the appropriate people to participate, based on the purpose, goal, and target market.

3. Ask open-ended questions.

4. Encourage customers to be brutally honest and be prepared for critical feedback.

5. Focus on listening, not talking.

6. Do not attempt to steer or influence the interviewee.

7. Ask follow-up questions.

8. Confirm what you heard by paraphrasing it back.

9. Ask for introductions to other customers.

10. Write up your notes as quickly as possible.

Source: Constable, Giff. "12 tips for customer development interviews." July 29, 2011. http://giffconstable.com.

launch to expose the expected benefits of the new product. Another widely used approach is to ask customers to compare two alternatives and to reflect on what they value about each of them. These comparisons can be quantified through conjoint analysis, where the researcher asks a respondent to make trade-off adjustments and decisions. Conjoint analysis provides a quantitative measure of the relative importance of one attribute as opposed to another. Although this method requires an investment of time and money in the research process, it may be worth it to avoid misreading customers' preferences [Aaker et al., 2001].

Focus groups, surveys, and customer interviews all face a challenge in that they have a limited ability to identify new problems and solutions. As Henry Ford, the automotive pioneer, once remarked, "If I'd asked my customers what they wanted, they'd have said a faster horse." Similarly, no potential customer ever asked for ATMs, personal computers, the Internet, or highly portable music players. Akio Marita, the founder of Sony, seized on this last opportunity. Marita directed his engineers to design a small portable radio and cassette player that would provide good audio quality and be attached to a person's head. Although no customer was asking for this product, the Sony Walkman became one of the twentieth century's most successful applications of miniaturized electronics. It fueled a market later addressed by the Apple iPod and then by mobile phones, such that people today take portable music for granted.

Since customers cannot always verbalize their problems and needs, direct observations are another important means of gathering customer information. As human factors expert Leon Segal says, "Innovation begins with an eye" [Kelley, 2001]. By studying potential customers engaged in their everyday activities, entrepreneurs can see firsthand the behaviors, frustrations, bottlenecks, and other cues that may indicate a need or problem—and, therefore, a potential opportunity. For example, the health care provider Kaiser Permanente had a project team conduct observations at four hospitals in order to improve both patient and medical-practitioner experiences. By carefully watching how patients and practitioners interacted, the team was able to quickly identify nursing-staff shift changes as a problem. They found that nurses spent a great deal of time trying to convey information to the new shift and that much of the most important information was still missed or miscommunicated since there was no easy or standardized means of sharing. These observation-based insights enabled Kaiser Permanente to introduce a new system that improved patient care and nurses' job satisfaction [Brown, 2008].

As another example, Logan Green had the idea for Lyft while traveling in Zimbabwe, where he noticed people often picking up hitchhikers. Back in the United States, by contrast, he noted that cars were nearly empty, and the roads were clogged with traffic. Green initially launched Lyft as Zimride (named for Zimbabwe), a method for arranging carpools.

There are several ways that entrepreneurs can act as effective observers. First, rather than rely on expertise to guide observations, entrepreneurs may find that naiveté is a gift. For example, Jane Goodall attributes her groundbreaking research on chimpanzees to the fact that she had little prior knowledge about chimpanzee behavior. She, therefore, was not blinded to novel findings by any preconceptions [Sutton, 2002]. Second, when selecting people to observe, it can be particularly effective to study "extreme" users—such as children—and "rule breakers" who face novel constraints or who apply products in new ways. Finally, observations are most effective when the observers themselves come from multiple backgrounds and perspectives. Diversity enables a team of entrepreneurs to imagine the world from multiple perspectives in order to identify meaningful problems and novel solutions [Kelley, 2001].

The customer development process and the product development process proceed in parallel. Thus, as entrepreneurs gather data from the market, they should also work to create and refine product mockups and prototypes. Eric Ries and Steve Blank are the leading supporters of the idea of a **lean startup.** Ries coined the term "lean startup," and Blank created a course called "The Lean Launchpad" that teaches entrepreneurs many of the concepts initially discussed by Ries [Ries, 2011]. When building lean startups, entrepreneurs focus on learning what customers may be interested in, and they proceed to build a **minimum viable product,** or MVP, in order to see if there is demand for their initial product offering. Thus, rather than waiting until the product is "perfect," entrepreneurs are advised to start selling early [Onyemah et al., 2013]. Additional product features can then be added over time. For example, when Apple developed the iPod, they began with a simple product that contained the essence of the offering: portable digital music. Over a period of three years, they drew on customer feedback to make numerous design changes and tweaks, moving from a simple product to a more complex one [Brown and Martin, 2015].

Typically, a minimum viable product is an actual product. For example, Embrace Innovations began when four Stanford graduate students decided to tackle the lack of a simple and affordable infant warmer for premature and low-weight babies. As the final project for a course on Design for Extreme Affordability, they modified a baby sleeping bag with a heatable wax insert. This MVP enabled them to attract funding and served as an initial prototype.

An MVP enables an entrepreneur to observe how potential customers or users interact with the product and to gain insight accordingly. When it isn't possible to create a minimally viable version of a product or service, however, entrepreneurs can instead create a high-level product specification, such as a brochure that outlines the offerings. Such a description should be specific about the proposed offering and how each aspect benefits the customer. Yet it also should stay at a high level to allow for rapid revision without investing too many resources [Aulet, 2013].

By beginning with a minimum viable product, startups that utilize the lean approach can be funded with smaller amounts of initial capital (since simple products can be faster and cheaper to build). They then seek incremental capital once the founders gain confidence that there is a market and have proven that they can build viable products. These startups also make heavy use of crowdsourcing, outsourcing, cloud computing, and Software as a Service (SaaS) in order to limit their cash outlays [McQuivey, 2013].

34 **CHAPTER 2** Opportunities

Sahl Khan followed this approach when launching the Khan Academy, a virtual school providing software and video tutorials in math, science, and other subjects. Kahn created almost all of the company's initial videos himself, often creating a video in just one or two days. His approach was to get videos out on the web quickly to see if they gained traction, thus testing the market and gathering feedback. Khan also runs his service on outsourced hardware. By following the lean approach, Khan proved his business model on very limited initial capital. By 2016, Khan Academy had received almost $10 million in grants and had extended its content to 36 languages reaching millions of students. The company is well on its way to revolutionizing the way education is taught and consumed.

2.3 Types and Sources of Innovation

Opportunities often reside at the nexus of a market need and a technological capability. Thus, entrepreneurs should simultaneously engage with the market and with the process of technological innovation. **Innovation** is defined as invention that has produced economic or social value in the marketplace. Innovations can be new products, new processes, new services, and new ways of doing business.

Often, innovations are combinations of multiple different components that are assembled in a particular way. For example, a simple fan might include a blade, a motor that turns the blade, a controller that turns the motor on and off, and a housing that contains the other components. Figure 2.4 illustrates how there are several different types of innovations, depending on whether one is changing the components, the way the components are put together, or both [Henderson and Clark, 1990].

Incremental innovation is characterized by faster, better, and/or cheaper versions of existing products. Thus, entrepreneurs engaged in incremental innovation take an existing idea and creatively expand on it. For example, imagine a new tablet that retains the same user interface and screen as its predecessor but adds a faster processor and more memory. To be successful, the incremental innovator must understand specific customer needs that are unmet by current offerings.

	Basic design concepts	
	Reinforced	Overturned
Linkages between modules Unchanged	Incremental innovation ("faster, better, cheaper")	Component or modular innovation
Changed	Architectural innovation	Radical or disruptive innovation ("brave new world")

FIGURE 2.4 Four types of innovation.

Like incremental innovation, architectural innovation leaves core design concepts relatively unchanged. But **architectural innovation** changes the way in which components of a product are linked together. Thus, the components remain unchanged, but the architecture of module connection is the innovation. (The overall architecture of the product describes how the components will work together.) For example, returning to the example of a fan, the move from large fans attached to the ceiling with their motors hidden from view to small portable fans would constitute an architectural innovation. The components remain largely the same, but they interact in new ways [Henderson and Clark, 1990].

By contrast, **modular innovation** is focused on the innovation of new components and modules, but without disrupting the overall pattern of connections between modules. For example, Nest Labs recognized that traditional thermostats were difficult to program and control and were aesthetically dull. They thus added a learning algorithm and WiFi capability to the thermostat, enabling it to program itself and to be easily controlled from devices like phones and tablets. (They made the thermostat look attractive, too.) The addition of new components or modules form the basis of the Nest thermostat innovation, but the basic functionality of the thermostat and its role in a heating/cooling system remain unchanged.

Finally, **radical innovation** or **disruptive innovation** uses new modules and new architecture to create new products. The Internet is an example of a network system with new modules and new architecture—a radical or disruptive innovation. Disruptive innovation transforms the relationship between customer and supplier, restructures markets, displaces current products, and often creates new product categories. Disruptive products also introduce a new value proposition [Christensen et al., 2015].

Salesforce.com introduced a disruptive application for sales force activity tracking. Salesforce.com started selling sales force automation on a Software as a Service (SaaS) basis, in which customers pay a monthly licensing fee. This arrangement contrasts dramatically with the way that the incumbent leaders in sales force automation, Oracle and SAP, were selling software: Oracle and SAP would charge a one-time license fee that could run into hundreds of thousands of dollars, and would additionally charge yearly maintenance fees. Furthermore, they made customers responsible for running and updating their own software. By contrast, Salesforce.com would run and maintain the customer's software. New customers implementing sales force automation were much more likely to try to implement their solution with lower up-front costs.

An emerging disruptive innovation is drone or unmanned aerial vehicle (UAV) technology. Drones enable aerial surveying, deliveries to remote locations, infrastructure inspections, and countless other tasks that were difficult or impossible to perform before. In the process, the use of drones is restructuring markets, displacing current offerings, and creating new product categories. Each year, drones are getting both more powerful and less expensive, leading to rapid expansion of the technology [Diamandis, 2016].

Other good examples of disruptive innovations include the photocopier, 3D printing, and driverless cars. These types of disruptive applications bring significant value to a product and cause an industry to grow exponentially. They also are associated with improved odds of success for an entrepreneur. New firms that try to make an incrementally better product and sell it to the same customers as existing firms experience only a 6 percent success rate; new firms that introduce disruptive innovations experience a 33 percent success rate [Christensen, 2002].

Sources of innovation include existing companies, research laboratories and universities, independent inventors and "user innovators," and open technical communities. Many companies are formed when employees in an existing enterprise have ideas for a new product and they decide that the best way to pursue it is as an independent venture. Of course, employees need to be careful about legal restrictions, which may restrain competition or require a license. Often, however, employees can take existing market insights and even technical knowledge and apply it to a new venture [Yeganegi et al., 2016].

Universities are another important source of innovation. Professors, graduate students, and other university researchers conduct an enormous amount of cutting-edge research. Since academic research typically is not driven by direct market needs, however, a major challenge in the commercialization of university breakthroughs lies in the need to move this research from lab prototypes and concepts into complete working products that can be manufactured reliably at a reasonable cost [Nelson, 2014]. To get the most benefit from a relationship with a university, a new venture should take a long-term view and imagine a partnership focused on both technical and strategic issues. When companies take a transactional approach to the relationship—attempting to pick technologies, sign a contract, and quickly commercialize them—they are likely to fail [Wright, 2008]. By contrast, when an inventor stays involved with product development as it moves from the university to a startup, the chances of success increase dramatically [Thursby and Thursby, 2004]. University-sourced innovations also present special legal challenges, which we will discuss in Chapter 11.

Many innovations come from end users themselves [Franke et al., 2016]. For example, snowboarding, skateboarding, and windsurfing trace their origins to users who experimented with new combinations of equipment [Shah, 2003]. Similarly, end users have developed innovations ranging from library information systems to baby strollers to chemical processing techniques [Shah and Tripsas, 2007]. Because users may understand their own needs and the limitations of existing products, they are uniquely positioned to innovate. Research shows that collaboration with users is especially beneficial in new technology areas and in the generation of radical innovations [Chatterji and Fabrizio, 2014].

Many user-innovators also participate in open technical communities [Baldwin and von Hippel, 2011]. These communities may be autonomous or sponsored, and their members may include both individuals and organizations. Open technical communities play a crucial role in helping new enterprises to develop and deploy innovations [West and O'Mahony, 2008]. Firms benefit from participating in open communities by gathering information on potential alliances, identifying new opportunities, and sharing work and risk. Furthermore, such communities offer the benefit of transparency of developments and ready accessibility to shared knowledge.

An **open source innovation** community may be defined as a collection of many firms and individuals collaborating to develop and deploy an innovation. These communities share a common goal and an agreed-to governance system. Open source software communities are important examples of open technical communities. Individual members of these communities share common goals, but not a common employer. Examples are the Mozilla and Hadoop communities.

Effective open source organizations enable new ventures to build on the ideas of others to create new innovations [Murray and O'Mahony, 2007]. Cumulative innovation is enabled by ready access, disclosure, and incentives associated with community activities. The sharing process enables knowledge to be reused, recombined, and accumulated, often in a modular format that all members can readily access and use.

One example of a good open source effort is the Collaborative Software Initiative (CSI), based in Portland, Oregon. Their enterprise software solutions are based on the efforts of contributors worldwide and are potentially more effective than individual or independent development. Other examples include Wikipedia, a free online encyclopedia that anyone can edit, and YouTube, which contains an ever-expanding video library based upon the contributions of users [Tapscott and Williams, 2008].

2.4 Trends and Convergence

Both market needs and technology developments tend to align with broader trends. Moreover, the convergence of different markets and technologies can point to new opportunities. For example, just 30 years ago both online shopping and the use of mobile phones to maintain social networks were far-off dreams. Today, hundreds of millions of people shop online, and mobile phones are widespread on every continent.

One of the most important trends lies in the globalization of business. Specifically, the Internet and overnight shipping have negated time and distance. This trend enables entrepreneurs to reach vastly larger markets and to build businesses that bring together a far more diverse set of resources. At the same time, of course, entrepreneurs face new competitors around the globe.

Growing environmental consciousness and associated challenges with climate change and pollution are other trends that shape the opportunity landscape. Consumers increasingly demand products that minimize negative environmental impacts. In turn, the redesign of products for sustainability presents enormous opportunities [Russo, 2010].

Social and cultural trends offer many examples of opportunity. Table 2.4 lists several social and cultural trends. One of the biggest current trends in America is the aging of the baby-boom generation—those born between 1946 and 1973. During those years, 107.5 million Americans were born, making up

TABLE 2.4 Social and cultural trends that will create opportunities.

■ Aging of the baby-boom generation	■ Changing role of religious organizations
■ Increasing ethnic diversity within countries	■ Changing role of women in society
■ Two-working-parent families	■ Pervasive influence of media and constant connectivity
■ Rising middle class of developing nations	■ Broadening access to education

50 percent of everyone alive in 1973 [Hoover, 2001]. Those born in the peak-birth year of 1961 will be 60 in 2021 and acting as consumers of goods and services such as new homes, travel, health care, and retirement plans. Other critical trends include the changing role of women in many societies and broadening access to education, including online education.

Entrepreneurs can sometimes study a trend to see how it might apply in other settings. Peer-to-peer services are one example. Airbnb is best known for enabling one person to work with another person to rent a room rather than staying in a more expensive hotel. That same model can be applied to many other services, such as car rentals and money transfers [de Boer, 2012]. For example, Lending Club and Prosper are establishing person-to-person lending, eliminating the bank as a middleman [Landes, 2012].

Opportunities often lie at the intersection of social and technological change. For example, new online education businesses are positioned at the intersection of growing interest in education and lifelong learning, on one hand, and increasing penetration of high-speed Internet and mobile Internet devices on the other hand. As another example, new businesses are forming at the intersection of unmanned aerial vehicles (UAVs) and regulatory changes that are permitting these UAVs to access U.S. airspace.

One of the most promising areas of science and engineering is based on several breakthroughs that enable the manipulation of matter at the molecular level. Mass production of products with these molecular adjustments now offers a world of possibilities. Nanotechnology will make materials lighter, more durable, and more stain resistant, and will enable the creation of products with wholly new capabilities. (One nanometer is one-billionth of a meter.)

With the need for security and safety of personal information, the emergence of personal identification cards, or smart cards, may be the next trend in the United States. A smart card is a plastic card incorporating an integrated circuit chip and memory that stores and transfers data such as personal data and identification information—for example, finger or palm print or facial scans. These cards have been adopted in several European and Asian countries and could spread worldwide. One form of smart card, the Octopus Card, is used in Hong Kong to pay for everything from subway rides to groceries. Another important use of smart cards would be a common approach for driver's licenses and personal information. Table 2.5 lists several other technology-related trends and opportunities.

TABLE 2.5 Trends and opportunities.

- Life science: Genetic engineering, genomics, biometrics

- Information technology: Internet, wireless device, cloud computing

- Food production: More efficient processes

- Video gaming: Learning, entertainment

- Speech recognition: Interface between computers and people

- Security devices and systems: Identification devices, scanners, protective gear

- Nanotechnology: Devices 100 nanometers or less for drug delivery, biosensors

- Clean energy: Solar cells and wind turbines

- Online education: Massive open courses and customized offerings

- Fuel cells: Electrochemical conversion of hydrogen or hydrocarbon fuels

- Superconductivity: Energy savings on utility power lines

- Designer enzymes: Protein catalysts that accelerate chemical reactions in living cells for consumers and health products

- Cell phones: Communications and computing

- Software security: Blocking e-mail spam and phishing, preventing hacks

- Robots: Teams of small coordinated robots for monitoring and safety

- Self-driving cars: Autonomous vehicles that can communicate with one another

- Virtual and augmented reality: Computer-enhanced information systems and entertainment

- Artificial intelligence: Algorithms for machine learning

- Drones: Delivery of household items, mapping for agriculture and security

- Outer space: Exploration, tourism, and resource extraction

Opportunities also emerge as the boundaries between many once-distinct businesses, from agribusiness and chemicals to energy and computing, continue to blur. The **convergence** of technologies or industries is the coming together or merging of several technologies or industries thought to be different or separate. Often, opportunities can be found in creative combinations that build on complementary technologies.

One example of industry convergence is that of computing and communications, which merged into the field of networks. Another example is convergence of a handheld computer and a mobile phone, now evident in Apple's iPhone and Samsung's Galaxy.

Satellite imaging and data and the handheld computer converged into global positioning system (GPS) devices, which are widely used, inexpensive devices that address the need for accurate locational data. Scanners, computers, and security systems converged into self-checkout systems for shoppers. Gene chips use semiconductor technology to speed up biochemistry lab analysis. Finally, medical and robotic technologies have converged to facilitate highly precise, minimally invasive robotic surgery. Intuitive Surgical's da Vinci medical robot has four arms and flexible wrists mounted with tools and cameras that can be controlled by a surgeon. The robots are being used for prostate surgeries, hysterectomies, and even more complicated surgeries like heart valve repair. As these examples highlight, effective entrepreneurs carefully examine social and technological trends. They strive to identify novel combinations that may point to significant opportunities.

2.5 Opportunity Evaluation

Alongside the identification of opportunities, entrepreneurs should work to evaluate these opportunities. In fact, a critical task of the entrepreneur is to distinguish between an idea and a true opportunity. Good opportunities have the potential to solve important and timely problems. As shown in Table 2.6, attractive opportunities also have the potential to be profitable and can be pursued under a favorable regulatory and industry context.

Choosing the right opportunity is both difficult and important. This choice is analogous to the selection of an equity investment in a company: Entrepreneurs will invest time, effort, and money in the venture they choose in a manner similar to how people invest in the stock of a company. Some sound investment principles that can be used for selecting opportunities are listed in Table 2.7.

TABLE 2.6 Five characteristics of an attractive opportunity.

■ Timely—a current need or problem	■ Profitable—the customer will pay for the solution and allow the enterprise to profit
■ Solvable—a problem that can be solved in the near future with accessible resource	
■ Important—the customer deems the problem or need important	■ Context—a favorable regulatory and industry situation

TABLE 2.7 Guiding principles for selecting good opportunities.

■ Remember that only one or two very good opportunities are needed in a lifetime.	■ If the opportunity is selected and turns out unfavorably, can you exit with minor losses?
■ Invest less time, money, and effort in the venture than it will be worth in the short run. Calculate the probability of a large return in the long term.	■ Does this opportunity provide a potential for a long-term success, or is it a fad? Go to where the potential future gains are significant.
■ Do not count on making a high-priced sale of your firm to the public or another company.	■ Can the management team execute the strategy selected for this opportunity?
■ Carry out a solid analysis of the current and expected conditions of the industry where the opportunity resides.	■ Will the customer enable your firm to profit from this venture?

The entrepreneur finds and thoroughly analyzes the best opportunities, since for many people, only one or two opportunities are needed to make a good life of entrepreneurial activity. One goal is to invest in a firm for which you pay less than it is worth; this provides some cushion for unforeseen challenges. Also, entrepreneurs try to find an opportunity with solid long-term potential in an industry they understand. They put together a good management team that can execute the strategy for this opportunity. And, they ensure that the customer will allow their firm to profit from the venture. Thus, they avoid industries that sell commodities where price is the basis of competition—unless they have a new, innovative business process that enables their firm to be the low-cost provider.

In 2008, iTunes was the largest supplier of digital music content. Yet Swedish startup Spotify AB thought iTunes' pay-per-song model was flawed, and it created an alternative "freemium" music streaming model. The company offers its product, Spotify, in two versions: free with ads or a paid subscription without ads. By 2016, Spotify had 40 million subscribers and an additional 55 million free users.

The review of opportunities will always include the evaluation of alternatives. The **opportunity cost** of an action is the value (cost) of the forgone alternative action. Selecting one opportunity will involve rejecting others. Chapter 1 discussed some of the considerations that people should use when deciding whether to become entrepreneurs by pursuing a specific opportunity. A critical part of this decision hinges on the quality of the opportunity in terms of a market assessment, feasibility of implementation, and differentiation of the product. There is an inherent tension in entrepreneurship in that much of this analysis requires additional information, yet a comprehensive analytical approach to evaluation of the opportunity does not suit most startups; entrepreneurs often lack the time and money to fully engage with all potential customers, analyze substitutes, reconstruct competitors' cost structures, and project alternative planning scenarios.

Most entrepreneurial teams instead follow a basic five-step process, as outlined in Table 2.8. The goal is to assess these five characteristics—capabilities,

TABLE 2.8 Basic five-step process of evaluating an opportunity.

1. **Capabilities:** Is the venture opportunity consistent with the capabilities, knowledge, and experience of the team members?

2. **Novelty:** Does the product or service have significant novel, proprietary, or differentiating qualities? Does it create significant value for the customer—enough so that the customer wants the product and will pay a premium for it?

3. **Resources:** Can the venture team attract the necessary financial, physical, and human resources consistent with the magnitude of the venture?

4. **Return:** Can the product be produced at a cost so that a profit can be obtained? Is the expected return of the venture consistent with the risk of the venture?

5. **Commitment:** Do the entrepreneurial team members feel compelled to commit to this venture? Are they passionate about the venture?

> ### The Twitter Opportunity
>
> In 2006, the board members of the podcasting company Odeo held a day-long brainstorming session to talk about the company. Jack Dorsey, then an undergraduate at New York University, proposed the idea of using an SMS service to send messages between a small group—much like Slack. Originally, the service was used as an internal communication tool for Odeo. In 2007, however, the founders of Twitter spun off the company. One of the founders, Evan Williams, admitted that "With Twitter, it wasn't clear what it was. They called it a social network, they called it microblogging, but it was hard to define, because it didn't replace anything." Through their commitment and belief in an opportunity, Williams and his partners were able to capitalize on a novel technological opportunity.

novelty, resources, return, and commitment—to quickly weed out unpromising ventures and thus conserve energy and time for the promising ones. The appropriate analytical effort and the issues that are most worthy of research and analysis depend on the characteristics of each venture. For example, the exploration process should be short for potential ventures with low degrees of novelty [Choi et al., 2008]. In general, however, an entrepreneur works through the five steps and eliminates the opportunities that do not pass muster. Those that do pass a quick review are worth looking into further.

The entrepreneur has to live with critical uncertainties, such as the number and relative competence of rivals, which are not easy to analyze. Who could have forecast, for example, that IBM would turn to Microsoft for an operating system for its personal computer, allow Microsoft to retain the rights to this operating system, and thus enable Microsoft to gain monopolistic dominance of the operating system marketplace? Entering a race requires faith in one's ability to finish ahead of whoever else might participate.

When evaluating an opportunity, the entrepreneur considers whether it fits or matches the contextual conditions, the team's capabilities and characteristics, and the team's ability to secure the necessary resources to initiate a new venture based on the opportunity. Figure 2.5 shows a diagram of fit or congruence that can be used to review an opportunity. A big diamond with high grades of fit are best.

Consider an opportunity that has existed for over 100 years—the electric automobile. We will assume that a capable set of engineers is available and the entrepreneurial team has the attitudes and capabilities required. However, the team is insecure about the risky nature of the venture, given the numerous failures over the past century. We will rate the entrepreneurial team at 75 percent on the team scale. The characteristics of the context are very mixed since regulations and support for electric cars are continually changing as potential customers and government organizations adjust their assessment of the

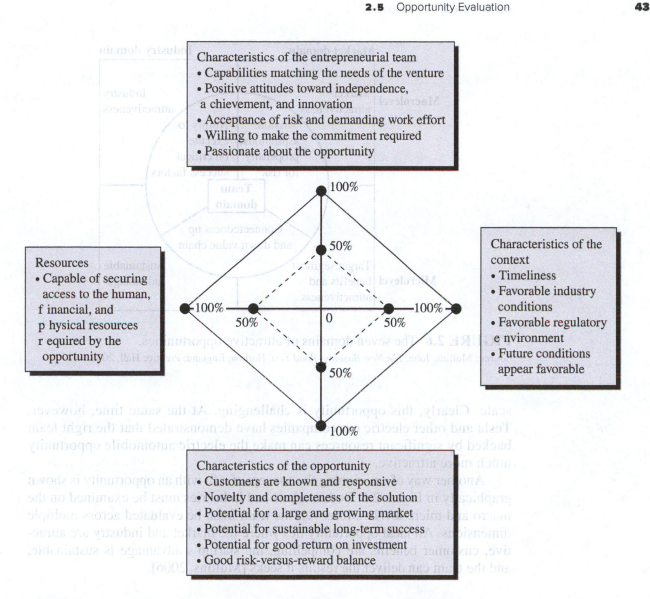

Characteristics of the entrepreneurial team
• Capabilities matching the needs of the venture
• Positive attitudes toward independence,
  achievement, and innovation
• Acceptance of risk and demanding work effort
• Willing to make the commitment required
• Passionate about the opportunity

Resources
• Capable of securing
  access to the human,
  financial, and
  physical resources
  required by the
  opportunity

Characteristics of the context
• Timeliness
• Favorable industry
  conditions
• Favorable regulatory
  environment
• Future conditions
  appear favorable

Characteristics of the opportunity
• Customers are known and responsive
• Novelty and completeness of the solution
• Potential for a large and growing market
• Potential for sustainable long-term success
• Potential for good return on investment
• Good risk-versus-reward balance

FIGURE 2.5 Diagram of the fit of an opportunity, the context, the entrepreneurial team, and the resources required. Rate each factor on a scale of 0 to 100 percent.

benefits and costs of these vehicles. We will rate this opportunity as 60 percent on the context scale. Next we turn to the opportunity, which has tremendous upside yet is challenged by costs, limited battery life, and short ranges before a recharge is required. The characteristics of the opportunity call for a rating of 75 percent on the opportunity scale. Given these ratings, most teams would be limited in their ability to secure the tens of millions of dollars required to launch this venture. Thus, we rate it only 60 percent on the resource

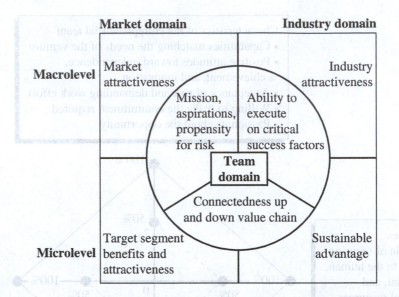

FIGURE 2.6 The seven domains of attractive opportunities.
Source: Mullins, John. *The New Business Road Test*. Harlow, England: Prentice Hall, 2006.

scale. Clearly, this opportunity is challenging. At the same time, however, Tesla and other electric car companies have demonstrated that the right team backed by significant resources can make the electric automobile opportunity much more attractive.

Another way of envisioning the concept of a fit with an opportunity is shown graphically in Figure 2.6. Both markets and industries must be examined on the macro and micro levels. Moreover, the team must be evaluated across multiple dimensions. An ideal opportunity lies where the market and industry are attractive, customer benefits are compelling, the startup's advantage is sustainable, and the team can deliver the results it seeks [Mullins, 2006].

A Big Opportunity in Television

What is the next big opportunity in television? As online streaming usurps traditional cable and satellite subscriptions, the living room screen is no longer the lone conduit for content. There are a number of opportunities arising from this shift. Google's Chromecast is a device that allows a user to mirror her computer screen on any USB-enabled display. Magic Leap is a startup that hopes to do away with screens altogether by selling a pair of glasses with a microcomputer that can simulate a television screen wherever a user wants it and as large as she want its. Netflix ingests data about what shows are most popular in order to produce its own perfectly optimized shows for every genre. Which of these opportunities pass the evaluation process of Table 2.8?

After evaluating an opportunity by using the factors in Table 2.8, the entrepreneurs should decide whether to act. With the knowledge generated by using the five-step process in Table 2.8, the entrepreneurs will tend to act on their estimate of the potential benefits and gains, B, while accounting for the total costs of the venture, C. Within the total cost accounting, there will need to be a recognition of their security needs and loss aversion. An individual will tend to act if the ratio B/C is greater than 1. The lucrative opportunity (high benefits and low losses) will tend to cause higher intention to act [McMullen and Shepherd, 2002]. If one acts and it is a false choice, the cost of that choice is important. Opportunities that can be attempted with low initial financial and time commitment costs may offer the chance for lucrative returns at a low initial cost.

Figure 2.7 shows the decision to act or not act. Then, the actual resulting quality of the opportunity is shown (this can be determined only after the decision). Life is about choices, and the best case is when we choose to act and it turns out we are right!

The entrepreneur tries to make a rational decision based on (1) his or her current psychological and financial assets, and (2) the possible consequences of the choice. The decision challenge is the task of turning incomplete knowledge of an opportunity into an action consistent with that knowledge. Competitive advantage comes from actually doing something that others cannot do; analyses and reports cannot substitute for action, and reworking a plan is no substitute for acting to get things done. In the end, an opportunity can be evaluated only so much [Pfeffer and Sutton, 2000]. Ambiguity remains, and the entrepreneur must act on or reject the opportunity. Fear of failure may overwhelm all but the best opportunities.

Actual quality of opportunity

	Poor	Very good
Act	2 False choice → Loss	1 Excellent choice → Hit
Do not act	Correct rejection → Save resources	Missed opportunity → Lost chance

Decision

FIGURE 2.7 Decision matrix.

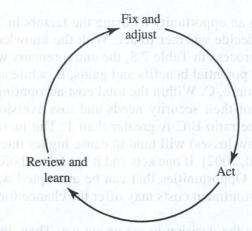

FIGURE 2.8 Act-learn-fix cycle of building a new venture.

Ultimately, identifying a good opportunity is less about making an initial selection and more about gathering data and refining the idea accordingly. Thus, while it is important to estimate fit, as in Figure 2.5, it is critical to act on the opportunity, trying it out in the marketplace of ideas and investors. Data gathered and lessons learned from these initial attempts can lead to refinement of the opportunity. Thus, effective entrepreneurs continually follow a PRRR process: plan, run, review, and revise [Rose, 2016]. Similarly, the act-review-fix cycle, as shown in Figure 2.8, summarizes the critical ability to act, review, and learn from the results, and then fix and adjust the business scheme as required.

2.6 Spotlight on Airbnb

Airbnb was founded by Brian Chesky and Joe Gebbia in 2007, with cofounder Nathan Blecharczyk joining in 2008. At first, Airbnb was called AirBed & Breakfast, with Chesky and Gebbia renting out a room in their own apartment to attendees of the Industrial Design conference. After limited traction, Airbnb joined the startup incubator Y Combinator in 2009, and the company's future turned around. In 2010, Airbnb closed a $7.2 million first round of financing from institutional investors. By 2016, Chesky and Gebbia were raising $850 million at a $30 billion valuation. Together they built a highly valued "unicorn," which is a term used to describe a privately owned company with a valuation over $1 billion.

Airbnb's rise to prominence emphasizes the increasing trend of the sharing economy, which takes underutilized items and rents them out to consumers for a fee. The sharing economy has reshaped how value is generated. With an increase in the amount of data available about users, companies like Airbnb capitalized on this trend. At the same time, Airbnb had an aggressive growth strategy that focused on getting big as quickly as possible, growing before the legality of the business could even be understood. Now Airbnb is large enough to handle the legal complications that often come with scaling.

In addition to capitalizing on a new opportunity driven by technological advancement, the founders of Airbnb focused on understanding and helping their customers. While reviewing New York listings, the founders realized people were not booking rentals due to low-quality pictures. Paul Graham, one of the Y Combinator founders, suggested the nonscalable, nontechnical solution of traveling to New York and taking high-resolution pictures for customers. This doubled Airbnb's weekly revenue to $400 at the time, establishing understanding the customer as a key Airbnb value.

2.7 Summary

The entrepreneur identifies numerous problems and needs that may point to good opportunities that can be made into great companies. However, he or she searches for the one that best fits the capabilities of the team, the economic and regulatory context, the characteristics of the opportunity, and the team's capability to secure the necessary resources. Then, the entrepreneur decides whether to act or not act on that best-fit opportunity.

The important ideas of the chapter are:

- Great opportunities are often disguised as problems that are difficult to describe.
- Opportunities can be tied to market demands and new technological capabilities.
- New technologies can arise from existing companies, universities, users, and open source communities.
- Social and technological trends shape opportunities.
- Entrepreneurs must engage with the market on a continual basis in order to identify and validate opportunities.
- Attractive opportunities are timely, solvable, important, and profitable, and they exist in a favorable context.
- The entrepreneurial team should cumulatively possess all the necessary capabilities.
- Entrepreneurs should, if possible, act on favorable opportunities in a timely manner.

Principle 2
The capable entrepreneur knows how to identify, select, describe, and communicate an opportunity that has good potential to become a successful enterprise.

Video Resources

Visit http://techventures.stanford.edu to view experts discussing content from this chapter.

Disruptive Technologies	John Doerr	KPCB
Pressure Points Around Opportunity	Brad Feld	Foundry Group
Internet of Everything	Padmasree Warrior	NextEV

2.8 Exercises

2.1 One approach to classifying market entry is by (a) creating a new market, (b) attacking an existing market, or (c) resegmenting an existing market. Using Table 2.1, indicate how each of these categories of opportunities would be applicable to these market-entry approaches.

2.2 What were some of the key customer, technology, and market trends that drove entrepreneurship during the last decade? What factors do you predict will drive entrepreneurial challenges in the next decade?

2.3 The next big wave of innovation may be the convergence of bio-, info-, and nanotechnologies. Each holds promise in its own right, but together in combination, they could give rise to many important products. Describe one opportunity motivated by the convergence of these new areas, and develop a story about the opportunity.

2.4 Some imagine that within a few years it will be possible, through the use of stem cells, to create new cells and eventually new organs to replace those that fail. Summarize the potential opportunity for stem cell enterprises. How would you begin to estimate the size of this opportunity? Develop a story depicting the opportunity.

2.5 As energy costs rise and the impact on the environment becomes clearer, clean tech has become an area of significant new investment. Quantify the trends driving this renewed investment interest. How would you evaluate and market size the clean tech opportunity?

2.6 Consider a software application you use regularly. What task(s) does it improve or enable? Suggest three ways the application could be improved. Would any of these improvements be considered an opportunity for a new venture? Why or why not?

2.7 Global sales of radio frequency identification tags (RFID) and related equipment have been forecasted to explode multiple times in the last decade. Describe the problems solved by RFID and the opportunities presented. What have been the barriers to commercialization of this technology? What types of opportunities will be created when RFID tags are widely adopted in products?

2.8 The trend of performance of two electronic technologies is given in Figure 2.9. Determine the performance trend of another technology. Prepare a chart of its performance over time.

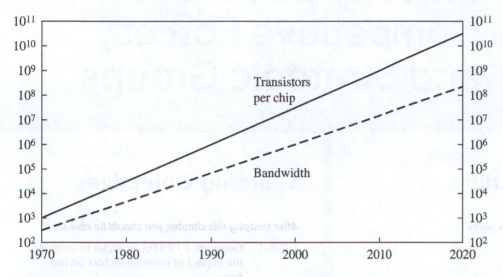

FIGURE 2.9 Technology trends: (a) transistors per chip; (b) bandwidth per household (bits/second).
Source: Dorf, R. C. (Ed.). *The Engineering Handbook,* 2nd ed. Boca Raton, FL: CRC Press, 2004.

VENTURE CHALLENGE

Consider the opportunity that you identified at the end of Chapter 1.

1. Using Table 2.1, attempt to categorize the type of opportunity you have selected.

2. How could you develop your customer at the same time as developing your product or service as shown in Figure 2.3?

3. Evaluate your opportunity using Table 2.7's principles and Table 2.8's process. Sketch a diagram using Figure 2.5 to illustrate your results.

CHAPTER

3

External Analysis: Industry Structure, Competitive Forces, and Strategic Groups

Chapter Outline

Learning Objectives

After studying this chapter, you should be able to:

LO 3-1 Generate a PESTEL analysis to evaluate the impact of external factors on the firm.

LO 3-2 Differentiate the roles of firm effects and industry effects in determining firm performance.

LO 3-3 Apply Porter's five competitive forces to explain the profit potential of different industries.

LO 3-4 Examine how competitive industry structure shapes rivalry among competitors.

LO 3-5 Describe the strategic role of complements in creating positive-sum co-opetition.

LO 3-6 Explain the five choices required for market entry.

LO 3-7 Appraise the role of industry dynamics and industry convergence in shaping the firm's external environment.

LO 3-8 Generate a strategic group model to reveal performance differences between clusters of firms in the same industry.

CHAPTER**CASE 3**　Part I

Airbnb: Disrupting the Hotel Industry

IN 2019, AIRBNB had 5 million listings in over 81,000 cities in some 190 countries, ranging from spare rooms to entire islands. With its "asset-light approach" based on its platform strategy, Airbnb is able to offer more accommodations than the three biggest hotel chains combined: Marriott, Hilton, and Intercontinental. And just like global hotel chains, Airbnb uses sophisticated pricing and reservation systems for guests to find, reserve, and pay for rooms to meet their travel needs. In this sense, Airbnb is a new entrant that competes in the global hotel industry.

Brian Chesky and Joe Gebbia, Airbnb founders, were roommates in San Francisco a little more than a decade earlier. Both were industrial designers, people who shape the form and function of everything from coffee cups to office furniture to airplane interiors. But since work opportunities were hit-and-miss, they found themselves struggling to make their rent payments. On a whim, they decided to e-mail everyone on the distribution list for an upcoming industrial design conference in their hometown: "If you're heading out to the [industrial design conference] in San Francisco next week and have yet to make accommodations, well, consider networking in your jam-jams. That's right. For an affordable alternative to hotels in the city, imagine yourself in a fellow design industry person's home, fresh awake from a snooze on the ol' air mattress, chatting about the day's upcoming events over Pop Tarts and OJ."[1]

Three people took up the offer, and the two roommates made some money to subsidize their rent payments. But more importantly, Chesky and Gebbia felt that they had stumbled upon a new business idea: Help people rent out their spare rooms. They then brought on computer scientist Nathan Blecharczyk, one of Gebbia's former roommates, to create a website where hosts and guests could meet and transact, naming their site AirBedandBreakfast.com (later

Nathan Blecharczyk, Joe Gebbia, and Brian Chesky founded Airbnb on a shoestring budget in 2008. Today, Airbnb is the largest hospitality platform globally.

Stefanie Keenan/Getty Images

shortened to Airbnb). The three entrepreneurs tested their new site at the 2008 South by Southwest (SXSW), an annual music, film, and interactive media conference. SXSW also serves as an informal launch pad for new ventures; for example, Twitter was unveiled at SXSW just a year earlier to great fanfare. Airbnb's launch at SXSW flopped, however, because the conference organizers had exclusive contracts with local hotels (which Airbnb founders learned about later), and so conference organizers didn't drive any traffic to Airbnb's site.

Not to be discouraged, Airbnb decided to take advantage of the anticipated shortage of hotel rooms in Denver, Colorado, the site of the Democratic National Convention (DNC) in the summer of 2008. After all hotels were booked, the founders prepared media releases with titles such as "Grassroots Housing for Grassroots Campaign," which Obama supporters loved. As luck would have it, Airbnb was covered in both *The New York Times* and *The Wall Street Journal*. And the newly designed Airbnb site worked! It facilitated about 100 rentals during the DNC. Soon after the event, however, website traffic to Airbnb's site fell back to zero. To keep going, Chesky and Gebbia decided to become cereal entrepreneurs, creating "Obama-O's: The breakfast of change" and "Cap'n McCains: A maverick in every bite," with illustrated images of the 2008 presidential candidates on 1,000 cereal boxes. After sending samples to their press contacts and subsequent coverage in the media, the limited edition cereal sold out quickly, providing enough cash to keep going with Airbnb a bit longer.

The fledgling venture's breakthrough came in 2009 when it was accepted into a program run by Y Combinator, a start-up accelerator that has spawned famous tech companies such as Dropbox, Stripe, and Twitch.tv. In exchange for equity in the new venture, these start-up accelerators provide office space, mentoring, and networking opportunities, including with venture capitalists looking to fund the next "big thing." In 2010, Airbnb received funding from Sequoia Capital, one of the most prestigious venture capital firms in

Silicon Valley, having provided early-stage capital to companies such as Apple, Google, Oracle, PayPal, YouTube, and WhatsApp. Although not a first mover in the peer-to-peer rental space, Airbnb, with support of Y Combinator, was the first one to figure out that a sleek website design comprising professional photos of available rentals made all the difference. In addition, Airbnb developed a seamless transaction experience between hosts and guests and was able to earn a little over 10 percent on each transaction conducted on its site. Timing was now much more fortuitous; with the global financial crisis in full swing, people were looking for low-cost

accommodations while hosts were trying to pay rent or mortgages to keep their homes.

In 2019, Airbnb was valued at a whopping $31 billion. This makes Airbnb the fourth most valuable private startup on the planet, just after Didi Chuxing, China's version of Uber ($56 billion), WeWork ($47 billion), and JUUL ($38 billion). Even more stunning, Airbnb's valuation approaches that of Marriott ($39 billion in 2019), the world's largest hotel chain with over $20 billion in annual revenues.[2]

Part II of this ChapterCase appears in Section 3.5.

HOW CAN AN INTERNET startup based on the idea of home sharing disrupt the global hotel industry, long dominated by corporate giants such as Marriott, Hilton, and Intercontinental? One reason is that Airbnb, now the world's largest accommodation provider, owns no real estate. Instead, it uses a business model innovation to circumvent traditional entry barriers into the hotel industry. Just like Uber, Facebook, or Amazon, Airbnb provides an online platform for sellers (hosts) and buyers (renters) to connect and transact (we'll take a closer look at "Platform Strategy" in Chapter 7). While traditional hotel chains need years and millions of dollars in real estate investments to add additional capacity (finding properties, building hotels, staffing and running them, etc.), Airbnb's inventory is basically unlimited as long as it can sign up users with spare rooms to rent. Even more importantly, Airbnb does not need to deploy millions of dollars in capital to acquire and manage physical assets or manage a large cadre of employees. For example, Marriott has almost 250,000 employees, while Airbnb's headcount is approximately 2,500 employees (only 1 percent of Marriott's). Thus, Airbnb can grow much faster and respond much more quickly to local circumstances affecting the demand and supply of accommodations. The competitive intensity in the hotel industry is likely to increase, especially in high-traffic metropolitan cities such as New York, Paris, Dubai, and Seoul.

In this chapter, we present a set of frameworks to analyze the firm's *external environment*—that is, the industry in which the firm operates, and the competitive forces that surround the firm from the outside. We move from a more macro perspective to a more micro understanding of how the external environment affects a firm's quest for competitive advantage. We begin with the PESTEL framework, which allows us to scan, monitor, and evaluate changes and trends in the firm's macroenvironment. Next, we study Porter's five forces model of competition, which helps us to determine an industry's profit potential. Depending on the firm's strategic position, these forces can affect its performance for good or ill. We also take a closer look at the choices firms must make when considering entry into an industry. We then move from a static analysis of a firm's industry environment to a dynamic understanding of how industries and competition change over time. We also discuss how to think through entry choices once an attractive industry has been identified. Next we introduce the strategic group model for understanding performance differences among clusters of firms in the same industry. Finally, we offer practical *Implications for Strategic Leaders*.

LO 3-1

Generate a PESTEL analysis to evaluate the impact of external factors on the firm.

3.1 The PESTEL Framework

A firm's external environment consists of all factors outside the firm that can affect its potential to gain and sustain a competitive advantage. By analyzing the factors in the firm's external environment, strategic leaders can mitigate threats and leverage opportunities. One

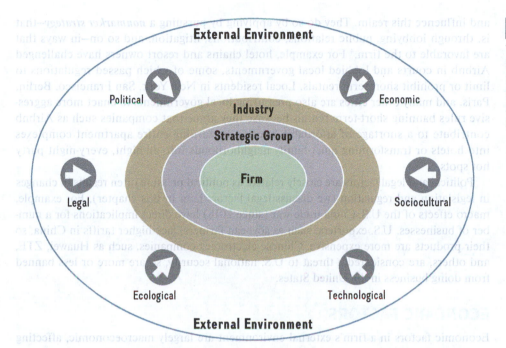

EXHIBIT 3.1

The Firm within Its External Environment, Industry, and Strategic Group, Subject to PESTEL Factors

common approach to understanding how external factors impinge upon a firm is to consider the source or proximity of these factors. For example, external factors in the firm's *general environment* are ones that strategic leaders have little direct influence over, such as macroeconomic factors (e.g., interest or currency exchange rates). In contrast, external factors in the firm's *task environment* are ones that strategic leaders do have some influence over, such as the composition of their strategic groups (a set of close rivals) or the structure of the industry. We will now look at each of these environmental layers in detail, moving from a firm's general environment to its task environment. Following along in Exhibit 3.1, we will be working from the outer ring to the inner ring.

The **PESTEL model** groups the factors in the firm's general environment into six segments:

- Political
- Economic
- Sociocultural
- Technological
- Ecological
- Legal

> **PESTEL model** A framework that categorizes and analyzes an important set of external factors (political, economic, sociocultural, technological, ecological, and legal) that might impinge upon a firm. These factors can create both opportunities and threats for the firm.

Together these form the acronym PESTEL. The PESTEL model provides a relatively straightforward way to *scan, monitor,* and *evaluate* the important external factors and trends that might impinge upon a firm. Such factors create both opportunities and threats.

POLITICAL FACTORS

Political factors result from the processes and actions of government bodies that can influence the decisions and behavior of firms.[3]

Although political factors are located in the firm's general environment, where firms traditionally wield little influence, companies nevertheless increasingly work to shape

nonmarket strategy
Strategic leaders' activities outside market exchanges where firms sell products or provide services to influence a firm's general environment through, for example, lobbying, public relations, contributions, and litigation in ways that are favorable to the firm.

and influence this realm. They do so by applying by pursuing a *nonmarket strategy*—that is, through lobbying, public relations, contributions, litigation, and so on—in ways that are favorable to the firm.[4] For example, hotel chains and resort owners have challenged Airbnb in courts and lobbied local governments, some of which passed regulations to limit or prohibit short-term rentals. Local residents in New York, San Francisco, Berlin, Paris, and many other cities are also pressuring local governments to enact more aggressive rules banning short-term rentals because they argue that companies such as Airbnb contribute to a shortage of affordable housing by turning entire apartment complexes into hotels or transforming quiet family neighborhoods into all-night, every-night party hot spots.

Political and legal factors are closely related, as political pressure often results in changes in legislation and regulation (we discuss legal factors later in this chapter). For example, macro effects of the U.S.-China trade war (since 2016) have direct implications for a number of businesses. U.S. exporters, such as soybean farmers, face higher tariffs in China, so their products are more expensive. Chinese electronics companies, such as Huawei, ZTE, and others, are considered a threat to U.S. national security, so are more or less banned from doing business in the United States.

ECONOMIC FACTORS

Economic factors in a firm's external environment are largely macroeconomic, affecting economy-wide phenomena. Strategic leaders need to consider how the following five macroeconomic factors can affect firm strategy:

- Growth rates.
- Levels of employment.
- Interest rates.
- Price stability (inflation and deflation).
- Currency exchange rates.

GROWTH RATES. The overall economic *growth rate* is a measure of the change in the amount of goods and services produced by a nation's economy. Strategic leaders look to the *real growth rate,* which adjusts for inflation. This real growth rate indicates the current business cycle of the economy—that is, whether business activity is expanding or contracting. In periods of economic expansion, consumer and business demands are rising, and competition among firms frequently decreases. During economic booms, businesses expand operations to satisfy demand and are more likely to be profitable. The reverse is generally true for recessionary periods, although certain companies that focus on low-cost solutions may benefit from economic contractions because demand for their products or services rises in such times. For customers, expenditures on luxury products are often the first to be cut during recessionary periods. For instance, you might switch from a $5 venti latte at Starbucks to a $1 alternative from McDonald's.

Occasionally, boom periods can overheat and lead to speculative asset bubbles. In the early 2000s, the United States experienced an asset bubble in real estate.[5] Easy credit, made possible by the availability of subprime mortgages and other financial innovations, fueled an unprecedented demand in housing. Real estate, rather than stocks, became the investment vehicle of choice for many Americans, propelled by the common belief that house prices could only go up. When the housing bubble burst, the deep economic recession of 2008–2009 began, impacting in some way nearly all businesses in the United States and worldwide.

LEVELS OF EMPLOYMENT. Growth rates directly affect the *level of employment*. In boom times, unemployment tends to be low, and skilled human capital becomes a scarce and more expensive resource. As the price of labor rises, firms have an incentive to invest more into capital goods such as cutting-edge equipment or artificial intelligence (AI).[6] In economic downturns, unemployment rises. As more people search for employment, skilled human capital is more abundant and wages usually fall.

INTEREST RATES. Another key macroeconomic variable for strategic leaders to track is real *interest rates*—the amount that creditors are paid for use of their money and the amount that debtors pay for that use, adjusted for inflation. The economic boom during the early years in the 21st century, for example, was fueled by cheap credit. Low real interest rates have a direct bearing on consumer demand. When credit is cheap because interest rates are low, consumers buy homes, condos, automobiles, computers, smartphones, and vacations on credit; in turn, all of this demand fuels economic growth. During periods of low real interest rates, firms can easily borrow money to finance growth. Borrowing at lower real rates reduces the cost of capital and enhances a firm's competitiveness. These effects reverse, however, when real interest rates are rising. Consumer demand slows, credit is harder to come by, and firms find it more difficult to borrow money to support operations, possibly deferring investments.

PRICE STABILITY. *Price stability*—the lack of change in price levels of goods and services—is rare. Therefore, companies will often have to deal with changing price levels, which is a function of the amount of money in any economy. When there is too much money in an economy, we tend to see rising prices—*inflation*. Indeed, a popular economic definition of inflation is *too much money chasing too few goods and services.*[7] Inflation tends to go with lower economic growth. Countries such as Argentina, Brazil, Mexico, Poland, and Venezuela experienced periods of hyperinflation in the recent past.

Deflation describes a decrease in the overall price level. A sudden and pronounced drop in demand generally causes deflation, which in turn forces sellers to lower prices to motivate buyers. Because many people automatically think of lower prices from the buyer's point of view, a decreasing price level seems at first glance to be attractive. However, deflation is actually a serious threat to economic growth because it distorts expectations about the future.[8] For example, once price levels start falling, companies will not invest in new production capacity or innovation because they expect a further decline in prices. In recent decades, the Japanese economy has been plagued with deflation.

CURRENCY EXCHANGE RATES. The *currency exchange rate* determines how many dollars one must pay for a unit of foreign currency. It is a critical variable for any company that buys or sells products and services across national borders. For example, if the U.S. dollar appreciates against the euro, and so increases in real value, firms need more euros to buy one dollar. This in turn makes U.S. exports such as Boeing aircraft, Intel chips, John Deere tractors, or American soybeans more expensive for European buyers and reduces demand for U.S. exports overall. This process reverses when the dollar depreciates (decreases in real value) against the euro. In this scenario it would take more dollars to buy one euro, and European imports such as LVMH luxury accessories or Porsche automobiles become more expensive for U.S. buyers.

In a similar fashion, if the Chinese yuan appreciates in value, Chinese goods imported into the United States become relatively more expensive. At the same time, Chinese purchasing power increases, which in turn allows their businesses to purchase more U.S. capital goods such as sophisticated machinery and other cutting-edge technologies. The reverse holds true if the Chinese yuan depreciates in value.

In summary, economic factors affecting businesses are ever-present and rarely static. Strategic leaders need to fully appreciate the power of these factors, in both domestic and global markets, to assess their effects on firm performance.

SOCIOCULTURAL FACTORS

Sociocultural factors capture a society's cultures, norms, and values. Because sociocultural factors not only are constantly in flux but also differ across groups, strategic leaders need to closely monitor such trends and consider the implications for firm strategy. In recent years, for example, a growing number of U.S. consumers have become more health-conscious about what they eat. This trend led to a boom for businesses such as Chipotle, Subway, and Whole Foods. At the same time, traditional fast food companies McDonald's and Burger King, along with grocery chains such as Albertsons and Kroger, have all had to scramble to provide healthier choices in their product offerings.

Demographic trends are also important sociocultural factors. These trends capture population characteristics related to age, gender, family size, ethnicity, sexual orientation, religion, and socioeconomic class. Like other sociocultural factors, demographic trends present opportunities but can also pose threats. Recent U.S. census data reveals that 59 million Americans (18.1 percent of the total population) are Hispanic. It is now the largest minority group in the United States and growing fast. On average, Hispanics are also younger and their incomes are climbing quickly. This trend is not lost on companies trying to benefit from this opportunity. For example, MundoFox and ESPN Deportes (specializing in soccer) have joined Univision and NBC's Telemundo in the Spanish-language television market. In the United States, Univision is now the fifth most popular network overall, just behind the four major English-language networks (ABC, NBC, CBS, and Fox). Likewise, advertisers are pouring dollars into the Spanish-language networks to promote their products and services.[9]

TECHNOLOGICAL FACTORS

Technological factors capture the application of knowledge to create new processes and products. Major innovations in process technology include lean manufacturing, Six Sigma quality, and biotechnology. The nanotechnology revolution, which is just beginning, promises significant upheaval for a vast array of industries ranging from tiny medical devices to new-age materials for earthquake-resistant buildings.[10] Recent product innovations include the smartphone, wearable devices such as smart watches, and high-performing electric cars such as the Tesla Model S.

Continued advances in artificial intelligence (AI) and machine learning promise to fundamentally alter the way we work and live.[11] While we are familiar with early AI applications such Amazon's Alexa, Apple's Siri, and Google's Assistant, the future will bring much more significant changes, including autonomous driving as well as the internet of things. The transportation industry is seeing early signs of disruption with autonomous vehicles and trucks, which can drive themselves from coast to coast, 24/7, with no breaks for the driver needed (other than recharging or exchanging battery packs). Our cities will be filled with autonomous taxis, which are already on the road in some places in the United States. The internet of things will connect all sorts of devices such as vehicles, airplanes, home appliances, computers, manufacturing facilities, power grids, and so forth to exchange data and to manage systems in a more holistic and smarter fashion to reduce, for example, energy consumption or letting the user know when a system is in need of maintenance long before it breaks down.

As discussed in the ChapterCase, Airbnb launched a process innovation of offering and renting rooms based on a business model leveraging the sharing economy. If one thing seems certain, technological progress is relentless and seems to be picking up speed.[12] Not surprisingly, changes in the technological environment bring both opportunities and threats for companies. Given the importance of a firm's innovation strategy to competitive advantage, we discuss the effect of technological factors in greater detail in Chapter 7.

Strategy Highlight 3.1 details how the once mighty video rental chain Blockbuster fell when it failed to pay sufficient attention to the PESTEL factors.

Strategy Highlight **3.1**

Blockbuster's Bust

Blockbuster was not only a pioneer in the video rental business, but it was also the undisputed industry leader from the mid-1980s to the early 2000s. At its peak, Blockbuster opened a new store every 17 hours, for a total of 9,000 stores across the United States, and earned $6 billion in annual revenue. As such, Blockbuster was a mainstay of American culture and an essential element of family movie night. But in 2010, the once mighty Blockbuster filed for bankruptcy. What went wrong?

Blockbuster was unable to respond effectively to technological changes in the industry. A first wave of disruption hit the TV industry in the 1980s and 1990s when cable networks started offering hundreds of channels, challenging the cozy oligopoly of the three old-line broadcast networks ABC, CBS, and NBC. With the arrival of the cable networks, Blockbuster's fortunes began to dim as reflected in a double-digit decline in its market valuation. Unable to address the technological challenge posed by cable network content as a substitute to video rentals, Blockbuster's creator and owner, Wayne Huizenga, sold the company to the media conglomerate Viacom in 1994.

By the late 1990s and early 2000s, Blockbuster was also challenged more directly by low-cost substitutes such as Netflix's mail-order DVD service and Redbox's automated DVD rental kiosks. In 1997, annoyed for having to pay more than $40 in late fees for a Blockbuster video, Reed Hastings decided to start Netflix—a subscription-based business model that offered consumers DVD rentals online. When the dot-com bubble burst in 2000, however, Netflix reached near bankruptcy. Hastings approached Blockbuster and proposed selling Netflix to it for a mere

$50 million and rebranding the chain Blockbuster.com. The idea was that Netflix would become Blockbuster's online branch. Thinking that it would be a small niche business at best, Blockbuster turned Netflix down.

Netflix managed to stay afloat. Its low-cost option for at-home viewing via higher-quality DVD technology (compared to lower-quality VHS tapes) attracted more and more subscribers; this allowed the firm to weather the dot-com crash. To fund future growth, Netflix went public in 2002 at a valuation of $310 million. Just a year later, Netflix surpassed 1 million subscribers. After seeing Netflix's success, Blockbuster began to mimic its online subscription model. Unlike Netflix, however, which did not charge late fees given Reed Hastings' aversion to penalizing customers, Blockbuster continued to do so. The firm relied on late fees because fees were, unfortunately, one of the most profitable aspects of its business model.

Technological progress continued at a rapid clip. The next wave of technological disruption hit the home media industry in the mid-2000s. The ability to stream content directly onto a host of devices, such as laptops, tablets, smartphones, and newer internet-based TVs, turned basically any screen into a personal media conduit. Prevalence of high-speed internet connections combined with advances in mobile devices, changed the way people consumed entertainment. The days where people needed to go to a brick-and-mortar store to rent a videotape or DVD were gone. With on-demand video streaming, consumers could choose from a near unlimited inventory of movies while sitting on their couch in the living room. In the end, Blockbuster's attempts to change were too little, too late. In 2010, the once mighty Blockbuster filed for bankruptcy. And in 2019, Netflix was valued at close to $160 billion.[13]

ECOLOGICAL FACTORS

Ecological factors involve broad environmental issues such as the natural environment, global warming, and sustainable economic growth. Organizations and the natural environment coexist in an interdependent relationship. Managing these relationships in a responsible and sustainable way directly influences the continued existence of human societies and the organizations we create. Strategic leaders can no longer separate the natural and the business worlds; they are inextricably linked.[14]

Unfortunately, many business organizations have contributed to the pollution of air, water, and land, as well as the depletion of the world's natural resources. One infamous example that comes readily to mind is the 2010 BP oil spill in the Gulf of Mexico. The spill destroyed fauna and flora along the U.S. shoreline from Texas to Florida. It led to a drop in fish and wildlife populations, triggered a decline in the fishery and tourism industries, and threatened the livelihood of thousands of people. It also cost BP more than $50 billion and one-half of its market value.

The relationship between organizations and the natural environment need not be adversarial, however. Ecological factors can also provide business opportunities. As we saw in ChapterCase 1, Tesla is addressing environmental concerns regarding the carbon emissions of gasoline-powered cars by building zero-emission battery-powered vehicles. To generate the needed energy to charge the batteries in a sustainable way, Tesla acquired SolarCity to provide integrated, clean-tech energy services for its customers, including decentralized solar power generation and storage via its Powerwall.

LEGAL FACTORS

Legal factors include the official outcomes of political processes as manifested in laws, mandates, regulations, and court decisions—all of which can have a direct bearing on a firm's profit potential. In fact, regulatory changes tend to affect entire industries at once. Many industries in the United States have been deregulated over the past few decades, including airlines, telecom, energy, and trucking, among others.

As noted earlier, legal factors often coexist with or result from political will. Governments especially can directly affect firm performance by exerting both political pressure and legal sanctions, including court rulings and industry regulations. Consider how several European countries and the European Union (EU) apply political and legal pressure on U.S. tech companies. European targets include Apple, Amazon, Facebook, Google, and Microsoft—the five largest U.S. tech companies—but also startups such as Uber. Europe's policy makers seek to retain control over important industries, including transportation and the internet, to ensure that profits earned in Europe by Silicon Valley firms are taxed locally. The European Parliament even proposed legislation to break up "digital monopolies" such as Google. This proposal would require Google to offer search services independently as a standalone company from its other online services, including Google Drive, a cloud-based file storage and synchronization service.

But the EU's wariness extends beyond tax revenue: It has much stronger legal requirements and cultural expectations concerning data privacy. In 2018, for instance, the EU implemented the General Data Protection Regulation (GDPR), which gives individuals wide-reaching control over their personal data as well as secured protection of these data. Personal data comprise any information related to a person such as a name, home address, e-mail address, phone number, location details, photos, videos, social media postings, computer IP addresses, and so forth. GDPR grants all EU residents far-reaching rights concerning their personal data, including the right to access, the right to be forgotten, the right to data portability across providers, the right to be notified, and so forth. All U.S. companies such as Google and Facebook had to change their policies to comply with the GDPR and thus be permitted to continue doing business in Europe. The data protection and privacy regulations that internet companies face in the EU are currently much more stringent than those in the United States, an aspect that came to the fore during the Facebook crisis regarding alleged foreign interference in U.S. elections and the siphoning off of private data for an unauthorized use by third parties (see ChapterCase 2).

Taken together, political/legal factors, along with other PESTEL factors, can have a direct bearing on a firm's performance—consider the implementation of autonomous vehicles for commercial and private use. Companies such as Uber, Waymo (a unit of Alphabet, the parent company of Google), and Tesla are ready to deploy autonomous vehicles, but political and legal factors are providing serious challenges and are delaying their widespread use.

The Waymo autonomous vehicle marks another step in an effort to revolutionize the way people get around. Instead of driving themselves, people will be chauffeured in self-driving cars if Waymo, Tesla, and ride-hailing services such as Uber realize their vision. Traditional automakers such as GM, Ford, and VW also invest tremendous amounts of money into autonomous vehicles. Taken together, the automobile industry is likely to be upended in the next few years, including who the key players will be and if individuals still want to own a car or prefer catching a ride in an autonomous vehicle available for a per-ride usage fee ("pay as you go") rather than requiring fairly large upfront investments when purchasing or leasing a vehicle.
Sundry Photography/ Shutterstock

3.2 Industry Structure and Firm Strategy: The Five Forces Model

INDUSTRY VS. FIRM EFFECTS IN DETERMINING FIRM PERFORMANCE

Firm performance is determined primarily by two factors: industry and firm effects. **Industry effects** describe the underlying economic structure of the industry. They attribute firm performance to the industry in which the firm competes. The structure of an industry is determined by elements common to all industries, such as entry and exit barriers, number and size of companies, and types of products and services offered. **Firm effects** attribute firm performance directly to the actions strategic leaders take.

In a series of empirical studies, academic researchers show that industry effects explain roughly 20 percent of overall firm performance, while firm effects (i.e., specific managerial actions) explain about 55 percent. In Chapter 4, we look inside the firm to understand why firms within the same industry differ and how differences among firms can lead to competitive advantage. For now, the important point is that external and internal factors combined explain roughly 75 percent of overall firm performance. The remaining 25 percent relates partly to business cycles and other effects.[15] Exhibit 3.2 shows these findings.

To better understand how external factors affect firm strategy and performance, and what strategic leaders can do about it, we take a closer look in this chapter at an industry's underlying structure. As such, we now move one step closer to the firm (in the center of Exhibit 3.1) and come to the industry in which it competes.

An **industry** is a group of incumbent firms facing more or less the same set of suppliers and buyers. Firms competing in the same industry tend to offer similar products or services

LO 3-2

Differentiate the roles of firm effects and industry effects in determining firm performance.

Industry effects Firm performance attributed to the structure of the industry in which the firm competes.

Firm effects Firm performance attributed to the actions strategic leaders take.

industry A group of incumbent companies that face more or less the same set of suppliers and buyers.

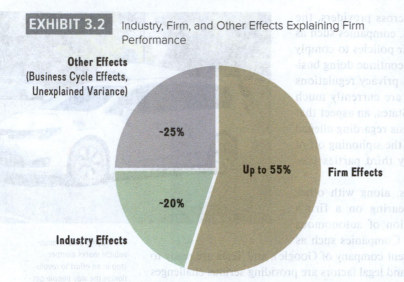

EXHIBIT 3.2   Industry, Firm, and Other Effects Explaining Firm Performance

Other Effects
(Business Cycle Effects, Unexplained Variance)

~25%

Up to 55%   **Firm Effects**

~20%

Industry Effects

to meet specific customer needs. Although the PESTEL framework allows us to scan, monitor, and evaluate the external environment to identify opportunities and threats, **industry analysis** provides a more rigorous basis not only to identify an industry's profit potential—the level of profitability that can be expected for the *average* firm—but also to derive implications for one firm's strategic position within an industry. A firm's **strategic position** relates to its ability to create value for customers (V) while containing the cost to do so (C). Competitive advantage flows to the firm that is able to create as large a gap as possible between the value the firm's product or service generates and the cost required to produce it ($V - C$).

COMPETITION IN THE FIVE FORCES MODEL

LO 3-3

Apply Porter's five competitive forces to explain the profit potential of different industries.

Michael Porter developed the highly influential **five forces model** to help strategic leaders understand the profit potential of different industries and how they can position their respective firms to gain and sustain competitive advantage.[16] By combining theory from industrial organization economics with detailed case studies, Porter derived two key insights that form the basis of his seminal five forces model:

1. *Competition is viewed more broadly in the five forces model.* Rather than defining competition narrowly as the firm's closest competitors to explain and predict a firm's performance, competition must be viewed more broadly to also encompass the other forces in an industry: buyers, suppliers, potential new entry of other firms, and the threat of substitutes.

2. *Profit potential is a function of the five competitive forces.* The profit potential of an industry is neither random nor entirely determined by industry-specific factors. Rather, it is a function of the five forces that shape competition: *threat of entry, power of suppliers, power of buyers, threat of substitutes,* and *rivalry among existing firms.*

COMPETITION BROADLY DEFINED. We start with the concept of competition, which, in Porter's model, is more broadly defined to include other industry forces: buyers, suppliers, potential new entry of other firms, and the threat of substitutes. Strategy addresses the question of how to deal with competition. In the five forces model, any of those forces is viewed as a potential competitor attempting to extract value from the industry. In particular, competition describes the struggle among these forces to capture as much of the economic value created in an industry as possible. A firm's strategic leaders, therefore, must be concerned not only with the intensity of rivalry among direct competitors (e.g., Nike versus Under

---

industry analysis A method to (1) identify an industry's profit potential and (2) derive implications for a firm's strategic position within an industry.

strategic position A firm's strategic profile based on the difference between value creation and cost ($V - C$).

five forces model A framework that identifies five forces that determine the profit potential of an industry and shape a firm's competitive strategy.

Armour, The Home Depot versus Lowe's, Merck versus Pfizer, and so on), but also with the strength of the other competitive forces that are attempting to extract part or all of the economic value that the firm creates.

Recall that firms create economic value by expanding as much as possible the gap between the perceived value (V) the firm's product or service generates and the cost (C) to produce it. *Economic value* thus equals ($V - C$). To succeed, creating value is not enough. Firms must also be able to *capture* a significant share of the value created to gain and sustain a competitive advantage. When faced with competition in this broader sense, strategy explains how a firm should position itself to enhance the chances of achieving superior performance.

PROFIT POTENTIAL. The five forces model enables strategic leaders to not only understand the firm's industry environment but also to shape firm strategy. As a rule of thumb, *the stronger the five forces, the lower the industry's profit potential*—making the industry less attractive for competitors. The reverse is also true: *the weaker the five forces, the greater the industry's profit potential*—making the industry more attractive. Therefore, from the perspective of a strategic leader of an existing firm competing for advantage in an established industry, the company should be positioned in a way that relaxes the constraints of strong forces and leverages weak forces. The goal of crafting a strategic position is of course to improve the firm's ability to achieve and sustain a competitive advantage.

As Exhibit 3.3 shows, Porter's model identifies five key competitive forces that strategic leaders need to consider when analyzing the industry environment and formulating competitive strategy:

1. Threat of entry.
2. Power of suppliers.
3. Power of buyers.
4. Threat of substitutes.
5. Rivalry among existing competitors.

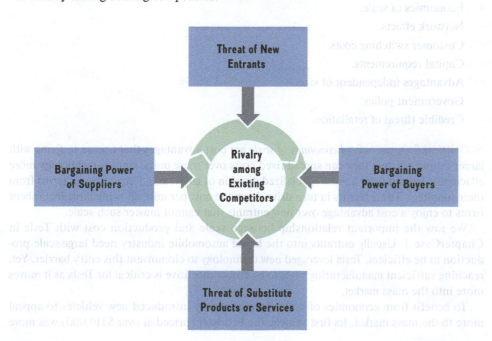

EXHIBIT 3.3

Porter's Five Forces Model

Source: M. E. Porter (2008, January). "The five competitive forces that shape strategy," *Harvard Business Review.*

THE THREAT OF ENTRY

The **threat of entry** describes the risk of potential competitors entering the industry. Potential new entry depresses industry profit potential in two major ways:

1. *Reduces the industry's overall profit potential.* With the threat of additional capacity coming into an industry, incumbent firms may lower prices to make the entry appear less attractive to the potential new competitors, which in turn would reduce the industry's overall profit potential, especially in industries with slow or no overall growth in demand. Consider the market for new microwaves. Demand consists of the replacement rate for older models and the creation of new households. Since this market grows slowly, if at all, any additional entry would likely lead to excess capacity and lower prices overall.

2. *Increases spending among incumbent firms.* The threat of entry by additional competitors may force incumbent firms to spend more to satisfy their existing customers. This spending reduces an industry's profit potential, especially if firms can't raise prices. Consider how Starbucks has chosen to constantly upgrade and refresh its stores and service offerings. Starbucks has over 14,000 U.S. stores and more than 28,000 global locations. By raising the value of its offering in the eyes of consumers, it slows others from entering the industry or from rapidly expanding. This allows Starbucks to keep at bay both smaller regional competitors, such as Peet's Coffee & Tea with fewer than 200 stores mostly on the West Coast, and smaller national chains, such as Caribou Coffee, with 415 stores nationally. Starbucks is willing to accept a lower profit margin to maintain its market share.

Of course, the more profitable an industry, the more attractive it is for new competitors to enter. However, a number of important barriers exist that can reduce that threat. **Entry barriers**, which are advantageous for incumbent firms, are obstacles that determine how easily a firm can enter an industry. Incumbent firms can benefit from several important sources of entry barriers:

- Economies of scale.
- Network effects.
- Customer switching costs.
- Capital requirements.
- Advantages independent of size.
- Government policy.
- Credible threat of retaliation.

ECONOMIES OF SCALE. *Economies of scale* are cost advantages that accrue to firms with larger output because they can spread fixed costs over more units, employ technology more efficiently, benefit from a more specialized division of labor, and demand better terms from their suppliers. These factors in turn drive down the cost per unit, allowing large incumbent firms to enjoy a cost advantage over new entrants that cannot muster such scale.

We saw the important relationship between scale and production cost with Tesla in ChapterCase 1. Usually entrants into the broad automobile industry need large-scale production to be efficient. Tesla leveraged new technology to circumvent this entry barrier. Yet, reaching sufficient manufacturing scale to be cost-competitive is critical for Tesla as it moves more into the mass market.

To benefit from economies of scale, Tesla gradually introduced new vehicles to appeal more to the mass market. Its first vehicle, the Roadster (priced at over $110,000) was more or less a prototype to prove the viability of an all-electric car that can outperform high-performance traditional sports cars. For consumers, it created a new mind-set of what electric cars can do. Tesla ended production of the Roadster to focus more fully on its next model: the family sedan Model S (with a baseline price of $70,000). With this model, Tesla's manufacturing scale increased more than 50-fold, from 2,500 Roadsters to 125,000 Model S's. Tesla is now hoping for an even broader customer appeal with its Model 3, a smaller and lower-priced vehicle (starting at $35,000) that will allow the company to break into the mass market and manufacture many more cars. Tesla's product introductions over time are motivated by an attempt to capture benefits that accrue to economies of scale. To capture benefits from economies of scale, including lower unit cost, Elon Musk hopes Tesla can increase its production volume to 1 million vehicles a year by 2020 (an increase by a factor of 20, from the 50,000 vehicles Tesla produced in 2015).

NETWORK EFFECTS. **Network effects** describe the positive effect that one user of a product or service has on the value of that product or service for other users. When network effects are present, the value of the product or service increases with the number of users. This is an example of a *positive externality*. The threat of potential entry is reduced when network effects are present.

> **network effects** The value of a product or service for an individual user increases with the number of total users.

For example, Facebook, with over 2 billion active users worldwide, enjoys tremendous network effects, making it difficult for such other social media entrants such as Twitter or Snap to compete effectively. Likewise, Brian Chesky, CEO of Airbnb, argues that Airbnb is able to benefit from global network effects because of listings in 81,000 cities around the globe at all different price points, combined with an inventory of 5 million homes and apartments. This global network effect only grows stronger as more and more guests use the service and become hosts themselves. Given their importance in the *digital economy,* we will discuss network effects in much more detail in Chapter 7.

CUSTOMER SWITCHING COSTS. *Switching costs* are incurred by moving from one supplier to another. Changing vendors may require the buyer to alter product specifications, retrain employees, and/or modify existing processes. Switching costs are onetime sunk costs, which can be quite significant and a formidable barrier to entry. For example, a firm that has used enterprise resource planning (ERP) software from SAP for many years will incur significant switching costs when implementing a new ERP system from Oracle.

CAPITAL REQUIREMENTS. *Capital requirements* describe the "price of the entry ticket" into a new industry. How much capital is required to compete in this industry, and which companies are willing and able to make such investments? Frequently related to economies of scale, capital requirements may encompass investments to set up plants with dedicated machinery, run a production process, and cover start-up losses.

Tesla made a sizable capital investment of roughly $150 million when it purchased from Toyota its Fremont, California, manufacturing plant, which it then upgraded with an automated production process that uses robots to produce high-quality cars at large scale.[17] It then invested another $5 billion in a battery gigafactory in Nevada.[18] With this new factory, Tesla is not only able to secure supplies of lithium-ion batteries, the most critical and expensive component of an all-electric car, but it also now has the capability to build as many as 1 million vehicles a year.[19] Any potential new entrant, however, must

Facebook CEO Mark Zuckerberg speaks about Graph Search, a key component in finding information from within a user's network of friends. With over 2 billion active monthly users, Facebook benefits from winner-take-all network effects and thus is often described as a digital monopoly.
Jeff Chiu/AP Images

carefully weigh the required capital investments, the cost of capital, and the expected return on investment.

Taken together, the threat of entry is high when capital requirements are low in comparison to the expected returns. If an industry is attractive enough, efficient capital markets are likely to provide the necessary funding to enter an industry. Capital, unlike proprietary technology and industry-specific know-how, is a *fungible* resource that can be relatively easily acquired in the face of attractive returns.

ADVANTAGES INDEPENDENT OF SIZE. Incumbent firms often possess cost and quality advantages that are independent of size. These advantages can be based on brand loyalty, proprietary technology, preferential access to raw materials and distribution channels, favorable geographic locations, and cumulative learning and experience effects.

Brand Loyalty. Tesla's loyal customers strengthen the firm's competitive position and reduce the threat of entry into the all-electric car segment, at least by other start-up companies.[20] Unlike GM or Ford, which spend billions each year on advertising, Tesla doesn't have a large marketing budget. Rather, it relies on word of mouth. Like Apple in its early days, Tesla has its own "cool factor," as evidenced by its beautifully designed, top-notch quality cars. In fact, when *Consumer Reports* tested the Model S, the usually understated magazine concluded: "The Tesla Model S is the best car we ever tested."[21] In addition, many Tesla owners feel an emotional connection to the company because they deeply believe in the company's vision "to accelerate the world's transition to sustainable energy."

Preferential Access. Preferential access to raw materials and key components can bestow absolute cost advantages. For example, the lithium-ion batteries that are so critical to all-electric vehicles are not only the most expensive component, but they are also in short supply. With its new battery gigafactory, however, Tesla can afford independence from the few worldwide suppliers (such as Panasonic) and also enjoy an absolute cost advantage.[22] This should further reduce the threat of new entry in the all-electric vehicle segment, assuming no radical technological changes are to be expected in battery-cell technology in the next few years.

Favorable Locations. Favorable locations, such as Silicon Valley for Tesla, often present advantages that other locales cannot match easily, including access to human and venture capital, and world-class research and engineering institutions.

Cumulative Learning and Experience. Finally, incumbent firms often benefit from cumulative learning and experience effects accrued over long periods of time. Tesla now has more than a dozen years of experience in designing and building high-performance all-electric vehicles of superior quality and design. Attempting to obtain such deep knowledge within a shorter time frame is often costly, if not impossible due to *time compression diseconomies,* which in turn constitutes a formidable barrier to entry.

GOVERNMENT POLICY. Frequently government policies restrict or prevent new entrants. Until recently, India did not allow foreign retailers such as Walmart or IKEA to own stores and compete with domestic companies in order to protect the country's millions of small vendors and wholesalers. China frequently requires foreign companies to enter joint ventures with domestic ones and to share technology.

In contrast, deregulation in industries such as airlines, telecommunications, and trucking have generated significant new entries. Therefore, the threat of entry is high when restrictive government policies do not exist or when industries become deregulated.

CREDIBLE THREAT OF RETALIATION. Potential new entrants must also anticipate how incumbent firms will react. A credible threat of retaliation by incumbent firms often deters entry. Should entry still occur, however, incumbents are able to retaliate quickly, through initiating a price war, for example. The industry profit potential can in this case easily fall below the cost of capital. Incumbents with deeper pockets than new entrants are able to withstand price competition for a longer time and wait for the new entrants to exit the industry—then raise prices again. Other weapons of retaliation include increased product and service innovation, advertising, sales promotions, and litigation.

Potential new entrants should expect a strong and vigorous response beyond price competition by incumbent firms in several scenarios. If the current competitors have deep pockets, unused excess capacity, reputational clout with industry suppliers and buyers, a history of vigorous retaliation during earlier entry attempts, or heavy investments in resources specific to the core industry and ill-suited for adaptive use, then they are likely to press these advantages. Moreover, if industry growth is slow or stagnant, incumbents are more likely to retaliate against new entrants to protect their market share, often initiating a price war with the goal of driving out these new entrants.

For example, in the southeastern United States, TV cable company Comcast has entered the market for residential and commercial telephone services and internet connectivity (as an ISP, internet service provider), emerging as a direct competitor for AT&T. Comcast also acquired NBC Universal, combining delivery and content. AT&T responded to Comcast's threat by introducing U-verse, a product combining high-speed internet access with cable TV and telephone service, all provided over its fast fiber-optic network. To combine media content with delivery capabilities, AT&T acquired TimeWarner in 2018, bringing in-house content providers such as Warner Bros., HBO, and Turner to compete more effectively against Comcast and others.

In contrast, the threat of entry is high when new entrants expect that incumbents will not or cannot retaliate.

THE POWER OF SUPPLIERS

The bargaining power of suppliers captures pressures that industry suppliers can exert on an industry's profit potential. This force reduces a firm's ability to obtain superior performance for two reasons:

1. Powerful suppliers can raise the cost of production by demanding higher prices for their inputs or by reducing the quality of the input factor or service level delivered.
2. Powerful suppliers are a threat to firms because they reduce the industry's profit potential by capturing part of the economic value created.

To compete effectively, companies generally need a wide variety of inputs into the production process, including raw materials and components, labor (via individuals or labor unions, when the industry faces collective bargaining), and services. The relative bargaining power of suppliers is high when

- The supplier's industry is more concentrated than the industry it sells to.
- Suppliers do not depend heavily on the industry for a large portion of their revenues.
- Incumbent firms face significant switching costs when changing suppliers.
- Suppliers offer products that are differentiated.
- There are no readily available substitutes for the products or services that the suppliers offer.
- Suppliers can credibly threaten to forward-integrate into the industry.

THE POWER OF BUYERS

In many ways, the bargaining power of buyers is the flip side of the bargaining power of suppliers. Buyers are the customers of an industry. The power of buyers relates to the pressure an industry's customers can put on the producers' margins by demanding a lower price or higher product quality. When buyers successfully obtain price discounts, it reduces a firm's top line (revenue). When buyers demand higher quality and more service, it generally raises production costs. Strong buyers can therefore reduce industry profit potential and a firm's profitability. Powerful buyers are a threat to the producing firms because they reduce the industry's profit potential by capturing part of the economic value created.

As with suppliers, an industry may face many different types of buyers. The buyers of an industry's product or service may be individual consumers—like you or me when we decide which provider we want to use for our wireless devices. In many areas, you can choose between several providers such as AT&T, Verizon, and T-Mobile (which merged with Sprint in a $26 billion deal). Although we might be able to find a good deal when carefully comparing their individual service plans, as individual consumers, we generally do not have significant buyer power. On the other hand, large institutions such as businesses or universities have significant buyer power when deciding which provider to use for their wireless services; this is because they are able to sign up or move several thousand employees at once.

FACTORS THAT INCREASE BUYER POWER.   The power of buyers is high when

- There are a few buyers and each buyer purchases large quantities relative to the size of a single seller.
- The industry's products are standardized or undifferentiated commodities.
- Buyers face low or no switching costs.
- Buyers can credibly threaten to backwardly integrate into the industry.

Niloo138/123RF

The retail giant Walmart provides perhaps the most potent example of tremendous buyer power. Walmart is not only the largest retailer worldwide (with 12,000 stores and over 2 million employees), but it is also one of the largest companies in the world (with $530 billion in revenues in 2019). Walmart is one of the few large big-box global retail chains and frequently purchases large quantities from its suppliers. Walmart leverages its buyer power by exerting tremendous pressure on its suppliers to lower prices and to increase quality or risk losing access to shelf space at the largest retailer in the world. Walmart's buyer power is so strong that many suppliers colocate offices next to Walmart's headquarters in Bentonville, Arkansas, because such proximity enables Walmart's strategic leaders to test the suppliers' latest products and negotiate prices.

The bargaining power of buyers also increases when their switching costs are low. Having multiple suppliers of a product category located close to its headquarters allows Walmart to demand further price cuts and quality improvements because it can easily switch from one supplier to the next. This threat is even more pronounced if the products are non-differentiated commodities from the consumer's perspective. For example, Walmart can easily switch from Rubbermaid plastic containers to Sterlite containers by offering more shelf space to the producer that offers the greatest price cut or quality improvement.

Buyers are also powerful when they can credibly threaten backward integration. Backward integration occurs when a buyer moves upstream in the industry value chain, into the seller's business. Walmart has exercised the threat to backward-integrate by producing a number of products as private-label brands such as Equate health and beauty items, Ol'Roy dog food, and Parent's Choice baby products.

Powerful buyers have the ability to extract a significant amount of the value created in the industry, leaving little or nothing for producers. In addition, strategic leaders need to be aware of situations when buyers are especially price sensitive. This is the case when

- The buyer's purchase represents a significant fraction of its cost structure or procurement budget.
- Buyers earn low profits or are strapped for cash.
- The quality (cost) of the buyers' products and services is not affected much by the quality (cost) of their inputs.

CONTEXT-DEPENDENCIES ON BUYER POWER. With regards to any of the five forces that shape competition, it is important to note that their relative strengths are context-dependent. For example, the Mexican multinational CEMEX, one of the world's leading cement producers, faces very different buyer power in the United States than domestically. In the United States, cement buyers consist of a few large and powerful construction companies that account for a significant percentage of CEMEX's output. The result? Razor-thin margins. In contrast, the vast majority of CEMEX customers in its Mexican home market are numerous, small, individual customers facing a few large suppliers, with CEMEX being the biggest. CEMEX earns high profit margins in its home market. With the same undifferentiated product, CEMEX competes in two different industry scenarios in terms of buyer strength.

THE THREAT OF SUBSTITUTES

Substitutes meet the same basic customer needs as the industry's product but in a different way. The threat of substitutes is the idea that products or services available from *outside the given industry* will come close to meeting the needs of current customers.[23] For example, many software products are substitutes to professional services, at least at the lower end. Tax preparation software such as Intuit's TurboTax is a substitute for professional services offered by H&R Block and others. LegalZoom, an online legal documentation service, is a threat to professional law firms. Other examples of substitutes are energy drinks versus coffee, videoconferencing versus business travel, e-mail versus express mail, gasoline versus biofuel, and wireless telephone services versus internet-enabled voice and video apps such as Skype, FaceTime (Apple), WhatsApp (Facebook), and WeChat (Tencent).

A high threat of substitutes reduces industry profit potential by limiting the price the industry's competitors can charge for their products and services. The threat of substitutes is high when

- The substitute offers an attractive price-performance trade-off.
- The buyers cost of switching to the substitute is low.

PRICE-PERFORMANCE TRADE-OFF. The movie rental company Redbox, which uses over 40,000 kiosks in the United States to make movie rentals available for just $2, is a substitute for buying movie DVDs. For buyers, video rental via Redbox offers an attractive price-performance trade-off with low switching costs in comparison to DVD ownership. Moreover, for customers that view only a few movies a month, Redbox is also a substitute for Netflix's basic on-demand internet movie streaming service, which costs $8.99 a month. Rather than a substitute, however, Redbox is a direct competitor to Netflix's DVD rental business, where plans cost $7.99 a month (for one DVD out at a time).

LOW-SWITCHING COSTS. In addition to a lower price, substitutes may also become more attractive by offering a higher value proposition.[24] In Spain, some 6 million people travel annually between Madrid and Barcelona, roughly 400 miles apart. The trip by car or train takes most of the day, and 90 percent of travelers would choose to fly, creating a highly profitable business for local airlines. This all changed when the Alta Velocidad Española (AVE), an ultramodern high-speed train, was completed in 2008. Taking into account total time involved, high-speed trains are faster than short-haul flights. Passengers travel in greater comfort than airline passengers and commute from one city center to the next, with only a short walk or cab ride to their final destinations.

The AVE example highlights the two fundamental insights provided by Porter's five forces framework. First, *competition must be defined more broadly to go beyond direct industry competitors.* In this case, rather than defining competition narrowly as the firm's closest competitors, airline executives in Spain must look beyond other airlines and consider substitute offerings such as high-speed trains. Second, *any of the five forces on its own, if sufficiently strong, can extract industry profitability.* In the AVE example, the threat of substitutes is limiting the airline industry's profit potential. With the arrival of the AVE, the airlines' monopoly on fast transportation between Madrid and Barcelona vanished, and with it the airlines' high profits. The strong threat of substitutes in this case increased the rivalry among existing competitors in the Spanish air transportation industry.

RIVALRY AMONG EXISTING COMPETITORS

LO 3-4

Examine how competitive industry structure shapes rivalry among competitors.

Rivalry among existing competitors describes the intensity with which companies within the same industry jockey for market share and profitability. It can range from genteel to cut-throat. The other four forces—threat of entry, the power of buyers and suppliers, and the threat of substitutes—all exert pressure upon this rivalry, as indicated by the arrows pointing toward the center in Exhibit 3.3. *The stronger the forces, the stronger the expected competitive intensity, which in turn limits the industry's profit potential.*

Competitors can lower prices to attract customers from rivals. When intense rivalry among existing competitors brings about price discounting, industry profitability erodes. Alternatively, competitors can use non-price competition to create more value in terms of product features and design, quality, promotional spending, and after-sales service and support. When non-price competition is the primary basis of competition, costs increase, which can also have a negative impact on industry profitability. However, when these moves create unique products with features tailored closely to meet customer needs and willingness to pay, then average industry profitability tends to increase because producers are able to raise prices and thus increase revenues and profit margins.

The intensity of rivalry among existing competitors is determined largely by the following factors:

competitive industry structure Elements and features common to all industries, including the number and size of competitors, the firms' degree of pricing power, the type of product or service offered, and the height of entry barriers.

- Competitive industry structure.
- Industry growth.
- Strategic commitments.
- Exit barriers.

COMPETITIVE INDUSTRY STRUCTURE. The **competitive industry structure** refers to elements and features common to all industries. The structure of an industry is largely captured by

- The number and size of its competitors.
- The firm's degree of pricing power.

EXHIBIT 3.4   Industry Competitive Structures along the Continuum from Fragmented to Consolidated

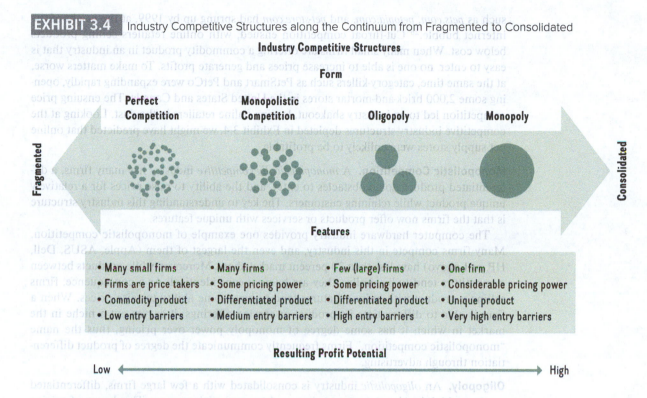

Industry Competitive Structures

Form

| Perfect Competition | Monopolistic Competition | Oligopoly | Monopoly |

Fragmented → Consolidated

Features

• Many small firms	• Many firms	• Few (large) firms	• One firm
• Firms are price takers	• Some pricing power	• Some pricing power	• Considerable pricing power
• Commodity product	• Differentiated product	• Differentiated product	• Unique product
• Low entry barriers	• Medium entry barriers	• High entry barriers	• Very high entry barriers

Resulting Profit Potential

Low ←——————————————→ High

- The type of product or service (commodity or differentiated product).
- The height of entry barriers.[25]

Exhibit 3.4 shows different industry types along a continuum from fragmented to consolidated structures. At one extreme, a *fragmented industry* consists of many small firms and tends to generate low profitability. At the other end of the continuum, a *consolidated industry* is dominated by a few firms, or even just one firm, and has the potential to be highly profitable. The four main competitive industry structures are

1. Perfect competition
2. Monopolistic competition
3. Oligopoly
4. Monopoly

Perfect Competition. A *perfectly competitive* industry is fragmented and has many small firms, a commodity product, ease of entry, and little or no ability for each individual firm to raise its prices. The firms competing in this type of industry are approximately similar in size and resources. Consumers make purchasing decisions solely on price, because the commodity product offerings are more or less identical. The resulting performance of the industry shows low profitability. Under these conditions, firms in perfect competition have difficulty achieving even a temporary competitive advantage and can achieve only competitive parity. Although perfect competition is a rare industry structure in its pure form, markets for commodities such as natural gas, copper, and iron tend to approach this structure.

Modern high-tech industries are also not immune to the perils of perfect competition. Many internet entrepreneurs learned the hard way that it is difficult to beat the forces of perfect competition. Fueled by eager venture capitalists, about 100 online pet supply stores such as *pets.com, petopia.com,* and *pet-store.com* had sprung up by 1999, at the height of the internet bubble.[26] Cut-throat competition ensued, with online retailers selling products below cost. When many small firms are offering a commodity product in an industry that is easy to enter, no one is able to increase prices and generate profits. To make matters worse, at the same time, category-killers such as PetSmart and PetCo were expanding rapidly, opening some 2,000 brick-and-mortar stores in the United States and Canada. The ensuing price competition led to an industry shakeout, leaving online retailers in the dust. Looking at the competitive industry structures depicted in Exhibit 3.4, we might have predicted that online pet supply stores were unlikely to be profitable.

Monopolistic Competition. A *monopolistically competitive* industry has many firms, a differentiated product, some obstacles to entry, and the ability to raise prices for a relatively unique product while retaining customers. The key to understanding this industry structure is that the firms now offer products or services with unique features.

The computer hardware industry provides one example of monopolistic competition. Many firms compete in this industry, and even the largest of them (Apple, ASUS, Dell, HP, or Lenovo) have less than 20 percent market share. Moreover, while products between competitors tend to be similar, they are by no means identical. As a consequence, firms selling a product with unique features tend to have some ability to raise prices. When a firm is able to differentiate its product or service offerings, it carves out a niche in the market in which it has some degree of monopoly power over pricing, thus the name "monopolistic competition." Firms frequently communicate the degree of product differentiation through advertising.

Oligopoly. An *oligopolistic* industry is consolidated with a few large firms, differentiated products, high barriers to entry, and some degree of pricing power. The degree of pricing power depends, just as in monopolistic competition, on the degree of product differentiation.

A key feature of an oligopoly is that the competing firms are *interdependent.* With only a few competitors in the mix, the actions of one firm influence the behaviors of the others. Each competitor in an oligopoly, therefore, must consider the strategic actions of the other competitors. This type of industry structure is often analyzed using *game theory,* which attempts to predict strategic behaviors by assuming that the moves and reactions of competitors can be anticipated.[27] Due to their strategic interdependence, companies in oligopolies have an incentive to coordinate their strategic actions to maximize joint performance. Although explicit coordination such as price fixing is illegal in the United States, tacit coordination such as "an unspoken understanding" is not.

The express-delivery industry is an example of an oligopoly. The main competitors in this space are FedEx and UPS. Any strategic decision made by FedEx (e.g., to expand delivery services to ground delivery of larger-size packages) directly affects UPS; likewise, any decision made by UPS (e.g., to guarantee next-day delivery before 8:00 a.m.) directly affects FedEx. Other examples of oligopolies include the soft drink industry (Coca-Cola versus Pepsi), airframe manufacturing business (Boeing versus Airbus), home-improvement retailing (The Home Depot versus Lowe's), toys and games (Hasbro versus Mattel), and detergents (P&G versus Unilever).[28]

Companies in an oligopoly tend to have some pricing power if they are able to differentiate their product or service offerings from those of their competitors. *Non-price competition,* therefore, is the preferred mode of competition. This means competing by offering unique product features or services rather than competing based on price alone. When one firm in an oligopoly cuts prices to gain market share from its competitor, the competitor typically will respond in kind and also cut prices. This process initiates a price war, which can be especially detrimental to firm performance if the products are close rivals.

In the early years of the soft drink industry, for example, whenever PepsiCo lowered prices, Coca-Cola followed suit. These actions only resulted in reduced profitability for both companies. In recent decades, both Coca-Cola and PepsiCo have repeatedly demonstrated that they have learned this lesson. They shifted the basis of competition from price-cutting to new product introductions and lifestyle advertising. Any price adjustments are merely short-term promotions. By leveraging innovation and advertising, Coca-Cola and PepsiCo have moved to non-price competition, which in turn allows them to charge higher prices and to improve industry and company profitability.[29]

Monopoly. An industry is a *monopoly* when there is only one, often large firm supplying the market. The firm may offer a unique product, and the challenges to moving into the industry tend to be high. The monopolist has considerable pricing power. As a consequence, firm and thus industry profit tends to be high. The one firm is the industry.

In some instances, the government will grant one firm the right to be the sole supplier of a product or service. This is often done to incentivize a company to engage in a venture that would not be profitable if there was more than one supplier. For instance, public utilities incur huge fixed costs to build plants and to supply a certain geographic area. Public utilities supplying water, gas, and electricity to businesses and homes are frequently monopolists. Georgia Power is the only supplier of electricity for some 2.5 million customers in the southeastern United States. Philadelphia Gas Works is the only supplier of natural gas in the city of Philadelphia, serving some 500,000 customers. These are so-called *natural monopolies*. Without them, the governments involved believe the market would not supply these products or services. In the past few decades, however, more and more of these natural monopolies have been deregulated in the United States, including airlines, telecommunications, railroads, trucking, and ocean transportation. This deregulation has allowed competition to emerge, which frequently leads to lower prices, better service, and more innovation.

While natural monopolies appear to be disappearing from the competitive landscape, so-called *near monopolies* are of much greater interest to strategists. These are firms that have accrued significant market power, for example, by owning valuable patents or proprietary technology. In the process, they are changing the industry structure in their favor, generally from monopolistic competition or oligopolies to near monopolies. These near monopolies are firms that have accomplished product differentiation to such a degree that they are in a class by themselves, just like a monopolist. The European Union, for example, views Google with its 90 percent market share in online search as a *digital monopoly*.[30] This is an enviable position in terms of the ability to extract profits by leveraging its data to provide targeted online advertising and other customized services, so long as Google can steer clear of monopolistic behavior, which may attract antitrust regulators and lead to legal repercussions.

INDUSTRY GROWTH. Industry growth directly affects the intensity of rivalry among competitors. In periods of high growth, consumer demand rises, and price competition among firms frequently decreases. Because the pie is expanding, rivals are focused on capturing part of that larger pie rather than taking market share and profitability away from one another.

The demand for knee replacements, for example, is a fast-growing segment in the medical products industry. In the United States, robust demand is driven by the need for knee replacements for an aging population as well as for an increasingly obese population. The leading competitors are Zimmer Biomet, DePuy, and Stryker, with a significant share held by Smith & Nephew. Competition is primarily based on innovative design, improved implant materials, and differentiated products such as gender solutions and a range of high-flex knees. With improvements to materials and procedures, younger patients are also increasingly choosing early surgical intervention. Competitors are able to avoid price competition and, instead, focus on differentiation that allows premium pricing.

In contrast, rivalry among competitors becomes fierce during slow or even negative industry growth. Price discounts, frequent new product releases with minor modifications, intense promotional campaigns, and fast retaliation by rivals are all tactics indicative of an industry with slow or negative growth. Competition is fierce because rivals can gain only at the expense of others; therefore, companies are focused on taking business away from one another. Demand for traditional fast food providers such as McDonald's, Burger King, and Wendy's has been declining in recent years. Consumers have become more health-conscious and demand has shifted to alternative restaurants such as Subway, Chick-fil-A, and Chipotle. Attempts by McDonald's, Burger King, and Wendy's to steal customers from one another include frequent discounting tactics such as dollar menus. Such competitive tactics are indicative of cut-throat competition and a low profit potential in the traditional hamburger fast food industry.

Competitive rivalry based solely on cutting prices is especially destructive to profitability because it transfers most, if not all, of the value created in the industry to the customers—leaving little, if anything, for the firms in the industry. While this may appear attractive to customers, firms that are not profitable are not able to make the investments necessary to upgrade their product offerings or services to provide higher value, and they eventually leave the industry. Destructive price competition can lead to limited choices, lower product quality, and higher prices for consumers in the long run if only a few large firms survive.

STRATEGIC COMMITMENTS. If firms make strategic commitments to compete in an industry, rivalry among competitors is likely to be more intense. **Strategic commitments** are firm actions that are costly, long-term oriented, and difficult to reverse. Strategic commitments to a specific industry can stem from large, fixed cost requirements, but also from noneconomic considerations.[31]

> **strategic commitments** Firm actions that are costly, long-term oriented, and difficult to reverse.

EXIT BARRIERS. The rivalry among existing competitors is also a function of an industry's **exit barriers**, the obstacles that determine how easily a firm can leave that industry. Exit barriers comprise both economic and social factors. They include fixed costs that must be paid regardless of whether the company is operating in the industry or not. A company exiting an industry may still have contractual obligations to suppliers, such as employee health care, retirement benefits, and severance pay. Social factors include elements such as emotional attachments to certain geographic locations. In Michigan, entire communities still depend on GM, Ford, and Chrysler. If any of those carmakers were to exit the industry, communities would suffer. Other social and economic factors include ripple effects through the supply chain. When one major player in an industry shuts down, its suppliers are adversely impacted as well.

> **exit barriers** Obstacles that determine how easily a firm can leave an industry.

An industry with low exit barriers is more attractive because it allows underperforming firms to exit more easily. Such exits reduce competitive pressure on the remaining firms because excess capacity is removed. In contrast, an industry with high exit barriers reduces its profit potential because excess capacity still remains.

To summarize our discussion of the five forces model, Exhibit 3.5 provides a checklist that you can apply to any industry when assessing the underlying competitive forces that shape strategy. The key take-away from the five forces model is that the stronger the forces, the lower the industry's ability to earn above-average profits, and correspondingly, the lower the firm's ability to gain and sustain a competitive advantage. Conversely, the weaker the forces, the greater the industry's ability to earn above-average profits, and correspondingly,

The threat of entry is high when

✓ The minimum efficient scale to compete in an industry is low.

✓ Network effects are not present.

✓ Customer switching costs are low.

✓ Capital requirements are low.

✓ Incumbents do not possess:
  ○ Brand loyalty.
  ○ Proprietary technology.
  ○ Preferential access to raw materials.
  ○ Preferential access to distribution channels.
  ○ Favorable geographic locations.
  ○ Cumulative learning and experience effects.

✓ Restrictive government regulations do not exist.

✓ New entrants expect that incumbents will not or cannot retaliate.

The power of suppliers is high when

✓ Supplier's industry is more concentrated than the industry it sells to.

✓ Suppliers do not depend heavily on the industry for their revenues.

✓ Incumbent firms face significant switching costs when changing suppliers.

✓ Suppliers offer products that are differentiated.

✓ There are no readily available substitutes for the products or services that the suppliers offer.

✓ Suppliers can credibly threaten to forward-integrate into the industry.

The power of buyers is high when

✓ There are a few buyers and each buyer purchases large quantities relative to the size of a single seller.

✓ The industry's products are standardized or undifferentiated commodities.

✓ Buyers face low or no switching costs.

✓ Buyers can credibly threaten to backwardly integrate into the industry.

The threat of substitutes is high when

✓ The substitute offers an attractive price-performance trade-off.

✓ The buyer's cost of switching to the substitute is low.

The rivalry among existing competitors is high when

✓ There are many competitors in the industry.

✓ The competitors are roughly of equal size.

✓ Industry growth is slow, zero, or even negative.

✓ Exit barriers are high.

✓ Incumbent firms are highly committed to the business.

✓ Incumbent firms cannot read or understand each other's strategies well.

✓ Products and services are direct substitutes.

✓ Fixed costs are high and marginal costs are low.

✓ Excess capacity exists in the industry.

✓ The product or service is perishable.

EXHIBIT 3.5

The Five Forces
Competitive Analysis
Checklist

Source: Adapted from M.E.
Porter (2008, January), "The
five competitive forces that
shape strategy," *Harvard
Business Review.*

the greater the firm's ability to gain and sustain competitive advantage. Therefore, strategic leaders need to craft a strategic position for their company that leverages weak forces into opportunities and mitigates strong forces because they are potential threats to the firm's ability to gain and sustain a competitive advantage.

APPLYING THE FIVE FORCES MODEL TO THE U.S. AIRLINE INDUSTRY

Applying the model to the U.S. domestic airline industry provides a neat examination of the five competitive forces that shape strategy.[32]

THREAT OF ENTRY. *Entry barriers* in the airline industry are relatively low, resulting in new airlines popping up occasionally. To enter the industry (on a small scale, serving a few select cities), a prospective new entrant needs only a couple of airplanes, which can be rented; a few pilots and crew members; some routes connecting city pairs; and gate access in airports. Despite notoriously low industry profitability, Virgin America entered the U.S. market in 2007. Virgin America is the brainchild of Sir Richard Branson, founder and chairman of the Virgin Group, a UK conglomerate of hundreds of companies using the Virgin brand, including the international airline Virgin Atlantic. Virgin America's business strategy was to offer low-cost service between major metropolitan cities on the American East and West coasts. In 2016, Alaska Airlines acquired Virgin America for $2.6 billion.

POWER OF SUPPLIERS. In the airline industry, the *supplier power* is also strong. The providers of airframes (e.g., Boeing and Airbus), makers of aircraft engines (e.g., GE and Rolls-Royce), aircraft maintenance companies (e.g., Goodrich), caterers (e.g., Marriott), labor unions, and airports controlling gate access all bargain away the profitability of airlines.

Let's take a closer look at one important supplier group to this industry: Boeing and Airbus, the makers of large commercial jets. Airframe manufacturers are powerful suppliers to airlines because their industry is much more concentrated (only two firms) than the industry it sells to. Compared to two airframe suppliers, there are hundreds of commercial airlines around the world. Given the trend of large airlines merging to create even larger mega-airlines, however, increasing buyer power may eventually balance this out a bit. Nonetheless, the airlines face nontrivial switching costs when changing suppliers because pilots and crew would need to be retrained to fly a new type of aircraft, maintenance capabilities would need to be expanded, and some routes may even need to be reconfigured due to differences in aircraft range and passenger capacity. Moreover, while some aircraft can be used as substitutes, Boeing and Airbus offer differentiated products. This fact becomes clearer when considering some of the more recent models from each company. Boeing introduced the 787 Dreamliner to capture long-distance point-to-point travel (close to an 8,000-mile range, sufficient to fly nonstop from Los Angeles to Sydney), while Airbus introduced the A-380 Superjumbo to focus on high-volume transportation (close to 900 passengers) between major airport hubs (e.g., Tokyo's Haneda Airport and Singapore's Changi Airport).

When considering long-distance travel, there are no readily available substitutes for commercial airliners, a fact that strengthens supplier power. Thus, the supplier power of commercial aircraft manufacturers is quite significant. This puts Boeing and Airbus in a strong position to extract profits from the airline industry, thus reducing the profit potential of the airlines themselves.

Although the supplier power of Boeing and Airbus is strong, several factors further moderate their bargaining positions somewhat. First, the suppliers of commercial airliners depend heavily on the commercial airlines for their revenues. Given the less than expected demand for the A-380, for instance, Airbus announced that it will stop producing the Superjumbo in 2021.[33] Rather, Airbus will focus more on its newer and smaller A-350 model, a versatile and fuel-efficient airplane to be deployed on high-traffic point-to-point routes, and thus a direct competitor to Boeing's 787. As the recent strategic moves by Airbus and Boeing have shown, even a *duopoloy* (a industry with only two suppliers) in the airframe manufacturing business is not immune to changes in customer demand (power of buyers).

Second, Boeing and Airbus are unlikely to threaten forward integration and become commercial airlines themselves. Third, Bombardier of Canada and Embraer of Brazil, both manufacturers of smaller commercial airframes, have begun to increase the size of the jets they offer and thus now compete with some of the smaller planes such as the Boeing 737 and Airbus A-320. Finally, industry structures are not static, but can change over time. Several of the remaining large domestic U.S. airlines have merged (Delta and Northwest, United and Continental, and American and U.S. Airways), which changed the industry structure in their favor. There are now fewer airlines, but they are larger. This fact increases their buyer power, which we turn to next.

POWER OF BUYERS. Large corporate customers contract with airlines to serve all of their employees' travel needs; such *powerful buyers* further reduce profit margins for air carriers. To make matters worse, consumers primarily make decisions based on price as air travel is viewed as a commodity with little or no differentiation across domestic U.S. carriers. In inflation-adjusted dollars, ticket prices have been falling since industry deregulation in 1978. Thanks to internet travel sites such as Orbitz, Travelocity, and Kayak, price comparisons are effortless. Consumers benefit from cut-throat price competition between carriers and capture significant value. Low switching costs and nearly perfect information in real time combine to strengthen buyer power.

THREAT OF SUBSTITUTES. To make matters worse, *substitutes* are also readily available: If prices are seen as too high, customers can drive a car or use the train or bus. For example, the route between Atlanta and Orlando (roughly 400 miles) used to be one of Delta's busiest and most profitable. Given the increasing security requirements at airports and other factors, more people now prefer to drive. Taken together, the competitive forces are quite unfavorable for generating a profit potential in the airline industry: low entry barriers, high supplier power, high buyer power combined with low customer switching costs, and the availability of low-cost substitutes. This type of hostile environment leads to intense rivalry among existing airlines and low overall industry profit potential.

RIVALRY AMONG EXISTING COMPETITORS. As a consequence of the powerful industry forces discussed above, the *nature of rivalry* among airlines has become incredibly intense. Moreover, the required strategic commitments combined with exit barriers further increase the competitive intensity in the U.S. domestic airline industry.

Strategic Commitments. Significant strategic commitments are required to compete in the airline industry when using a hub-and-spoke system to provide not only domestic but also international coverage. U.S.-based airlines Delta, United, and American have large fixed costs to maintain their network of routes that affords global coverage, frequently in conjunction with foreign partner airlines. These fixed costs in terms of aircraft, gate leases, hangars, maintenance facilities, baggage facilities, and ground transportation all accrue before the airlines sell any tickets. High fixed costs create tremendous pressure to fill empty seats. An airline seat on a specific flight, just like an unbooked hotel room, is perishable. Empty airline seats are often filled through price-cutting. Given similar high fixed costs, other airlines respond in kind. Eventually, a vicious cycle of price-cutting ensues, driving average industry profitability to zero, or even negative numbers (where the companies are losing money). To make matters worse, given their strategic commitments, airlines are unlikely to exit an industry. Excess capacity remains, further depressing industry profitability.

In other cases, strategic commitments to a specific industry may be the result of more political than economic considerations. Airbus, for example, was created by a number of European governments through direct subsidies to provide a countervailing power to Boeing. The European Union in turn claims that Boeing is subsidized by the U.S. government indirectly via defense contracts. Given these political considerations and large-scale strategic commitments, neither Airbus nor Boeing is likely to exit the aircraft manufacturing industry even if industry profit potential falls to zero.

Exit Barriers. The U.S. domestic airline industry is characterized by high exit barriers, which further reduces the industry's overall profit potential. All the large U.S. airlines (American, Delta, and United) have filed for bankruptcy at one point. Due to a unique feature of U.S. Chapter 11 bankruptcy law, companies may continue to operate and reorganize while being temporarily shielded from their creditors and other obligations until renegotiated. This implies that excess capacity is not removed from the industry, and by putting pressure on prices further reduces industry profit potential.

CONCLUSION. Although many of the mega-airlines have lost billions of dollars over the past few decades and continue to struggle to generate consistent profitability, other players in the industry have been quite profitable because they were able to extract some of the economic value created. The surprising conclusion, therefore, is that while the mega-airlines themselves frequently struggle to achieve consistent profitability over time, the other players in the industry—such as the suppliers of airframes and aircraft engines, aircraft maintenance companies, IT companies providing reservation and logistics services, caterers, airports, and so on—are quite profitable, all extracting significant value from the air transportation industry. Customers also are better off, as ticket prices have decreased and travel choices increased.

During the mid-2010s, the cash-strapped airlines benefited from a windfall as the price of jet fuel fell from a high of $3.25 per gallon (in the spring of 2011) all the way to $0.80 per gallon (in early 2016), before climbing back to $1.80 (in early 2019). The cost of jet fuel is roughly 50 percent of an airline's total operating costs. Nonetheless, competition remains intense in this industry.

Taking a closer look at the U.S. domestic airline industry shows how the five forces framework is a powerful and versatile tool to analyze industries. The five forces model allows strategic leaders to analyze all players using a wider industry lens, which in turn enables a deeper understanding of an industry's profit potential. Moreover, a five forces analysis provides the basis for how a firm should position itself to gain and sustain a competitive advantage. We will take up the topic of competitive positioning in Chapter 6 when studying business-level strategy in much more detail.

LO 3-5

Describe the strategic role of complements in creating positive-sum co-opetition.

A SIXTH FORCE: THE STRATEGIC ROLE OF COMPLEMENTS

As valuable as the five forces model is for explaining the profit potential and attractiveness of industries, the value of Porter's five forces model can be further enhanced if one also considers the availability of complements.[34]

A **complement** is a product, service, or competency that adds value to the original product offering when the two are used in tandem.[35] Complements increase demand for the primary product, thereby enhancing the profit potential for the industry and the firm. A company is a **complementor** to your company if customers value your product or service offering more when they are able to combine it with the other company's product or service.[36] Firms may choose to provide the complements themselves or work with another company to accomplish this.

CO-OPETITION.   For example, in the smartphone industry, Alphabet's Google complements Samsung. The Korean high-tech company's smartphones are more valuable when they come with Google's Android mobile operating system installed. At the same time, Google and Samsung are increasingly becoming competitors. With Google's acquisition of Motorola Mobility, the online search company launched its own line of smartphones and Chromebooks. This development illustrates the process of **co-opetition**, which is cooperation by competitors to achieve a strategic objective. Samsung and Google cooperate as complementors to compete against Apple's strong position in the mobile device industry, while at the same time Samsung and Google are increasingly becoming competitive with one another. While Google retained Motorola's patents to use for development in its future phones and to defend itself against competitors such as Samsung and Apple, Alphabet (Google's parent company) sold the manufacturing arm of Motorola to Lenovo, a Chinese maker of computers and mobile devices.

In 2017, Google acquired HTC's smartphone engineering group for $1.1 billion. The Taiwanese smartphone maker developed the Google Pixel phone. With this acquisition, Google is making a commitment to handset manufacturing, unlike in the Motorola deal, which was more motivated by intellectual property considerations. Integrating HTC's smartphone unit within Google will allow engineers to more tightly integrate hardware and software. This in turn will allow Google to differentiate its high-end Pixel phones from the competition, especially Apple's iPhones and Samsung's Galaxy line of phones.

3.3 Changes over Time: Entry Choices and Industry Dynamics

ENTRY CHOICES

One of the key insights of the five forces model is that the more profitable an industry, the more attractive it becomes to competitors. Let's assume a firm's strategic leaders are aware of potential barriers to entry (discussed earlier), but would nonetheless like to contemplate potential market entry because the industry profitability is high and thus quite attractive. Exhibit 3.6 shows an integrative model that can guide the entry choices firms make. Rather

complement A product, service, or competency that adds value to the original product offering when the two are used in tandem.	**complementor** A company that provides a good or service that leads customers to value your firm's offering more when the two are combined.	**co-opetition** Cooperation by competitors to achieve a strategic objective.

EXHIBIT 3.6   Entry Choices

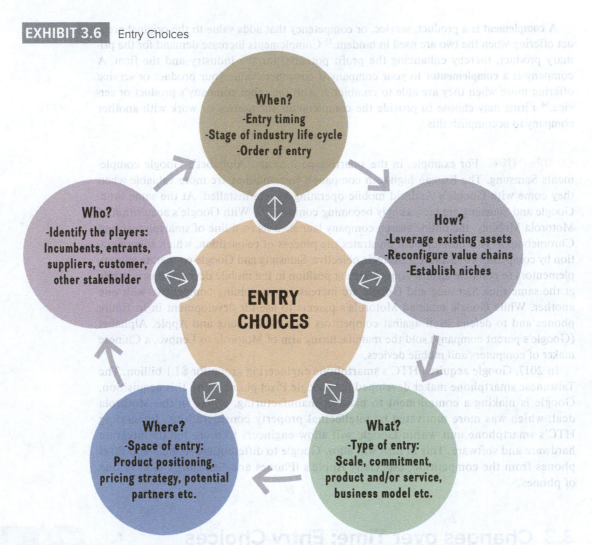

Source: Based on and adapted from M.A., Zachary, P.T. Gianiodis, G. Tyge Payne, and G.D. Markman (2014), "Entry timing: enduring lessons and future directions," *Journal of Management* 41: 1409; and Bryce, D.J., and J.H. Dyer (2007, May), "Strategies to crack well-guarded markets," *Harvard Business Review*: 84–92.

than considering firm entry as a discrete event (i.e., simple yes or no decision), or a discrete event composed of five parts, this model suggests that the entry choices firms make constitute a strategic process unfolding over time.

In particular, to increase the probability of successful entry, strategic leaders need to consider the following five questions:[37]

1. *Who are the players?* Building on Porter's insight that competition must be viewed in a broader sense beyond direct competitors, the *who are the players* question allows strategic leaders to not only identify direct competitors but also focus on other external and internal stakeholders necessary to successfully compete in an industry, such as customers, employees, regulators, and communities (see discussion of stakeholder strategy in Chapter 2).

2. *When to enter?* This question concerns the *timing of entry.* Given that our perspective is that of a firm considering potential entry into an *existing* industry, any first-mover advantages are bygones. Nonetheless, the potential new entrant needs to consider at which stage of the industry life cycle (introduction, growth, shakeout, maturity, or decline) it should enter. We take a deep dive into the industry life cycle and how it unfolds in Chapter 7.

3. *How to enter?* One of the challenges that strategic leaders face is that often the most attractive industries in terms of profitability are also the hardest to break into because they are protected by entry barriers. Thus, the *how to enter* question goes to the heart of this problem.

   ▪ One option is to *leverage existing assets,* that is to think about a new combination of resources and capabilities that firms already possess, and if needed to combine them with partner resources through strategic alliances. Although Circuit City went bankrupt as an electronics retailer, losing out to Best Buy and Amazon, a few years earlier it recombined its existing expertise in big-box retailing including optimization of supply and demand in specific geographic areas to create CarMax, now the largest used-car dealer in the United States and a Fortune 500 company.

   ▪ Another option is to *reconfigure value chains.* This approach allowed Skype to enter the market for long-distance calls by combining value chains differently (offering VoIP rather than relying on more expensive fiber-optic cables), and thus compete with incumbents such as AT&T.

   ▪ The third option is to *establish a niche* in an existing industry, and then use this beachhead to grow further. This is the approach the Austrian maker of Red Bull used when entering the U.S. soft drink market, long dominated by Coca-Cola and PepsiCo. Its energy drink was offered in a small 8.4-ounce (250 ml) can, but priced at multiples compared to Coke or Pepsi. This allowed retailers to stock Red Bull cans in small spaces such as near the checkout counter. In addition, Red Bull initially used many nontraditional outlets as points of sale such as nightclubs and gas stations. This approach created a loyal following from which the energy drink maker could expand its entry into the mainstream carbonated beverage drink in the United States and elsewhere. Indeed, energy drinks are now one of the fastest growing segments in this industry.

4. *What type of entry?* The *what* question of entry refers to the type of entry in terms of product market (e.g., smartphones), value chain activity (e.g., R&D for smartphone chips or manufacturing of smartphones), geography (e.g., domestic and/or international), and type of business model (e.g., subsidizing smartphones when providing services). Depending on the market under consideration for entry, firms may face unique competitive and institutional challenges. For example, discount carrier Spirit Airlines' unbundling of its services by charging customers separately for elements such as checked luggage, assigned seating, carry-on items, and other in-flight perks such as drinks met with considerable backlash in 2007 when introduced. Yet this marked the starting point of Spirit Airlines' strategic positioning as an ultra-low-cost carrier and enabled the company to add many attractive routes, and thus to enter geographic markets it was not able to compete in previously.

5. *Where to enter?* After deciding on the type of entry, the *where* to enter question refers to more fine-tuned aspects of entry such as product positioning (high end versus low end), pricing strategy, potential partners, and so forth.

LO 3-7

Appraise the role of industry dynamics and industry convergence in shaping the firm's external environment.

INDUSTRY DYNAMICS

Although the five forces plus complements model is useful in understanding an industry's profit potential, it provides only a point-in-time snapshot of a moving target. With this model (as with other static models), one cannot determine the changing speed of an industry or the rate of innovation. This drawback implies that strategic leaders must repeat their analysis over time to create a more accurate picture of their industry. It is therefore important that strategic leaders consider industry dynamics.

Industry structures are not stable over time. Rather, they are dynamic. Since a consolidated industry tends to be more profitable than a fragmented one (see Exhibit 3.4), firms have a tendency to change the industry structure in their favor, making it more consolidated through horizontal mergers and acquisitions. Having fewer competitors generally equates to higher industry profitability. Industry incumbents, therefore, have an incentive to reduce the number of competitors in the industry. With fewer but larger competitors, incumbent firms can mitigate more effectively the threat of strong competitive forces such as supplier or buyer power.

The U.S. domestic airline industry has witnessed several large, horizontal mergers between competitors, including Delta and Northwest, United and Continental, Southwest and AirTran, as well as American and U.S. Airways. These moves allow the remaining carriers to enjoy a more benign industry structure. It also allows them to retire some of the excess capacity in the industry as the merged airlines consolidate their networks of routes. The merger activity in the airline industry provides one example of how firms can proactively reshape industry structure in their favor. A more consolidated airline industry is likely to lead to higher ticket prices and fewer choices for customers, but also more profitable airlines.

In contrast, consolidated industry structures may also break up and become more fragmented. This generally happens when there are external shocks to an industry such as deregulation, new legislation, technological innovation, or globalization. For example, the widespread use of the internet moved the stock brokerage business from an oligopoly controlled by full-service firms such as Merrill Lynch and Morgan Stanley to monopolistic competition with many generic online brokers such as Ameritrade, E*Trade, and Scottrade.

industry convergence A process whereby formerly unrelated industries begin to satisfy the same customer need.

Another dynamic to be considered is **industry convergence**, a process whereby formerly unrelated industries begin to satisfy the same customer need. Industry convergence is often brought on by technological advances. For years, many players in the media industries have been converging due to technological progress in AI, telecommunications, and digital media. Media convergence unites computing, communications, and content, thereby causing significant upheaval across previously distinct industries. Content providers in industries such as newspapers, magazines, TV, movies, radio, and music are all scrambling to adapt. Many standalone print newspapers are closing up shop, while others are trying to figure out how to offer online news content for which consumers are willing to pay.[38] Internet companies such as Google, Facebook, Instagram (acquired by Facebook), LinkedIn (acquired by Microsoft), Snapchat, Pinterest, and Twitter are changing the industry structure by constantly morphing their capabilities and forcing old-line media companies such as News Corp., Time Warner (now part of AT&T), and Disney to adapt. A wide variety of mobile devices, including smartphones, tablets, and e-readers, provide a new form of content delivery that has the potential to make print media obsolete.

Finally, the convergence of different technology can also lead to the emergence of entirely new industries. Strategy Highlight 3.2 documents the recent rise of the e-sports industry.

Strategy Highlight **3.2**

From League of Legends to Fortnite: The Rise of e-Sports

League of Legends (LoL), the popular multiplayer online battle arena (MOBA) game developed and launched in 2009 by Riot Games of Los Angeles, went from being a small niche game to a billion-dollar business, sparking the explosive growth of the e-sports industry. Although online games have been around for a while, Riot Games was the first company to put e-sports on the map and to bring it into the mainstream culture.

Within just two years of its launch, LoL managed to accrue 1.4 million daily players and 3.5 million monthly average users (MAU). Since then, it has garnered 30 million daily players and made more than $7 billion in revenues. For nearly a decade, LoL was the world's most popular video game—until Fortnite took over. The explosive growth and global popularity of LoL did not go unnoticed: In 2011, the Chinese tech company Tencent (also owner of WeChat, the world's largest social media

and mobile payment app with some 1 billion daily users) bought Riot Games for $400 million. Exhibit 3.7 shows the annual revenues of LoL and Fortnite (FN) over time.

League of Legends is free to download and free to play. Game updates released by Riot Games are also free of charge. How has Riot Games been able to make so much money using this "freemium" business model? It relies on four key tactics in its business model: in-game and ancillary transactions, live e-sport events, live-streamed e-sport events, and merchandise sales.

In-game and ancillary transactions are the first source of revenue. Riot Games makes the bulk of its money by selling "champions" (the avatars that fight in the battles; each champion has unique abilities and you unlock more abilities as you go along and win) as well as their "skins" (which change the appearance of the champions) to its extensive user base, offering more than 140 champions with some 800 skins and other accessories, such as

EXHIBIT 3.7 League of Legends and Fortnite Annual Revenues (in $bn)

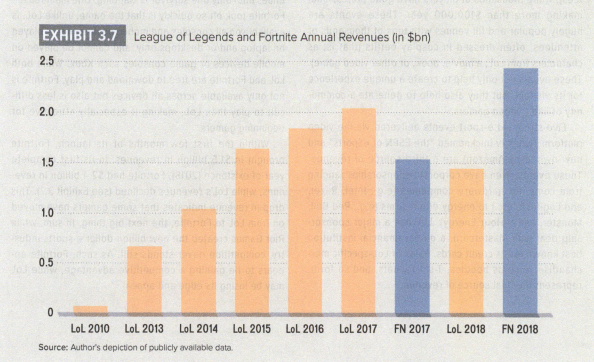

Source: Author's depiction of publicly available data.

(*Continued*)

name changes. LoL accepts two types of currency: Blue Essence, which are points that can be earned through playing (accomplishing specific missions in a game, for instance) and Riot Points, which are points that can be purchased with real money using prepaid cards. Since each battle consists of two teams comprising five players, the possible permutations of champions and skins can add up to the billions, and all encounters are unique. Furthermore the LoL in-game store is digital, which means its inventory of items is potentially unlimited. Players also have their own personal stores based on their selected champions and other individual characteristics. Here, players often find items recommended uniquely for them.

Live e-sport events are a second source of revenue. One key differentiator between LoL and previous e-sports games is its competitive focus. Riot Games hosts a League Championship Series (LCS), which attracts vast audiences and significant media and sponsorship attention. It controls all aspects of the LCS: the music, broadcasting, and decisions about where to run LoL tournaments, which are hosted in several global locations. Top professional players can earn millions of dollars a year (in prize money, sponsorship, and streaming fees), while thousands of players have gone professional making more than $100,000 year. These events are hugely popular and fill venues with tens of thousands of attendees, often dressed in cosplay outfits (that is, as characters from LoL, a movie, book, or other video game). These events not only help to create a unique experience for its visitors, but they also help to generate a community of like-minded gamers.

Live-streamed e-sport events delivered via the video platform Twitch.tv (nicknamed "the ESPN of eSports" and now owned by Amazon) are a third source of revenue. These events often have corporate sponsorships ranging from computer hardware companies (e.g., Intel, Razer, and Logitech, etc.) to energy drinks firms (e.g., Red Bull, Monster, and 5-Hour Energy). LoL has a major sponsorship deal with Mastercard, a global financial institution best known for its credit cards. Sales of LoL-specific merchandise, such as hoodies, T-shirts, hats, and so forth, represent the final source of revenue.

Riot Games maintains its revenues even as the game continuously evolves. The constant evolution of the game keeps gamers challenged, creative, and engaged. Many can be found in online chat rooms such as Reddit rethinking and discussing their strategy with other players, and thus further expanding the gaming community and its global reach. Currently, most of the world's ranked players are from the United States, China, South Korea, Germany, France, and Sweden (in rank order). The demographics of the players are highly sought after by advertisers because most players are between the ages of 15 and 35 years old, a notoriously difficult audience to reach. Yet, it is also highly skewed in terms of gender: 85 percent of the players are male. With virtually no barriers to entry, Riot Games managed to build a huge gamer base that continues to grow exponentially and thus created a new industry.

During LoL's rise to success, however, Riot Games found itself contending with competitors such as Minecraft (which Microsoft bought for $2.5 billion in 2014), Dota 2, and others. LoL dominated its competitors until the fall of 2017, when Epic Games (also owned in part by Tencent) released Fortnite. Fortnite is known as a "Battle Royale Game," that is a multiplayer online game that continues until only one survivor is standing. One main reason Fortnite took off so quickly is that the game, unlike LoL, is available on all consoles and mobile devices. LoL is played on laptop and/or desktops only, and cannot be played on mobile devices or game consoles such Xbox. While both LoL and Fortnite are free to download and play, Fortnite is not only available across all devices but also is less difficult to play than LoL, making it especially attractive for beginning gamers.

Within the first few months of its launch, Fortnite brought in $1.5 billion in revenues. In its first complete year of existence (2018), Fortnite had $2.4 billion in revenues, while LoL's revenues declined (see Exhibit 3.7). This drop in revenue indicates that some gamers have moved on from LoL to Fortnite, the next big thing. In sum, while Riot Games created the new billion-dollar e-sports industry, competition never stands still. As such, Fortnite appears to be gaining a competitive advantage, while LoL may be losing its edge and appeal.[39]

3.4 Performance Differences within the Same Industry: Strategic Groups

In further analyzing the firm's external environment to explain performance differences, we now move to firms *within the same industry*. As noted earlier in the chapter, a firm occupies a place within a **strategic group**, a set of companies that pursue a similar strategy within a specific industry in their quest for competitive advantage (see Exhibit 3.1).[40] Strategic groups differ from one another along important dimensions such as expenditures on research and development, technology, product differentiation, product and service offerings, market segments, distribution channels, and customer service.

To explain differences in firm performance within the same industry, the **strategic group model** clusters different firms into groups based on a few key strategic dimensions.[41] Even within the same industry, firm performances differ depending on strategic group membership. Some strategic groups tend to be more profitable than others. This difference implies that firm performance is determined not only by the industry to which the firm belongs, but also by its strategic group membership.

The distinct differences across strategic groups reflect the business strategies that firms pursue. Firms in the same strategic group tend to follow a similar strategy. Companies in the same strategic group, therefore, are direct competitors. The rivalry among firms *within* the same strategic group is generally more intense than the rivalry *among* strategic groups: *Intra-group rivalry exceeds inter-group rivalry.* The number of different business strategies pursued within an industry determines the number of strategic groups in that industry. In most industries, strategic groups can be identified along a fairly small number of dimensions. In many instances, two strategic groups are in an industry based on two different business strategies: one that pursues a low-cost strategy and a second that pursues a differentiation strategy (see Exhibit 3.8). We'll discuss each of these generic business strategies in detail in Chapter 6.

EXHIBIT 3.8

Strategic Groups and Mobility Barrier in U.S. Domestic Airline Industry

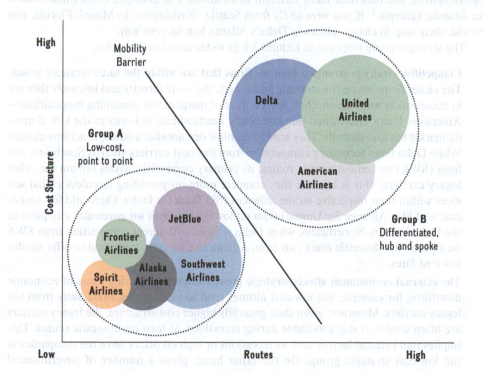

THE STRATEGIC GROUP MODEL

To understand competitive behavior and performance within an industry, we can map the industry competitors into strategic groups. We do this by

- Identifying the most important strategic dimensions such as expenditures on research and development, technology, product differentiation, product and service offerings, cost structure, market segments, distribution channels, and customer service. These dimensions are strategic commitments based on managerial actions that are costly and difficult to reverse.

- Choosing two key dimensions for the horizontal and vertical axes, which expose important differences among the competitors.

- Graphing the firms in the strategic group, indicating each firm's market share by the size of the bubble with which it is represented.[42]

The U.S. domestic airline industry provides an illustrative example. Exhibit 3.8 maps companies active in this industry. The two strategic dimensions on the axes are cost structure and routes. As a result of this mapping, two strategic groups become apparent, as indicated by the dashed circles: Group A, low-cost, point-to-point airlines (Alaska Airlines, Frontier Airlines, JetBlue, Southwest Airlines, and Spirit Airlines), and Group B, differentiated airlines using a hub-and-spoke system (American, Delta, and United). The low-cost, point-to-point airlines are clustered in the lower-left corner because they tend to have a lower cost structure but generally serve fewer routes due to their point-to-point operating system.

The differentiated airlines in Group B, offering full services using a hub-and-spoke route system, comprise the so-called legacy carriers. They are clustered in the upper-right corner because of their generally higher cost structures. The legacy carriers usually offer many more routes than the point-to-point low-cost carriers, made possible by use of the hub-and-spoke system, and thus offer many different destinations. For example, Delta's main hub is in Atlanta, Georgia.[43] If you were to fly from Seattle, Washington, to Miami, Florida, you would likely stop to change planes in Delta's Atlanta hub on your way.

The strategic group mapping in Exhibit 3.8 provides additional insights:

- **Competitive rivalry is strongest between firms that are within the same strategic group.** The closer firms are on the strategic group map, the more directly and intensely they are in competition with one another. After a wave of mergers, the remaining mega-airlines—American, Delta, and United—are competing head-to-head, not only in the U.S. domestic market but also globally. They tend to monitor one another's strategic actions closely. While Delta faces secondary competition from low-cost carriers such as Southwest Airlines (SWA) on some domestic routes, its primary competitive rivals remain the other legacy carriers. This is because they compete more on providing seamless global services within their respective airline alliances (SkyTeam for Delta, Oneworld for American, and Star Alliance for United) than on low-cost airfares for particular city pairs in the United States. Nonetheless, when Delta is faced with direct competition from SWA on a particular domestic route (say from Atlanta to Chicago), both tend to offer similar low-cost fares.

- **The external environment affects strategic groups differently.** During times of economic downturn, for example, the low-cost airlines tend to take market share away from the legacy carriers. Moreover, given their generally higher cost structure, the legacy carriers are often unable to stay profitable during recessions, at least on domestic routes. This implies that external factors such as recessions or high oil prices favor the companies in the low-cost strategic group. On the other hand, given a number of governmental restrictions on international air travel, the few airlines that are able to compete globally usually make a tidy profit in this specific industry segment.

- **The five competitive forces affect strategic groups differently.** *Barriers to entry,* for example, are higher in the hub-and-spoke (differentiated) airline group than in the point-to-point (low-cost) airline group. Following deregulation, many airlines entered the industry, but all of these new players used the point-to-point system. Since hub-and-spoke airlines can offer worldwide service and are protected from foreign competition by regulation to some extent, they often face weaker *buyer power,* especially from business travelers. While the hub-and-spoke airlines compete head-on with the point-to-point airlines when they are flying the same or similar routes, the *threat of substitutes* is stronger for the point-to-point airlines. This is because they tend to be regionally focused and compete with the viable substitutes of car, train, or bus travel. The threat of *supplier power* tends to be stronger for the airlines in the point-to-point, low-cost strategic group because they are much smaller and thus have weaker negotiation power when acquiring new aircraft, for example. To get around this, these airlines frequently purchase used aircraft from legacy carriers. This brief application of the five forces model leads us to conclude that rivalry among existing competitors in the low-cost, point-to-point strategic group is likely to be more intense than within the differentiated, hub-and-spoke strategic group.

- **Some strategic groups are more profitable than others.** Historically, airlines clustered in the lower-left corner tend to be more profitable when considering the U.S. domestic market only. Why? Because they create similar, or even higher, value for their customers in terms of on-time departure and arrival, safety, and fewer bags lost, while keeping their cost structure well below those of the legacy carriers. The point-to-point airlines have generally lower costs than the legacy carriers because they are faster in turning their airplanes around, keep them flying longer, use fewer and older airplane models, focus on high-yield city pairs, and tie pay to company performance, among many other activities that all support their low-cost business model. The point-to-point airlines, therefore, are able to offer their services at a lower cost and a higher perceived value, resulting in more pricing options, and thus creating the basis for a competitive advantage.

MOBILITY BARRIERS

Although some strategic groups tend to be more profitable and therefore more attractive than others, **mobility barriers** restrict movement between groups. These are industry-specific factors that separate one strategic group from another.[44] The dimensions to determine a strategic group are mobility barriers, which are strategic commitments. These are actions that are costly and not easily reversed such as the firm's underlying cost structure because it is based on managerial commitments resulting in hard-to-reverse investments.

The two groups identified in Exhibit 3.8 are separated by the fact that offering international routes necessitates the hub-and-spoke model. Frequently, the international routes tend to be the remaining profitable routes left for the legacy carriers; albeit the Persian Gulf region carriers, in particular Emirates, Etihad Airways, and Qatar Airways, are beginning to threaten this profit sanctuary.[45]

This economic reality implies that if carriers in the lower-left cluster wanted to compete globally, they would likely need to change their point-to-point operating model to a hub-and-spoke model. Or they could select a few profitable international routes and service them with long-range aircrafts such as Boeing 787s or Airbus A-380s. Adding international service to the low-cost model, however, would require managerial commitments resulting in significant capital investments and a likely departure from a well-functioning business

mobility barriers
Industry-specific factors that separate one strategic group from another.

model. Additional regulatory hurdles reinforce these mobility barriers, such as the difficulty of securing landing slots at international airports around the world.

Despite using its point-to-point operating system, SWA experienced these and many other challenges when it began offering international flights to selected resort destinations such as Aruba, Cabo San Lucas, Cancun, the Bahamas, and Jamaica: changes to its reservation system, securing passports for crew members, cultural-awareness training, learning instructions in foreign languages, and performing drills in swimming pools on how to evacuate passengers onto life rafts. All of these additional requirements result in a somewhat higher cost for SWA in servicing international routes.[46]

3.5 Implications for Strategic Leaders

At the start of the strategic management process, it is critical for strategic leaders to conduct a thorough analysis of the firm's external environment to identify threats and opportunities. The initial step is to apply a PESTEL analysis to scan, monitor, and evaluate changes and trends in the firm's macroenvironment. This versatile framework allows strategic leaders to track important trends and developments based on the *source* of the external factors: political, economic, sociocultural, technological, ecological, and legal. When applying a PESTEL analysis, the guiding consideration for strategic leaders should be the question of how the external factors identified affect the firm's industry environment.

Exhibit 3.1 delineates external factors based on the *proximity* of these external factors by gradually moving from the general to the task environment. The next layer for strategic leaders to understand is the industry. Applying Porter's five forces model allows strategic leaders to understand the profit potential of an industry and to obtain clues on how to carve out a strategic position that makes gaining and sustaining a competitive advantage more likely. Follow these steps to apply the five forces model:[47]

1. **Define the relevant industry.** In the five forces model, industry boundaries are drawn by identifying a group of incumbent companies that face more or less the same suppliers and buyers. This group of competitors is likely to be an industry if it also has the same entry barriers and a similar threat from substitutes. In this model, therefore, an industry is defined by commonality and overlap in the five competitive forces that shape competition.

2. **Identify the key players in each of the five forces and attempt to group them into different categories.** This step aids in assessing the relative strength of each force. For example, while makers of jet engines (GE, Rolls-Royce, Pratt & Whitney) and local catering services are all suppliers to airlines, their strengths vary widely. Segmenting different players within each force allows you to assess each force at a fine-grained level.

3. **Determine the underlying drivers of each force.** Which forces are strong, and which are weak? And why? Keeping with the airline example, why is the supplier power of jet engine manufacturers strong? Because they are supplying a mission-critical, highly differentiated product for airlines. Moreover, there are only a few suppliers of jet engines worldwide and no viable substitutes.

4. **Assess the overall industry structure.** What is the industry's profit potential? Here you need to identify forces that directly influence industry profit potential, because not all forces are likely to have an equal effect. Focus on the most important forces that drive industry profitability.

The final step in industry analysis is to draw a strategic group map. This exercise allows you to unearth and explain *performance differences within the same industry.* When analyzing a firm's external environment, it is critical to apply the three frameworks introduced in this chapter (PESTEL, Porter's five forces, and strategic group mapping). Taken together, the external environment can determine up to roughly one-half of the performance differences across firms (see Exhibit 3.2).

Although the different models discussed in this chapter are an important step in the strategic management process, they are not without shortcomings. First, all the models presented are *static*. They provide a snapshot of what is actually a moving target and do not allow for consideration of industry dynamics. However, changes in the external environment can appear suddenly, for example, through black swan events. Industries can be revolutionized by innovation. Strategic groups can be made obsolete through deregulation or technological progress. To overcome this important shortcoming, strategic leaders must conduct external analyses at different points in time to gain a sense of the underlying *dynamics*. The frequency with which these tools need to be applied is a function of the rate of change in the industry. The mobile app industry is changing extremely fast, while the railroad industry experiences a less volatile environment.

Second, the models presented in this chapter do not allow strategic leaders to fully understand *why* there are performance differences among firms in the *same* industry or strategic group. To better understand differences in firm performance, we must look *inside the firm* to study its resources, capabilities, and core competencies. We do this in the next chapter by moving from external to internal analysis.

CHAPTER**CASE 3**   Part II

EVEN THOUGH AIRBNB IS, at $31 billion, one of the most valuable private startups in the world and offers more accommodations than the three largest hotel chains (Marriott, Hilton, and Intercontinental) combined, not all is smooth sailing. In particular, PESTEL factors discussed in this chapter are creating major headwinds for Airbnb. Take regulation, for example.

In 2016, New York state strengthened legislation first passed in 2010 that makes it illegal to rent out entire apartments in residential blocks in New York City for less than 30 days. It remains legal if the renter is living in the apartment at the same time, so "true space sharing" is still possible. Fines start at $1,000 for the first offense and rise to $7,500 for repeat offenders. Paris, Berlin, and Barcelona face similar problems and have passed laws with even stiffer penalties, fining offenders up to $100,000. This legislation creates major problems for Airbnb because New York City is by far its largest market, with more than 50,000 accommodations available for rent. In 2018, the city of New York went a step further and sued residential brokerage firms (as well as some of their employees) for allegedly using Airbnb in an illegal apartment rental scheme that earned them an estimated $20 million.

The issue for Airbnb is that about one-third of its listings in major metropolitan areas such as New York City are from hosts with multiple offerings in the same city. Commercial landlords realized quickly that it is more profitable to convert some apartments into short-term rentals and to offer them via Airbnb than to sign long-term rentals with just one tenant, which often fall under some form of rent control. Although this tactic increases the landlord's return on investment and profits, it creates all kinds of negative externalities. Neighbors complain about noisy tourists partying all night. Some apartments get ransacked or are used for illegal activities such as drug deals and prostitution. New Yorkers expressed their frustration by scrawling on Airbnb posters: "The dumbest person in your building is passing out keys to your front door!"[48]

Hotel chains and resort owners have challenged Airbnb in courts and lobbied local governments to pass regulations to limit or prohibit short-term rentals—some of which already have. Residents in New York City, San Francisco, Berlin, Paris, and many other cities have joined this lobby, arguing that companies like Airbnb contribute to a shortage of affordable housing because they turn entire apartment complexes into hotels and quiet family neighborhoods into daily, all-night party venues. Airbnb is also being criticized for accelerating gentrification in some cities.[49]

Questions

1. How was an internet startup able to disrupt the hotel industry, long dominated by giants such as Marriott and Hilton, which took decades to become successful worldwide hospitality chains? Explain.

2. Why is it that PESTEL factors can have such a strong impact on the future of a business? Do you support legislation such as that passed in New York (and elsewhere), or do you think it has more to do with protecting vested interests such as the hotel industry?

3. Citing the Digital Millennium Copyright Act (DMCA), Airbnb is challenging the New York law and others in the United States, arguing that it merely operates a digital marketplace, and thus is not responsible for the content that users place on its site. Do you think Airbnb has a strong argument? Why or why not?

4. Are you concerned that the concept of the sharing economy could be abused by unscrupulous "entrepreneurs" and thus give the entire novel concept a bad reputation? Why or why not? Explain.

mySTRATEGY

Is My New Job Going to Be Around in the Next 10 Years?

When we think about starting a new job, say, as we finish up a college degree, traditionally it is advisable to check out the relevant industry trends first. For instance, raises and promotion opportunities tend to be more abundant in industries that are growing rather than retracting. Overall, professional pay scales are better in industries with higher profit margins (such as financial services and pharmaceuticals) than lower profits (such as retailing). Today though, other technological, global, and environmental factors should be considered. We can see examples of ride-hailing firms upending the taxi and rental car industries and online retailing diminishing brick and mortar stores, but what do these changes portend for the employment market? A full-time taxi driver used to be a pathway to the middle class in the United States and many other countries. Now these jobs are being replaced by "gig economy" workers, who often have it as a second or third job to try to make ends meet.

Autonomous driving could have significant impacts on employment options across the entire transportation sector.

However, far more wide-reaching is the still-developing role of artificial intelligence (AI) on business, governments, and the economy as a whole. There are widely ranging viewpoints on how the inevitable increase of AI will impact the national and global labor markets in the coming years. Thus, there are technological uncertainties for this generation that while not unique, will likely have major effects on employment paths moving forward.

1. Many people approach the job market by thinking about particular firms. What are some advantages of broadening this thought process to consider the industry-level factors of a potential new employer?

2. What industries do you think may offer the best U.S. (or domestic) job opportunities in the future? Which industries do you think may offer the greatest job opportunities in the global market in the future? Use the PESTEL framework and the five forces model to think through a logical set of reasons that some fields will have higher job growth trends than others.

3. Do these types of macroenvironmental and industry trends affect your thinking about selecting a career field after college? Why or why not? Explain.

TAKE-AWAY CONCEPTS

This chapter demonstrated various approaches to analyzing the firm's *external environment,* as summarized by the following learning objectives and related take-away concepts.

LO 3-1 / Generate a PESTEL analysis to evaluate the impact of external factors on the firm.

- A firm's macroenvironment consists of a wide range of political, economic, sociocultural, technological, ecological, and legal (PESTEL) factors that can affect industry and firm performance. These external factors have both domestic and global aspects.
- Political factors describe the influence governmental bodies can have on firms.
- Economic factors to be considered are growth rates, interest rates, levels of employment, price stability (inflation and deflation), and currency exchange rates.
- Sociocultural factors capture a society's cultures, norms, and values.
- Technological factors capture the application of knowledge to create new processes and products.
- Ecological factors concern a firm's regard for environmental issues such as the natural environment, global warming, and sustainable economic growth.
- Legal factors capture the official outcomes of the political processes that manifest themselves in laws, mandates, regulations, and court decisions.

LO 3-2 / Differentiate the roles of firm effects and industry effects in determining firm performance.

- A firm's performance is more closely related to its managers' actions (firm effects) than to the external circumstances surrounding it (industry effects).
- Firm and industry effects, however, are interdependent. Both are relevant in determining firm performance.

LO 3-3 / Apply Porter's five competitive forces to explain the profit potential of different industries.

- The profit potential of an industry is a function of the five forces that shape competition: (1) threat

of entry, (2) power of suppliers, (3) power of buyers, (4) threat of substitutes, and (5) rivalry among existing competitors.
- The stronger a competitive force, the greater the threat it represents. The weaker the competitive force, the greater the opportunity it presents.
- A firm can shape an industry's structure in its favor through its strategy.

LO 3-4 / Examine how competitive industry structure shapes rivalry among competitors.

- The competitive structure of an industry is largely captured by the number and size of competitors in an industry, whether the firms possess some degree of pricing power, the type of product or service the industry offers (commodity or differentiated product), and the height of entry barriers.
- A perfectly competitive industry is characterized by many small firms, a commodity product, low entry barriers, and no pricing power for individual firms.
- A monopolistic industry is characterized by many firms, a differentiated product, medium entry barriers, and some pricing power.
- An oligopolistic industry is characterized by few (large) firms, a differentiated product, high entry barriers, and some degree of pricing power.
- A monopoly exists when there is only one (large) firm supplying the market. In such instances, the firm may offer a unique product, the barriers to entry may be high, and the monopolist usually has considerable pricing power.

LO 3-5 / Describe the strategic role of complements in creating positive-sum co-opetition.

- Co-opetition (cooperation among competitors) can create a positive-sum game, resulting in a larger pie for everyone involved.
- Complements increase demand for the primary product, enhancing the profit potential for the industry and the firm.
- Attractive industries for co-opetition are characterized by high entry barriers, low exit barriers, low buyer and supplier power, a low threat of substitutes, and the availability of complements.

LO 3-6 / **Explain the five choices required for market entry.**

- The more profitable an industry, the more attractive it becomes to competitors, who must consider the *who, when, how, what,* and *where* of entry.

- The five choices constitute more than parts of a single decision point; their consideration forms a strategic process unfolding over time. Each choice involves multiple decisions including many dimensions.

- *Who* includes questions about the full range of stakeholders, and not just competitors; *when,* questions about the industry life cycle; *how,* about overcoming barriers to entry; *what,* about options among product market, value chain, geography, and business model; and *where,* about product positioning, pricing strategy, and potential partners.

LO 3-7 / **Appraise the role of industry dynamics and industry convergence in shaping the firm's external environment.**

- Industries are dynamic—they change over time.

- Different conditions prevail in different industries, directly affecting the firms competing in these industries and their profitability.

- In industry convergence, formerly unrelated industries begin to satisfy the same customer need. Such convergence is often brought on by technological advances.

LO 3-8 / **Generate a strategic group model to reveal performance differences between clusters of firms in the same industry.**

- A strategic group is a set of firms within a specific industry that pursue a similar strategy in their quest for competitive advantage.

- Generally, there are two strategic groups in an industry based on two different business strategies: one that pursues a low-cost strategy and a second that pursues a differentiation strategy.

- Rivalry among firms of the same strategic group is more intense than the rivalry between strategic groups: intra-group rivalry exceeds inter-group rivalry.

- Strategic groups are affected differently by the external environment and the five competitive forces.

- Some strategic groups are more profitable than others.

- Movement between strategic groups is restricted by mobility barriers—industry-specific factors that separate one strategic group from another.

KEY TERMS

Competitive industry structure *(p. 90)*

Complement *(p. 99)*

Complementor *(p. 99)*

Co-opetition *(p. 99)*

Entry barriers *(p. 84)*

Exit barriers *(p. 94)*

Firm effects *(p. 81)*

Five forces model *(p. 82)*

Industry *(p. 81)*

Industry analysis *(p. 82)*

Industry convergence *(p. 102)*

Industry effects *(p. 81)*

Mobility barriers *(p. 107)*

Network effects *(p. 85)*

Nonmarket strategy *(p. 76)*

PESTEL model *(p. 75)*

Strategic commitments *(p. 94)*

Strategic group *(p. 105)*

Strategic group model *(p. 105)*

Strategic position *(p. 82)*

Threat of entry *(p. 84)*

DISCUSSION QUESTIONS

1. Why is it important for any organization (firms, nonprofits, etc.) to study and understand its external environment?

2. How do the five competitive forces in Porter's model affect the average profitability of an industry? For example, in what way might weak forces

increase industry profits, and in what way do strong forces reduce industry profits? Identify an industry in which many of the competitors seem to be having financial performance problems. Which of the five forces seems to be strongest?

3. This chapter covers the choices firms make in entering new markets. Reflect on ChapterCase 3 and

discuss how Airbnb might have answered these questions in Exhibit 3.6.

4. How do mobility barriers affect the structure of an industry? How do they help us explain differences in firm performance?

ENDNOTES

1. As quoted in Parker, G.G., M.W. Van Alstyne, S.P. Choudary (2016), *Platform Revolution: How Networked Markets Are Transforming the Economy—And How to Make Them Work for You* (New York: Norton).

2. This ChapterCase is based on: "All eyes on the sharing economy," *The Economist* (2013, Mar. 9); "New York deflates Airbnb," *The Economist* (2016, Oct. 27); Austin, S., C. Canipe, and S. Slobin (2015, Feb. 18), "The billion dollar startup club," *The Wall Street Journal* (updated January 2017), http://graphics.wsj.com/billion-dollar-club/; Parker, G.G., M.W. Van Alstyne, S.P. Choudary (2016), *Platform Revolution: How Networked Markets Are Transforming the Economy—And How to Make Them Work for You* (New York: Norton); Pressler, J. (2014, Sept. 23), "The dumbest person in your building is passing out keys to your front door!" *New York*; Stone, B. (2017), *The Upstarts: How Uber, Airbnb, and the Killer Companies of the New Silicon Valley Are Changing the World* (New York: Little, Brown and Co.); Tabarrok, A. (2017, Jan. 30), "How Uber and Airbnb won," *The Wall Street Journal*. "Interview with Brian Chesky, co-founder and CEO Airbnb." (34:24 min) Code 2018. Recode, www.youtube.com/watch?v=nc90n-6dQRo&t=673s.

3. For a detailed treatise on how institutions shape the economic climate and with it firm performance, see: North, D.C. (1990), *Institutions, Institutional Change, and Economic Performance* (New York: Random House).

4. De Figueireo, R.J.P., and G. Edwards (2007), "Does private money buy public policy? Campaign contributions and regulatory outcomes in telecommunications," *Journal of Economics & Management Strategy* 16: 547–576; and Hillman, A.J., G. D. Keim, and D. Schuler (2004), "Corporate political activity: A review and research agenda," *Journal of Management* 30: 837–857.

5. Lowenstein, R. (2010), *The End of Wall Street* (New York: Penguin Press).

6. Brynjolfsson, E., and A. McAfee (2014), *The Second Machine Age: Work, Progress, and Prosperity in a Time of Brilliant Technologies* (New York: Norton).

7. "Professor Emeritus Milton Friedman dies at 94," University of Chicago press release (2006, Nov. 16).

8. Lucas, R. (1972), "Expectations and the neutrality of money," *Journal of Economic Theory* 4: 103–124.

9. U.S. Census Bureau (2017, Jul. 1), "Population estimates," www.census.gov/quickfacts/fact/table/US/PST045217; "Media companies are piling into the Hispanic market. But will it pay off?" *The Economist* (2012, Dec. 15).

10. Woolley, J.L., and R. M. Rottner (2008), "Innovation policy and nanotech entrepreneurship," *Entrepreneurship Theory and Practice* 32: 791–811; and Rothaermel, F.T., and M. Thursby (2007), "The nanotech vs. the biotech revolution: Sources of incumbent productivity in research," *Research Policy* 36: 832–849.

11. See for example: Brynjolfsson, E., and A. McAfee (2014). *The Second Machine Age: Work, Progress, and Prosperity in a Time of Brilliant Technologies* (New York: W. W. Norton & Co.); and McAfee, A., and E. Brynjolfsson (2017). *Machine, Platform, Crowd: Harnessing Our Digital Future* 1st ed., Kindle edition (New York: W. W. Norton & Co.).

12. Afuah, A. (2009), *Strategic Innovation: New Game Strategies for Competitive Advantage* (New York: Routledge); Hill, C.W.L., and F.T. Rothaermel (2003), "The performance of incumbent firms in the face of radical technological innovation," *Academy of Management Review* 28: 257–274; and Bettis, R., and M.A. Hitt (1995), "The new competitive landscape," *Strategic Management Journal* 16 (Special Issue): 7–19.

13. For an in-depth discussion of technological changes in the media industry, see: Rothaermel, F.T., and A. Guenther (2018),

Netflix, Inc., case study MH0043, http://create.mheducation.com; and Sandomirjune, R. (1991, Jun. 9), "Entrepreneurs: Wayne Huizenga's growth complex," *The New York Times Magazine*; "Blockbuster files for bankruptcy," *The Economist* (2010, Sept. 23); Gandel, S. (2010, Oct. 17), "How Blockbuster failed at failing," *Time*; Satel, G. (2014, Sept. 5), "A look back at why Blockbuster really failed and why it didn't have to," *Forbes*; Schmidt, S. (2017, Apr. 26), "Blockbuster has survived in the most curious of places—Alaska," *The Washington Post*.

14. Academy of Management, ONE Division, 2013 domain statement; Anderson, R.C. (2009), *Confessions of a Radical Industrialist: Profits, People, Purpose–Doing Business by Respecting the Earth* (New York: St. Martin's Press); and Esty, D.C., and A.S. Winston (2009), *Green to Gold: How Smart Companies Use Environmental Strategy to Innovate, Create Value, and Build Competitive Advantage*, revised and updated (Hoboken, NJ: John Wiley & Sons).

15. This interesting debate unfolds in the following articles, among others: Misangyi, V.F., H. Elms, T. Greckhamer, and J.A. Lepine (2006), "A new perspective on a fundamental debate: A multilevel approach to industry, corporate, and business unit effects," *Strategic Management Journal* 27: 571–590; Hawawini, G., V. Subramanian, and P. Verdin (2003), "Is performance driven by industry- or firm-specific factors? A new look at the evidence," *Strategic Management Journal* 24: 1–16; McGahan, A.M., and M.E. Porter (1997), "How much does industry matter, really?" *Strategic Management Journal* 18: 15–30; Rumelt, R.P. (1991), "How much does industry matter?" *Strategic Management Journal* 12: 167–185; and Hansen, G.S., and B. Wernerfelt (1989), "Determinants of firm performance: The relative importance of economic and organizational factors," *Strategic Management Journal* 10: 399–411.

16. The discussion in this section is based on: Magretta, J. (2012), *Understanding Michael Porter: The Essential Guide to Competition and Strategy* (Boston: Harvard Business Review Press); Porter, M.E, (2008, January), "The five competitive forces that shape strategy," *Harvard Business Review;* Porter, M.E. (1980), *Competitive Strategy: Techniques for Analyzing Industries and Competitors* (New York: Free Press); and Porter, M.E. (1979, March–April), "How competitive forces shape strategy," *Harvard Business Review:* 137–145.

17. Hull, D. (2014, Jul. 22), "Tesla idles Fremont production line for Model X upgrade," *San Jose Mercury News;* and Vance, A. (2013, Jul. 18), "Why everybody loves Tesla," *Bloomberg Businessweek.*

18. Ramsey, M. (2014, Sept. 3), "Tesla to choose Nevada for battery factory," *The Wall Street Journal.*

19. Ramsey, M. (2014, Feb. 26), "Tesla plans $5 billion battery factory," *The Wall Street Journal.*

20. Walsh, T. (2014, Sept. 2), "The cult of Tesla Motors Inc: Why this automaker has the most loyal customers," *The Motley Fool.*

21. "Tesla Model S road test," *Consumer Reports,* www.consumerreports.org/cro/tesla/model-s/road-test.htm.

22. Wang, U. (2013, Nov. 5), "Tesla considers building the world's biggest lithium-ion battery factory," *Forbes.*

23. Whether a product is a substitute (complement) can be estimated by the cross-elasticity of demand. The cross-elasticity estimates the percentage change in the quantity demanded of good X resulting from a 1 percent change in the price of good Y. If the cross-elasticity of demand is greater (less) than zero, the products are substitutes (complements). For a detailed discussion, see: Allen, W.B., K. Weigelt, N. Doherty, and E. Mansfield (2009), *Managerial Economics Theory, Application, and Cases,* 7th ed. (New York: Norton).

24. This example, as with some others in the section on the five forces, is drawn from: Magretta, J. (2012), *Understanding Michael Porter: The Essential Guide to Competition and Strategy* (Boston: Harvard Business Review Press).

25. Because the threat of entry is one of the five forces explicitly recognized in Porter's model, we discuss barriers to entry when introducing the threat of entry above. The competitive industry structure framework is frequently referred to as the structure-conduct-performance (SCP) model. For a detailed discussion, see: Allen, W.B., K. Weigelt, N. Doherty, and E. Mansfield (2009), *Managerial Economics Theory,*

Application, and Cases, 7th ed. (New York: Norton); Carlton, D.W., and J.M. Perloff (2000), *Modern Industrial Organization,* 3rd ed. (Reading, MA: Addison-Wesley); Scherer, F.M., and D. Ross (1990), *Industrial Market Structure and Economic Performance,* 3rd ed. (Boston: Houghton Mifflin); and Bain, J.S. (1968), *Industrial Organization* (New York: John Wiley & Sons).

26. Besanko, D., E. Dranove, M. Hanley, and S. Schaefer (2010), *The Economics of Strategy,* 5th ed. (Hoboken, NJ: John Wiley & Sons).

27. Dixit, A., S. Skeath, and D.H. Reiley (2009), *Games of Strategy,* 3rd ed. (New York: Norton).

28. When there are only two main competitors, it's called a *duopoly* and is a special case of oligopoly.

29. Yoffie, D.B., and R. Kim (2011, June), "Coca-Cola in 2011: In Search of a New Model," Harvard Business School Case 711-504 (revised August 2012). See also: Yoffie, D.B., and Y. Wang (2002, January), "Cola Wars Continue: Coke and Pepsi in the Twenty-First Century," Harvard Business School Case 702-442 (revised January 2004, et seq).

30. "Trustbusting in the internet age: Should digital monopolies be broken up?" *The Economist* (2014, Nov. 29); and "Internet monopolies: Everybody wants to rule the world," *The Economist* (2014, Nov. 29).

31. See: Chang, S-J., and B. Wu (2013), "Institutional barriers and industry dynamics," *Strategic Management Journal* 35: 1103–1123. Discussion of this new and insightful research offers an opportunity to link the PESTEL analysis to the five forces analysis. The study focuses on the competitive interaction between incumbents and new entrants as a driver of industry evolution. It investigates the impact of institutional characteristics (political, legal, and sociocultural norms in PESTEL analysis) unique to China on productivity and exit hazards of incumbents versus new entrants. China's environment created a divergence between productivity and survival that shaped industry evolution. It also offers an illustration of the role that liability of newness plays in new entrant survival.

32. This example is drawn from: Porter, M.E. (2008), "The five competitive forces that shape strategy," *An Interview with Michael E. Porter: The Five Competitive Forces that Shape Strategy,* Harvard BusinessPublishing video; "Everyone else in the travel business makes money off airlines," *The Economist* (2012, Aug. 25); "How airline ticket prices fell 50% in 30 years (and nobody noticed)," *The Atlantic* (2013, Feb. 28); U.S. gallon of jet fuel prices; author's interviews with Delta Air Lines executives.

33. Wall, R. (2019, Feb. 14), "Airbus to retire the A380, the superjumbo that never quite took off," *The Wall Street Journal.*

34. Brandenburger, A.M., and B. Nalebuff (1996), *Co-opetition* (New York: Currency Doubleday); and Grove, A.S. (1999), *Only the Paranoid Survive* (New York: Time Warner).

35. Milgrom, P., and J. Roberts (1995), "Complementarities and fit strategy, structure, and organizational change in manufacturing," *Journal of Accounting and Economics* 19, no. 2-3: 179–208; and Brandenburger, A.M., and B. Nalebuff (1996), *Co-opetition* (New York: Currency Doubleday).

36. In this recent treatise, Porter also highlights positive-sum competition. See: Porter, M.E. (2008, January), "The five competitive forces that shape strategy," *Harvard Business Review.*

37. This discussion is based on: Zachary, M.A., P.T. Gianiodis, G. Tyge Payne, and G.D. Markman (2014), "Entry timing: Enduring lessons and future directions," *Journal of Management* 41: 1388–1415; and Bryce, D.J., and J.H. Dyer (2007, May), "Strategies to crack well-guarded markets," *Harvard Business Review:* 84-92. I also gratefully acknowledge the additional input received by Professors Zachary, Gianiodis, Tyge Payne, and Markman.

38. "Reading between the lines," *The Economist* (2009, Mar. 26); and "New York Times is near web charges," *The Wall Street Journal* (2010, Jan. 19).

39. Based on: Chokshi, N. (2018, Aug. 27), "What you might not know about e-sports, soon to be a $1 billion industry," *The New York Times;* Grey, A. (2018, July 3), "The explosive growth of eSports," *World Economic Forum;* Fisher, S.D. (2014, January/February), "The rise of eSports: League of Legends article series," white paper, Foster Pepper PLLC; Segal, D. (2014, Oct. 10), "Behind League of Legends, e-sports' main attraction," *The New York Times;* and data drawn from statista.com and "How much money does League of Legends make?" www.youtube.com/watch?v=1ug-YKLwkaA.

40. Porter, M.E. (1980), *Competitive Strategy: Techniques for Analyzing Industries and Competitors* (New York: Free Press); Hatten, K.J., and D.E. Schendel (1977), "Heterogeneity within an industry: Firm conduct in the U.S. brewing industry," *Journal of Industrial Economics* 26: 97–113; and Hunt, M.S. (1972), *Competition in the Major Home Appliance Industry, 1960-1970,* unpublished doctoral dissertation, Harvard University.

41. This discussion is based on: McNamara, G., D.L. Deephouse, and R. Luce (2003),

"Competitive positioning within and across a strategic group structure: The performance of core, secondary, and solitary firms," *Strategic Management Journal* 24: 161–181; Nair, A., and S. Kotha (2001), "Does group membership matter? Evidence from the Japanese steel industry," *Strategic Management Journal* 22: 221–235; Cool, K., and D. Schendel (1988), "Performance differences among strategic group members," *Strategic Management Journal* 9: 207–223; Hunt, M.S. (1972), *Competition in the Major Home Appliance Industry, 1960–1970,* unpublished doctoral dissertation, Harvard University; Hatten, K.J., and D.E. Schendel (1977), "Heterogeneity within an industry: Firm conduct in the U.S. brewing industry," *Journal of Industrial Economics* 26: 97–113; and Porter, M.E. (1980), *Competitive Strategy: Techniques for*

Analyzing Industries and Competitors (New York: Free Press), 102.

42. In Exhibit 3.8, United Airlines is the biggest bubble because it merged with Continental in 2010, creating the largest airline in the United States. Delta is the second-biggest airline in the United States after merging with Northwest Airlines in 2008.

43. American's hub is at Dallas-Fort Worth; Continental's is at Newark, New Jersey; United's is at Chicago; and U.S. Airways' is at Charlotte, North Carolina.

44. Caves, R.E., and M.E. Porter (1977), "From entry barriers to mobility barriers," *Quarterly Journal of Economics* 91: 241–262.

45. Carey, S. (2015, Mar. 16.), "U.S. airlines battling gulf carriers cite others' experience," *The Wall Street Journal.*

46. Carey, S. (2014, Oct. 14), "Steep learning curve for Southwest Airlines as it flies overseas," *The Wall Street Journal.*

47. Porter, M.E. (2008, January), "The five competitive forces that shape strategy," *Harvard Business Review*; and Magretta, J. (2012), *Understanding Michael Porter: The Essential Guide to Competition and Strategy* (Boston: Harvard Business Review Press): 56–57.

48. Pressler, J. (2014, Sept. 23), "The dumbest person in your building is passing out keys to your front door!" *New York Magazine.*

49. Greenberg, Z. (2018, Jul. 18), "New York City looks to crack down on Airbnb amid housing crisis," *The New York Times*; and Barbanel, J. (2018, Nov. 11), "New York City raids condo building in crackdown on Airbnb rentals," *The Wall Street Journal.*

CHAPTER FOUR

4 Defining the Project

LEARNING OBJECTIVES

After reading this chapter you should be able to:

4-1 Identify key elements of a project scope statement and understand why a complete scope statement is critical to project success.

4-2 Describe the causes of scope creep and ways to manage it.

4-3 Understand why it is important to establish project priorities in terms of cost, time, and performance.

4-4 Demonstrate the importance of a work breakdown structure (WBS) to the management of projects and how it serves as a database for planning and control.

4-5 Demonstrate how the organization breakdown structure (OBS) establishes accountability to organization units.

4-6 Describe a process breakdown structure (PBS) and when to use it.

4-7 Create responsibility matrices for small projects.

4-8 Create a communication plan for a project.

OUTLINE

4.1 Step 1: Defining the Project Scope

4.2 Step 2: Establishing Project Priorities

4.3 Step 3: Creating the Work Breakdown Structure

4.4 Step 4: Integrating the WBS with the Organization

4.5 Step 5: Coding the WBS for the Information System

4.6 Process Breakdown Structure

4.7 Responsibility Matrices

4.8 Project Communication Plan

Summary

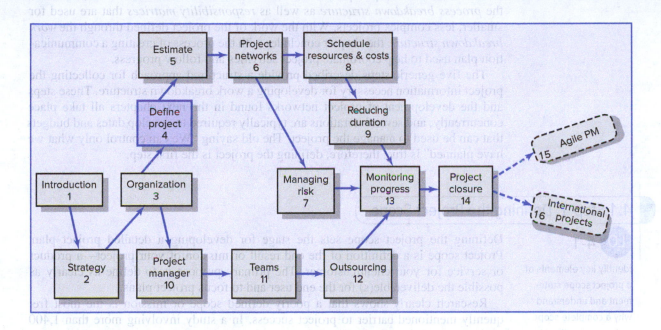

Select a dream

Use your dream to set a goal

Create a plan

Consider resources

Enhance skills and abilities

Spend time wisely

Start! Get organized and go

. . . it is one of those acro-whatevers, said Pooh.

—*Roger E. Allen and Stephen D. Allen,* Winnie-the-Pooh on Success *(New York: Penguin, 1997), p. 10.*

Project managers in charge of a single small project can plan and schedule the project tasks without much formal planning and information. However, when the project manager must manage several small projects or a large, complex project, a threshold is quickly reached in which the project manager can no longer cope with the detail.

This chapter describes a disciplined, structured method for selectively collecting information to use through all phases of the project life cycle, to meet the needs of all stakeholders (e.g., customer, project manager), and to measure performance against the strategic plan of the organization. The suggested method is a selective outline of the project called the *work breakdown structure*. The early stages of developing the outline ensure that all tasks are identified and that project participants have an understanding of what is to be done. Once the outline and its detail are defined, an integrated information system can be developed to schedule work and allocate budgets. This baseline information is later used for control.

In addition, the chapter presents a variant of the work breakdown structure called the *process breakdown structure* as well as *responsibility matrices* that are used for smaller, less complex projects. With the work of the project defined through the *work breakdown structure*, the chapter concludes with the process of creating a communication plan used to help coordinate project activities and follow progress.

The five generic steps described provide a structured approach for collecting the project information necessary for developing a work breakdown structure. These steps and the development of project networks found in the next chapters all take place concurrently, and several iterations are typically required to develop dates and budgets that can be used to manage the project. The old saying "We can control only what we have planned" is true; therefore, defining the project is the first step.

4.1 Step 1: Defining the Project Scope

LO 4-1

Identify key elements of a project scope statement and understand why a complete scope statement is critical to project success.

Defining the project scope sets the stage for developing a detailed project plan. Project scope is a definition of the end result or mission of your project—a product or service for your client/customer. The primary purpose is to define as clearly as possible the deliverable(s) for the end user and to focus project plans.

Research clearly shows that a poorly defined scope or mission is the most frequently mentioned barrier to project success. In a study involving more than 1,400 project managers in the United States and Canada, Gobeli and Larson (1990) found that approximately 50 percent of the planning problems relate to unclear definition of scope and goals. This and other studies suggest a strong correlation between project success and clear scope definition (Ashley et al., 1987; Pinto & Slevin, 1988; Standish Group, 2009). The scope document directs focus on the project purpose throughout the life of the project for the customer and project participants.

The scope should be developed under the direction of the project manager, customer, and other significant stakeholders. The project manager is responsible for seeing that there is agreement with the owner on project objectives, deliverables at each stage of the project, technical requirements, and so forth. For example, a deliverable in the early stage might be specifications; for the second stage, three prototypes for production; for the third, a sufficient quantity to introduce to market; and finally, marketing promotion and training.

Your project scope definition is a document that will be published and used by the project owner and project participants for planning and measuring project success. *Scope* describes what you expect to deliver to your customer when the project is complete. Your project scope should define the results to be achieved in specific, tangible, and measurable terms.

Employing a Project Scope Checklist

Clearly project scope is the keystone interlocking all elements of a project plan. To ensure that scope definition is complete, you may wish to use the following checklist:

Project Scope Checklist

1. Project objective
2. Product scope description
3. Justification
4. Deliverables
5. Milestones
6. Technical requirements
7. Limits and exclusions
8. Acceptance criteria

---

1. **Project objective.** The first step of project scope definition is to define the overall objective to meet your customer's need(s). For example, as a result of extensive market research a computer software company decides to develop a program that automatically translates verbal sentences in English to Russian. The project should be completed within three years at a cost not to exceed $1.5 million. Another example is to design and construct a portable hazardous-waste thermal treatment system in 13 months at a cost not to exceed $13 million. The project objective answers the questions of what, when, how much, and at times where.

2. **Product scope description.** This step is a detailed description of the characteristics of the product, service, or outcome of the project. The description is progressively elaborated throughout the project. The product scope answers the question "What end result is wanted?" For example, if the product is a cell phone, its product scope will be its screen size, battery, processor, camera type, memory, and so on.

3. **Justification.** It is important that project team members and stakeholders know why management authorized the project. What is the problem or opportunity the project is addressing? This is sometimes referred to as the *business case* for the project, since it usually includes cost/benefit analysis and strategic significance. For example, on a new-release project, the justification may be an expected ROI of 30 percent and an enhanced reputation in the marketplace.

4. **Deliverables.** The next step is to define major deliverables—the expected, measurable outputs over the life of the project. For example, deliverables in the early design phase of a project might be a list of specifications. In the second phase deliverables might be software coding and a technical manual. The next phase might be the prototype. The final phase might be final tests and approved software. Note: Deliverables and requirements are often used interchangeably.

5. **Milestones.** A **milestone** is a significant event in a project that occurs at a point in time. The milestone schedule shows only major segments of work; it represents first, rough-cut estimates of time, cost, and resources for the project. The milestone schedule is built using the deliverables as a platform to identify major segments of work and an end date—for example, testing complete and finished by July 1 of the same year. Milestones should be natural, important control points in the project. Milestones should be easy for all project participants to recognize.

SNAPSHOT FROM PRACTICE 4.1   Big Bertha ERC II versus the USGA's COR Requirement*

In 1991 Callaway Golf Equipment introduced their Big Bertha driver and revolutionized the golf equipment business. Big Bertha—named after the World War I German long-distance cannon—was much larger than conventional woods and lacked a hosel (the socket in the head of the club into which the shaft is inserted) so that the weight could be better distributed throughout the head. This innovative design gave the clubhead a larger sweet spot, which allowed a player to strike the golf ball off-center and not suffer much loss in distance or accuracy.

In 2000 Callaway introduced the Big Bertha ERC II forged titanium driver. "Designing the ERC II was a dream experience," said Richard C. Helmstetter, senior executive vice president of research and development and chief of new products. "We had no restrictions, so we were able to think outside the box to accomplish our goal of making the energy transfer from club to ball as efficient as possible. This allows golfers to generate more ball speed without swinging harder, which leads to greater distance. We used a combination of advanced new computer design technology and hands-on research with golfers from around the world. As a result, we created some design elements that go beyond any previous driver designs. Feedback from the players who have tested this driver indicates that our efforts dramatically improved the performance all golfers can expect to get from these drivers."[1]

However, there was a big problem. The new version of Bertha did not conform to the coefficient of restitution (COR) requirement established by the United States Golf Association (USGA). As a result it was barred from use by golfers in North America who intended to play by the USGA's Rules of Golf.

The USGA felt that the integrity of the game was being threatened by technological advances. Players were hitting balls so much farther and straighter that golf courses around the world were being redesigned to make them longer and more difficult. This was expensive.

thoermer/123RF

So in 1998 the USGA established performance thresholds for all new golf equipment. In order to prevent manufacturers from developing more powerful clubs, the USGA limited the COR of new golf equipment to 0.83. The COR was calculated by firing a golf ball at a driver out of a cannonlike machine at 109 miles per hour. The speed that the ball returned to the cannon could not exceed 83 percent of its initial speed (90.47 mph). The USGA called the ratio of incoming to outgoing velocity the coefficient of restitution (COR). Studies indicated that a 0.01 increase in COR resulted in 2 extra yards of carry. The Big Bertha ERC II's COR was 0.86.

After numerous efforts to get USGA to change its technical requirements, Callaway's engineers went back to the drawing board and in 2002 introduced Great Big Bertha II, which conformed to USGA's 0.83 COR restriction. They also continued to produce the ERC II.

[1]Callaway Press Release. *Callaway Golf Introduces ERC II Forged Titanium Driver—Its Hottest and Most Forgiving Driver Ever*. Accessed 03 January, 2019, ir.callawaygolf.com.

6. **Technical requirements.** More frequently than not, a product or service will have technical requirements to ensure proper performance. Technical requirements typically clarify the deliverables or define the performance specifications. For example, a technical requirement for a personal computer might be the ability

SNAPSHOT FROM PRACTICE 4.2   Scope Statement

PROJECT OBJECTIVE

To construct a high-quality, custom house within five months at cost not to exceed $700,000 on lot 42A in Greendale, Oregon.

PRODUCT SCOPE DESCRIPTION

A 2,200-square-foot, 2½-bath, 3-bedroom, finished home.

DELIVERABLES

- A finished garage, insulated and sheetrocked.
- Kitchen appliances to include range, oven, microwave, and dishwasher.
- A high-efficiency gas furnace with programmable thermostat.
- Aluminum roofing.

MILESTONES

1. Permits approved—March 5.
2. Foundation poured—March 14.
3. Drywall in. Framing, sheathing, plumbing, electrical, and mechanical inspections passed—May 25.
4. Final inspection—June 7

TECHNICAL REQUIREMENTS

1. Home must meet local building codes.
2. All windows and doors must pass NFRC class 40 energy ratings.
3. Exterior wall insulation must meet an "R" factor of 21.
4. Ceiling insulation must meet an "R" factor of 38.
5. Floor insulation must meet an "R" factor of 25.
6. Garage will accommodate two large-size cars and one 20-foot Winnebago.
7. Structure must pass seismic stability codes.

Ufulum/Shutterstock

LIMITS AND EXCLUSIONS

1. House will be built to the specifications and design of the original blueprints provided by the customer.
2. Owner is responsible for landscaping.
3. Refrigerator is not included among kitchen appliances.
4. Air conditioning is not included but prewiring is included.
5. Contractor reserves the right to contract out services.
6. Contractor is responsible for subcontracted work.
7. Site work limited to Monday through Friday, 8:00 a.m. to 6:00 p.m.

CUSTOMER REVIEW

Linda and Dave Smith.

to accept 120-volt alternating current or 240-volt direct current without any adapters or user switches. Another well-known example is the ability of 911 emergency systems to identify the caller's phone number and the location of the phone. Examples from information systems projects include the speed and capacity of database systems and connectivity with alternative systems. For understanding the importance of key requirements, see Snapshot from Practice 4.1: Big Bertha ERC II versus the USGA's COR Requirement.

7. **Limits and exclusions.** The limits of scope should be defined. Failure to do so can lead to false expectations and to expending resources and time on the wrong problem. The following are examples of limits: work on-site is allowed only

between the hours of 8:00 p.m. and 5:00 a.m.; system maintenance and repair will be done only up to one month after final inspection; and the client will be billed for additional training beyond that prescribed in the contract. Exclusions further define the boundary of the project by stating what is not included. Examples include: data will be collected by the client, not the contractor; a house will be built, but no landscaping or security devices added; software will be installed, but no training given.

8. **Acceptance criteria.** Acceptance criteria are a set of conditions that must be met before the deliverables are accepted. The following are examples: all tasks and milestones are complete, new service processes begin with a less than 1 percent defect rate, third-party certification is required, and customer on-site inspection is required.

Scope statements are twofold. There is a short, one- to two-page summary of key elements of the scope, followed by extended documentation of each element (e.g., a detailed milestone schedule or risk analysis report). See Snapshot from Practice 4.2: Scope Statement for an example of a summary page.

The project scope checklist in Step 1 is generic. Different industries and companies will develop unique checklists and templates to fit their needs and specific kinds of projects. A few companies engaged in contracted work refer to scope statements as "statements of work (SOWs)." Other organizations use the term *project charter*. However, the term **project charter** has emerged to have a special meaning in the world of project management. A project charter is a document that authorizes the project manager to initiate and lead the project. This document is issued by upper management and provides the project manager with written authority to use organizational resources for project activities. Often the charter will include a brief scope description as well as such items as risk limits, business case, spending limits, and even team composition.

LO 4-2

Describe the causes of scope creep and ways to manage it.

Many projects suffer from **scope creep**, which is the tendency for the project scope to expand over time—usually by changing requirements, specifications, and priorities. Scope creep can have a positive or negative effect on the project, but in most cases scope creep means added costs and possible project delays. Changes in requirements, specifications, and priorities frequently result in cost overruns and delays. Examples are abundant—the Denver Airport baggage handling system, Boston's new freeway system ("The Big Dig"), the Sochi Winter Olympics, and the list goes on. On software development projects, scope creep is manifested in bloated products in which added functionality undermines ease of use.

Five of the most common causes of scope creep are

- **Poor requirement analysis.** Customers often don't really know what they want. "I'll know it when I see it" syndrome contributes to wasted effort and ambiguity.
- **Not involving users early enough.** Too often project teams think they know up front what the end user needs, only to find out later they were mistaken.
- **Underestimating project complexity.** Complexity and associated uncertainty naturally lead to changes in scope, since there are so many unknowns yet to be discovered.
- **Lack of change control.** A robust change control process is needed to ensure that only appropriate changes occur in the scope of the project.

- **Gold plating. Gold plating** refers to adding extra value to the project that is beyond the scope of the project. This is common on software projects where developers add features that they think the end user will like.

In many cases these causes reflect a misfit—traditional project management methods being applied to high-uncertainty projects (remember Figure 1.2!). Instead of trying to establish plans up front, Agile project management should be applied to discover what needs to be done. On Agile projects the scope is assumed to evolve rather than be prescribed. Scope creep is managed and reflects progress.

If the project scope needs to change, it is critical to have a sound change control process in place that records the change and keeps a log of all project changes. Change control is one of the topics of Chapter 7. Project managers in the field constantly suggest that dealing with changing requirements is one of their most challenging problems.

4.2 Step 2: Establishing Project Priorities

LO 4-3

Understand why it is important to establish project priorities in terms of cost, time, and performance.

Quality and the ultimate success of a project are traditionally defined as meeting and/or exceeding the expectations of the customer and/or upper management in terms of the cost (budget), time (schedule), and performance (scope) of the project (see Figure 4.1). The interrelationship among these criteria varies. For example, sometimes it is necessary to compromise the performance and scope of the project to get the project done quickly or less expensively. Often the longer a project takes, the more expensive it becomes. However, a positive correlation between cost and schedule may not always be true. Other times project costs can be reduced by using cheaper, less efficient labor or equipment that extends the duration of the project. Likewise, as will be seen in Chapter 9, project managers are often forced to expedite, or "crash," certain key activities by adding additional labor, thereby raising the original cost of the project.

One of the primary jobs of a project manager is to manage the trade-offs among time, cost, and performance. To do so, project managers must define and understand the nature of the priorities of the project. They need to have a candid discussion with the project customer and upper management to establish the relative importance of each criterion. For example, what happens when the customer keeps adding requirements? Or if midway through the project a trade-off must be made between cost and expediting, which criterion has priority?

FIGURE 4.1
Project Management Trade-offs

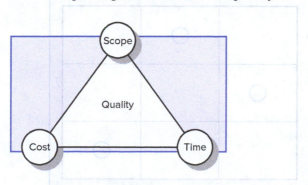

One technique that is useful for this purpose is completing a **priority matrix** for the project to identify which criterion is constrained, which should be enhanced, and which can be accepted:

Constrain. The original parameter is fixed. The project must meet the completion date, specifications and scope of the project, or budget.

Enhance. Given the scope of the project, which criterion should be optimized? In the case of time and cost, this usually means taking advantage of opportunities to either reduce costs or shorten the schedule. Conversely, with regard to performance, enhancing means adding value to the project.

Accept. For which criterion is it tolerable not to meet the original parameters? When trade-offs have to be made, is it permissible to allow the schedule to slip, to reduce the scope and performance of the project, or to go over budget?

Figure 4.2 displays the priority matrix for the development of a new wireless router. Because *time*-to-market is important to sales, the project manager is instructed to take advantage of every opportunity to reduce completion time. In doing so, going over *budget* is acceptable, though not desirable. At the same time, the original *performance* specifications for the router as well as reliability standards cannot be compromised.

Priorities vary from project to project. For example, for many software projects time-to-market is critical, and companies like Microsoft may defer original scope requirements to later versions in order to get to the market first. Alternatively, for special event projects (conferences, parades, tournaments) time is constrained once the date has been announced, and if the budget is tight the project manager will compromise the scope of the project in order to complete the project on time.

Some would argue that all three criteria are always constrained and that good project managers should seek to optimize each criterion. If everything goes well on a project and no major problems or setbacks are encountered, their argument may be valid. However, this situation is rare, and project managers are often forced to make tough decisions that benefit one criterion while compromising the other two. The purpose of this exercise is to define and agree on what the priorities and constraints of the project are so that when "push comes to shove," the right decisions can be made.

There are likely to be natural limits to the extent managers can constrain, enhance, or accept any one criterion. It may be acceptable for the project to slip one month

FIGURE 4.2
Project Priority Matrix

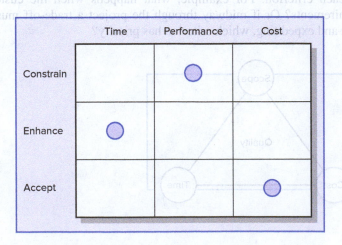

behind schedule but no further or to exceed the planned budget by as much as $20,000. Likewise, it may be desirable to finish a project a month early, but after that cost conservation should be the primary goal. Some project managers document these limits as part of creating the priority matrix.

In summary, developing a priority matrix for a project *before the project begins* is a useful exercise. It provides a forum for clearly establishing priorities with customers and top management so as to create shared expectations and avoid misunderstandings. The priority information is essential to the planning process, where adjustments can be made in the scope, schedule, and budget allocation. Finally, the matrix is useful midway in the project for approaching a problem that must be solved.

One caveat must be mentioned; during the course of a project, priorities may change. The customer may suddenly need the project completed one month sooner, or new directives from top management may emphasize cost-saving initiatives. The project manager needs to be vigilant in order to anticipate and confirm changes in priorities and make appropriate adjustments.

4.3 Step 3: Creating the Work Breakdown Structure

LO 4-4

Demonstrate the importance of a work breakdown structure (WBS) to the management of projects and how it serves as a database for planning and control.

Major Groupings in a WBS

Once the scope and deliverables have been identified, the work of the project can be successively subdivided into smaller and smaller work elements. The outcome of this hierarchical process is called the **work breakdown structure (WBS).** Use of a WBS helps to assure project managers that all products and work elements are identified, to integrate the project with the current organization, and to establish a basis for control. Basically, the WBS is an outline of the project with different levels of detail.

Figure 4.3 shows the major groupings commonly used in the field to develop a hierarchical WBS. The WBS begins with the project as the final deliverable. Major project work deliverables/systems are identified first; then the subdeliverables necessary to accomplish the larger deliverables are defined. The process is repeated until the subdeliverable detail is small enough to be manageable and one person can be responsible. This subdeliverable is further divided into work packages. Because the lowest subdeliverable usually includes several work packages, the work packages are grouped by type of work—for example, design and testing. These groupings within a subdeliverable are called cost accounts. This grouping facilitates a system for monitoring project progress by work, cost, and responsibility.

How a WBS Helps the Project Manager

The WBS defines all the elements of the project in a hierarchical framework and establishes their relationships to the project end item(s). Think of the project as a large work package that is successively broken down into smaller work packages; the total project is the summation of all the smaller work packages. This hierarchical structure facilitates the evaluation of cost, time, and technical performance at all levels in the organization over the life of the project. The WBS also provides management with information appropriate to each level. For example, top management deals primarily with major deliverables, while first-line supervisors deal with smaller subdeliverables and work packages.

FIGURE 4.3
Hierarchical Breakdown of the WBS

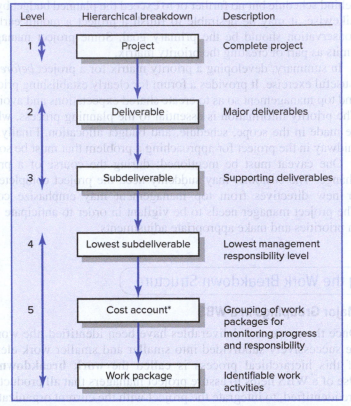

*This breakdown groups work packages by type of work within a deliverable and allows assignment of responsibility to an organization unit. This extra step facilitates a system for monitoring project progress (discussed in Chapter 13).

Each item in the WBS needs a time and cost estimate. With this information it is possible to plan, schedule, and budget the project. The WBS also serves as a framework for tracking cost and work performance.

As the WBS is developed, organization units and individuals are assigned responsibility for executing work packages. This integrates the work and the organization. In practice, this process is sometimes called the organization breakdown structure (OBS), which will be further discussed later in the chapter.

Use of the WBS provides the opportunity to "roll up" (sum) the budget and actual costs of the smaller work packages into larger work elements so that performance can be measured by organization units and work accomplishment.

The WBS can also be used to define communication channels and assist in understanding and coordinating many parts of the project. The structure shows the work and responsible organization units and suggests where written communication should be directed. Problems can be quickly addressed and coordinated because the structure integrates work and responsibility.

A Simple WBS Development

Figure 4.4 shows a simplified WBS to develop a new prototype tablet computer. At the top of the chart (level 1) is the project end item—the E-Slim Tablet x-13 Prototype. The subdeliverable levels (2–5) below level 1 represent further decomposition of work. The levels of the structure can also represent information for different levels

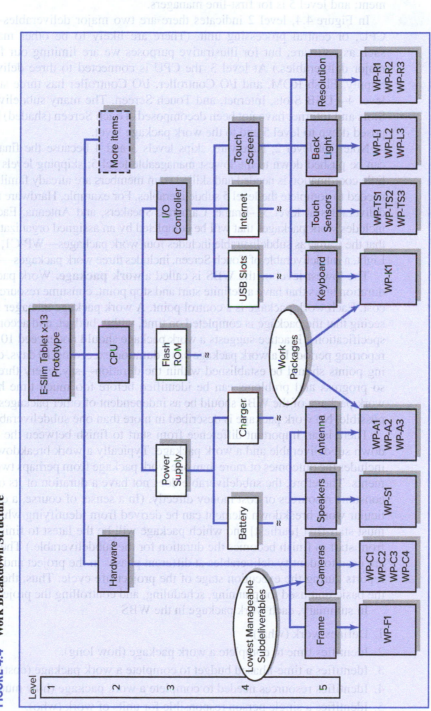

FIGURE 4.4   Work Breakdown Structure

of management. For example, level 1 information represents the total project objective and is useful to top management; levels 2, 3, and 4 are suitable for middle management; and level 5 is for first-line managers.

In Figure 4.4, level 2 indicates there are two major deliverables—Hardware and CPU, or central processing unit. (There are likely to be other major deliverables such as software, but for illustrative purposes we are limiting our focus to just two major deliverables.) At level 3, the CPU is connected to three deliverables—Power Supply, Flash ROM, and I/O Controller. I/O Controller has three subdeliverables at level 4—USB Slots, Internet, and Touch Screen. The many subdeliverables for USB Slots and Internet have not been decomposed. Touch Screen (shaded) has been decomposed down to level 5 and to the work package level.

Note that level 2, Hardware, skips levels 3 and 4 because the final subdeliverables can be pushed down to the lowest manageable level 5; skipping levels 3 and 4 suggests little coordination is needed and skilled team members are already familiar with the work needed to complete the level 5 subdeliverables. For example, Hardware requires four subdeliverables at level 5—Frame, Cameras, Speakers, and Antenna. Each subdeliverable includes work packages that will be completed by an assigned organization unit. Observe that the Cameras subdeliverable includes four work packages—WP-C1, 2, 3, and 4. Back Light, a subdeliverable of Touch Screen, includes three work packages—WP-L 1, 2, and 3.

The lowest level of the WBS is called a **work package.** Work packages are short-duration tasks that have a definite start and stop point, consume resources, and represent cost. Each work package is a control point. A work package manager is responsible for seeing that the package is completed on time, within budget, and according to technical specifications. Practice suggests a work package should not exceed 10 workdays or one reporting period. If a work package has a duration exceeding 10 days, check or monitoring points should be established within the duration—say, every three to five days—so progress and problems can be identified before too much time has passed. Each work package of the WBS should be as independent of other packages of the project as possible. No work package is described in more than one subdeliverable of the WBS.

There is an important difference from start to finish between the last work breakdown subdeliverable and a work package. Typically a work breakdown subdeliverable includes the outcomes of more than one work package from perhaps two or three departments. Therefore, the subdeliverable does not have a duration of its own and does not consume resources or cost money directly. (In a sense, of course, a duration for a particular work breakdown element can be derived from identifying which work package must start first [earliest] and which package will be the latest to finish; the difference from start to finish becomes the duration for the subdeliverable.) The higher elements are used to identify deliverables at different phases in the project and to develop status reports during the execution stage of the project life cycle. Thus, the work package is the basic unit used for planning, scheduling, and controlling the project.

In summary, each work package in the WBS

1. Defines work (what).
2. Identifies time to complete a work package (how long).
3. Identifies a time-phased budget to complete a work package (cost).
4. Identifies resources needed to complete a work package (how much).
5. Identifies a single person responsible for units of work (who).
6. Identifies monitoring points for measuring progress (how well).

Figure 4.4 represents the classic WBS in which the project is broken down to the lowest manageable deliverable and subsequent work packages. Many situations do not require this level of detail. This begs the question of how far you should break down the work. There is no set answer to this question. However, here are some tips given by project managers:

Break down the work until you can do an estimate that is accurate enough for your purposes. If you are doing a ballpark estimate to see if the project is worthy of serious consideration, you probably do not need to break it down beyond major deliverables. On the other hand, if you are pricing a project to submit a competitive bid, then you are likely to go down to the work package level.

The WBS should conform to how you are going to schedule work. For example, if assignments are made in terms of days, then tasks should be limited as best as possible to one day or more to complete.

Conversely, if hours are the smallest unit for scheduling, then work can be broken down to one-hour increments.

Final activities should have clearly defined start/end events. Avoid open-ended tasks like "research" or "market analysis." Take it down to the next level in which deliverables/outcomes are more clearly defined. Instead of ending with market analysis, include items such as "identify market share," "list user requirements," or "write a problem statement."

If accountability and control are important, then break the work down so that one individual is clearly responsible for the work. For example, instead of stopping at product design, take it to the next level and identify specific components of the design (e.g., electrical schematics or power source) that different individuals will be responsible for creating.

The bottom line is that the WBS should provide the level of detail needed to manage the specific project successfully.

Creating a WBS from scratch can be a daunting task. Project managers should take advantage of relevant examples from previous projects to begin the process.

WBSs are products of group efforts. If the project is small, the entire project team may be involved in breaking down the project into its components. For large, complex projects, the people responsible for the major deliverables are likely to meet to establish the first two levels of deliverables. In turn, further detail would be delegated to the people responsible for the specific work. Collectively this information would be gathered and integrated into a formal WBS by a project support person. The final version would be reviewed by the inner echelon of the project team. Relevant stakeholders (most notably customers) would be consulted to confirm agreement and revise when appropriate.

Project teams developing their first WBS frequently forget that the structure should be end-item, output oriented. First attempts often result in a WBS that follows the organization structure—design, marketing, production, finance. If a WBS follows the organization structure, the focus will be on the organization function and processes, rather than the project output or deliverables. In addition, a WBS with a process focus will become an accounting tool that records costs by function rather than a tool for "output" management. Every effort should be made to develop a WBS that is output oriented in order to concentrate on concrete deliverables. See Snapshot from Practice 4.3: Creating a WBS.

4.4 Step 4: Integrating the WBS with the Organization

LO 4-5

Demonstrate how the organization breakdown structure (OBS) establishes accountability to organization units.

The WBS is used to link the organization units responsible for performing the work. In practice, the outcome of this process is the **organization breakdown structure (OBS).** The OBS depicts how the firm has organized to discharge work responsibility. The purposes of the OBS are to provide a framework to summarize organization unit work performance, identify the organization units responsible for work packages, and tie the organization unit to cost control accounts. Recall that, cost accounts group similar work packages (usually under the purview of a department). The OBS defines the organization subdeliverables in a hierarchical pattern in successively smaller and smaller units. Frequently the traditional organization structure can be used. Even if the project is completely performed by a team, it is necessary to break down the team structure for assigning responsibility for budgets, time, and technical performance.

As in the WBS, the OBS assigns the lowest organization unit the responsibility for work packages within a cost account. Herein lies one major strength of using the WBS and OBS; they can be *integrated* as shown in Figure 4.5. The intersection of work packages and the organization unit creates a project control point **(cost account)** that integrates work and responsibility. For example, at level 5, Touch Sensors has three work packages that have been assigned to the Design, Quality Control Test, and Production Departments. The intersection of the WBS and OBS represents the set of work packages necessary to complete the subdeliverable located immediately above and the organization unit on the left responsible for accomplishing the packages at the intersection. Note that the Design Department is responsible for five different work packages across the Hardware and Touch Screen deliverables.

Later we will use the intersection as a cost account for management control of projects. For example, the Cameras element requires the completion of work packages whose primary responsibility will include the Design, QC Test, Production, and Outsourcing Departments. Control can be checked from two directions—outcomes and responsibility. In the execution phase of the project, progress can be tracked vertically on deliverables (client's interest) and tracked horizontally by organization responsibility (owner's interest).

4.5 Step 5: Coding the WBS for the Information System

Gaining the maximum usefulness of a breakdown structure depends on a coding system. The codes are used to define levels and elements in the WBS, organization elements, work packages, and budget and cost information. The codes allow reports to be consolidated at any level in the structure. The most commonly used scheme in practice is numeric indention. A portion of the E-Slim Tablet x-13 Prototype project is presented in Exhibit 4.1.

Note that the project identification is 1.0. Each successive indention represents a lower element or work package. Ultimately the numeric scheme reaches down to the work package level, and all tasks and elements in the structure have an identification code. The "cost account" is the focal point because all budgets, work assignments, time, cost, and technical performance come together at this point.

This coding system can be extended to cover large projects. Additional schemes can be added for special reports. For example, adding a "23" after the code could indicate a site location, an elevation, or a special account such as labor. Some letters can be used as special identifiers such as "M" for materials or "E" for engineers.

FIGURE 4.5 Integration of WBS and OBS

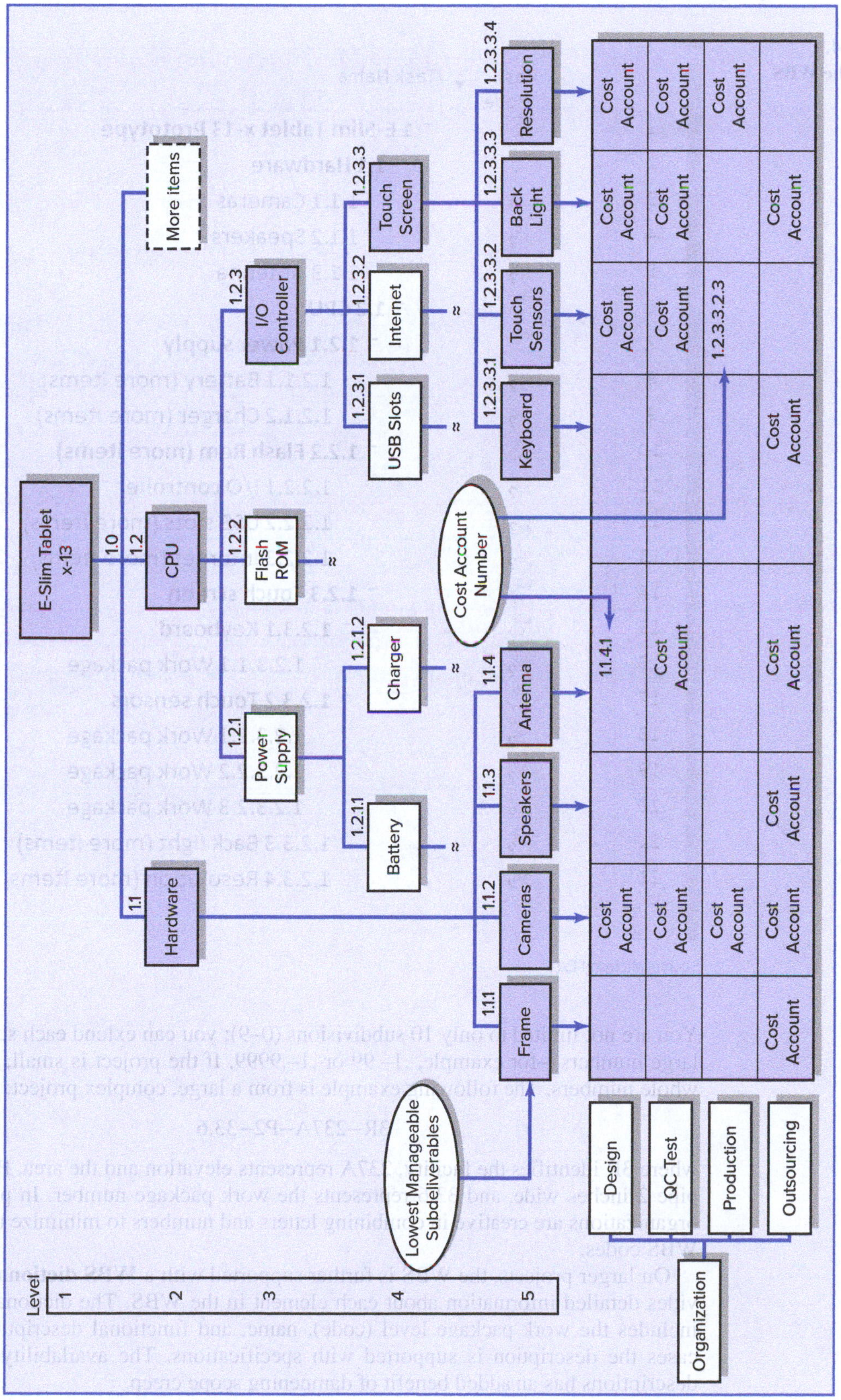

120   Chapter 4   *Defining the Project*

EXHIBIT 4.1
Coding the WBS

	ⓘ	Task Mode ▾	Task Name ▾
1		⇨	⊟ **1 E-Slim Tablet x-13 Prototype**
2		⇨	⊟ **1.1 Hardware**
3		⚲?	1.1.1 Cameras
4		⚲?	1.1.2 Speakers
5		⚲?	1.1.3 Antenna
6		⇨	⊟ **1.2 CPU**
7		⇨	⊟ **1.2.1 Power supply**
8		⚲?	1.2.1.1 Battery (more items)
9		⚲?	1.2.1.2 Charger (more items)
10		⇨	⊟ **1.2.2 Flash Rom (more items)**
11		⚲?	1.2.2.1 I/O controller
12		⚲?	1.2.2.2 USB slots (more items)
13		⚲?	1.2.2.3 Internet (more items)
14		⇨	⊟ **1.2.3 Touch screen**
15		⇨	⊟ **1.2.3.1 Keyboard**
16		⚲?	1.2.3.1.1 Work package
17		⇨	⊟ **1.2.3.2 Touch sensors**
18		⚲?	1.2.3.2.1 Work package
19		⚲?	1.2.3.2.2 Work package
20		⚲?	1.2.3.2.3 Work package
21		⚲?	1.2.3.3 Back light (more items)
22		⚲?	1.2.3.4 Resolution (more items)

Source: Microsoft Excel

You are not limited to only 10 subdivisions (0–9); you can extend each subdivision to large numbers—for example, .1–.99 or .1–.9999. If the project is small, you can use whole numbers. The following example is from a large, complex project:

$$3R–237A–P2–33.6$$

where 3R identifies the facility, 237A represents elevation and the area, P2 represents pipe 2 inches wide, and 33.6 represents the work package number. In practice most organizations are creative in combining letters and numbers to minimize the length of WBS codes.

On larger projects, the WBS is further supported with a **WBS dictionary** that provides detailed information about each element in the WBS. The dictionary typically includes the work package level (code), name, and functional description. In some cases the description is supported with specifications. The availability of detailed descriptions has an added benefit of dampening scope creep.

4.6 Process Breakdown Structure

 LO 4-6

Describe a process breakdown structure (PBS) and when to use it.

The WBS is best suited for design and build projects that have tangible outcomes such as an offshore mining facility or a new car prototype. The project can be decomposed, or broken down, into major deliverables, subdeliverables, further subdeliverables, and ultimately work packages. It is more difficult to apply WBS to less tangible, *process-oriented* projects in which the final outcome is a product of a series of steps or phases. Here, the big difference is that the project evolves over time with each phase affecting the next phase. Information systems projects typically fall in this category—for example, creating an extranet website or an internal software database system. Process projects are driven by performance requirements, not by plans/blueprints. Some practitioners choose to utilize a **process breakdown structure (PBS)** instead of the classic WBS.

Figure 4.6 provides an example of a PBS for a software development project. Instead of being organized around deliverables, the project is organized around phases. Each of the five major phases can be broken down into more specific activities until a sufficient level of detail is achieved to communicate what needs to be done to complete that phase. People can be assigned to specific activities, and a complementary OBS can be created, just as is done for the WBS. Deliverables are not ignored but are defined as outputs required to move to the next phase. The software industry often refers to a PBS as the "waterfall method," since progress flows downward through each phase.[1]

[1]The limitations of the waterfall method for software development have led to the emergence of Agile project management methods that are the subject of Chapter 15.

FIGURE 4.6 **PBS for Software Development Project**

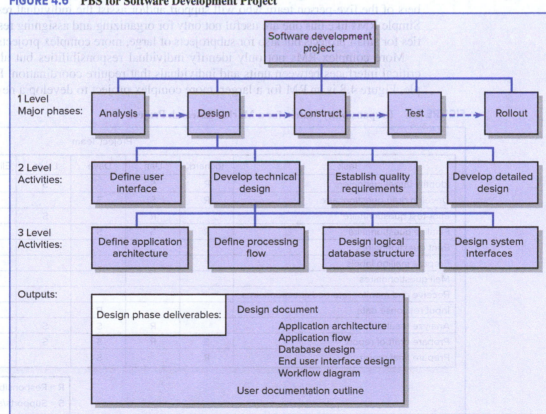

Checklists that contain the phase exit requirements are developed to manage project progress. These checklists provide the means to support phase walk-throughs and reviews. Checklists vary depending upon the project and activities involved but typically include the following details:

- Deliverables needed to exit a phase and begin a new one.
- Quality checkpoints to ensure that deliverables are complete and accurate.
- Sign-offs by all responsible stakeholders to indicate that the phase has been successfully completed and that the project should move on to the next phase.

As long as exit requirements are firmly established and deliverables for each phase are well defined, the PBS provides a suitable alternative to the standard WBS for projects that involve extensive development work.

4.7 Responsibility Matrices

LO 4-7

Create responsibility matrices for small projects.

In many cases, the size and scope of the project do not warrant an elaborate WBS or OBS. One tool that is widely used by project managers and task force leaders of small projects is the **responsibility matrix** (RM). The RM (sometimes called a linear responsibility chart) summarizes the tasks to be accomplished and who is responsible for what on a project. In its simplest form an RM consists of a chart listing all the project activities and the participants responsible for each activity. For example, Figure 4.7 illustrates an RM for a market research study. In this matrix the R is used to identify the committee member who is responsible for coordinating the efforts of other team members assigned to the task and making sure that the task is completed. The S is used to identify members of the five-person team who will support and/or assist the individual responsible. Simple RMs like this one are useful not only for organizing and assigning responsibilities for small projects but also for subprojects of large, more complex projects.

More complex RMs not only identify individual responsibilities but also clarify critical interfaces between units and individuals that require coordination. For example, Figure 4.8 is an RM for a larger, more complex project to develop a new piece of

FIGURE 4.7   **Responsibility Matrix for a Market Research Project**

Task	Richard	Dan	Dave	Linda	Elizabeth
Identify target customers	R	S		S	
Develop draft questionnaire	R	S	S		
Pilot-test questionnaire		R		S	
Finalize questionnaire	R	S	S	S	
Print questionnaire					R
Prepare mailing labels					R
Mail questionnaires					R
Receive and monitor returned questionnaires				R	S
Input response data			R		
Analyze results		R	S	S	
Prepare draft of report	S	R	S	S	
Prepare final report	R		S		

Project Team

R = Responsible
S = Supports/assists

FIGURE 4.8   Responsibility Matrix for the Conveyor Belt Project

Deliverables	Design	Development	Documentation	Assembly	Testing	Purchasing	Quality Assur.	Manufacturing
				Organization				
Architectural designs	1	2			2		3	3
Hardware specifications	2	1				2	3	
Kernel specifications	1	3						3
Utilities specifications	2	2			3			
Hardware design	1	1		3		3	3	3
Disk drivers	3	1	2		3			
Memory management	1	3			3			
Operating system documentation	2		1	1				
Prototypes	5	4	4		3	3	3	4
Integrated acceptance test	5	5	2		1		5	5

1 Responsible
2 Support
3 Consult
4 Notification
5 Approval

automated equipment. Notice that within each cell a numeric coding scheme is used to define the nature of involvement on that specific task. Such an RM extends the WBS/OBS and provides a clear and concise method for depicting responsibility, authority, and communication channels.

Responsibility matrices provide a means for all participants in a project to view their responsibilities and agree on their assignments. They also help clarify the extent or type of authority exercised by each participant in performing an activity in which two or more parties have overlapping involvement. By using an RM and by defining authority, responsibility, and communications within its framework, the relationship between different organization units and the work content of the project is made clear.

4.8 Project Communication Plan

LO 4-8

Create a communication plan for a project.

Once the project deliverables and work are clearly identified, creating an internal communication plan is vital. Stories abound of poor communication as a major contributor to project failure. Having a robust communication plan can go a long way toward mitigating project problems and can ensure that customers, team members, and other stakeholders have the information to do their jobs.

The communication plan is usually created by the project manager and/or the project team in the early stage of project planning.

Communication is a key component in coordinating and tracking project schedules, issues, and action items. The plan maps out the flow of information to different stakeholders and becomes an integral part of the overall project plan. The purpose of a project communication plan is to express what, who, how, and when information will be transmitted to project stakeholders so schedules, issues, and action items can be tracked.

Project communication plans address the following core questions:

- What information needs to be collected and when?
- Who will receive the information?
- What methods will be used to gather and store information?
- What are the limits, if any, on who has access to certain kinds of information?
- When will the information be communicated?
- How will it be communicated?

Developing a communication plan that answers these questions usually entails the following basic steps:

1. **Stakeholder analysis.** Identify the target groups. Typical groups could be the customer, sponsor, project team, project office, or anyone else who needs project information to make decisions and/or contribute to project progress. A common tool found in practice to initially identify and analyze major project stakeholders' communication needs is presented in Figure 4.9.[2] What is communicated and how are influenced by stakeholder interest and power. Some of these stakeholders may have the power to either block or enhance your project. By identifying stakeholders and prioritizing them on the "Power/Interest" map, you can plan the type and frequency of communications needed. (More on stakeholders will be discussed in Chapter 10.)

[2] For a more elaborate scheme for assessing stakeholders, see: Bourne, L. *Stakeholder Relationship Management* (Farnham, UK: Gower, 2009).

FIGURE 4.9
Stakeholder
Communications

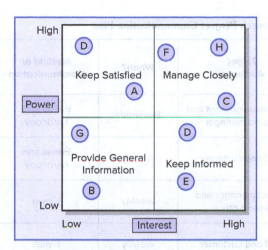

For example, on a typical project you want to manage closely the professionals doing the work, while you want to satisfy senior management and the project sponsor with periodic updates. Unions and operation managers interested in capacity should be kept informed, while you would only need to provide general information to the legal, public relations, and other departments.

2. **Information needs.** What information is pertinent to stakeholders who contribute to the project's progress? The simplest answer to this question can be obtained by asking the various individuals what information they need and when they need it. For example, top management needs to know how the project is progressing, whether it is encountering critical problems, and the extent to which project goals are being realized. This information is required so that they can make strategic decisions and manage the portfolio of projects. Project team members need to see schedules, task lists, specifications, and the like so they know what needs to be done next. External groups need to know any changes in the schedule and performance requirements of the components they are providing. Frequent information needs found in communication plans are

Project status reports	Deliverable issues
Changes in scope	Team status meetings
Gating decisions	Accepted request changes
Action items	Milestone reports

3. **Sources of information.** When the information needs are identified, the next step is to determine the sources of information. That is, where does the information reside? How will it be collected? For example, information relating to the milestone report, team meetings, and project status meetings would be found in the minutes and reports of various groups.

4. **Dissemination modes.** In today's world, traditional status report meetings are being supplemented by e-mail, teleconferencing, SharePoint, and a variety of database sharing programs to circulate information. In particular, many companies are using the Web to create a "virtual project office" to store project information. Project management software feeds information directly to the website so that different people have immediate access to relevant project information. In some cases appropriate information is routed automatically to key stakeholders. Backup paper hardcopy to specific stakeholders is still critical for many project changes and action items.

126   Chapter 4   *Defining the Project*

FIGURE 4.10   **Shale Oil Research Project Communication Plan**

What Information	Target Audience	When?	Method of Communication	Provider
Milestone report	Senior management and project manager	Bimonthly	E-mail and hardcopy	Project office
Project status reports & agendas	Staff and customer	Weekly	E-mail and hardcopy	Project manager
Team status reports	Project manager and project office	Weekly	E-mail	Team recorder
Issues report	Staff and customer	Weekly	E-mail	Team recorder
Escalation reports	Staff and customer	When needed	Meeting and hardcopy	Project manager
Outsourcing performance	Staff and customer	Bimonthly	Meeting	Project manager
Accepted change requests	Project office, senior mgmt., customer, staff, and project mgr.	Anytime	E-mail and hardcopy	Design department
Oversight gate decisions	Senior management and project manager	As required	E-mail meeting report	Oversight group or project office

5. **Responsibility and timing.** Determine who will send out the information. For example, a common practice is to have secretaries of meetings forward the minutes or specific information to the appropriate stakeholders. In some cases the responsibility lies with the project manager or project office. Timing and frequency of distribution appropriate to the information need to be established.

The advantage of establishing a communication plan is that instead of responding to information requests, you are controlling the flow of information. This reduces confusion and unnecessary interruptions, and it can provide project managers greater autonomy. Why? By reporting on a regular basis how things are going and what is happening, you allow senior management to feel more comfortable about letting the team complete the project without interference. See Figure 4.10 for a sample Shale Oil research project communication plan.

The importance of establishing a plan up front for communicating important project information cannot be overstated. Many of the problems that plague a project can be traced back to insufficient time devoted to establishing a well-grounded internal communication plan.

Summary

The project scope definition, priorities, and work breakdown structure are the keys to nearly every aspect of managing the project. The scope definition provides focus and emphasis on the end item(s) of the project. Establishing project priorities allows managers to make appropriate trade-off decisions. The WBS structure helps ensure that all tasks of the project are identified and provides two views of the project—one on deliverables and one on organization responsibility. The WBS avoids having the project driven by organization function or by a finance system. The structure forces attention to realistic requirements of personnel, hardware, and budgets. Use of the structure provides a powerful framework for project control that identifies deviations from the plan, identifies responsibility, and spots areas for improved performance. No well-developed project plan or control system is possible without a disciplined, structured approach. The WBS, OBS, and cost account codes provide this discipline. The WBS serves as the database for developing the project network, which establishes the timing of work, people, equipment, and costs.

The PBS is often used for process-based projects with ill-defined deliverables. In small projects responsibility matrices may be used to clarify individual responsibility.

Clearly defining your project is the first and most important step in planning. The absence of a clearly defined project plan consistently shows up as the major reason for project failures. Whether you use a WBS, PBS, or responsibility matrix will depend primarily on the size and nature of your project. Whatever method you use, definition of your project should be adequate to allow for good control as the project is being implemented. Follow-up with a clear communication plan for coordinating and tracking project progress will help you keep important stakeholders informed and avoid some potential problems.

Key Terms

Acceptance criteria, *110*
Cost account, *118*
Gold plating, *111*
Milestone, *107*
Organization breakdown structure (OBS), *118*
Priority matrix, *112*

Process breakdown structure (PBS), *121*
Product scope description, *107*
Project charter, *110*
Responsibility matrix, *122*

Scope creep, *110*
Scope statement, *110*
WBS dictionary, *120*
Work breakdown structure (WBS), *113*
Work package, *116*

Review Questions

1. What are the eight elements of a typical scope statement?
2. What questions does a project objective answer? What would be an example of a good project objective?
3. What does it mean if the priorities of a project include Time-constrain, Scope-accept, and Cost-enhance?
4. What kinds of information are included in a work package?
5. When would it be appropriate to create a responsibility matrix rather than a full-blown WBS?
6. How does a communication plan benefit the management of projects?

DISCUSSION QUESTIONS

4.1 *Big Bertha ERC II versus the USGA's COR Requirement*
1. How did Helmstetter's vision conflict with USGA rules?
2. How could this mistake have been avoided?

4.3 *Creating a WBS*
1. Why is it important that final activities not be open-ended?

128 Chapter 4   *Defining the Project*

Exercises

1. You are in charge of organizing a dinner-dance concert for a local charity. You have reserved a hall that will seat 30 couples and have hired a jazz combo.
   a. Develop a scope statement for this project that contains examples of all the elements. Assume that the event will occur in four weeks. Provide your best estimate of the dates for milestones.
   b. What would the priorities likely be for this project?
2. In small groups, identify real-life examples of a project that would fit each of the following priority scenarios:
   a. Time-constrain, Scope-enhance, Cost-accept
   b. Time-accept, Scope-constrain, Cost-accept
   c. Time-constrain, Scope-accept, Cost-enhance
3. Develop a WBS for a project in which you are going to build a bicycle. Try to identify all of the major components and provide three levels of detail.
4. You are the father or mother of a family of four (kids ages 13 and 15) planning a weekend camping trip. Develop a responsibility matrix for the work that needs to be done prior to starting your trip.
5. Develop a WBS for a local stage play. Be sure to identify the deliverables and organization units (people) responsible. How would you code your system? Give an example of the work packages in one of your cost accounts. Develop a corresponding OBS that identifies who is responsible for what.
6. Use an example of a project you are familiar with or are interested in. Identify the deliverables and organization units (people) responsible. How would you code your system? Give an example of the work packages in one of your cost accounts.
7. Develop a communication plan for an airport security project. The project entails installing the hardware and software system that (1) scans a passenger's eyes, (2) fingerprints the passenger, and (3) transmits the information to a central location for evaluation.
8. Go to an Internet search engine (e.g., Google) and type in "project communication plan." Check three or four results that have ".gov" as their source. How are they similar or dissimilar? What would be your conclusion concerning the importance of an internal communication plan?
9. Your roommate is about to submit a scope statement for a spring concert sponsored by the entertainment council at Western Evergreen State University (WESU). WESU is a residential university with over 22,000 students. This will be the first time in six years that WESU has sponsored a spring concert. The entertainment council has budgeted $40,000 for the project. The event is to occur on June 5. Since your roommate knows you are taking a class on project management she has asked you to review her scope statement and make suggestions for improvement. She considers the concert a resume-building experience and wants to be as professional as possible. Following is a draft of her scope statement. What suggestions would you make and why?

WESU Spring Music Concert

Project Objective
To organize and deliver a 6-hour music concert

Product Scope Description
An all-age, outdoor rock concert

Justification

Provide entertainment to WESU community and enhance WESU's reputation as a destination university

Deliverables

- Concert security
- Contact local newspapers and radio stations
- Separate beer garden
- Six hours of musical entertainment
- Design a commemorative concert T-shirt
- Local sponsors
- Food venues
- Event insurance
- Safe environment

Milestones

1. Secure all permissions and approvals
2. Sign big-name artist
3. Contact secondary artists
4. Secure vendor contracts
5. Advertising campaign
6. Plan set-up
7. Concert
8. Clean-up

Technical Requirements

1. Professional sound stage and system
2. At least five performing acts
3. Restroom facilities
4. Parking
5. Compliance with WESU and city requirements/ordinances

Limits and Exclusions

- Seating capacity for 8,000 students
- Performers are responsible for travel arrangement to and from WESU
- Performers must provide own liability insurance
- Performers and security personnel will be provided lunch and dinner on the day of the concert
- Vendors contribute 25 percent of sales to concert fund
- Concert must be over at 12:15 a.m.

Customer Review: WESU

References

Ashley, D. B., et al., "Determinants of Construction Project Success," *Project Management Journal,* vol. 18, no. 2 (June 1987), p. 72.

Chilmeran, A. H., "Keeping Costs on Track," *PM Network,* 2004 pp. 45–51.

Gary, L., "Will Project Scope Cost You—or Create Value?" *Harvard Management Update,* January 2005.

Gobeli, D. H., and E. W. Larson, "Project Management Problems," *Engineering Management Journal,* vol. 2 (1990), pp. 31–36.

Ingebretsen, M., "Taming the Beast," *PM Network,* July 2003, pp. 30–35.

Katz, D. M., "Case Study: Beware 'Scope Creep' on ERP Projects," CFO.com, March 27, 2001.

Kerzner, H., *Project Management: A Systems Approach to Planning,* 8th ed. (New York: Van Nostrand Reinhold, 2003).

Luby, R. E., D. Peel, and W. Swahl, "Component-Based Work Breakdown Structure," *Project Management Journal,* vol. 26, no. 2 (December 1995), pp. 38–44.

Murch, R., *Project Management: Best Practices for IT Professionals* (Upper Darby, NJ: Prentice Hall, 2001).

Pinto, J. K., and D. P. Slevin, "Critical Success Factors across the Project Life Cycle," *Project Management Journal,* vol. 19, no. 3 (June 1988), p. 72.

Pitagorsky, G., "Realistic Project Planning Promotes Success," *Engineer's Digest,* vol. 29, no. 1 (2001).

PMI Standards Committee, *Guide to the Project Management Body of Knowledge* (Newton Square, PA: Project Management Institute, 2017).

Posner, B. Z., "What It Takes to Be a Good Project Manager," *Project Management Journal,* vol. 18, no. 1 (March 1987), p. 52.

Raz, T., and S. Globerson, "Effective Sizing and Content Definition of Work Packages," *Project Management Journal,* vol. 29, no. 4 (1998), pp. 17–23.

The Standish Group, *CHAOS Summary 2009,* pp. 1–4.

Tate, K., and K. Hendrix, "Chartering IT Projects," *Proceedings, 30th Annual, Project Management Institute* (Philadelphia: Project Management Institute, 1999), CD.

Case 4.1

Celebration of Colors 5K

Brandon was having an ale with his girlfriend, Sierra, when the subject of the Omega Theta Pi 5K-run project came up. Brandon has been chosen to chair the 5K-charity run for his fraternity. At the time, Brandon thought it would look good on his resume and wouldn't be too difficult to pull off. This would be the first running event Omega Theta Pi had organized. In the past Delta Tau Chi always organized the spring running event. However, Delta Tau had been dissolved after a highly publicized hazing scandal.

Brandon and his brothers at Omega Theta Pi thought that organizing a 5K-run would be a lot more fun and profitable than the normal spring cleaning service they offered the local community. Early on in the discussions, everyone agreed that partnering with a sorority would be an advantage. Not only would they help manage the event, but they would have useful contacts to recruit sponsors and participants. Brandon pitched the fund raising idea to the sisters at Delta Nu, and they agreed to co-manage the event. Olivia Pomerleau volunteered and was named co-chair by Delta Nu.

Brandon told Sierra about the task force's first meeting, which was held last night and included five members from each living group. Olivia and Brandon tried, but failed, to meet beforehand due to scheduling conflicts. The meeting began with the attendees introducing themselves and telling what experience they had had with running events. Only one person had not run at past events, but no one had been involved in managing an event other than volunteering as intersection flaggers.

Olivia then said she thought the first thing they should decide on was the theme of the 5K-race. Brandon hadn't thought much about this, but everyone agreed that the race had to have a theme. People began to suggest themes and ideas based on other runs they knew about. The group seemed stumped when Olivia said, "Do you know that the last Friday in March is a full moon? In India, *Holi,* the celebration of colors, occurs on the last full moon in March. Maybe you've seen pictures of this, but this is where people go crazy tossing dye and color water balloons at each other. I looked it up and the Holi festival signifies a victory of good over evil, the arrival of spring and the end of winter. It is a day to meet others, play, laugh, and forgive and forget. I think it would be neat if we organized our 5K-run as a Holi festival. At different points in the race we would have people toss dye on runners. The run would end with a giant water balloon fight. We could even see if Evergreen [the local Indian restaurant] would cater the event!"

Brandon and the other boys looked at each other, while the girls immediately supported the idea. The deal maker occurred when Olivia showed a YouTube video of a similar event last year at a university in Canada that had over 700 participants and raised over $14,000.

Once the theme was decided the discussion turned into a free-for-all of ideas and suggestions. One member said she may know an artist who could create really neat T-shirts for the event. Others wondered where you get the dye and if it is safe. Another talked about the importance of a website and creating a digital account for registration. Others began to argue whether the run should be done on campus or through the streets of their small college town. One by one students excused themselves due to other commitments. With only a few members remaining Brandon and Olivia adjourned the meeting.

While Brandon took a sip of his IPA beer, Sierra pulled a book out of her knapsack. "Sounds like what you need to do is create what my project management professor calls a WBS for your project." She pointed to a page in her project management textbook showing a diagram of a WBS.

1. Make a list of the major deliverables for the 5k-run color project and use them to develop a draft of the work breakdown structure for the project that contains, when appropriate, at least three levels of detail.

2. How would developing a WBS alleviate some of the problems that occurred during the first meeting and help Brandon organize and plan the project?

 Case 4.2

The Home Improvement Project

Lukas Nelson and his wife, Anne, and their three daughters had been living in their house for over five years when they decided it was time to make some modest improvements. One area they both agreed needed an upgrade was the bathtub. Their current house had one standard shower/bathtub combination. Lukas was 6 feet four and could barely squeeze into it. In fact, he had taken only one bath since they moved in. He and Anne both missed soaking in the older, deep bathtubs they enjoyed when they lived back East.

Fortunately, the previous owners, who had built the house, had plumbed the corner of a large exercise room in the basement for a hot tub. They contacted a trusted remodeling contractor, who assured them it would be relatively easy to install a new bathtub and it shouldn't cost more than $1,500. They decided to go ahead with the project.

First the Nelsons went to the local plumbing retailer to pick out a tub. They soon realized that for a few hundred dollars more they could buy a big tub with water jets (a Jacuzzi). With old age on the horizon a Jacuzzi seemed like a luxury that was worth the extra money.

Originally the plan was to install the tub using the simple plastic frame the bath came with and install a splash guard around the tub. Once Anne saw the tub, frame, and splashguard in the room she balked. She did not like how it looked with the cedar paneling in the exercise room. After significant debate, Anne won out, and the Nelsons agreed to pay extra to have a cedar frame built for the tub and use attractive tile instead of the plastic splashguard. Lukas rationalized that the changes would pay for themselves when they tried to sell the house.

The next hiccup occurred when it came time to address the flooring issue. The exercise room was carpeted, which wasn't ideal when getting out of a bathtub. The original idea was to install relatively cheap laminated flooring in the drying and undressing area adjacent to the tub. However, the Nelsons couldn't agree on the pattern to use. One of Anne's friends said it would be a shame to put such cheap flooring in such a nice room. She felt they should consider using tile. The contractor agreed and said he knew a tile installer who needed work and would give them a good deal.

Lukas reluctantly agreed that the laminated options just didn't fit the style or quality of the exercise room. Unlike the laminated floor debate, both Anne and Lukas immediately liked a tile pattern that matched the tile used around the tub. Anxious not to delay the project, they agreed to pay for the tile flooring.

Once the tub was installed and the framing was almost completed, Anne realized that something had to be done about the lighting. One of her favorite things to do was to read while soaking in the tub. The existing lights didn't provide sufficient illumination for doing so. Lukas knew this was "nonnegotiable" and they hired an electrician to install additional lighting over the bathtub.

While the lighting was being installed and the tile was being laid, another issue came up. The original plan was to tile only the exercise room and use remnant rugs to cover the area away from the tub where the Nelsons did their exercises. The Nelsons were very happy with how the tile looked and fit with the overall room. However, it clashed with the laminated flooring in the adjacent bathroom. Lukas agreed with Anne that it really made the adjacent bathroom look cheap and ugly. He also felt the bathroom was so small it wouldn't cost much more.

After a week the work was completed. Both Lukas and Anne were quite pleased with how everything turned out. It cost much more than they had planned, but they planned to live in the house until the girls graduated from college, so they felt it was a good long-term investment.

Anne had the first turn using the bathtub, followed by their three girls. Everyone enjoyed the Jacuzzi. It was 10:00 p.m. when Lukas began running water for his first bath. At first the water was steaming hot, but by the time he was about to get in, it was lukewarm at best. Lukas groaned, "After paying all of that money I still can't enjoy a bath."

The Nelsons rationed bathing for a couple weeks, until they decided to find out what, if anything, could be done about the hot water problem. They asked a reputable heating contractor to assess the situation. The contractor reported that the hot water tank was insufficient to service a family of five. This had not been discovered before because baths were rarely taken in the past. The contractor said it would cost $2,200 to replace the existing water heater with a larger one that would meet their needs. The heating contractor also said if they wanted to do it right they should replace the existing furnace with a more energy-efficient one. A new furnace would not only heat the house but also indirectly heat the water tank. Such a furnace would cost $7,500, but with the improved efficiency and savings in the gas bill, the furnace would pay for itself in 10 years. Besides, the Nelsons would likely receive tax credits for the more fuel-efficient furnace.

Three weeks later, after the new furnace was installed, Lukas settled into the new bathtub. He looked around the room at all the changes that had been made and muttered to himself, "And to think that all I wanted was to soak in a nice, hot bath."

1. What factors and forces contributed to scope creep in this case?
2. Is this an example of good or bad scope creep? Explain.
3. How could scope creep have been better managed by the Nelsons?

CHAPTER FIVE

5 Estimating Project Times and Costs

LEARNING OBJECTIVES

After reading this chapter you should be able to:

5-1   Understand estimating project times and costs is the foundation for project planning and control.

5-2   Describe guidelines for estimating time, costs, and resources.

5-3   Describe the methods, uses, and advantages and disadvantages of top-down and bottom-up estimating methods.

5-4   Distinguish different kinds of costs associated with a project.

5-5   Suggest a scheme for developing an estimating database for future projects.

5-6   Understand the challenge of estimating mega projects and describe steps that lead to better informed decisions.

5-7   Define a "white elephant" in project management and provide examples.

A5-1 Use learning curves to improve task estimates.

OUTLINE

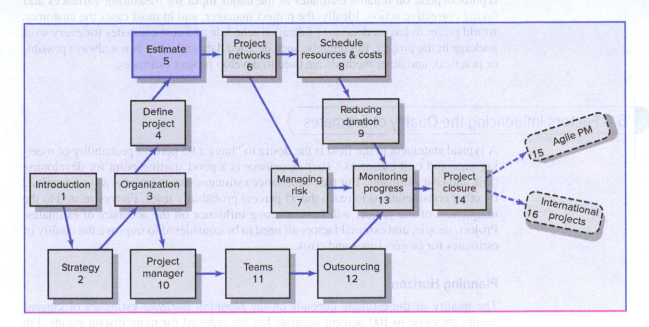

Plans are of little importance, but planning is essential.
— Winston Churchill, former British prime minister

Understand estimating project times and costs is the foundation for project planning and control.

Estimating is the process of forecasting or approximating the time and cost of completing project deliverables. Estimating processes are frequently classified as top-down and bottom-up. Top-down estimates are usually done by senior management. Management will often derive estimates from analogy, group consensus, or mathematical relationships. Bottom-up estimates are typically performed by the people who are doing the work. Their estimates are based on estimates of elements found in the work breakdown structure. Exhibit 5.1 summarizes some of the key reasons for estimating.

All project stakeholders prefer accurate cost and time estimates, but they also understand the inherent uncertainty in all projects. Inaccurate estimates lead to false expectations and consumer dissatisfaction. Accuracy is improved with greater effort, but is it worth the time and cost? Estimating costs money! Project estimating becomes a trade-off, balancing the benefits of better accuracy against the costs for securing increased accuracy.

136   Chapter 5   *Estimating Project Times and Costs*

- Estimates are needed to support good decisions.
- Estimates are needed to schedule work.
- Estimates are needed to determine how long the project should take and its cost.
- Estimates are needed to determine whether the project is worth doing.
- Estimates are needed to develop cash flow needs.
- Estimates are needed to determine how well the project is progressing.

Cost, time, and budget estimates are the lifeline for control; they serve as the standard for comparison of actual and plan throughout the life of the project. Project status reports depend on reliable estimates as the major input for measuring variances and taking corrective action. Ideally, the project manager, and in most cases the customer, would prefer to have a database of detailed schedule and cost estimates for every work package in the project. Regrettably, such detailed data gathering is not always possible or practical, and other methods are used to develop project estimates.

5.1 Factors Influencing the Quality of Estimates

A typical statement in the field is the desire to "have a 95 percent probability of meeting time and cost estimates." *Past experience* is a good starting point for developing time and cost estimates. But past experience estimates must almost always be refined by other considerations to reach the 95 percent probability level. Factors related to the uniqueness of the project will have a strong influence on the accuracy of estimates. Project, people, and external factors all need to be considered to improve the quality of estimates for project times and costs.

Planning Horizon

The quality of the estimate depends on the *planning horizon;* estimates of current events are close to 100 percent accurate but are reduced for more distant events. For example, cost estimates for a party you are organizing this weekend should be much more accurate than the estimates for a party that will take place in six months. Now imagine how difficult it would be to estimate the total cost of a four-year transportation project. The accuracy of time and cost estimates should improve as you move from the conceptual phase to the point where individual work packages are defined.

Project Complexity

Time to implement new *technology* has a habit of expanding in an increasing, nonlinear fashion. Sometimes poorly written scope specifications for new technology result in errors in estimating times and costs.

People

The *people* factor can influence the quality of time and cost estimates. For example, accuracy of estimates depends on the skills of the people making the estimates. How familiar are they with the task they are estimating?

Project Structure and Organization

Which *project structure* is chosen to manage the project will influence time and cost estimates. One of the major advantages of a dedicated project team is the speed gained from concentrated focus and localized project decisions. This speed comes at an additional cost of tying up personnel full time. Conversely, projects operating in a matrix environment may reduce costs by more efficiently sharing personnel across projects but may take longer to complete, since attention is divided and coordination demands are higher.

Padding Estimates

In some cases people are inclined to *pad estimates*. For example, if you are asked how long it takes you to drive to the airport, you might give an average time of 30 minutes, assuming a 50/50 chance of getting there in 30 minutes. If you are asked the fastest you could possibly get there, you might reduce the driving time to 20 minutes. Finally, if you are asked how long the drive would take if you absolutely had to be there to meet with the president, it is likely you would increase the estimate to, say, 50 minutes to ensure not being late.

In work situations where we are asked for time and cost estimates, most of us are inclined to add a little padding to reduce the risk of being late. If everyone at all levels of the project adds a little padding to reduce risk, the project duration and cost are seriously overstated. This phenomenon causes some managers or owners to call for a 10–15 percent cut in time and/or cost for the project. Of course, the next time the game is played, the person estimating cost and/or time will pad the estimate to 20 percent or more. Clearly such games defeat chances for realistic estimates, which is what is needed to be competitive.

Organizational Culture

Organizational culture can significantly influence project estimates. In some organizations padding estimates is tolerated and even privately encouraged. Other organizations place a premium on accuracy and strongly discourage estimating gamesmanship. Organizations vary in the importance they attach to estimates. The prevailing belief in some organizations is that detailed estimating takes too much time and is not worth the effort or that it's impossible to predict the future. Other organizations subscribe to the belief that accurate estimates are the bedrock of effective project management. Organizational culture shapes every dimension of project management; estimating is not immune to this influence.

Other Factors

Finally, *nonproject factors* can impact time and cost estimates. For example, equipment down-time can alter time estimates. National holidays, vacations, and legal limits can influence project estimates. Project priority can influence resource assignment and impact time and cost.

Project estimating is a complex process. The quality of time and cost estimates can be improved when these variables are considered in making the estimates. Estimates of time and cost together allow the manager to develop a time-phased budget, which is imperative for project control. Before discussing macro and micro estimating methods for times and costs, a review of estimating guidelines will remind us of some of the important "rules of the game" that can improve estimating.

5.2 Estimating Guidelines for Times, Costs, and Resources

LO 5-2

Describe guidelines for estimating time, costs, and resources.

Managers recognize time, cost, and resource estimates must be accurate if project planning, scheduling, and controlling are to be effective. However, there is substantial evidence suggesting poor estimates are a major contributor to projects that have failed. Therefore, every effort should be made to see that initial estimates are as accurate as possible, since the choice of no estimates leaves a great deal to luck and is not palatable to serious project managers. Even though a project has never been done before, a manager can follow seven guidelines to develop useful work package estimates.

1. **Responsibility.** At the work package level, estimates should be made by the person(s) most familiar with the task. Draw on their expertise! Except for supertechnical tasks, those responsible for getting the job done on schedule and within budget are usually first-line supervisors or technicians who are experienced and familiar with the type of work involved. These people will not have some preconceived, imposed duration for a deliverable in mind. They will give an estimate based on experience and best judgment. A secondary benefit of using those responsible is the hope they will "buy in" to seeing that the estimate materializes when they implement the work package. If those involved are not consulted, it will be difficult to hold them responsible for failure to achieve the estimated time. Finally, drawing on the expertise of team members who will be responsible helps to build communication channels early.

2. **The use of several people to estimate.** It is well known that a cost or time estimate usually has a better chance of being reasonable and realistic when several people with relevant experience and/or knowledge of the task are used (sometimes called "crowdsourcing"). True, people bring different biases based on their experience. But discussion of the individual differences in their estimate leads to consensus and tends to eliminate extreme estimate errors.

3. **Normal conditions.** When task time, cost, and resource estimates are determined, they are based on certain assumptions. *Estimates should be based on normal conditions, efficient methods, and a normal level of resources.* Normal conditions are sometimes difficult to discern, but it is necessary to have a consensus in the organization as to what normal conditions mean in this project. If the normal workday is eight hours, the time estimate should be based on an eight-hour day. Similarly, if the normal workday is two shifts, the time estimate should be based on a two-shift workday. Any time estimate should reflect efficient methods for the resources normally available. The time estimate should represent the normal level of resources—people or equipment. For example, if three programmers are available for coding or two road graders are available for road construction, time and cost estimates should be based on these normal levels of resources unless it is anticipated the project will change what is currently viewed as "normal." In addition, possible conflicts in demand for resources on parallel or concurrent activities should not be considered at this stage. The need for adding resources will be examined when resource scheduling is discussed in a later chapter.

4. **Time units.** Specific time units to use should be selected early in the development phase of the project network. *All task time estimates need consistent time units.* Estimates of time must consider whether normal time is represented by calendar days, workdays, workweeks, person days, single shift, hours, minutes, etc. In practice the use of workdays is the dominant choice for expressing task duration. However, in projects such as a heart transplant operation, minutes probably would be

more appropriate as a time unit. One such project that used minutes as the time unit was the movement of patients from an old hospital to an elegant new one across town. Since there were several life-endangering moves, minutes were used to ensure patient safety so that proper emergency life-support systems would be available if needed. The point is, network analysis requires a standard unit of time. When computer programs allow more than one option, some notation should be made of any variance from the standard unit of time. If the standard unit of time is a five-day workweek and the estimated activity duration is in calendar days, it must be converted to the normal workweek.

5. **Independence.** Estimators should treat each task as independent of other tasks that might be integrated by the WBS. Use of first-line managers usually results in considering tasks independently; this is good. Top managers are prone to aggregate many tasks into one time estimate and then deductively make the individual task time estimates add to the total. If tasks are in a chain and performed by the same group or department, it is best not to ask for all the time estimates in the sequence at once to avoid the tendency for a planner or a supervisor to look at the whole path and try to adjust individual task times in the sequence to meet an arbitrary imposed schedule or some rough "guesstimate" of the total time for the whole path or segment of the project. This tendency does not reflect the uncertainties of individual activities and generally results in optimistic task time estimates. In summary, each task time estimate should be considered independently of other activities.

6. **Contingencies.** *Work package estimates should not include allowances for contingencies.* The estimate should assume normal or average conditions, even though every work package will not materialize as planned. For this reason top management needs to create an extra fund for contingencies that can be used to cover unforeseen events.

7. **Risk assessment added to the estimate to avoid surprises to stakeholders.** It is obvious some tasks carry more time and cost risks than others. For example, a new technology usually carries more time and cost risks than a proven process. Simply identifying the degree of risk lets stakeholders consider alternative methods and alter process decisions. A simple breakdown by optimistic, most likely, and pessimistic for task time could provide valuable information regarding time and cost. See Chapter 7 for further discussion of project risk.

Where applicable, these guidelines will greatly help to avoid many of the pitfalls found so often in practice.

5.3 Top-Down versus Bottom-Up Estimating

LO 5-3

Describe the methods, uses, and advantages and disadvantages of top-down and bottom-up estimating methods.

Since estimating efforts cost money, the time and detail devoted to estimating are important decisions. Yet when estimating is considered, you as a project manager may hear statements such as these:

Rough order of magnitude is good enough. Spending time on detailed estimating wastes money.

Time is everything; our survival depends on getting there first! Time and cost accuracy is not an issue.

The project is internal. We don't need to worry about cost.

The project is so small, we don't need to bother with estimates. Just do it.

140   Chapter 5   *Estimating Project Times and Costs*

TABLE 5.1

Conditions for Preferring Top-Down or Bottom-Up Time and Cost Estimates

Condition	Top-Down Estimates	Bottom-Up Estimates
Strategic decision making	X	
Cost and time important		X
High uncertainty	X	
Internal, small project	X	
Fixed-price contract		X
Customer wants details		X
Unstable scope	X	

However, there are sound reasons for using top-down or bottom-up estimates. Table 5.1 depicts conditions that suggest when one approach is preferred over another.

Top-down estimates usually are derived from someone who uses experience and/ or information to determine the project duration and total cost. However, these estimates are sometimes made by top managers who have very little knowledge of the component activities used to complete the project. For example, a mayor of a major city making a speech noted that a new law building would be constructed at a cost of $23 million and would be ready for occupancy in two and one-half years. Although the mayor probably asked for an estimate from someone, the estimate could have come from a luncheon meeting with a local contractor who wrote an estimate (guesstimate) on a napkin. This is an extreme example, but in a relative sense this scenario is frequently played out in practice. See Snapshot from Practice 5.1: Portland Aerial Tram for another example of this. The question actually is, do these estimates represent low-cost, efficient methods? Seldom. The fact that the estimate came from the top can influence people responsible to "do what it takes to make the estimate."

If possible and practical, you want to push the estimating process down to the work package level for **bottom-up estimates** that establish low-cost, efficient methods. This process can take place after the project has been defined in detail. Good sense suggests project estimates should come from the people most knowledgeable about the estimate needed. The use of several people with relevant experience with the task can improve the time and cost estimate. The bottom-up approach at the work package level can serve as a check on cost elements in the WBS by rolling up the work packages and associated cost accounts to major deliverables. Similarly, resource requirements can be checked. Later, the time, resource, and cost estimates from the work packages can be consolidated into time-phased networks, resource schedules, and budgets that are used for control.

The bottom-up approach also provides the customer with an opportunity to compare the low-cost, efficient method approach with any imposed restrictions. For example, if the project completion duration is imposed at two years and your bottom-up analysis tells you the project will take two and one-half years, the client can now consider the trade-off of the low-cost method versus compressing the project to two years—or in rare cases canceling the project. Similar trade-offs can be compared for different levels of resources or increases in technical performance. The assumption is any movement away from the low-cost, efficient method will increase costs—e.g., overtime. The preferred approach in defining the project is to make rough top-down estimates, develop the WBS/OBS, make bottom-up estimates, develop schedules and budgets, and reconcile differences between top-down and bottom-up estimates. These steps should be done *before* final negotiation with either an internal or external customer.

SNAPSHOT FROM PRACTICE 5.1   Portland Aerial Tram*

The Portland Tram is an aerial tramway in Portland, Oregon. The tram carries passengers between the city's south waterfront and the main Oregon Health & Science University (OHSU) campus, which is located high on a bluff overlooking the waterfront. The tram ride takes four minutes and rises over 500 feet. The tram was jointly funded by OHSU, the city of Portland, and south waterfront property owners.

OHSU was the driving force behind the project. OHSU argued that the tram was needed so it could expand its operations to the south waterfront, where there were plans to build several major facilities. The tram would also reduce traffic congestions and make it easier for OHSU employees to commute to work. OHSU is a major player in the Oregon economy, with an estimated annual economic impact of over $4 billion and over 35,000 jobs.

The OHSU tram would be one of only two city trams in the United States, and advocates championed the idea that the tram would become an icon for the city like Seattle's Space Needle.

OHSU political clout helped gain approval by the Portland city council for the project in 2003. The initial cost estimate was $15 million, with the city directly responsible for $2 million. A public review in 2004 revealed a new cost estimate of $18.5 million. A second review in 2005 led to a cost readjustment of $40 million with a construction delay of six months.

In 2006 a change in city leadership led to an independent audit being conducted on the tram project. The audit revealed that OSHU managers knew as early as 2003 that the cost of the tram would be in excess of $15.5 million but withheld the information from city officials.

Public reaction was immediate and harsh. City Commissioner Randy Leonard accused the OHSU leadership of an "outrageous shell game . . . all at the expense of taxpayers." The city of Portland threatened to pull out of the project. OHSU protested vigorously, threatening a lawsuit, should the tram be canceled. Negotiations ensued.

Rigucci/Shutterstock

A revised funding plan and budget were agreed upon in April 2006, by a 3–2 vote of the city council. This plan required concessions from all parties involved and called for a final budget of $57 million, with direct contributions from the city of $8.5 million, or nearly 15 percent of the overall budget. This final budget was met, and the tram was opened to the public January 27, 2007.

Budget concerns were not the only problem facing the tram project. Many residents in the neighborhood beneath the tram were concerned that the tram would be an invasion of privacy and lead to lower property values. The residents were promised that the overhead power lines would be buried, but as a cost saving measure the plans were scrapped. One irate homeowner living below the track placed a sign on his backyard fence stating "F%&! The Tram." The sign was not visible from the street, only from the air. Lawsuits ensued.

The city ultimately negotiated with each resident living under the tramway and offered fair market value for their homes.

* R. Gragg and A. Scott, "From Controversy to Icon: Portland's Aerial Tram Turns 10," *Oregon Broadcasting Network*, February 12, 2017, www.opb.org/radio/. Accessed 2/14/19; S. Moore, "Audit: Tram Costs Shoot Skyward—Again," *Portland Mercury*, www.portlandmercury.com, February 2, 2006. Accessed 2/20/19; E. Njus, "Portland Aerial Tram Marks Its 10th Anniversary," *Oregonian*, www.oregon live.com. Accessed 2/2/19.

In conclusion, the ideal approach is for the project manager to allow enough time for both the top-down and bottom-up estimates to be worked out so that a complete plan based on reliable estimates can be offered to the customer. In this way false expectations are minimized for all stakeholders and negotiation is reduced.

5.4 Methods for Estimating Project Times and Costs

Top-Down Approaches for Estimating Project Times and Costs

At the strategic level, top-down estimating methods are used to evaluate the project proposal. Sometimes much of the information needed to derive accurate time and cost estimates is not available in the initial phase of the project—for example, design is not finalized. In these situations top-down estimates are used until the tasks in the WBS are clearly defined.

Consensus Method

This method simply uses the pooled experience of senior and/or middle managers to estimate the total project duration and cost. It typically involves a meeting where experts discuss, argue, and ultimately reach a decision as to their best guesstimate. Firms seeking greater rigor will use the Delphi Method to make these macro estimates. See Snapshot from Practice 5.2: The Delphi Method.

SNAPSHOT FROM PRACTICE 5.2   The Delphi Method

Originally developed by the RAND Corporation in 1969 for technological forecasting, the **Delphi Method** is a group decision process about the likelihood that certain events will occur. The Delphi Method makes use of a panel of experts familiar with the kind of project in question. The notion is that well-informed individuals, calling on their insights and experience, are better equipped to estimate project costs/times than theoretical approaches or statistical methods. Their responses to estimate questionnaires are anonymous, and they are provided with a summary of opinions.

Experts are then encouraged to reconsider, and if appropriate, to change their previous estimate in light of the replies of other experts. After two or three rounds it is believed that the group will converge toward the "best" response through this consensus process. The midpoint of responses is statistically categorized by the median score. In each succeeding round of questionnaires, the range of responses by the panelists will presumably decrease and the median will move toward what is deemed to be the "correct" estimate.

A movie exec would use the Delphi Method to decide whether to invest in the remaking of a classic film, like *Gunga Din*.[1] He is concerned because both the screenwriter and director insist on shooting the film on location in Rajasthan, India. He recruits

five experts who have worked on film projects overseas, two recently in India. He provides each of them with a detailed summary proposal that describes the requirements as well as the 75-day shooting schedule. He asks them to respond to an estimating questionnaire concerning the costs of certain deliverables (e.g., accommodations, sets) as well as total operational costs, ignoring the lead actors' contracts. He is surprised by the disparity between those who have worked in India and the others. After several rounds, where opinions and ideas are exchanged, he has a fairly good idea of what the total costs are likely to be as well as the risks involved. When he combines this information with market research, he concludes that the project is not worth the investment.

One distinct advantage of the Delphi Method is that the experts never need to be brought together physically. The process also does not require complete agreement by all panelists, since the majority opinion is represented by the median. Since the responses are anonymous, the pitfalls of ego, domineering personalities, and the bandwagon or halo effect in responses are all avoided.

[1] *Gunga Din* is a 1939 adventure film that tells the tale of three British officers in Rajasthan, India, who, thanks to a water boy (Gunga Din), survive a rebel revolt.

It is important to recognize that these first top-down estimates are only a rough cut and typically occur in the "conceptual" stage of the project. The top-down estimates are helpful in initial development of a complete plan. However, such estimates are sometimes significantly off the mark because little detailed information is gathered. At this level individual work items are not identified. Or in a few cases the top-down estimates are not realistic because top management "wants the project." Nevertheless, the initial top-down estimates are helpful in determining whether the project warrants more formal planning, which would include more detailed estimates. Be careful that macro estimates made by senior managers are not dictated to lower-level managers who might feel compelled to accept the estimates even if they believe resources are inadequate.

Ratio Method

Top-down methods (sometimes called parametric) usually use ratios, or surrogates, to estimate project times or costs. Top-down **ratio methods** are often used in the concept, or "need," phase of a project to get an initial duration and cost estimate for the project. For example, contractors frequently use number of square feet to estimate the cost and time to build a house; that is, a house of 2,700 square feet might cost $160 per square foot (2,700 feet × $160 per square foot equals $432,000). Likewise, knowing the square feet and dollars per square foot, experience suggests it should take approximately 100 days to complete. Two other common examples of top-down cost estimates are the cost for a new plant estimated by capacity size and a software product estimated by features and complexity.

Apportion Method

This method is an extension to the ratio method. **Apportionment** is used when projects closely follow past projects in features and costs. Given good historical data, estimates can be made quickly with little effort and reasonable accuracy. This method is very common in projects that are relatively standard but have some small variation or customization.

Anyone who has borrowed money from a bank to build a house has been exposed to this process. Given an estimated total cost for the house, banks and the FHA (Federal Housing Authority) authorize pay to the contractor by completion of specific segments of the house. For example, foundation might represent 3 percent of the total loan, framing 25 percent, plumbing and heating 15 percent, etc. Payments are made as these items are completed. An analogous process is used by some companies that apportion costs to deliverables in the WBS—given average cost percentages from past projects. Figure 5.1 presents an example similar to one found in practice. Assuming the total project cost is estimated, using a top-down estimate, to be $500,000, the costs are apportioned as a percentage of the total cost. For example, the costs apportioned to the "Document" deliverable are 5 percent of the total, or $25,000. The subdeliverables "Doc-1 and Doc-2" are allocated 2 and 3 percent of the total—$10,000 and $15,000, respectively.

Function Point Methods for Software and System Projects

In the software industry, software development projects are frequently estimated using weighted macro variables called **function points** or major parameters such as number of inputs, number of outputs, number of inquiries, number of data files, and number of interfaces. These weighted variables are adjusted for a complexity factor and added. The total adjusted count provides the basis for estimating the labor effort and cost

FIGURE 5.1 **Apportion Method of Allocating Project Costs Using the Work Breakdown Structure**

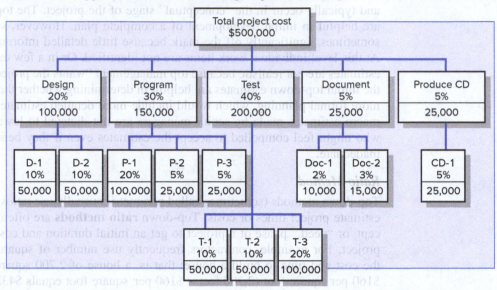

for a project (usually using a regression formula derived from data of past projects). This latter method assumes adequate historical data by type of software project for the industry—for example, MIS systems. In the U.S. software industry, one person-month represents on average five function points. A person working one month can generate on average (across all types of software projects) about five function points. Of course, each organization needs to develop its own average for its specific type of work. Such historical data provide a basis for estimating the project duration. Variations of this top-down approach are used by companies such as IBM, Bank of America, Sears Roebuck, HP, AT&T, Ford Motors, GE, DuPont, and many others. See Table 5.2 and Table 5.3 for a simplified example of function point count methodology.

From historical data the organization developed the weighting scheme for complexity found in Table 5.2. Function points are derived from multiplying the number of kinds of elements by weighted complexity.

Table 5.3 shows the data collected for a specific task or deliverable: Patient Admitting and Billing—the number of inputs, outputs, inquiries, files, and interfaces along with the expected complexity rating. Finally, the application of the element count is applied and the function point count total is 660. Given this count and the fact that 1 person-month has historically been equal to 5 function points, the job will require

TABLE 5.2
Simplified Basic Function Point Count Process for a Prospective Project or Deliverable

Element	Complexity Weighting			
	Low	Average	High	Total
Number of *inputs*	____ × 2 +	____ × 3 +	____ × 4	= ____
Number of *outputs*	____ × 3 +	____ × 6 +	____ × 9	= ____
Number of *inquiries*	____ × 2 +	____ × 4 +	____ × 6	= ____
Number of *files*	____ × 5 +	____ × 8 +	____ × 12	= ____
Number of *interfaces*	____ × 5 +	____ × 10 +	____ × 15	= ____

TABLE 5.3

Example: Function Point Count Method

Software Project 13: Patient Admitting and Billing			
15	Inputs	Rated complexity as low	(2)
5	Outputs	Rated complexity as average	(6)
10	Inquiries	Rated complexity as average	(4)
30	Files	Rated complexity as high	(12)
20	Interfaces	Rated complexity as average	(10)

Application of Complexity Factor					
Element	Count	Low	Average	High	Total
Inputs	15	× 2			= 30
Outputs	5		× 6		= 30
Inquiries	10		× 4		= 40
Files	30			× 12	= 360
Interfaces	20		× 10		= 200
				Total	660

132 person-months (660/5 = 132). Assuming you have 10 programmers who can work on this task, the duration would be approximately 13 months. The cost is easily derived by multiplying the labor rate per month times 132 person-months. For example, if the monthly programmer rate is $8,000, then the estimated cost would be $1,056,000 (132 × 8,000). Although function point metrics are useful, their accuracy depends on adequate historical data, the currency of the data, and the relevancy of the project/deliverable to past averages.

Learning Curves

Some projects require that the same task, group of tasks, or product be repeated several times. Managers know intuitively that the time to perform a task improves with repetition. This phenomenon is especially true of tasks that are labor intensive. In these circumstances the pattern of improvement phenomenon can be used to predict the reduction in time to perform the task. From empirical evidence across *all* industries, the pattern of this improvement has been quantified in the **learning curve** (also known as improvement curve, experience curve, and industrial progress curve), which is described by the following relationship:

Each time the output quantity doubles, the unit labor hours are reduced at a constant rate.

In practice the improvement ratio may vary from 60 percent, representing very large improvement, to 100 percent, representing no improvement at all. Generally as the difficulty of the work decreases the expected improvement also decreases and the improvement ratio that is used becomes greater. One significant factor to consider is the proportion of labor in the task in relation to machine-paced work. Obviously a lower percentage of improvement can occur only in operations with high labor content. Appendix 5.1 at the end of the chapter provides a detailed example of how the improvement phenomenon can be used to estimate time and cost for repetitive tasks.

The main disadvantage of top-down approaches to estimating is simply that the time and cost for a specific task are not considered. Grouping many tasks into a common basket encourages errors of omission and the use of imposed times and costs.

Micro, bottom-up estimating methods are usually more accurate than macro methods.

Bottom-Up Approaches for Estimating Project Times and Costs

Template Method

If the project is similar to past projects, then **template methods** can be used as a starting point for the new project. Templates are created based on the costs of previous, similar projects. Differences in the new project can be noted and past times and costs adjusted to reflect these differences. For example, a ship repair drydock firm has a set of standard repair projects (i.e., templates for overhaul, electrical, mechanical) that are used as starting points for estimating the cost and duration of any new project. Differences from the appropriate standardized project are noted (for times, costs, and resources) and changes are made. This approach enables the firm to develop a potential schedule, estimate costs, and develop a budget in a very short time span. Development of such templates in a database can quickly reduce estimate errors.

Parametric Procedures Applied to Specific Tasks

Just as parametric techniques such as cost per square foot can be the source of top-down estimates, the same technique can be applied to specific tasks. For example, as part of an MS Office conversion project, 36 different computer workstations needed to be converted. Based on past conversion projects, the project manager determined that on average one person could convert three workstations per day. Therefore the task of converting the 36 workstations would take three technicians four days [(36/3)/3]. Similarly, to estimate the wallpapering allowance on a house remodel, the contractor figured a cost of $5 per square yard of wallpaper and $2 per yard to install it, for a total cost of $7. By measuring the length and height of all the walls, she was able to calculate the total area in square yards and multiply it by $7.

Range Estimating

When do you use range estimating? **Range estimating** works best when work packages have significant uncertainty associated with the time or cost to complete. If the work package is routine and carries little uncertainty, using a person most familiar with the work package is usually the best approach. He is likely to know best how to estimate work packages durations and costs. However, when work packages have significant uncertainty associated with the time or cost to complete, it is a prudent policy to require three time estimates—low, average, and high (borrowed from PERT methodology that uses probability distributions). The low to high give a range within which the average estimate will fall. Determining the low and high estimates for the activity is influenced by factors such as complexity, technology, newness, and familiarity.

How do you get the estimates? Since range estimating works best for work packages that have significant uncertainty, having a group determine the low, average, and high cost or duration gives best results. Group estimating tends to refine extremes by bringing more evaluative judgments to the estimate and potential risks. The judgment of others in a group helps to moderate extreme perceived risks associated with a time or cost estimate. Involving others in making activity estimates gains buy-in and credibility to the estimate.

Figure 5.2 presents an abridged estimating template using three time estimates for work packages developed by a cross-functional group or groups of project stakeholders. The group estimates show the low, average, and high for each work package. The Risk Level column is the group's independent assessment of the degree of confidence that the actual time will be very close to the estimate. In a sense this number

FIGURE 5.2

Range Estimating Template

	A	B	C	D	E	F	G	H
1	Project number: 18				Project Manager: Dawn O'Connor			
2	Project description: New Organic Wine Launch				Date: 2/17/2xxx			
3			Organic Wine Launch Project					
4			Range Estimates					
5								
6	WBS	Description	Low	Average	High	Range	Risk	
7	ID		Estimate	Estimate	Estimate		Level	
8			Days	Days	Days	Days		
9								
10	102	Approval	1	1	3	2	low	
11	103	Design packaging	4	7	12	8	medium	
12	104	ID potential customers	14	21	35	21	high	
13	105	Design bottle logo	5	7	10	5	low	
14	106	Contract kiosk space	8	10	15	7	medium	
15	107	Construct kiosk	4	4	8	4	medium	
16	108	Design fair brochure	6	7	12	6	high	
17	109	Trade journal advertising	10	12	15	5	medium	
18	110	Production test	10	14	20	10	high	
19	111	Produce to inventory	5	5	10	5	high	
20	112	Business card scanner hookup	1	2	3	2	low	
21	113	Video hook up	2	2	4	2	medium	
22	114	Event rehearsal	2	2	5	3	high	

Source: Microsoft Excel

represents the group's evaluation of many factors (e.g., complexity, technology) that might impact the average time estimate. In our example, the group feels work packages 104, 108, 110, 111, and 114 have a high chance that the average time may vary from expected. Likewise, the group's confidence feels the risk of work packages 102, 105, and 112 not materializing as expected is low.

How do you use the estimate? Group range estimating gives the project manager and owner an opportunity to assess the confidence associated with project times (and/ or costs). For example, a contractor responsible for building a high-rise apartment building can tell the owner that the project will cost between $3.5 and $4.1 million and take between six and nine months to complete. The approach helps to reduce surprises as the project progresses. The range estimating method also provides a basis for assessing risk, managing resources, and determining the project contingency fund. (See Chapter 7 for a discussion of contingency funds.) Range estimating is popular in software and new product projects where up-front requirements are fuzzy and not well known. Group range estimating is often used with phase estimating, which is discussed next.

A Hybrid: Phase Estimating

This approach begins with a top-down estimate for the project and then refines estimates for phases of the project as it is implemented. Some projects by their nature cannot be rigorously defined because of the uncertainty of design or the final product. These projects are often found in aerospace projects, IT projects, new technology projects, and construction projects where design is incomplete. In these projects, phase or life-cycle estimating is frequently used.

Phase estimating is used when an unusual amount of uncertainty surrounds a project and it is impractical to estimate times and costs for the entire project. Phase estimating uses a two-estimate system over the life of the project. A detailed estimate is developed for the immediate phase and a macro estimate is made for the remaining phases of the project. Figure 5.3 depicts the phases of a project and the progression of estimates over its life.

148   Chapter 5   *Estimating Project Times and Costs*

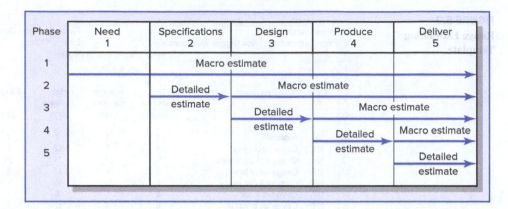

FIGURE 5.3

Phase Estimating over Project Life Cycle

For example, when the project need is determined, a macro estimate of the project cost and duration is made so analysis and decisions can be made. Simultaneously a detailed estimate is made for deriving project specifications and a macro estimate for the remainder of the project. As the project progresses and specifications are solidified, a detailed estimate for design is made and a macro estimate for the remainder of the project is computed. Clearly, as the project progresses through its life cycle and more information is available, the reliability of the estimates should be improving. See Snapshot from Practice 5.3: Estimate Accuracy.

Phase estimating is preferred by those working on projects where the final product is not known and the uncertainty is very large—for example, the development of reusable rockets or domestic robots. The commitment to cost and schedule is only necessary over the next phase of the project, and commitment to unrealistic future schedules and costs based on poor information is avoided. This progressive macro/micro method provides a stronger basis for using schedule and cost estimates to manage progress during the next phase.

SNAPSHOT FROM PRACTICE 5.3   Estimate Accuracy

The smaller the element of a work package, the more accurate the overall estimate is likely to be. The extent of this improvement varies by type of project. The following table is developed to reflect this observation. For example, information technology projects that determine their time and cost estimates in the conceptual stage can expect their "actuals" to err up to 200 percent over cost and duration and, perhaps, as much as 30 percent under estimates. Conversely, estimates for buildings, roads, and so on, made after the work packages are clearly defined, have a smaller error in actual costs and times of 15 percent over estimate and 5 percent less than estimate. Although these estimates vary by project, they can serve as ballpark numbers for project stakeholders selecting how project time and cost estimates will be derived.

Time and Cost Estimate Accuracy by Type of Project

	Bricks and Mortar	Information Technology
Conceptual stage	+60% to −30%	+200% to −30%
Deliverables defined	+30% to −15%	+100% to −15%
Work packages defined	+15% to − 5%	+ 50% to − 5%

FIGURE 5.4
Top-Down and
Bottom-Up Estimates

Top-Down Estimates	Bottom-Up Estimates
Intended Use	**Intended Use**
Feasibility/conceptual phase	Budgeting
Rough time/cost estimate	Scheduling
Fund requirements	Resource requirements
Resource capacity planning	Fund timing
Preparation Cost	**Preparation Cost**
1/10 to 3/10 of a percent of total project cost	3/10 of a percent to 1.0 percent of total project cost
Accuracy	**Accuracy**
Minus 20%, to plus 60%	Minus 10%, to plus 30%
Method	**Method**
Consensus	Template
Ratio	Parametric
Apportion	WBS packages
Function point	Range estimates
Learning curves	

Unfortunately, your customer—internal or external—will want an accurate estimate of schedule and cost the moment the decision is made to implement the project. Additionally, the customer who is paying for the project often perceives phase estimating as a blank check because costs and schedules are not firm over most of the project life cycle. Even though the reasons for phase estimating are sound and legitimate, most customers have to be sold on its legitimacy. A major advantage for the customer is the opportunity to change features, re-evaluate the project, or even cancel it in each new phase. In conclusion, phase estimating is very useful in projects that possess huge uncertainties concerning the final nature (shape, size, features) of the project.

See Figure 5.4 for a summary of the differences between top-down and bottom-up estimates.

Obtaining accurate estimates is a challenge. Committed organizations accept the challenge of coming up with meaningful estimates and invest heavily in developing their capacity to do so. Accurate estimates reduce uncertainty and support a discipline for effectively managing projects.

5.5 Level of Detail

Level of detail is different for different levels of management. At any level the detail should be no more than is necessary and sufficient. Top management interests usually center on the total project and major milestone events that mark major accomplishments—for example, "build oil platform in the north sea" or "complete prototype." Middle management might center on one segment of the project or one milestone. First-line managers' interests may be limited to one task or work package. One of the beauties of WBS is the ability to aggregate network information so each level of management can have the kind of information necessary to make decisions.

Getting the level of detail in the WBS to match management needs for effective implementation is crucial, but the delicate balance is difficult to find. See Snapshot from Practice 5.4: Level of Detail. The level of detail in the WBS varies with the

150   Chapter 5   *Estimating Project Times and Costs*

complexity of the project; the need for control; the project size, cost, and duration; and other factors. If the structure reflects excessive detail, there is a tendency to break the work effort into department assignments. This tendency can become a barrier to success, since the emphasis will be on departmental outcomes rather than on deliverable outcomes. Excessive detail also means more unproductive paperwork. Note that if the level of the WBS is increased by one, the number of cost accounts may increase geometrically. On the other hand, if the level of detail is not adequate, an organization unit may find the structure falls short of meeting its needs. Fortunately, the WBS has built-in flexibility. Participating organization units may expand their portion of the structure to meet their special needs. For example, the Engineering Department may wish to further break their work on a deliverable into smaller packages by electrical, civil, and mechanical. Similarly, the Marketing Department may wish to break their new product promotion into TV, radio, periodicals, and newspapers.

5.6 Types of Costs

LO 5-4

Distinguish different kinds of costs associated with a project.

Assuming work packages are defined, detailed cost estimates can be made. Here are typical kinds of costs found in a project:

1. Direct costs
   a. Labor   b. Materials
   c. Equipment   d. Other
2. Direct project overhead costs
3. General and administrative (G&A) overhead costs

The total project cost estimate is broken down in this fashion to sharpen the control process and improve decision making.

Direct Costs

These costs are clearly chargeable to a specific work package. **Direct costs** can be influenced by the project manager, project team, and individuals implementing the work package. These costs represent real cash outflows and must be paid as the project progresses; therefore, direct costs are usually separated from overhead costs. Lower-level project rollups frequently include only direct costs.

Direct Project Overhead Costs

Direct overhead rates more closely pinpoint which resources of the organization are being used in the project. Direct project **overhead costs** can be tied to project deliverables or work packages. Examples include the salary of the project manager and temporary rental space for the project team. Although overhead is not an immediate out-of-pocket expense, it is *real* and must be covered in the long run if the firm is to remain viable. These rates are usually a ratio of the dollar value of the resources used—e.g., direct labor, materials, equipment. For example, a direct labor burden rate of 20 percent would add a direct overhead charge of 20 percent to the direct labor cost estimate. A direct charge rate of 50 percent for materials would carry an additional 50 percent charge to the material cost estimate. Selective direct overhead charges provide a more accurate project (job or work package) cost than does using a blanket overhead rate for the whole project.

General and Administrative (G&A) Overhead Costs

These represent organization costs that are not directly linked to a specific project. They are carried for the duration of the project. Examples include organization costs across all products and projects such as advertising, accounting, and senior management above the project level. Allocation of G&A costs varies from organization to organization. However, G&A costs are usually allocated as a percent of total direct cost or a percent of the total of a specific direct cost such as labor, materials, or equipment.

Given the totals of direct and overhead costs for individual work packages, it is possible to cumulate the costs for any deliverable or for the entire project. A percentage can be added for profit if you are a contractor. A breakdown of costs for a proposed contract bid is presented in Figure 5.5.

Perceptions of costs and budgets vary depending on their users. The project manager must be very aware of these differences when setting up the project budget and when communicating these differences to others. Figure 5.6 depicts these different perceptions.

FIGURE 5.5
Contract Bid Summary Costs

Direct costs	$80,000
Direct overhead	$20,000
Total direct costs	$100,000
G&A overhead (20%)	$20,000
Total costs	$120,000
Profit (20%)	$24,000
Total bid	$144,000

152   Chapter 5   *Estimating Project Times and Costs*

FIGURE 5.6
Three Views of Cost

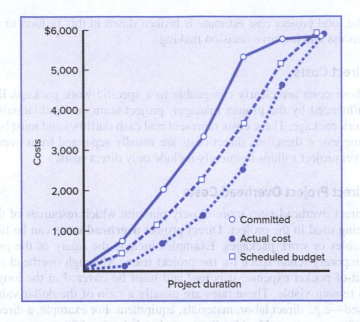

The project manager can commit costs months before the resource is used. This information is useful to the financial officer of the organization in forecasting future cash outflows. The project manager is interested in when the budgeted cost is expected to occur and when the budgeted cost actually is charged (earned); the respective timings of these two cost figures are used to measure project schedule and cost variances.

5.7 Refining Estimates

As described in Chapter 4, detailed work package estimates are aggregated and "rolled up" by deliverable to estimate the total direct cost of the project. Similarly, estimated durations are entered into the project network to establish the project schedule and determine the overall duration of the project. Experience tells us that for many projects the total estimates do not materialize and the actual costs and schedule of some projects significantly exceed original work package–based estimates. In order to compensate for the problem of actual cost and schedule exceeding estimates, some project managers adjust total costs by some multiplier (e.g., total estimated costs × 1.20).

The practice of adjusting original estimates by 20 percent or even 100 percent begs the question of why, after investing so much time and energy on detailed estimates, the numbers could be so far off. There are a number of reasons for this, most of which can be traced to the estimating process and the inherent uncertainty of predicting the future. Following are some of those reasons.

- **Interaction costs are hidden in estimates.** According to the guidelines, each task estimate is supposed to be done independently. However, tasks are rarely completed in a vacuum. Work on one task is dependent upon prior tasks, and the hand-offs between tasks require time and attention. For example, people working on prototype development need to interact with design engineers after the design is completed, whether to simply ask clarifying questions or to make adjustments in the original design. Similarly, the time necessary to coordinate activities is typically not reflected in independent estimates. Coordination is reflected in meetings and briefings as well as time necessary to resolve disconnects between tasks. Time, and therefore cost, devoted to managing interactions rises exponentially as the number of people and different disciplines involved increases on a project.

- **Normal conditions do not apply.** Estimates are supposed to be based on normal conditions. While this is a good starting point, it rarely holds true in real life, especially when it comes to the availability of resources. Resource shortages, whether in the form of people, equipment, or materials, can extend original estimates. For example, under normal conditions four bulldozers are typically used to clear a certain site size in five days, but the availability of only three bulldozers would extend the task duration to eight days. Similarly, the decision to outsource certain tasks can increase costs as well as extend task durations, since time is added to acclimating outsiders to the particulars of the project and the culture of the organization.

- **Things go wrong on projects.** Design flaws are revealed after the fact, extreme weather conditions occur, accidents happen, and so forth. Although you shouldn't plan for these risks to happen when estimating a particular task, the likelihood and impact of such events need to be considered.

- **Project scope and plans change.** As one gets further and further into the project, a manager obtains a better understanding of what needs to be done to accomplish the project. This may lead to major changes in project plans and costs. Likewise, if the project is a commercial project, changes often have to be made midstream to respond to new demands by the customer and/or competition. Unstable project scopes are a major source of cost overruns. While every effort should be made up front to nail down the project scope, it is becoming increasingly difficult to do so in our rapidly changing world.

- **People are overly optimistic.** There is solid research indicating that people tend to overestimate how quickly they can get things done (Buehler, Griffin, & Ross, 1994; Lovallo & Kahneman, 2003).

- **People engage in strategic misrepresentation.** There is growing evidence that some project promoters underestimate the costs of projects and overestimate project benefits in order to win approval. This appears to be particularly true for large-scale public works projects, which have a notorious habit of coming in way over budget (remember Snapshot from Practice 5.1: Portland Aerial Tram).

The reality is that for many projects not all of the information needed to make accurate estimates is available, and it is impossible to predict the future. The challenge is further compounded by human nature and the political dynamics associated with gaining project approval. The dilemma is that without solid estimates the credibility of the project plan is eroded. Deadlines become meaningless, budgets become rubbery, and accountability becomes problematic.

Such challenges will influence the final time and cost estimates. Even with the best estimating efforts, it may be necessary to revise estimates based on relevant information *prior to* establishing a baseline schedule and budget.

Effective organizations adjust estimates of specific tasks once the risks, resources, and particulars of the situation have been more clearly defined. They recognize that the rolled-up estimates generated from a detailed estimate based on the WBS are just the starting point. As they delve further into the project-planning process, they make appropriate revisions in both the time and cost of specific activities. They factor the final assignment of resources into the project budget and schedule. For example, when they realize that only three instead of four bulldozers are available to clear a site, they adjust both the time and cost of that activity. They adjust estimates to account for specific actions to mitigate potential risks on the project. For example, to reduce the chances of design code errors, they add the cost of independent testers to the schedule and budget. Finally, organizations adjust estimates to take into account abnormal conditions. For example, if soil samples reveal excessive ground water, then they adjust foundation costs and times.

There will always be some mistakes, omissions, and adjustments that will require additional changes in estimates. Fortunately, every project should have a change management system in place to accommodate these situations and any impact on the project baseline. Change management and contingency funds will be discussed in Chapter 7.

5.8 Creating a Database for Estimating

LO 5-5

Suggest a scheme for developing an estimating database for future projects.

The best way to improve estimates is to collect and archive data on past project estimates and actuals. Saving historical data—estimates and actuals—provides a knowledge base for improving project time and cost estimating. Creating an estimating data-base is a "best practice" among leading project management organizations.

Some organizations, such as Boeing and IBM, have large estimating departments of professional estimators that have developed large **time and cost databases.** Others collect these data through the project office. This database approach allows the project estimator to select a specific work package item from the database for inclusion. The estimator then makes any necessary adjustments concerning the materials, labor, and equipment. Of course, any items not found in the database can be added to the project—and ultimately to the database if desired. Again, the quality of the database estimates depends upon the experience of the estimators, but over time the data quality should improve. Such structured databases serve as feedback for estimators and as benchmarks for cost and time for each project. In addition, comparison of estimate and actual for different projects can suggest the degree of risk inherent in estimates. See Figure 5.7 for the structure of a database similar to those found in practice.

FIGURE 5.7
Estimating Database Templates

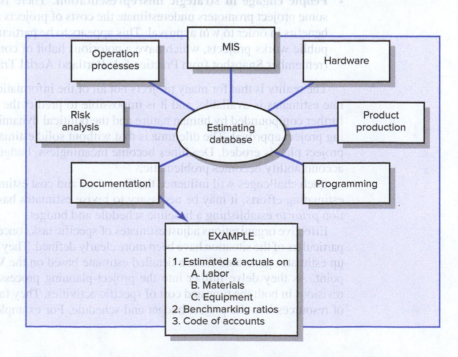

5.9 Mega Projects: A Special Case

 LO 5-6

Understand the challenge of estimating mega projects and describe steps that lead to better informed decisions.

Mega projects are large-scale, complex ventures that typically cost $1 billion or more, take many years to complete, and involve multiple private and public stakeholders. They are often transformational, and impact millions of people (Flyvbjerg, 2014). Examples include high-speed rail lines, airports, healthcare reform, the Olympics, development of new aircraft, and so forth. What do these projects have in common beyond scope and complexity? They all tend to go way over budget and fall behind schedule. For example, the new Denver airport that opened in 1995 had cost overruns of 200 percent and was completed two years later than planned. The "Chunnel," the 31-mile-plus tunnel that connects France with England, was 80 percent over budget. These are but two examples of many public works and other large-scale projects in which costs came in way over than planned. In a study of government infrastructure projects, Flyvbjerg found costs for bridges and tunnels, roads, and rails to be underestimated 34 percent, 20 percent, and 45 percent, respectively, from baseline estimates (Flyvbjerg, Bruzelius, & Rothengatter, 2003)!

Mega projects often involve a double whammy. Not only did they cost much more than expected, but they underdelivered on benefits they were to provide. The Denver airport realized only 55 percent of forecasted traffic during its first year of operation. The Chunnel traffic revenues have been one-half of what was predicted with internal rate of return of −14.5 percent! Again Flyvbjerg's study revealed a consistent pattern of underusage on most infrastructure projects (Flyvbjerg et al., 2003), including only a 5 percent forecasted usage for the Kolkata (Calcutta) metro in India!

So why does there appear to be a consistent pattern of overestimating benefits and underestimating costs? Many argue the sheer complexity and long time horizon make it impossible to accurately estimate costs and benefits. While this is certainly true, Flyvbjerg and his colleagues' research suggests that other factors come in to play. They concluded that in most cases project promoters use deception to promote projects not for public good but for personal gain, political or economic. Deception may be deliberate, or may be the product of overzealousness, optimism, and ignorance (Flyvbjerg et al., 2003). In some cases, promoters rationalize that nothing great would ever get built if people knew in advance what the real costs and challenges involved were (Hirschman, 1967).

On some mega projects, there is a triple whammy. Not only are they over budget and under value, but the cost of maintaining them exceeds the benefits received. These kinds of projects are called **white elephants.**

LO 5-7

Define a "white elephant" in project management and provide examples.

A "white elephant" suggests a valuable, but burdensome, possession, which its owner cannot easily dispose of and whose cost (particularly upkeep) is out of proportion with its usefulness. The term derives from the story that the Kings of Siam (now Thailand) would often make a present of a white elephant to courtiers who had fallen out of favor with the king. At first glance, it was a great honor to receive such a revered beast from the king. However, the true intent was to ruin the recipient by forcing him to absorb the costs of taking care of the animal.

Examples of white elephants abound. While traveling across southern China one of the authors was struck by the palatial stature of the Trade Expo buildings each city had. It was as if each city had tried to outdo its neighbor in terms of grandeur. When asked how often they were used, city officials would say once or twice a year. The 2015 FIFA scandal brought attention to the hidden costs of hosting the World Cup. South Africa built six new world-class stadiums for the 2010 competition. None of the post–World Cup revenue generated from these stadiums exceeds their maintenance cost (Molloy & Chetty, 2015).

White elephants are not limited to buildings and stadiums. Air France had to mothball the Concorde, the world's fastest commercial airline, because maintenance costs and noise restrictions did not justify a three-flights-a-week schedule. It is not uncommon in our personal lives to acquire white elephants, such as underutilized vacation homes or yachts.

Flyvbjerg and others argue that cost overrun is not the price of doing big things and that we are capable of making better informed decisions on mega projects. The first step is to assume there is optimism bias and even deception on the part of promoters. Proposals should require a thorough review by impartial observers who do not have vested interest in the project. Some if not all financial risk should be absorbed by promoters and those who benefit financially from the project. Sustainable business practices should be used and maintenance costs be integrated into the forecasted cost/benefit analyses of projects. See Snapshot from Practice 5.5: Avoiding the Curse of the White Elephant to see how British organizers tried to avoid the curse of the white elephant in the 2012 Olympic games.

In particular, Flyvbjerg advocates an external view based on the outcome of similar projects completed in the past. It is called **reference class forecasting (RCF)** and involves three major steps:

1. Select a reference class of projects similar to your potential project, for example, cargo ships or bridges.

2. Collect and arrange outcome data as a distribution. Create a distribution of cost overruns as a percentage of the original project estimate (low to high).

3. Use the distribution data to arrive at a realistic forecast. Compare the original cost estimate for the project with the reference class projects. Take, for example, a three-mile-long rail tunnel project. Tunnel advocates estimate that it will cost $100 million. Analyses of similar tunnel projects in the region indicate that on average they are 34 percent over budget. If the proponents cannot come up with a reasonable explanation for why this project will be different, decision makers should assume that the tunnel will cost at least $134 million.

The benefits of RCF are compelling:

- Outside empirical data mitigates human bias.
- Political, strategic, and promoter forces have difficulty ignoring outside RCF information.
- RCF serves as a reality check for funding large projects.
- RCF helps executives avoid unsound optimism.
- RCF leads to improved accountability.
- RCF provides a basis for project contingency funds.

The use of RCF is increasing as governments and organizations require this method be used to temper project promoters' estimates and reduce cost/benefit inaccuracies.

SNAPSHOT FROM PRACTICE 5.5

Avoiding the Curse of the White Elephant*

Once, hosting the Olympics was considered the crown prize and a tremendous source of national pride. Seven cities competed to host the 1992 Winter Olympics. For the 2022 Winter Olympics only Beijing and Almaty (Kazakhstan) submitted bids. Oslo (Norway), the favorite, withdrew application due to a lack of public support. Likewise, Boston withdrew application for the 2024 Summer Olympics in the face of public outcry.

Why the outcry? Because of the legacy of exorbitant cost overruns and draining maintenance costs. The Olympics has a long history of expensive white elephants. For example, the Beijing National Stadium, nicknamed the *Bird's Nest,* built at a cost of $480 million for the 2008 Olympic games, requires over $10 million each year to maintain and has no regular tenant.

Some have attributed the Greek economic meltdown to exorbitant debt accrued from hosting the 2004 summer games (Flyvbjerg, 2014). "It felt good at the time because we were the center of the world, and we got to show off our country," says gymnast Christos Libanovnos of the Hellenic Gymnastics Federation. "But what did it cost? So much money—billions of euros. And now we are bankrupt, and everything just gets worse and worse every day. It's hard not to see a connection. It's hard not to think that maybe it wasn't worth it."[1]

Perhaps the most infamous example of an Olympic white elephant is the 1976 Montreal Olympic Stadium. Originally nicknamed the *Big O,* due to its unique doughnut design, the stadium soon became known across Canada as the *Big Owe.* Estimated to cost $134 million, it took Canadian taxpayers 30 years to pay off the final $1.1 billion debt. To make matters worse, the stadium was not completely finished by the time the Olympics opened. The stadium has not had a main tenant since 2004, when the successful Montreal Expos moved to Washington, D.C.

The London 2012 Olympics organizers were committed to reducing the Olympic financial hangover. In particular, they were well aware of hidden post-Olympic maintenance costs of buildings that were no

© Sophie Vigneault /123RF

longer in demand. One advantage they had over less developed countries is that the infrastructure and many of the arenas were already in place and the Olympics provided a necessary upgrade. They built temporary arenas for less popular sports. For example, after the games the water polo arena was deconstructed and materials recycled. The 12,000-seat basketball arena was designed to be portable so it could be used in future Olympics. Scalability was another key consideration. For example, during the Olympics over 17,000 people watched swimming events in the newly constructed aquatic center. The aquatic center was downsized to a 2,500-person capacity after the Olympics and is now open to the public.

In recognition of its achievements, London 2012 Olympics won Gold in the Environmental and Sustainability category of the 6th International Sports Events awards. "We set out with a huge promise to the world, to deliver the most sustainable Olympic Games of modern times," says David Stubbs, London 2012's Head of Sustainability. "Seven years, nine million visitors, and 2,484 medals later, that's exactly what we achieved."

[1] Sanborn, J., "Was It Worth It? Debit-Ridden Greeks Question the Cost of the 2004 Olympics," *Time,* July 9, 2012, p. 33.
*"London 2012's Sustainability Legacy Lives On," Olympic .org. Accessed 10/10/15.

Summary

Quality time and cost estimates are the bedrock of project control. Past experience is the best starting point for these estimates. The quality of estimates is influenced by other factors such as people, technology, and downtimes. Companies that excel record past experiences and create an estimation database that provides quick and accurate information on the cost of specific work packages.

Using top-down estimates is good for initial and strategic decision making or in situations where the costs associated with developing better estimates have little benefit. However, in most cases the bottom-up approach to estimating is preferred and more reliable because it assesses each work package, rather than the whole project, section, or deliverable of a project. Estimating time and costs for each work package facilitates development of the project schedule and a time-phased budget, which are needed to control the project as it is implemented. Using the estimating guidelines will help eliminate many common mistakes made by those unacquainted with estimating times and costs for project control.

The level of time and cost detail should follow the old phrase "no more than is necessary and sufficient." Managers must remember to differentiate among committed outlays, actual costs, and scheduled costs. It is well known that up-front efforts in clearly defining project objectives, scope, and specifications vastly improve time and cost estimate accuracy.

Culture plays a significant role in estimating. If the focus is on what went wrong instead of who is to blame, then people should be more forthright in sharing their experiences and insights. However, if you work in a punitive organizational culture that is only concerned with results, you are likely to be much more guarded in what you share and may even pad estimates out of self-protection.

Finally, large-scale mega projects like subway systems or football stadiums often suffer from underestimated costs and overestimated benefits. They also can evolve into white elephants whose cost of maintenance exceeds benefits. Steps must be taken to remove bias and compare mega project estimates with similar projects that have been done in the past.

Key Terms

Apportionment, *143*	Overhead costs, *151*	Template method, *146*
Bottom-up estimates, *140*	Phase estimating, *147*	Time and cost
Delphi Method, *142*	Range estimating, *146*	databases, *154*
Direct costs, *151*	Ratio method, *143*	Top-down estimates, *140*
Function points, *143*	Reference class	White elephant, *155*
Learning curve, *145*	forecasting (RCF), *157*	

Review Questions

1. Why are accurate estimates critical to effective project management?
2. How does the culture of an organization influence the quality of estimates?
3. What are the differences between bottom-up and top-down estimating approaches? Under what conditions would you prefer one over the other?
4. What are the major types of costs? Which costs are controllable by the project manager?
5. Why is it difficult to estimate mega project (e.g., airport, stadium) costs and benefits?
6. Define a white elephant in project management. Provide a real-life example.

SNAPSHOT FROM PRACTICE

Discussion Questions

5.1 *Portland Aerial Tram*

1. Can you think of a local public project that had significant cost overruns like the Portland Tram project?

2. Do you agree with the statement that "nothing great would ever be built if people knew in advance what the real costs and challenges were"?

5.2 *The Delphi Method*

1. What kinds of estimates are best suited for this method?

5.3 *Estimate Accuracy*

1. Why is the range so much higher for IT projects than construction projects?

5.5 *Avoiding the Curse of the White Elephant*

1. Can you identify personal examples of white elephants?

2. What else do you think Olympic organizers could do to make the event more sustainable?

Exercises

1. Calculate the direct cost of labor for a project team member using the following data:

   Hourly rate: $50/hr

   Hours needed: 120

   Overhead rate: 40%

2. Calculate the direct and total direct costs of labor for a project team member using the following data:

   Hourly rate: $50/hr

   Hours needed: 100

   Overhead rate: 30%

3. The Munsters have been saving money in order to buy a house. They figure that, given current interest rates, they could afford a $400,000 home. Before looking at houses on the market they decide to explore the possibility of building a new home. The Munsters figure they could buy a suitable lot for $70,000–$75,000. At a minimum they want to build a 2,400-square-foot house. The cost for a house of the quality they desire is $160 per square foot. Given this information, should the Munsters pursue the option of building a new house?

4. Mrs. Publinsky and her husband, Xander, are planning their dream house. The lot for the house sits high on a hill with a beautiful view of the White Mountains. The plans show the size of the house to be 2,900 square feet. The average price for a lot and house similar to this one has been $150 per square foot. Fortunately, Xander is a retired plumber and feels he can save money by installing the plumbing himself. Mrs. Publinsky feels she can take care of the interior decorating. They both feel they can complete the exterior painting with the help of their two sons.

   The following average cost information is available from a local bank that makes loans to local contractors and dispenses progress payments to contractors when specific tasks are verified as complete.

25%	Excavation and framing complete	4%	Plumbing fixtures installed
8%	Roof and fireplace complete	5%	Exterior painting complete
3%	Wiring roughed in	4%	Light fixtures installed, finish hardware installed
6%	Plumbing roughed in		
5%	Siding on	6%	Carpet and trim installed
17%	Windows, insulation, walks, plaster, and garage complete	4%	Interior decorating
		4%	Floors laid and finished
9%	Furnace installed		

    a. What is the estimated cost for the Publinskys' house if they use contractors to complete all of the house?

    b. Estimate what the cost of the house would be if the Publinskys used their talents to do some of the work themselves.

5. Exercise Figure 5.1 is a project WBS with cost apportioned by percentages. If the total project cost is estimated to be $800,000, what are the estimated costs for the following deliverables?

    a. Design

    b. Programming

    c. In-house testing

What weaknesses are inherent in this estimating approach?

EXERCISE FIGURE 5.1
WBS Figure

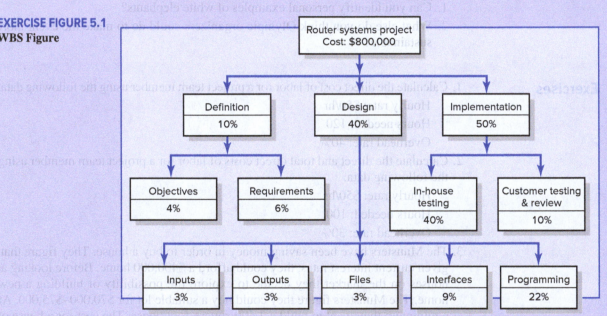

6. Assume you are the project manager for the Tidal 2 software project. You have been asked to calculate the expected cost for the project. Your company's database indicates that developers can handle eight function points each person-month and that the cost per developer at your firm is $5,000 per month. You and your team of five developers have come up with the following requirements:

Elements	Count	Complexity
Inputs	10	Low
Outputs	4	Low
Inquiries	4	High
Files	28	Medium
Interfaces	18	High

Using the "complexity weighting" scheme shown in Table 5.2 and the information provided, calculate the total number of function points, the estimated cost, and the estimated duration of the Tidal 2 project.

7. Omega 2 Project. Using the "complexity weighting" scheme shown in Table 5.2 and the following function point complexity weight table, estimate the total function point count. Assume historical data suggest five function points equal one person a month and six people have been assigned to work on the project.

Complexity Weight Table

Number of inputs	15	Rated complexity low
Number of outputs	20	Rated complexity average
Number of inquiries	10	Rated complexity average
Number of files	30	Rated complexity average
Number of interfaces	50	Rated complexity high

a. What is the estimated project duration?

b. If 20 people are available for the project, what is the estimated project duration?

c. If the project must be completed in six months, how many people will be needed for the project?

References

Buehler, R., D. Griffin, and M. Ross, "Exploring the 'Planning Fallacy': Why People Underestimate Their Task Completion Times," *Journal of Personality and Social Psychology,* vol. 67, no. 3 (1994), pp. 366–81.

Dalkey, N. C., D. L. Rourke, R. Lewis, and D. Snyder, *Studies in the Quality of Life: Delphi and Decision Making* (Lexington, MA: Lexington Books, 1972).

Flyvbjerg, B., "Curbing Optimism Bias and Strategic Misrepresentation in Planning: Reference Class Forecasting in Practice," *European Planning Studies,* vol. 16, no. 1 (January 2008), pp. 3–21.

Flyvbjerg, B., "From Nobel Prize to Project Management: Getting Risks Right," *Project Management Journal,* August 2006, pp. 5–15.

Flyvbjerg, B., "What You Should Know about Megaprojects and Why: An Overview," *Project Management Journal,* vol. 45, no. 2 (April/May 2014), pp. 6–19.

Flyvbjerg, B., N. Bruzelius, and W. Rothengatter, *Mega Projects and Risk: An Anatomy of Ambition* (UK: Cambridge University Press, 2003).

Gray, N. S., "Secrets to Creating the Elusive 'Accurate Estimate,'" *PM Network,* August 2001, p. 56.

Hirschman. A. O., "The Principle of the Hiding Hand," *The Public Interest,* Winter 1967, pp. 10–23.

Jeffery, R., G. C. Low, and M. Barnes, "A Comparison of Function Point Counting Techniques," *IEEE Transactions on Software Engineering,* vol. 19, no. 5 (1993), pp. 529–32.

Jones, C., *Applied Software Measurement* (New York: McGraw-Hill, 1991).

Jones, C., *Estimating Software Costs* (New York: McGraw-Hill, 1998).

Kharbanda, O. P., and J. K. Pinto, *What Made Gertie Gallop: Learning from Project Failures* (New York: Von Nostrand Reinhold, 1996).

Lovallo, D., and D. Kahneman, "Delusions of Success: How Optimism Undermines Executives' Decisions," *Harvard Business Review,* July 2003, pp. 56–63.

Magne, E., K. Emhjellenm, and P. Osmundsen, "Cost Estimation Overruns in the North Sea," *Project Management Journal,* vol. 34, no. 1 (2003), pp. 23–29.

McLeod, G., and D. Smith, *Managing Information Technology Projects* (Cambridge, MA: Course Technology, 1996).

Molloy, E., and T. Chetty, "The Rocky Road to Legacy: Lessons from the 2010 FIFA World Cup South Africa Stadium Program," *Project Management Journal,* vol. 46, no. 3 (June/July 2015), pp. 88–107.

Symons, C. R., "Function Point Analysis: Difficulties and Improvements," *IEEE Transactions on Software Engineering,* vol. 14, no. 1 (1988), pp. 2–11.

Walters, D. J., P. Fernbach, C. Fox, and S. Sloman, "Known Unknowns: A Critical Determinant of Confidence and Calibration," *Management Science,* vol. 63, no. 12 (2017), pp. 3999–4446.

Case 5.1

Sharp Printing, AG

Three years ago the Sharp Printing (SP) strategic management group set a goal of having a color laser printer available for the consumer and small business market for less than $200. A few months later the senior management met off-site to discuss the new product. The results of this meeting were a set of general technical specifications along with major deliverables, a product launch date, and a cost estimate based on prior experience.

Shortly afterward a meeting was arranged for middle management explaining the project goals, major responsibilities, project start date, and importance of meeting the product launch date within the cost estimate. Members of all departments involved attended the meeting. Excitement was high. Although everyone saw the risks as high, the promised rewards for the company and the personnel were emblazoned in their minds. A few participants questioned the legitimacy of the project duration and cost estimates. A couple of R&D people were worried about the technology required to produce the high-quality product for less than $200. But given the excitement of the moment, everyone agreed the project was worth doing and doable. The color laser printer project was to have the highest project priority in the company.

Lauren was selected to be the project manager. She had 15 years of experience in printer design and manufacture, which included successful management of several projects related to printers for commercial markets. Since she was one of those uncomfortable with the project cost and time estimates, she felt getting good bottom-up time and cost estimates for the deliverables was her first concern. She quickly had a meeting with the significant stakeholders to create a WBS identifying the work packages and organization unit responsible for implementing the work packages. Lauren stressed that she wanted time and cost estimates from those who would do the work or were the most knowledgeable, if possible. Getting estimates from more than one source was encouraged. Estimates were due in two weeks.

The compiled estimates were placed in the WBS/OBS. The corresponding cost estimate seemed to be in error. The cost estimate was $1,250,000 over the top-down senior management estimate; this represented about a 20 percent overrun! Furthermore, the bottom-up time estimate based on the project network was four months longer than the top management time estimate. Another meeting was scheduled with the significant stakeholders to check the estimates and to brainstorm for alternative solutions. At this meeting everyone agreed the bottom-up cost and time estimates appeared to be accurate. Following are some of the suggestions from the brainstorming session.

- Change scope.
- Outsource technology design.
- Use the priority matrix (found in Chapter 4) to get top management to clarify their priorities.
- Partner with another organization or build a research consortium to share costs and to share the newly developed technology and production methods.
- Cancel the project.
- Commission a break-even study for the laser printer.

Very little in the way of concrete savings was identified, although there was consensus that time could be compressed to the market launch date, but at additional costs.

Lauren met with the marketing (Connor), production (Kim), and design (Gage) managers, who yielded some ideas for cutting costs, but nothing significant enough to have a large impact. Gage remarked, "I wouldn't want to be the one to deliver the message to top management that their cost estimate is $1,250,000 off! Good luck, Lauren."

1. At this point, what would you do if you were the project manager?
2. Was top management acting correctly in developing an estimate?
3. What estimating techniques should be used for a mission-critical project such as this?

Case 5.2

Post-Graduation Adventure

Josh and Mike met as roommates during freshman year at Macalester College in St. Paul, Minnesota. Despite a rocky start they became best friends. They are planning a two-week adventure together to celebrate their graduation in June. Josh has never been to Europe and wants to visit France or Spain. Mike spent a semester abroad in Aarhus, Denmark, and traveled extensively in northern Europe. Even though Mike has never been to France or Spain, he wants to go to someplace more exotic, like South Africa or Vietnam. For the past week they have been arguing over where they should go. Josh argues that it will cost too much to fly to South Africa or Vietnam, while Mike counters that it will be much cheaper to travel in Vietnam or South Africa once they are there. They agree that they can spend no more than $3,500 each on the trip and could be gone for only two weeks.

One evening when they were arguing with each other over beers with friends, Sara said, "Why don't you use what you learned in your project management class to decide what to do?" Josh and Mike looked at each other and agreed that made perfect sense.

1. Assume you are either Mike or Josh; how would you go about making a decision using project management methodology?
2. Looking first at only cost, what decision would you make?
3. After cost, what other factors should be considered before making a decision?

Appendix 5.1

LEARNING OBJECTIVES

After reading this appendix you should be able to:

A5-1 Use learning curves to improve task estimates.

Learning Curves for Estimating

LO A5-1

Use learning curves to
improve task estimates.

A forecast estimate of the time required to perform a work package or task is a basic necessity for scheduling the project. In some cases the manager simply uses judgment and past experience to estimate work package time or uses historical records of similar tasks.

Most managers and workers intuitively know that improvement in the amount of time required to perform a task or group of tasks occurs with repetition. A worker can perform a task better/quicker the second time and each succeeding time she performs it (without any technological change). It is this pattern of improvement that is important to the project manager and project scheduler.

This improvement from repetition generally results in a reduction of labor hours for the accomplishment of tasks and results in lower project costs. From empirical evidence across *all* industries, the pattern of this improvement has been quantified in the *learning curve* (also known as improvement curve, experience curve, and industrial progress curve), which is described by the following relationship:

Each time the output quantity doubles, the unit labor hours are reduced at a constant rate.

For example, assume that a manufacturer has a new contract for 16 prototype units and a total of 800 labor hours were required for the first unit. Past experience has indicated that on similar types of units the improvement rate has been 80 percent. This relationship of improvement in labor hours is shown below:

Unit		Labor Hours
1		800
2	800 × .80 =	640
4	640 × .80 =	512
8	512 × .80 =	410
16	410 × .80 =	328

By using Table A5.1 unit values, similar labor hours per unit can be determined. Looking across the 16 unit level and down the 80 percent column, we find a ratio of .4096. By multiplying this ratio times the labor hours for the first unit, we obtain the per unit value:

$$.4096 \times 800 = 328 \text{ hours, or } 327.68$$

That is, the 16th unit should require close to 328 labor hours, assuming an 80 percent improvement ratio.

Obviously a project manager may need more than a single unit value for estimating the time for some work packages. The cumulative values in Table A5.2 provide factors for computing the cumulative total labor hours of all units. In the previous example, for the first 16 units, the total labor hours required would be

$$800 \times 8.920 = 7,136 \text{ hours}$$

TABLE A5.1
Learning Curves
Unit Values

Units	60%	65%	70%	75%	80%	85%	90%	95%
1	1.0000	1.0000	1.0000	1.0000	1.0000	1.0000	1.0000	1.0000
2	.6000	.6500	.7000	.7500	.8000	.8500	.9000	.9500
3	.4450	.5052	.5682	.6338	.7021	.7729	.8462	.9219
4	.3600	.4225	.4900	.5625	.6400	.7225	.8100	.9025
5	.3054	.3678	.4368	.5127	.5956	.6857	.7830	.8877
6	.2670	.3284	.3977	.4754	.5617	.6570	.7616	.8758
7	.2383	.2984	.3674	.4459	.5345	.6337	.7439	.8659
8	.2160	.2746	.3430	.4219	.5120	.6141	.7290	.8574
9	.1980	.2552	.3228	.4017	.4930	.5974	.7161	.8499
10	.1832	.2391	.3058	.3846	.4765	.5828	.7047	.8433
12	.1602	.2135	.2784	.3565	.4493	.5584	.6854	.8320
14	.1430	.1940	.2572	.3344	.4276	.5386	.6696	.8226
16	.1296	.1785	.2401	.3164	.4096	.5220	.6561	.8145
18	.1188	.1659	.2260	.3013	.3944	.5078	.6445	.8074
20	.1099	.1554	.2141	.2884	.3812	.4954	.6342	.8012
22	.1025	.1465	.2038	.2772	.3697	.4844	.6251	.7955
24	.0961	.1387	.1949	.2674	.3595	.4747	.6169	.7904
25	.0933	.1353	.1908	.2629	.3548	.4701	.6131	.7880
30	.0815	.1208	.1737	.2437	.3346	.4505	.5963	.7775
35	.0728	.1097	.1605	.2286	.3184	.4345	.5825	.7687
40	.0660	.1010	.1498	.2163	.3050	.4211	.5708	.7611
45	.0605	.0939	.1410	.2060	.2936	.4096	.5607	.7545
50	.0560	.0879	.1336	.1972	.2838	.3996	.5518	.7486
60	.0489	.0785	.1216	.1828	.2676	.3829	.5367	.7386
70	.0437	.0713	.1123	.1715	.2547	.3693	.5243	.7302
80	.0396	.0657	.1049	.1622	.2440	.3579	.5137	.7231
90	.0363	.0610	.0987	.1545	.2349	.3482	.5046	.7168
100	.0336	.0572	.0935	.1479	.2271	.3397	.4966	.7112
120	.0294	.0510	.0851	.1371	.2141	.3255	.4830	.7017
140	.0262	.0464	.0786	.1287	.2038	.3139	.4718	.6937
160	.0237	.0427	.0734	.1217	.1952	.3042	.4623	.6869
180	.0218	.0397	.0691	.1159	.1879	.2959	.4541	.6809
200	.0201	.0371	.0655	.1109	.1816	.2887	.4469	.6757
250	.0171	.0323	.0584	.1011	.1691	.2740	.4320	.6646
300	.0149	.0289	.0531	.0937	.1594	.2625	.4202	.5557
350	.0133	.0262	.0491	.0879	.1517	.2532	.4105	.6482
400	.0121	.0241	.0458	.0832	.1453	.2454	.4022	.6419
450	.0111	.0224	.0431	.0792	.1399	.2387	.3951	.6363
500	.0103	.0210	.0408	.0758	.1352	.2329	.3888	.6314
600	.0090	.0188	.0372	.0703	.1275	.2232	.3782	.6229
700	.0080	.0171	.0344	.0659	.1214	.2152	.3694	.6158
800	.0073	.0157	.0321	.0624	.1163	.2086	.3620	.6098
900	.0067	.0146	.0302	.0594	.1119	.2029	.3556	.6045
1,000	.0062	.0137	.0286	.0569	.1082	.1980	.3499	.5998
1,200	.0054	.0122	.0260	.0527	.1020	.1897	.3404	.5918
1,400	.0048	.0111	.0240	.0495	.0971	.1830	.3325	.5850
1,600	.0044	.0102	.0225	.0468	.0930	.1773	.3258	.5793
1,800	.0040	.0095	.0211	.0446	.0895	.1725	.3200	.5743
2,000	.0037	.0089	.0200	.0427	.0866	.1683	.3149	.5698
2,500	.0031	.0077	.0178	.0389	.0606	.1597	.3044	.5605
3,000	.0027	.0069	.0162	.0360	.0760	.1530	.2961	.5530

TABLE A5.2
Learning Curves
Cumulative Values

Units	60%	65%	70%	75%	80%	85%	90%	95%
1	1.000	1.000	1.000	1.000	1.000	1.000	1.000	1.000
2	1.600	1.650	1.700	1.750	1.800	1.850	1.900	1.950
3	2.045	2.155	2.268	2.384	2.502	2.623	2.746	2.872
4	2.405	2.578	2.758	2.946	3.142	3.345	3.556	3.774
5	2.710	2.946	3.195	3.459	3.738	4.031	4.339	4.662
6	2.977	3.274	3.593	3.934	4.299	4.688	5.101	5.538
7	3.216	3.572	3.960	4.380	4.834	5.322	5.845	6.404
8	3.432	3.847	4.303	4.802	5.346	5.936	6.574	7.261
9	3.630	4.102	4.626	5.204	5.839	6.533	7.290	8.111
10	3.813	4.341	4.931	5.589	6.315	7.116	7.994	8.955
12	4.144	4.780	5.501	6.315	7.227	8.244	9.374	10.62
14	4.438	5.177	6.026	6.994	8.092	9.331	10.72	12.27
16	4.704	5.541	6.514	7.635	8.920	10.38	12.04	13.91
18	4.946	5.879	6.972	8.245	9.716	11.41	13.33	15.52
20	5.171	6.195	7.407	8.828	10.48	12.40	14.64	17.13
22	5.379	6.492	7.819	9.388	11.23	13.38	15.86	18.72
24	5.574	6.773	8.213	9.928	11.95	14.33	17.10	20.31
25	5.668	6.909	8.404	10.19	12.31	14.80	17.71	21.10
30	6.097	7.540	9.305	11.45	14.02	17.09	20.73	25.00
35	6.478	8.109	10.13	12.72	15.64	19.29	23.67	28.86
40	6.821	8.631	10.90	13.72	17.19	21.43	26.54	32.68
45	7.134	9.114	11.62	14.77	18.68	23.50	29.37	36.47
50	7.422	9.565	12.31	15.78	20.12	25.51	32.14	40.22
60	7.941	10.39	13.57	17.67	22.87	29.41	37.57	47.65
70	8.401	11.13	14.74	19.43	25.47	33.17	42.87	54.99
80	8.814	11.82	15.82	21.09	27.96	36.80	48.05	62.25
90	9.191	12.45	16.83	22.67	30.35	40.32	53.14	69.45
100	9.539	13.03	17.79	24.18	32.65	43.75	58.14	76.59
120	10.16	14.16	19.57	27.02	37.05	50.39	67.93	90.71
140	10.72	15.08	21.20	29.67	41.22	56.78	77.46	104.7
160	11.21	15.97	22.72	32.17	45.20	62.95	86.80	118.5
180	11.67	16.79	24.14	34.54	49.03	68.95	95.96	132.1
200	12.09	17.55	25.48	36.80	52.72	74.79	105.0	145.7
250	13.01	19.28	28.56	42.08	61.47	88.83	126.9	179.2
300	13.81	20.81	31.34	46.94	69.66	102.2	148.2	212.2
350	14.51	22.18	33.89	51.48	77.43	115.1	169.0	244.8
400	15.14	23.44	36.26	55.75	84.85	127.6	189.3	277.0
450	15.72	24.60	38.48	59.80	91.97	139.7	209.2	309.0
500	16.26	25.68	40.58	63.68	98.85	151.5	228.8	340.6
600	17.21	27.67	44.47	70.97	112.0	174.2	267.1	403.3
700	18.06	29.45	48.04	77.77	124.4	196.1	304.5	465.3
800	18.82	31.09	51.36	84.18	136.3	217.3	341.0	526.5
900	19.51	32.60	54.46	90.26	147.7	237.9	376.9	587.2
1,000	20.15	34.01	57.40	96.07	158.7	257.9	412.2	647.4
1,200	21.30	36.59	62.85	107.0	179.7	296.6	481.2	766.6
1,400	22.32	38.92	67.85	117.2	199.6	333.9	548.4	884.2
1,600	23.23	41.04	72.49	126.8	218.6	369.9	614.2	1001.
1,800	24.06	43.00	76.85	135.9	236.8	404.9	678.8	1116.
2,000	24.83	44.84	80.96	144.7	254.4	438.9	742.3	1230.
2,500	26.53	48.97	90.39	165.0	296.1	520.8	897.0	1513.
3,000	27.99	52.62	98.90	183.7	335.2	598.9	1047.	1791.

By dividing the total cumulative hours (7,136) by the units, the average unit labor hours can be obtained:

$$7,136 \text{ labor hours}/16 \text{ units} = 446 \text{ average labor hours per unit}$$

Note how the labor hours for the 16th unit (328) differs from the average for all 16 units (446). The project manager, knowing the average labor costs and processing costs, could estimate the total prototype costs. (The mathematical derivation of factors found in Tables A5.1 and A5.2 can be found in Jelen, F. C., and J. H. Black, *Cost and Optimization Engineering,* 2nd ed. (New York: McGraw-Hill, 1983.)

FOLLOW-ON CONTRACT EXAMPLE

Assume the project manager gets a follow-on order of 74 units; how should he estimate labor hours and cost? Going to the cumulative Table A5.2 we find at the 80 percent ratio and 90 total units intersection—a 30.35 ratio.

800 × 30.35 =	24,280 labor hours for 90 units
Less previous 16 units =	7,136
Total follow-on order =	17,144 labor hours
17,144/74 equals 232 average labor hours per unit	

Labor hours for the 90th unit can be obtained from Table A5.1: .2349 × 800 = 187.9 labor hours. (For ratios between given values, simply estimate.)

Exercise A5.1

Norwegian Satellite Development Company (NSDC)
Cost Estimates
for
World Satellite Telephone Exchange Project

NSDC has a contract to produce eight satellites to support a worldwide telephone system (for Alaska Telecom, Inc.) that allows individuals to use a single, portable telephone in any location on earth to call in and out. NSDC will develop and produce the eight units. NSDC has estimated that the R&D costs will be NOK (Norwegian Krone) 12,000,000. Material costs are expected to be NOK 6,000,000. They have estimated that the design and production of the first satellite will require 100,000 labor hours, and an 80 percent improvement curve is expected. Skilled labor cost is NOK 300 per hour. Desired profit for all projects is 25 percent of total costs.

A. How many labor hours should the eighth satellite require?
B. How many labor hours for the whole project of eight satellites?
C. What price would you ask for the project? Why?
D. Midway through the project your design and production people realize that a 75 percent improvement curve is more appropriate. What impact does this have on the project?
E. Near the end of the project, Deutsch Telefon AG requests a cost estimate for four satellites identical to those you have already produced. What price will you quote them? Justify your price.

Design elements: Snapshot from Practice, Highlight box, Case icon: ©Sky Designs/Shutterstock

CHAPTER
6

Business Strategy: Differentiation, Cost Leadership, and Blue Oceans

Chapter Outline

6.1 Business-Level Strategy: How to Compete for Advantage
Strategic Position
Generic Business Strategies

6.2 Differentiation Strategy: Understanding Value Drivers
Product Features
Customer Service
Complements

6.3 Cost-Leadership Strategy: Understanding Cost Drivers
Cost of Input Factors
Economies of Scale
Learning Curve
Experience Curve

6.4 Business-Level Strategy and the Five Forces: Benefits and Risks
Differentiation Strategy: Benefits and Risks
Cost-Leadership Strategy: Benefits and Risks

6.5 Blue Ocean Strategy: Combining Differentiation and Cost Leadership
Value Innovation
Blue Ocean Strategy Gone Bad: "Stuck in the Middle"

6.6 Implications for Strategic Leaders

Learning Objectives

After studying this chapter, you should be able to:

LO 6-1 Define business-level strategy and describe how it determines a firm's strategic position.

LO 6-2 Examine the relationship between value drivers and differentiation strategy.

LO 6-3 Examine the relationship between cost drivers and cost-leadership strategy.

LO 6-4 Assess the benefits and risks of differentiation and cost-leadership strategies vis-à-vis the five forces that shape competition.

LO 6-5 Evaluate value and cost drivers that may allow a firm to pursue a blue ocean strategy.

LO 6-6 Assess the risks of a blue ocean strategy, and explain why it is difficult to succeed at value innovation.

CHAPTER**CASE 6**   Part I

JetBlue Airways: En Route to a New Blue Ocean?

IN 2019, JETBLUE AIRWAYS became the sixth-largest airline in the United States, following the "big four" (American, Delta, Southwest, and United) and Alaska Airlines, which beat out JetBlue in acquiring Virgin America in 2016. Jet-Blue offers approximately 1,000 flights daily, employs 22,000 crew members, and services 42 million customers annually.

When JetBlue took to the skies in 2000, founder David Neeleman set out to pursue a blue ocean strategy. This type of competitive strategy combines differentiation and cost-leadership activities. To reconcile the inherent trade-offs in these two distinct strategic positions, it used value innovation. How did Neeleman accomplish this strategy and where did his ideas come from?

At the age of 25, the young entrepreneur co-founded Morris Air, a charter air service that was purchased by Southwest Airlines (SWA) in 1993. Morris Air was a low-fare airline that pioneered many cost-saving practices that later became standard in the industry, such as e-ticketing. After a stint as an airline executive for SWA, Neeleman went on to launch JetBlue. His strategy was to provide air travel at even lower costs than SWA. At the same time, he wanted to offer service and amenities that were better and more than those offered by such legacy carriers as American, Delta, and United. According to JetBlue's Customer Bill of Rights, its primary mission is to bring humanity back to air travel.

To implement a blue ocean strategy, JetBlue focused on lowering operating costs while driving up perceived customer value in its service offerings. Specifically, it copied

In an attempt to differentiate its service offering, JetBlue provides its Mint luxury experience, which includes a lie-flat bed up to 6 feet 8 inches long, a high-resolution personal screen, and free in-flight high-speed Wi-Fi, on many domestic U.S. routes. Other U.S. competitors offer such amenities only on a few selected routes.
Carlosyudica/123RF

and improved upon many of SWA's cost-reducing activities. It used just one type of airplane (the Airbus A-320) to lower the costs of aircraft maintenance and pilot and crew training (but has since expanded its fleet). It also specialized in transcontinental flights connecting the East Coast (from its home base in New York) to the West Coast (e.g., Los Angeles). This model, known as the point-to-point model, focuses on directly connecting fewer but more highly trafficked city pairs, unlike American, Delta, and United's hub-and-spoke system, which connects many different locations via layovers at airport hubs. JetBlue's point-to-point model lowers costs in mainly two ways: flying longer distances and transporting more passengers per flight than SWA, further driving down its costs. As a consequence, Jet-Blue enjoys one of the lowest cost per available seat-mile (an important performance metric in the airline industry) in the United States.

To enhance its differential appeal, JetBlue drove up its perceived value by implementing its mantra: combining *high-touch*—to enhance the customer experience—and *high-tech*—to drive down costs. JetBlue also had a highly functional website for making reservations and planning other travel-related services. But because research showed that roughly one-third of customers prefer speaking to live reservation agents, it decided to add live agents, all of whom were U.S.-based, work-from-home employees rather than outsourced ones, as per the industry best practice.

To further enhance its value for customers, JetBlue added to its fleet high-end, 100-seat Embraer regional jets—each equipped with leather seats, free movie and television programming via DirecTV, and XM Satellite Radio, and each staffed with friendly and attentive on-board service attendants. Additional amenities included its Mint class, a luxury version of first-class travel featuring small private suites with lie-flat beds of up to 6 feet 8 inches long, a high-resolution personal viewing screen offering a large library of free and on-demand movies, live TV, and free in-flight high-speed Wi-Fi ("Fly-Fi"). JetBlue also offered personal check-in and early boarding, free bag check and priority bag retrieval after flight, and complimentary gourmet food and alcoholic beverages in flight.

In its early years, pursuing a blue ocean strategy by combining a cost-leadership position with a differentiation strategy resulted in a competitive advantage. JetBlue used value innovation to drive up perceived customer value even while lowering operating costs. This approach can work when an airline is small and connecting a few highly profitable city routes. However, it is quite difficult to implement because it involves simultaneous execution of cost-leadership and differentiation activities—two very distinct strategic strategies. Pursuing them simultaneously results in trade-offs that work against each other. For instance, higher perceived customer value (e.g., by providing leather seats and free Wi-Fi throughout the entire aircraft) comes with higher costs. These trade-offs eventually caught up with JetBlue.

Between 2007 and 2015, the airline faced several high-profile mishaps (e.g., emergency landings and erratic pilot and crew behaviors). Following the 2007 "snowmageddon," when JetBlue was forced to cancel about 1,600 flights and passengers were stranded for up to nine hours sitting on the tarmac aboard full airplanes, the board removed founder Neeleman as CEO and replaced him with David Barger, formerly JetBlue's chief operating officer. These public relations nightmares compounded the fundamental difficulty of resolving the need to limit costs while providing superior customer service and in-flight amenities. Meanwhile, Barger was unable to overcome JetBlue's competitive disadvantage; by 2015, the airline was lagging the Dow Jones U.S. Airline Index by more than 180 percentage points. In that same year, JetBlue's board replaced Barger, appointing Robin Hayes, who had been with British Airways for almost 20 years, as the new CEO.

JetBlue's situation went from bad to worse. In 2017, JetBlue ranked dead last in the annual WSJ survey of U.S. airlines based on objective data such as on-time arrival, tarmac and flight delays, cancelled flights, involuntary bumping of passengers, mishandled bags, and numerous other customer complaints.

So Hayes set out to sharpen JetBlue's strategic profile, doubling down on its blue ocean strategy. He attempted once again to lower operating costs while increasing perceived value creation. To drive down costs, he decided to add more seats to each plane, reducing legroom in coach (now on par with the legacy carriers). He identified other cost-savings opportunities, mainly in aircraft maintenance and crew scheduling. At the same time, Hayes also expanded its Mint class service to many more flights, providing a product that customers loved and some other airlines lacked. JetBlue also added a new airplane, the Airbus A-321, to its fleet, which scores significantly higher in customer satisfaction surveys than the older A-320.[1]

Part II of this ChapterCase appears in Section 6.6.

THE CHAPTERCASE illustrates how JetBlue ran into trouble by pursuing two different business strategies at the same time—a *cost-leadership* strategy, focused on low cost, and a *differentiation* strategy, focused on delivering unique features and service. Although the idea of combining different business strategies seems appealing, it is quite difficult to execute a cost-leadership and differentiation position at the same time. This is because cost leadership and differentiation are distinct strategic positions. Pursuing them simultaneously results in trade-offs that work against each other. Providing higher perceived customer value tends to generate higher costs.

Many firms that attempt to combine cost-leadership and differentiation strategies end up being *stuck in the middle*. In this situation, strategic leaders have failed to carve out a clear *strategic position*. In their attempt to be everything to everybody, these firms end up being neither a low-cost leader nor a differentiator (thus the phrase *stuck in the middle* between the two distinct strategic positions). This common strategic failure contributed to JetBlue's sustained competitive disadvantage from 2007 to 2019. Strategic leaders need to be aware to avoid being *stuck in the middle* between distinct business strategies. A clear strategic position—either as differentiator *or* low-cost leader—is more likely to form the basis for competitive advantage. Although quite attractive at first glance, a *blue ocean strategy* is difficult to implement because of the trade-offs between the two distinct strategic positions (low-cost leadership and differentiation), unless the firm is successful in *value innovation* that allows a reconciliation of these inherent trade-offs (discussed in detail later).

This chapter, the first in Part 2 on strategy *formulation*, takes a close look at business-level strategy, frequently also referred to as *competitive strategy*. It deals with *how* to compete for advantage. Based on the analysis of the external and internal environments (presented in Part 1), the second step in the *AFI Strategy Framework* is to formulate a business strategy that enhances the firm's chances of achieving a competitive advantage.

We begin our discussion of strategy formulation by defining *business-level strategy, strategic position*, and *generic business strategies*. We then look at two key generic business strategies: *differentiation* and *cost leadership*. We pay special attention to value and cost drivers that managers can use to carve out a clear strategic profile. Next, we relate the two business-level strategies to the external environment, in particular, to the five forces, to highlight their respective benefits and risks. We then introduce the notion of *blue ocean strategy*—using *value innovation* to combine a differentiation and cost-leadership strategic position. We also look at changes in competitive positioning over time before concluding with practical *Implications for Strategic Leaders*.

6.1 Business-Level Strategy: How to Compete for Advantage

Business-level strategy details the goal-directed actions managers take in their quest for competitive advantage when competing in a single product market.[2] It may involve a single product or a group of similar products that use the same distribution channel. It concerns the broad question, "How should we compete?" To formulate an appropriate business-level strategy, managers must answer the who, what, why, and how questions of competition:

- *Who* are the customer segments we will serve?
- *What* customer needs, wishes, and desires will we satisfy?
- *Why* do we want to satisfy them?
- *How* will we satisfy them?[3]

To formulate an effective business strategy, managers need to keep in mind that competitive advantage is determined jointly by *industry* and *firm* effects. As shown in Exhibit 6.1, one route to competitive advantage is shaped by *industry effects*, while a second route is determined by *firm effects*. As discussed in Chapter 3, an industry's profit potential can be assessed using the five forces framework plus the availability of complements. Managers need to be certain that the business strategy is aligned with the five forces that shape competition. They can evaluate performance differences among clusters of firms in the same industry by conducting a strategic-group analysis. The concepts introduced in Chapter 4 are key in understanding firm effects because they allow us to look inside firms and explain why they differ based on their resources, capabilities, and competencies. It is also important to note that industry and firm effects are not independent, but rather they are *interdependent*, as shown by the two-pointed arrow connecting industry effects and firm effects in Exhibit 6.1. At the firm level, performance is determined by value and cost positions *relative* to competitors. This is the firm's *strategic position*, to which we turn next.

LO 10-1

Define business-level strategy and describe how it determines a firm's strategic position.

business-level strategy The goal-directed actions managers take in their quest for competitive advantage when competing in a single product market.

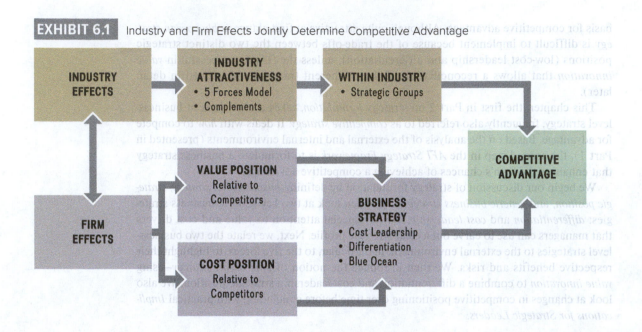

EXHIBIT 6.1 Industry and Firm Effects Jointly Determine Competitive Advantage

STRATEGIC POSITION

We noted in Chapter 5 that competitive advantage is based on the difference between the *perceived value* a firm is able to create for consumers (V), captured by how much consumers are willing to pay for a product or service, and the total cost (C) the firm incurs to create that value. The greater the *economic value created* ($V - C$), the greater is a firm's potential for competitive advantage. To answer the business-level strategy question of how to compete, managers have two primary competitive levers at their disposal: value (V) and cost (C).

A firm's business-level strategy determines its *strategic position*—its strategic profile based on value creation and cost—in a specific product market. A firm attempts to stake out a valuable and unique position that meets customer needs while simultaneously creating as large a gap as possible between the value the firm's product creates and the cost required to produce it. Higher value creation tends to require higher cost. To achieve a desired strategic position, managers must make **strategic trade-offs**—choices between a cost *or* value position. Managers must address the tension between value creation and the pressure to keep cost in check so as not to erode the firm's economic value creation and profit margin.

As shown in the ChapterCase, JetBlue experienced a competitive disadvantage for a number of years because it was unable to effectively address the strategic trade-offs inherent in pursuing a cost-leadership *and* differentiation strategy at the same time. A business strategy is more likely to lead to a competitive advantage if a firm has a clear strategic profile, either as differentiator *or* a low-cost leader. A *blue ocean strategy* is only successful, in contrast, if the firm can implement some type of value innovation that reconciles the inherent trade-off between value creation and underlying costs.

GENERIC BUSINESS STRATEGIES

There are two fundamentally different generic business strategies—*differentiation* and *cost leadership*. A **differentiation strategy** seeks to create higher value for customers than the value that competitors create, by delivering products or services with unique features while

strategic trade-offs Choices between a cost *or* value position. Such choices are necessary because higher value creation tends to generate higher cost.

differentiation strategy Generic business strategy that seeks to create higher value for customers than the value that competitors create, while containing costs.

keeping costs at the same or similar levels, allowing the firm to charge higher prices to its customers. A **cost-leadership strategy**, in contrast, seeks to create the same or similar value for customers by delivering products or services at a lower cost than competitors, enabling the firm to offer lower prices to its customers.

These two business strategies are called *generic strategies* because they can be used by any organization—manufacturing or service, large or small, for-profit or nonprofit, public or private, domestic or foreign—in the quest for competitive advantage, independent of industry context. Differentiation and cost leadership require distinct strategic positions, and in turn increase a firm's chances to gain and sustain a competitive advantage.[4] Because value creation and cost tend to be positively correlated, however, important trade-offs exist between value creation and low cost. A business strategy, therefore, is more likely to lead to a competitive advantage if it allows a firm to either *perform similar activities differently* or *perform different activities* than its rivals that result in creating more value or offering similar products or services at lower cost.[5]

When considering different business strategies, strategic leaders also must define the **scope of competition**—whether to pursue a specific, narrow part of the market or go after the broader market.[6] The automobile industry provides an example of the *scope of competition*. Alfred P. Sloan, longtime president and CEO of GM, defined the carmaker's mission as providing a car for every purse and purpose. GM was one of the first to implement a multi-divisional structure in order to separate the brands into strategic business units, allowing each brand to create its unique strategic position (with its own profit and loss responsibility) within the broad automotive market. For example, GM's product lineup ranges from the low-cost-positioned Chevy brand to the differentiated Cadillac brand. In this case, Chevy is pursuing a broad cost-leadership strategy, while Cadillac is pursuing a broad differentiation strategy. The two different business strategies are integrated at the corporate level at GM (more on *corporate strategy* in Chapters 8 and 9).

On the other hand, Tesla, the maker of all-electric cars (featured in ChapterCase 1), offers a highly differentiated product and pursues only a small market segment. At this point, it uses a *focused differentiation strategy*. In particular, Tesla focuses on environmentally conscious consumers that want to drive a high-performance car and who are willing to pay a premium price. Going forward, Tesla is hoping to broaden its competitive scope with its Model 3, priced at roughly half of the Model S sedan and Model X sport utility crossover. Moreover, Elon Musk hopes the Tesla Model Y (a smaller, compact SUV) will sell even better than the Model 3. Taken together, GM's competitive scope is broad—with a focus on the mass automotive market—while Tesla's competitive scope is narrow—with a focus on all-electric luxury cars.

Now we can combine the dimensions describing a firm's strategic position (*differentiation versus cost*) with the scope of competition (*narrow versus broad*). As shown in Exhibit 6.2, by doing so we get the two major broad business strategies (*cost leadership* and *differentiation*), shown as the top two boxes in the matrix, and the *focused* version of each, shown as the

cost-leadership strategy Generic business strategy that seeks to create the same or similar value for customers at a lower cost.

scope of competition The size—narrow or broad—of the market in which a firm chooses to compete.

EXHIBIT 6.2   Strategic Position and Competitive Scope: Generic Business Strategies

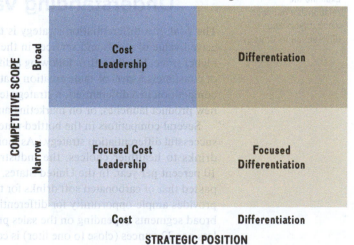

Source: Adapted from M.E. Porter (1980), *Competitive Strategy. Techniques for Analyzing Industries and Competitors* (New York: Free Press).

focused cost-leadership strategy   Same as the cost-leadership strategy except with a narrow focus on a niche market.

focused differentiation strategy   Same as the differentiation strategy except with a narrow focus on a niche market.

bottom two boxes in the matrix. The focused versions of the two business strategies—**focused cost-leadership strategy** and **focused differentiation strategy**—are essentially the same as the broad generic strategies *except* that the competitive scope is narrower. For example, the manufacturing company BIC pursues a focused cost-leadership strategy, designing and producing disposable pens and cigarette lighters at a low cost, while Mont Blanc pursues a focused differentiation strategy, offering exquisite pens—what it calls "writing instruments"—frequently priced at several hundred dollars.

As discussed in ChapterCase 6, JetBlue attempts to combine a focused cost-leadership position with a focused differentiation position. Although initially successful, for the last several years, JetBlue has been consistently outperformed by airlines that do not attempt to straddle different strategic positions, but rather have clear strategic profiles as either differentiators or low-cost leaders. For example, Southwest Airlines competes clearly as a broad cost leader (and would be placed squarely in the upper-left quadrant of Exhibit 6.2). The legacy carriers—Delta, American, and United—all compete as broad differentiators (and would be placed in the upper-right quadrant). Regionally, we find smaller airlines that are ultra low cost, such as Allegiant Air, Frontier Airlines, and Spirit Airlines, with very clear strategic positions. These smaller airlines would be placed in the lower-left quadrant of Exhibit 6.2 because they are pursuing a focused cost-leadership strategy. Based on a clear strategic position, these airlines have outperformed JetBlue over many years. JetBlue appears to be stuck between different strategic positions, trying to combine a focused cost-leadership position with focused differentiation. And, as the airline grew, the problems inherent in attempting to combine different strategic positions also grew—and more severe at that because of its attempt to also straddle the (broad) cost-leadership position with the (broad) differentiation position. In essence, JetBlue was trying to be everything to everybody. Being *stuck in the middle* of different strategic positions is a recipe for inferior performance and competitive disadvantage—and this is exactly what JetBlue experienced between 2007 and 2019, when it underperformed the Dow Jones Airlines Index, lagging behind the big four airlines (American, Delta, Southwest, and United) as well as smaller airlines such as Alaska Airlines, Allegiant Air, and Spirit.

LO 6-2

Examine the relationship between value drivers and differentiation strategy.

6.2 Differentiation Strategy: Understanding Value Drivers

The goal of a differentiation strategy is to add unique features that will increase the perceived value of goods and services in the minds of consumers so they are willing to pay a higher price. Ideally, a firm following a differentiation strategy aims to achieve in the minds of consumers a level of value creation that its competitors cannot easily match. The focus of competition in a differentiation strategy tends to be on unique product features, service, and new product launches, or on marketing and promotion rather than price.

Several competitors in the bottled-water industry provide a prime example of pursuing a successful differentiation strategy.[7] As more and more consumers shift from carbonated soft drinks to healthier choices, the industry for bottled water is booming—growing about 10 percent per year. In the United States, the per person consumption of bottled water surpassed that of carbonated soft drinks for the first time in 2016. Such a fast-growing industry provides ample opportunity for differentiation. In particular, the industry is split into two broad segments depending on the sales price. Bottled water with a sticker price of $1.30 or less per 32 ounces (close to one liter) is considered low-end, while those with a higher price tag are seen as luxury items. For example, PepsiCo's Aquafina and Coca-Cola's Dasani are considered low-end products, selling purified tap water at low prices, often in bulk at big-box retailers such as Walmart. On the premium end, PepsiCo introduced Lifewtr with a splashy ad during Super Bowl LI in 2017, while Jennifer Aniston markets Smartwater, Coca-Cola's premium water.

The idea of selling premium water is not new, however. Evian (owned by Danone, a French consumer products company) and S.Pellegrino (owned by Nestlé of Switzerland) have long focused on differentiating their products by emphasizing the uniqueness of their respective natural sources (Evian hails from the French Alps while Pellegrino comes from San Pellegrino Terme in Italy's Lombardy region). Recent entrants into the luxury segment for bottled water have taken the differentiation of their products to new heights. Some purveyors, such as Svalbardi, are able to charge super premium prices. At upscale retailer Harrods in London, a bottle of Svalbardi costs about $100 for 25 ounces; the water, sold in a heavy glass bottle, hails from Norwegian icebergs some 4,000 years old. Ordering premium bottled water in the United States to accompany lunch has become a status symbol. Indeed, many restaurants now feature water lists besides the more traditional wine selection. "Energy waters" enhanced with minerals and vitamins are the fastest growing segment. Although flavored waters make up less than 5 percent of the overall market for bottled water, they rack up 15 percent of total revenues. And this is nothing to be snuffed at: The market for bottled water globally reached some $150 billion and continues to grow fast. Although a free substitute can be had from most taps in industrialized countries, the success of many luxury brands in the bottled-water industry shows the power of differentiation strategy.

Anythings/Shutterstock

A company that uses a differentiation strategy can achieve a competitive advantage as long as its economic value created $(V - C)$ is greater than that of its competitors. Firm A in Exhibit 6.3 produces a generic commodity. Firm B and Firm C represent two efforts at differentiation. Firm B not only offers greater value than Firm A, but also maintains *cost parity,* meaning it has the same costs as Firm A. However, even if a firm fails to achieve cost parity (which is often the case because higher value creation tends to go along with higher costs in terms of higher-quality raw materials, research and development, employee training to provide superior customer service, and so on), it can still gain a competitive advantage if its economic value creation exceeds that of its competitors. Firm C represents just such a competitive advantage. For the approach shown *either* in Firm B or Firm C, economic value creation, $(V - C)_B$ or $(V - C)_C$, is greater than that of Firm A $(V - C)_A$. Either Firm B or C, therefore, achieves a competitive advantage because it has a higher value gap over Firm A $[(V - C)_B > (V - C)_A$, or $(V - C)_C > (V - C)_A]$, which allows it to charge a premium price, reflecting its higher value creation. To complete the relative comparison, although both companies pursue a differentiation strategy, Firm B also has a competitive advantage over Firm C because although both offer identical value, Firm B has lower costs, thus $(V - C)_B > (V - C)_C$.

Although increased value creation is a defining feature of a differentiation strategy, managers must also control costs. Rising costs reduce economic value created and erode profit margins. Indeed, if cost rises too much as the firm attempts to create more perceived value for customers, its value gap shrinks, negating any differentiation advantage. One reason JetBlue could not maintain an initial competitive advantage was because it was unable to keep its costs down sufficiently. JetBlue's current management team put measures in place to lower the airline's cost structure such as charging fees for checked bags and reducing leg space to increase passenger capacity on each of its planes. These cost-saving initiatives should increase its economic value creation.

200   CHAPTER 6   Business Strategy: Differentiation, Cost Leadership, and Blue Oceans

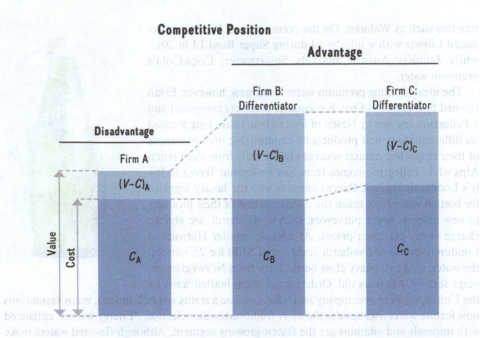

Although a differentiation strategy is generally associated with premium pricing, strategic leaders have an important second pricing option. When a firm is able to offer a differentiated product or service and can control its costs at the same time, it is able to gain market share from other firms in the industry by charging a similar price but offering more perceived value. By leveraging its differentiated appeal of superior customer service and quality, for example, Marriott offers a line of different hotels: its flagship Marriott full-service business hotel equipped to host large conferences; Residence Inn for extended stay; Marriott Courtyard for business travelers; and Marriott Fairfield Inn for inexpensive leisure and family travel.[8] Although these hotels are roughly comparable to competitors in price, they generally offer a higher perceived value. With this line of different hotels, Marriott can benefit from economies of scale and scope, and thus keep its cost structure in check. *Economies of scale* denote decreases in cost per unit as output increases (more in the next section when we discuss cost-leadership strategy). **Economies of scope** describe the savings that come from producing two (or more) outputs at less cost than producing each output individually, even though using the same resources and technology. This larger difference between cost and value allows Marriott to achieve greater economic value than its competitors, and thus to gain market share and post superior performance.

Managers can adjust a number of different levers to improve a firm's strategic position. These levers either increase perceived value or decrease costs. Here, we will study the most salient *value drivers* that strategic leaders have at their disposal (we look at cost drivers in the next section).[9] They are

- Product features
- Customer service
- Complements

These value drivers are related to a firm's expertise in, and organization of, different internal value chain activities. Although these are the most important value drivers, no such list can be complete. Applying the concepts introduced in this chapter should allow strategic leaders to identify other important value and cost drivers unique to their business.

When attempting to increase the perceived value of the firm's product or service offerings, managers must remember that the different value drivers contribute to competitive advantage *only if* their increase in value creation (ΔV) exceeds the increase in costs (ΔC). The condition of $\Delta V > \Delta C$ must be fulfilled if a differentiation strategy is to strengthen a firm's strategic position and thus enhance its competitive advantage.

PRODUCT FEATURES

One of the obvious but most important levers that strategic leaders can adjust is product features, thereby increasing the perceived value of the product or service offering. Adding unique product attributes allows firms to turn commodity products into differentiated products commanding a premium price. Strong R&D capabilities are often needed to create superior product features. In the kitchen-utensil industry, OXO follows a differentiation strategy, highlighting product features. By adhering to its philosophy of making products that are easy to use for the largest variety of possible users,[10] OXO differentiates its kitchen utensils through its patent-protected ergonomically designed soft black rubber grips.

CUSTOMER SERVICE

Managers can increase the perceived value of their firms' product or service offerings by focusing on customer service. For example, the online retailer Zappos earned a reputation for superior customer service by offering free shipping both ways: to the customer and for returns.[11] Although several online retailers now offer free shipping both ways, Zappos has done so since its inception in 1999, that is, long before more recent imitators. Perhaps more important, Zappos makes the return process hassle free by providing a link to a prepaid shipping label. All the customer needs to do is drop the box off at the nearby UPS store, all free of charge. Zappos's strategic leaders didn't view free shipping both ways as an additional expense but rather as part of the marketing budget. Moreover, Zappos does not outsource its customer service, and its associates do not use predetermined scripts. They are instead encouraged to build a relationship of trust with each individual customer. Indeed, it is quite fun to interact with Zappos customer service reps. There seemed to be a good return on investment as word spread through the online shopping community. Competitors took notice, too; Amazon bought Zappos for over $1 billion.[12]

COMPLEMENTS

When studying industry analysis in Chapter 3, we identified the availability of complements as an important force determining the profit potential of an industry. Complements add value to a product or service when they are consumed in tandem. Finding complements, therefore, is an important task for strategic leaders in their quest to enhance the value of their offerings.

A prime example of complements is smartphones and cellular services. A

Trader Joe's has some 475 stores, about half of which are in California and the rest in another 43 states plus Washington, D.C. The chain is known for good products, value for money, and great customer service. As just one example, stores stock local products as requested by their communities.[13]

QualityHD/Shutterstock

smartphone without a service plan is much less useful than one with a data plan. Traditionally, the providers of phones such as Apple, Samsung, and others did not provide wireless services. AT&T and Verizon are by far the two largest service providers in the United States, jointly holding some 70 percent of market share. To enhance the attractiveness of their phone and service bundles, phone makers and service providers frequently sign exclusive deals. When first released, for instance, service for the iPhone was exclusively offered by AT&T. Thus, if you wanted an iPhone, you had to sign up for a two-year service contract with AT&T.

Google, a division of Alphabet, decided to offer the important complements of smartphones and wireless services in-house to attract more customers.[14] Google offers high-end phones such as the Pixel 3 with cutting-edge artificial intelligence built in (via its Google Assistant) at competitive prices. It combines this with discounted high-speed wireless services in its Project Fi, a complementary offering. Working in conjunction with smaller wireless service providers such as T-Mobile (which merged with Sprint), Google provides seamless wireless services by stitching together a nationwide network of services based on available free Wi-Fi hotspots (such as at Starbucks) and cellular networks offered by T-Mobile. This not only enables wide coverage, but also reduces data usage significantly because Google phones automatically switch to free Wi-Fi networks wherever available. In addition, rather than to pay for a predetermined amount of data each month, Google Fi charges users for data use "as they go," that is for actual data consumed without throttling services after consuming the data allowance (as do AT&T and Verizon).

Project Fi is intended to drive more demand for Google's phone; sales have been lackluster thus far. Stronger demand for Google's phones locks more users into the Google ecosystem as its wireless services are available only with its own phones. This provides an example where complementary product and service offerings not only reinforce demand for one another, but also create a situation where network externalities can arise. As more users sign up for Project Fi, Google is able to offer faster and more reliable services through investing more into the latest technology, such as 5G, making its network and with it its Google phones more attractive to more users, and so forth.

In summary, by choosing the differentiation strategy as the strategic position for a product, managers focus their attention on adding value to the product through its unique features that respond to customer preferences, customer service during and after the sale, or effective marketing that communicates the value of the product's features. Although this positioning involves increased costs (for example, higher-quality inputs or innovative research and development activities), customers are generally willing to pay a premium price for the product or service that satisfies their needs and preferences. In the next section, we will discuss how strategic leaders formulate a cost-leadership strategy.

LO 6-3

Examine the relationship between cost drivers and cost-leadership strategy.

6.3 Cost-Leadership Strategy: Understanding Cost Drivers

The goal of a cost-leadership strategy is to reduce the firm's cost below that of its competitors while offering adequate value. The *cost leader,* as the name implies, focuses its attention and resources on reducing the cost to manufacture a product or on lowering the operating cost to deliver a service in order to offer lower prices to its customers. The cost leader attempts to optimize all of its value chain activities to achieve a low-cost position. Although staking out the lowest-cost position in the industry is the overriding strategic objective, a cost leader still needs to offer products and services of acceptable value. As an example, GM and Korean car manufacturer Kia offer some models that compete directly with one another, yet Kia's cars tend to be produced at lower cost, while providing a similar value proposition.

A cost leader can achieve a competitive advantage as long as its economic value created $(V - C)$ is greater than that of its competitors. Firm A in Exhibit 6.4 produces a product with a cost structure vulnerable to competition. Firms B and C show two different approaches to cost leadership. Firm B achieves a competitive advantage over Firm A because Firm B not only has lower cost than Firm A, but also achieves *differentiation parity* (meaning it creates the same value as Firm A). As a result, Firm B's economic value creation, $(V - C)_B$, is greater than that of Firm A, $(V - C)_A$. For example, as the low-cost leader, Walmart took market share from Kmart, which subsequently filed for bankruptcy.

What if a firm fails to create differentiation parity? Such parity is often hard to achieve because value creation tends to go along with higher costs, and Firm B's strategy is aimed at lower costs. A firm can still gain a competitive advantage as long as its economic value creation exceeds that of its competitors. Firm C represents this approach to cost leadership. Even with lower value (no differentiation parity) but lower cost, Firm C's economic value creation, $(V - C)_C$, still is greater than that of Firm A, $(V - C)_A$.

In both approaches to cost leadership in Exhibit 6.4, Firm B's economic value creation is greater than that of Firm A and Firm C. Yet, both firms B and C achieve a competitive advantage over Firm A. Either one can charge prices similar to its competitors and benefit from a greater profit margin per unit, or it can charge lower prices than its competition and gain higher profits from higher volume. Both variations of a cost-leadership strategy can result in competitive advantage. Although Firm B has a competitive advantage over both firms A and C, Firm C has a competitive advantage in comparison to Firm A.

Although companies successful at cost leadership must excel at controlling costs, this doesn't mean that they can neglect value creation. Kia signals the quality of its cars with a five-year, 60,000-mile warranty, one of the more generous warranties in the

EXHIBIT 6.4 Cost-Leadership Strategy: Achieving Competitive Advantage

Pursuing a cost-leadership strategy, firms that can keep their cost at the lowest point in the industry while offering acceptable value are able to gain a competitive advantage. Firm A has not managed to take advantage of possible cost savings and thus experiences a competitive disadvantage. The offering from Firm B has the same perceived value as Firm A but through more effective cost containment creates more economic value (over both Firm A and Firm C because $(V - C)_B > (V - C)_C > (V - C)_A$. The offering from Firm C has a lower perceived value than that of Firm A or B and has the same reduced product cost as with Firm B; as a result, Firm C still generates higher economic value than Firm A.

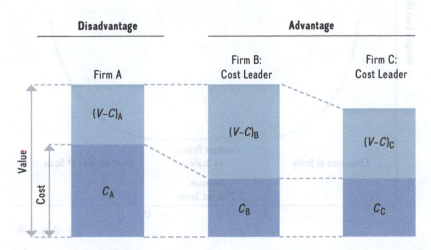

Competitive Position

industry. Walmart offers products of acceptable quality, including many brand-name products.

The most important *cost drivers* that strategic leaders can manipulate to keep their costs low are

- Cost of input factors.
- Economies of scale.
- Learning-curve effects.
- Experience-curve effects.

However, this list is only a starting point; managers may consider other cost drivers, depending on the situation.

COST OF INPUT FACTORS

One of the most basic advantages a firm can have over its rivals is access to lower-cost input factors such as raw materials, capital, labor, and IT services. In the market for international long-distance travel, one of the potent competitive threats facing U.S. legacy carriers— American, Delta, and United—comes from three airlines located in the Persian Gulf states— Emirates, Etihad, and Qatar. These airlines achieve a competitive advantage over their U.S. counterparts thanks to lower-cost inputs—raw materials (access to cheaper fuel), capital (interest-free government loans), labor—and fewer regulations (for example, regarding nighttime take-offs and landings, or in adding new runways and building luxury airports with swimming pools, among other amenities).[15] To benefit from lower-cost IT services, the Gulf carriers also outsource some value chain activities such as booking and online customer service to India. Together, these distinct cost advantages across several key input factors add up to create a greater economic value creation for the Gulf carriers vis-à-vis U.S. competitors, leading to a competitive advantage.

ECONOMIES OF SCALE

economies of scale Decreases in cost per unit as output increases.

Firms with greater market share might be in a position to reap **economies of scale**, decreases in cost per unit as output increases. This relationship between unit cost and output is depicted in the first (left-hand) part of Exhibit 6.5: Cost per unit falls as output increases up

EXHIBIT 6.5

Economies of Scale, Minimum Efficient Scale, and Diseconomies of Scale

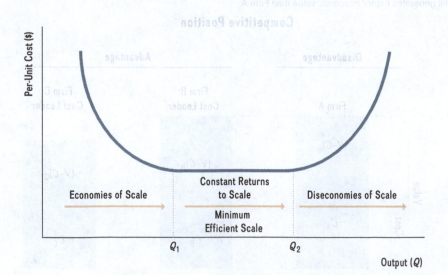

to point Q_1. A firm whose output is closer to Q_1 has a cost advantage over other firms with less output. In this sense, bigger is better.

In the airframe-manufacturing industry, for example, reaping economies of scale and learning is critical for cost-competitiveness. The market for commercial airplanes is often not large enough to allow more than one competitor to reach sufficient scale to drive down unit cost. Boeing chose not to compete with Airbus in the market for superjumbo jets; rather, it decided to focus on a smaller, fuel-efficient airplane (the 787 Dreamliner, priced at roughly $250 million) that allows for long-distance, point-to-point connections. By spring 2019, it had built 800 Dreamliners with more than 600 orders for the new airplane.[16] Boeing can expect to reap significant economies of scale and learning, which will lower per-unit cost. At the same time, Airbus had delivered 290 A-380 superjumbos (sticker price: $450 million) with 64 orders remaining on its books.[17] If both companies would have chosen to compete head-on in each market segment, the resulting per-unit cost for each airplane would have been much higher because neither could have achieved significant economies of scale (overall their market share split is roughly 50-50).

What causes per-unit cost to drop as output increases (up to point Q_1)? Economies of scale allow firms to

- Spread their fixed costs over a larger output.
- Employ specialized systems and equipment.
- Take advantage of certain physical properties.

SPREADING FIXED COSTS OVER LARGER OUTPUT. Larger output allows firms to spread their fixed costs over more units. That is why gains in market share are often critical to drive down per-unit cost. This relationship is even more pronounced in many high-tech industries because most of the cost occurs before a single product or service is sold. Take operating systems software as an example. Microsoft spends over $10 billion a year on research and development (R&D).[18] Between 2011 and 2015, a good part of this was spent on developing Windows 10, its most recent operating system software. This R&D expense was a fixed cost Microsoft had to incur before a single copy of Windows 10 was sold. However, once the initial version of the new software was completed, the marginal cost of each additional copy was basically zero, especially for copies sold in digital form online. Given that Microsoft dominates the operating system market for personal computers (PCs) with more than 90 percent market share, it expects to sell several hundred million copies of Windows 10, thereby spreading its huge fixed cost of development over a large output. Microsoft's huge installed base of Windows operating systems throughout the world allowed it to capture a large profit margin for each copy of Windows sold, after recouping its initial investment. Microsoft's Windows 10 also drives sales for complementary products such as the ubiquitous Microsoft Office Suite made up of Word, Excel, PowerPoint, and Outlook, among other programs (as discussed in ChapterCase 5).

EMPLOYING SPECIALIZED SYSTEMS AND EQUIPMENT. Larger output also allows firms to invest in more specialized systems and equipment, such as enterprise resource planning (ERP) software or manufacturing robots. Tesla's strong demand for its Model 3 sedan allows it to employ cutting-edge robotics in its Fremont, California, manufacturing plant to produce cars of high quality at large scale, and thus driving down costs. Tesla is expecting even more demand for the Model 3 and the newly launched Model Y in China, thus it will employ more specialized systems and equipment in the new and much larger Shanghai, China, factory in its quest for economies of scale.

TAKING ADVANTAGE OF CERTAIN PHYSICAL PROPERTIES. Economies of scale also occur because of certain physical properties. One such property is known as the *cube-square rule:* The volume of a body such as a pipe or a tank increases disproportionately more than its surface. This same principle makes big-box retail stores such as Walmart or The Home Depot cheaper to build and run. They can also stock much more merchandise and handle inventory more efficiently. Their huge size makes it difficult for department stores or small retailers to compete on cost and selection.

Look again at Exhibit 6.5. The output range between Q_1 and Q_2 in the figure is considered the **minimum efficient scale (MES)** to be cost-competitive. Between Q_1 and Q_2, the returns to scale are constant. It is the output range needed to bring the cost per unit down as much as possible, allowing a firm to stake out the lowest-cost position achievable through economies of scale. With more than 10 million Prius cars sold worldwide since its introduction in 1997, Toyota has been able to reach the minimum efficient scale part of the per-unit cost curve. This allows the company to offer the car at a relatively low price and still make a profit.

The concept of minimum efficient scale applies not only to manufacturing processes but also to managerial tasks such as how to organize work. Due to investments in specialized technology and equipment (e.g., electric arc furnaces), Nucor is able to reach MES with much smaller batches of steel than larger, fully vertically integrated steel companies using older technology. Nucor's optimal plant size is about 500 people, which is much smaller than at larger integrated steelmakers such as U.S. Steel which often employ thousands of workers per plant.[19] Of course, minimum efficient scale depends on the specific industry: The average per-unit cost curve, depicted conceptually in Exhibit 6.5, is a reflection of the underlying production function, which is determined by technology and other input factors.

Benefits to scale cannot go on indefinitely, though. Bigger is not always better; in fact, sometimes bigger is worse. Beyond *Q*2 in Exhibit 6.5, firms experience **diseconomies of scale**—increases in cost as output increases. As firms get too big, the complexity of managing and coordinating the production process raises the cost, negating any benefits to scale. Large firms also tend to become overly bureaucratic, with too many layers of hierarchy. They grow inflexible and slow in decision making. To avoid problems associated with diseconomies of scale, Gore Associates, maker of GORE-TEX fabric, Glide dental floss, and many other innovative products, breaks up its company into smaller units. Gore Associates found that employing about 150 people per plant allows it to avoid diseconomies of scale. It uses a simple decision rule:[20] "We put 150 parking spaces in the lot, and when people start parking on the grass, we know it's time to build a new plant."[21]

Finally, there are also physical limits to scale. Airbus is pushing the envelope with its A-380 aircraft, which can hold more than 850 passengers and can fly 9,520 miles (from Newark, New Jersey, to Singapore, for instance). The goal, of course, is to drive down the cost of the average seat-mile flown (CASM, a standard cost metric in the airline industry). It appears, however, that the A-380 superjumbo did not allow airlines to operate at minimum efficient scale, and thus failed to deliver the lowest cost per unit (CASM) possible. Rather, it turned out that the A-380 was simply too large to be efficient, thus causing *diseconomies of scale*. For example, boarding and embarking procedures needed to be completely revamped and streamlined to accommodate more than 850 people in a timely and safe manner. Airports around the world needed to be retrofitted with longer and wider runways to allow the superjumbo to take off and land. To prove the point, Airbus announced in early 2019 that it will cease production of the A-380 in 2021 as demand declined for the superjumbo in recent years.[22]

Scale economies are critical to driving down a firm's cost and strengthening a cost-leadership position. Although strategic leaders need to increase output to operate at a

---

minimum efficient scale (MES) Output range needed to bring down the cost per unit as much as possible, allowing a firm to stake out the lowest-cost position that is achievable through economies of scale.

diseconomies of scale Increases in cost per unit when output increases.

minimum efficient scale (between $Q1$ and $Q2$ in Exhibit 6.5), they also need to be watchful not to drive scale beyond $Q2$, where they would encounter diseconomies. In sum, if the firm's output range is less than Q_1 or more than Q_2, the firm is at a cost disadvantage; reaching an output level between $Q1$ and $Q2$ is optimal in regards to driving down costs. Monitoring the firm's cost structure closely over different output ranges allows managers to fine-tune operations and benefit from economies of scale.

LEARNING CURVE

Do learning curves go up or down? Looking at the challenge of learning, many people tend to see it as an uphill battle, and assume the learning curve goes up. But if we consider our productivity, learning curves go down, as it takes less and less time to produce the same output as we learn how to be more efficient—learning by doing drives down cost. As individuals and teams engage repeatedly in an activity, whether writing computer code, developing new medicines, or building submarines, they learn from their cumulative experience.[23] *Learning curves* were first documented in aircraft manufacturing as the United States ramped up production in the 1930s, before its entry into World War II.[24] Every time production was doubled, the per-unit cost dropped by a predictable and constant rate (approximately 20 percent).[25]

It is not surprising that a learning curve was first observed in aircraft manufacturing. Highly complex, a modern commercial aircraft can contain more than 5 million parts, compared with a few thousand for a car. The more complex the underlying process to manufacture a product or deliver a service, the more learning effects we can expect. As cumulative output increases, managers learn how to optimize the process, and workers improve their performance through repetition and specialization.

TESLA'S LEARNING CURVE. Tesla's production of its Model S vehicle provides a more recent example, depicted in Exhibit 6.6, with the horizontal axis showing cumulative output in units and the vertical axis showing per-unit cost in thousands of dollars.[26]

The California-based designer and manufacturer of all-electric cars made headlines in 2017 when its market capitalization overtook both GM and Ford. This was the first time in U.S. history that the most valuable U.S. car company is not based in Detroit, Michigan, but in Silicon Valley. In 2016, Tesla sold some 80,000 vehicles, while GM sold some 10 million. How can a start-up company that makes less than 1 percent as many vehicles as GM have a higher market valuation? The answer: Future expected growth. Investors bidding up Tesla's share price count on the maker of all-electric cars to sell millions of its newer Model 3 (compact sedan) and Model Y (compact SUV). When the Model 3 was announced in 2016, Tesla garnered some 400,000 preorders from future owners for a car that was not yet produced, let alone test-driven by any potential buyer. The Model Y was announced in 2019 and is expected to be ready for delivery in 2021.

Tesla's learning curve is critical in justifying such lofty stock market valuations, because as production volume increases, production cost per car falls, and the company becomes profitable. Based on a careful analysis of production reports for the Model S between 2012 and 2014[27], Exhibit 6.6 shows how Tesla was able to drive down the unit cost for each car as production volume ramped up. Initially, Tesla lost a significant amount of money on each Model S sold because of high upfront R&D spending to develop the futuristic self-driving car. When producing only 1,000 vehicles, unit cost was $140,000. As production volume of the Model S reached some 12,000 units per year (in 2014), unit cost fell to about $57,000. Although still high, Tesla was able to start making money on each car, because the average selling price for a Model S was about $90,000.

208   **CHAPTER 6**   Business Strategy: Differentiation, Cost Leadership, and Blue Oceans

EXHIBIT 6.6

Tesla's Learning
Curve Producing the
Model S

Source: Depiction of
functional relationship
estimated in J. Dyer and H.
Gregersen (2016, Aug. 24),
"Tesla's innovations are
transforming the auto
industry," *Forbes*.

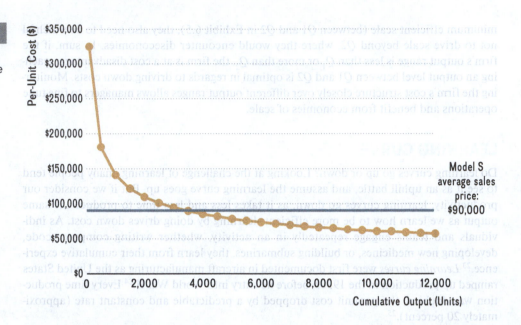

The relationship between production volume and per-unit cost for Tesla (depicted in Exhibit 6.6) suggests that it is an 80 percent learning curve. In an 80 percent learning curve, per-unit cost drops 20 percent every time output is doubled. Assuming a similar relationship holds for the Model 3 production, then per-unit cost would fall to $16,000 per Model 3 with a cumulative production volume of 400,000 (which is the number of preorders Tesla received within one week of announcing this new vehicle). Although the Model 3 base price is pegged at $35,000, the estimated average selling price is more like $50,000 given additional features and eventual expiration of a $7,500 federal tax credit for electric vehicles (when a manufacturer hits 200,000 units). Riding down an 80 percent learning curve, Tesla could make a profit of an estimated $34,000 per Model 3. This would translate to a cumulative profit for Tesla of more than $13.5 billion for the Model 3 preorders alone. As Tesla is reducing the price for the Model 3, the expected profits would decline accordingly. This back-of-the-envelope calculation shows some of the rationale behind Tesla's market capitalization exceeding that of GM and Ford.

Taken together, this example highlights not only the power of the learning curve in driving down per-unit costs, but also how critical cost containment is in gaining a competitive advantage when pursuing a differentiation strategy as Tesla does.

DIFFERENCES IN LEARNING CURVES. Let's now compare different learning curves, and explore their implications for competitive advantage. The steeper the learning curve, the more learning has occurred. As cumulative output increases, firms move down the learning curve, reaching lower per-unit costs. Exhibit 6.7 depicts two different learning curves: a 90 percent and an 80 percent learning curve. In a 90 percent learning curve, per-unit cost drops 10 percent every time output is doubled. The steeper 80 percent learning curve indicates a 20 percent drop every time output is doubled (this was the case in the Tesla example above). It is important to note that the learning-curve effect is driven by increasing cumulative output within the existing technology over time. That implies that the only difference between two points on the same learning curve is the size of the cumulative output. The underlying technology remains the same. The speed of

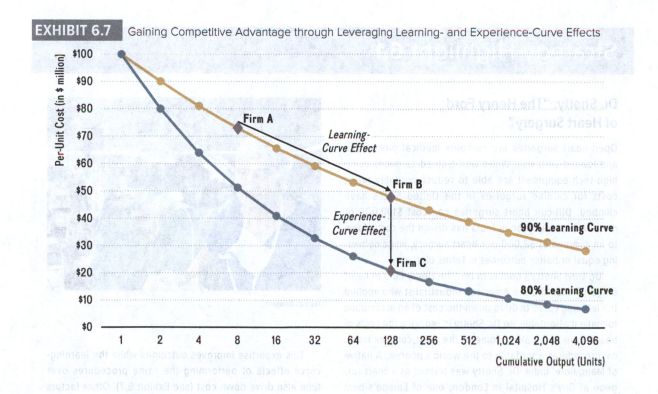

EXHIBIT 6.7   Gaining Competitive Advantage through Leveraging Learning- and Experience-Curve Effects

learning determines the slope of the learning curve, or how steep the learning curve is (e.g., 80 percent is steeper than a 90 percent learning curve because costs decrease by 20 percent versus a mere 10 percent each time output doubles). In this perspective, *economies of learning* allow movement down a *given* learning curve based on current production technology.

By moving further down a given learning curve than competitors, a firm can gain a competitive advantage. Exhibit 6.7 shows that Firm B is further down the 90 percent learning curve than Firm A. Firm B leverages *economies of learning* due to larger cumulative output to gain an advantage over Firm A. The only variable that has changed is cumulative output; the technology underlying the 90 percent learning curve remained the same.

Let's continue with the example of manufacturing airframes. To be more precise, as shown in Exhibit 6.7, Firm A produces eight aircraft and reaches a per-unit cost of $73 million per aircraft.[28] Firm B produces 128 aircraft using the same technology as Firm A (because both firms are on the same [90 percent] learning curve), but given a much larger cumulative output, its per unit-cost falls to only $48 million. Thus, Firm B has a clear competitive advantage over Firm A, assuming similar or identical quality in output. We will discuss Firm C when we formally introduce the impact of changes in technology and process innovation.

Learning curves are a robust phenomenon observed in many industries, not only in manufacturing processes but also in alliance management, franchising, and health care.[29] For example, physicians who perform only a small number of cardiac surgeries per year can have a patient mortality rate five times higher than physicians who perform the same surgery more frequently.[30] Strategy Highlight 6.1 features Dr. Devi Shetty of India who reaped huge benefits by applying learning-curve principles to open-heart surgery, driving down cost while improving quality at the same time.

Strategy Highlight **6.1**

Dr. Shetty: "The Henry Ford of Heart Surgery"

Open-heart surgeries are complex medical procedures and loaded with risk. While well-trained surgeons using high-tech equipment are able to reduce mortality rates, costs for cardiac surgeries in the United States have climbed. Difficult heart surgeries can cost $100,000 or more. A heart surgeon in India has driven the costs down to an average of $2,000 per heart surgery, while delivering equal or better outcomes in terms of quality.

Dr. Devi Shetty's goal is to be "the Henry Ford of heart surgery." Just like the American industrialist who applied the learning curve to drive down the cost of an automobile to make it affordable, so Dr. Shetty is reducing the costs of health care and making some of the most complex medical procedures affordable to the world's poorest. A native of Mangalore, India, Dr. Shetty was trained as a heart surgeon at Guy's Hospital in London, one of Europe's best medical facilities. He first came to fame in the 1990s when he successfully conducted an open-heart bypass surgery on Mother Teresa, after she suffered a heart attack.

Dr. Shetty believes that the key to driving down costs in health care is not product innovation, but process innovation. He is able to drive down the cost of complex medical procedures from $100,000 to $2,000 not by doing one big thing, but rather by focusing on doing a thousand small things. Dr. Shetty is applying the concept of the learning curve to make a complex procedure routine and comparatively inexpensive. Part of the Narayana Health group, Dr. Shetty's hospital in Bangalore, India, performs so many cardiac procedures per year that doctors are able to get a great deal of experience quickly, which allows them to specialize in one or two complex procedures. The Narayana surgeons perform two or three procedures a day for six days a week, compared to U.S. surgeons who perform one or two procedures a day for five days a week. The difference adds up. Some of Dr. Shetty's surgeons perform more specialized procedures by the time they are in their 30s than their U.S. counterparts will perform throughout their entire careers. This volume of experienc e allows the cardiac surgeons to move down the learning curve quickly, because the more heart surgeries they perform, the more their skills improve. With this skill level, surgical teams develop robust standard operating procedures and processes, where team members become experts at their specific tasks.

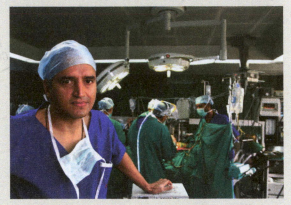

Namas Bhojani

This expertise improves outcomes while the learning-curve effects of performing the same procedures over time also drive down cost (see Exhibit 6.7). Other factors provide additional cost savings. At the same time, Dr. Shetty pays his cardiac surgeons the going rate in India, between $110,000 and $250,000 a year, depending on experience. Their U.S. counterparts earn two to three times the average Indian salary.

Dr. Shetty's health group also reduces costs through economies of scale. By performing thousands of heart surgeries a year, high fixed costs such as the purchase of expensive medical equipment can be spread over a much larger volume. The Narayana hospital in Bangalore has 1,000 beds (many times larger than the average U.S. hospital with 160 beds) and some 20 operating rooms that stay busy pretty much around the clock. This scale allows the Narayana heart clinic to cost-effectively employ specialized high-tech equipment. Given the large size of Dr. Shetty's hospital, it also has significant buying power, driving down the costs of the latest high-tech equipment from vendors such as GE and Siemens. Wherever possible, Dr. Shetty sources lower-cost inputs such as sutures locally, rather than from the more expensive companies such as Johnson & Johnson. Further, the Narayana heart clinic shares common services, such as laboratories and blood bank and more mundane services such as catering, with the 1,400-bed cancer clinic next door. Taken together, all of these small changes result in significant cost savings, and so create a reinforcing system of low-cost value chain activities.

While many worry that high volume compromises quality, the data suggest the opposite: Narayana Health's medical outcomes in terms of mortality rate are equal to or even lower than the best hospitals in the United States. The American College of Cardiology frequently sends surgeons and administrators to visit the Narayana heart clinic. The college concluded that the clinic provides high-tech and high-quality care at low cost. Dr. Shetty now brings top-notch care at low cost to the masses in India.

Narayana Health runs a chain of over 30 hospitals in 20 locations throughout India and performs some 100,000 heart surgeries a year.

Dr. Shetty is also bringing his high-quality, low-cost health care solutions closer to American patients. In 2014, his group opened the doors to Health City Cayman Islands, a fully accredited cardiac and cardiothoracic surgery clinic, a bit over one hour from Miami by air.[31]

Learning effects differ from economies of scale (discussed earlier) as shown:

- **Differences in timing.** Learning effects occur *over time* as output accumulates, while economies of scale are captured at *one point in time* when output increases. The improvements in Tesla's production costs, featured earlier, resulted from some 12,000 units in cumulative output, but it took two years to reach this volume (see Exhibit 6.6). Although learning can decline or flatten (see Exhibit 6.7), there are no *diseconomies to learning* (unlike *diseconomies to scale* in Exhibit 6.5).

- **Differences in complexity.** In some production processes (e.g., the manufacture of steel rods), effects from economies of scale can be quite significant, while learning effects are minimal. In contrast, in some professions (brain surgery or the practice of estate law), learning effects can be substantial, while economies of scale are minimal.

Managers need to understand such differences to calibrate their business-level strategy. If a firm's cost advantage is due to economies of scale, a strategic leader should worry less about employee turnover (and a potential loss in learning) and more about drops in production runs. In contrast, if the firm's low-cost position is based on complex learning, a strategic leader should be much more concerned if a key employee (e.g., a star engineer) was to leave.

EXPERIENCE CURVE

In the *learning curve* just discussed, we assumed the underlying technology remained constant, while only cumulative output increased. In the *experience curve,* in contrast, we now change the underlying technology while holding cumulative output constant.[32]

In general, technology and production processes do not stay constant. *Process innovation*—a new method or technology to produce an existing product—may initiate a new and steeper curve. Assume that Firm C, on the same learning curve as Firm B, implements a new production process (such as lean manufacturing). In doing so, Firm C initiates an entirely new and steeper learning curve. Exhibit 6.7 shows this *experience-curve effect* based on a process innovation. Firm C jumps down to the 80 percent learning curve, reflecting the new and lower-cost production process. Although Firm B and Firm C produce the same cumulative output (each making 128 aircraft), the per-unit cost differs. Firm B's per-unit cost for each airplane, being positioned on the less-steep 90 percent learning curve, is $48 million.[33] In contrast, Firm C's per-unit cost, being positioned on the steeper 80 percent learning curve because of process innovation, is only $21 million per aircraft, and thus less than half that of Firm B. Clearly, Firm C has a competitive advantage over Firm B based on lower cost per unit (assuming similar quality).

Learning by doing allows a firm to lower its per-unit costs by moving down a given learning curve, while experience-curve effects based on process innovation allow a firm to leapfrog to a steeper learning curve, thereby driving down its per-unit costs.

In Strategy Highlight 6.1, we saw how Dr. Shetty leveraged learning-curve effects to save lives while driving down costs. One could argue that his Narayana Health group not only moved down a given learning curve using best industry practice, but it also jumped down to a new and steeper learning curve through process innovation. Dr. Shetty sums up his business strategy based on cost leadership: "Japanese companies reinvented the process of making cars (by introducing lean manufacturing). That's what we're doing in health care. What health care needs is process innovation, not product innovation."[34]

In a cost-leadership strategy, managers must focus on lowering the costs of production while maintaining a level of quality acceptable to the customer. If firms can share the benefits of lower costs with consumers, cost leaders appeal to the bargain-conscious buyer, whose main criterion is price. By looking to reduce costs in each value chain activity, managers aim for the lowest-cost position in the industry. They strive to offer lower prices than competitors and thus to increase sales. Cost leaders such as Walmart ("Every Day Low Prices") can be quite profitable by pursuing this strategic position over time.

LO 6-4

Assess the benefits and risks of differentiation and cost-leadership strategies vis-à-vis the five forces that shape competition.

6.4 Business-Level Strategy and the Five Forces: Benefits and Risks

The business-level strategies introduced in this chapter allow firms to carve out strong strategic positions that enhance the likelihood of gaining and sustaining competitive advantage. The five forces model introduced in Chapter 3 helps strategic leaders assess the forces—threat of entry, power of suppliers, power of buyers, threat of substitutes, and rivalry among existing competitors—that make some industries more attractive than others. With this understanding of industry dynamics, managers use one of the generic business-level strategies to protect themselves against the forces that drive down profitability.[35] Exhibit 6.8 details the relationship between competitive positioning and the five forces. In particular, it highlights the benefits and risks of differentiation and cost-leadership business strategies, which we discuss next.

DIFFERENTIATION STRATEGY: BENEFITS AND RISKS

A differentiation strategy is defined by establishing a strategic position that creates higher perceived value while controlling costs. The successful differentiator stakes out a unique strategic position, where it can benefit from imperfect competition (as discussed in Chapter 3) and command a premium price. A well-executed differentiation strategy reduces rivalry among competitors.

A successful differentiation strategy is likely to be based on unique or specialized features of the product, on an effective marketing campaign, or on intangible resources such as a reputation for innovation, quality, and customer service. A rival would need to improve the product features as well as build a similar or more effective reputation in order to gain market share. The threat of entry is reduced: Competitors will find such intangible advantages time-consuming and costly, and maybe impossible, to imitate. If the source of the differential appeal is intangible rather than tangible (e.g., reputation rather than observable product and service features), a differentiator is even more likely to sustain its advantage.

Moreover, if the differentiator is able to create a significant difference between perceived value and current market prices, the differentiator will not be so threatened by increases in input prices due to powerful suppliers. Although an increase in input factors could erode margins, a differentiator is likely able to pass on price increases to its customers as long as its value creation exceeds the price charged. Since a successful differentiator creates

EXHIBIT 6.8 Competitive Positioning and the Five Forces: Benefits and Risks of Differentiation and Cost-Leadership Business Strategies

Competitive Force	Differentiation		Cost Leadership	
	Benefits	**Risks**	**Benefits**	**Risks**
Threat of entry	• Protection against entry due to intangible resources such as a reputation for innovation, quality, or customer service	• Erosion of margins • Replacement	• Protection against entry due to economies of scale	• Erosion of margins • Replacement
Power of suppliers	• Protection against increase in input prices, which can be passed on to customers	• Erosion of margins	• Protection against increase in input prices, which can be absorbed	• Erosion of margins
Power of buyers	• Protection against decrease in sales prices, because well-differentiated products or services are not perfect imitations	• Erosion of margins	• Protection against decrease in sales prices, which can be absorbed	• Erosion of margins
Threat of substitutes	• Protection against substitute products due to differential appeal	• Replacement, especially when faced with innovation	• Protection against substitute products through further lowering of prices	• Replacement, especially when faced with innovation
Rivalry among existing competitors	• Protection against competitors if product or service has enough differential appeal to command premium price	• Focus of competition shifts to price • Increasing differentiation of product features that do not create value but raise costs • Increasing differentiation to raise costs above acceptable threshold	• Protection against price wars because lowest-cost firm will win	• Focus of competition shifts to non-price attributes • Lowering costs to drive value creation below acceptable threshold

Source: Based on M.E. Porter (2008, January), "The five competitive forces that shape strategy," *Harvard Business Review*; and M.E. Porter (1980), *Competitive Strategy: Techniques for Analyzing Industries and Competitors* (New York: Free Press).

perceived value in the minds of consumers and builds customer loyalty, powerful buyers demanding price decreases are unlikely to emerge. A strong differentiated position also reduces the threat of substitutes, because the unique features of the product have been created to appeal to customer preferences, keeping them loyal to the product. By providing superior quality beverages and other food items combined with a great customer experience and a global presence, Starbucks has built a strong differentiated appeal. It has cultivated a loyal following of customers who reward it with repeat business.

The viability of a differentiation strategy is severely undermined when the focus of competition shifts to price rather than value-creating features. This can happen when differentiated products become commoditized and an acceptable standard of quality has emerged across rival firms. Although the iPhone was a highly differentiated product when introduced in 2007, touch-based screens and other once-innovative features are now standard in smartphones. Indeed, Android-based smartphones hold some 75 percent market share globally, while Apple's iOS phones hold about 23 percent.[36] Several companies including Google; Samsung and LG, both of South Korea; and low-cost leaders Huawei and Xiaomi of China are attempting to challenge Apple's ability to extract significant profits from the smartphone industry based on its iPhone franchise. A differentiator also needs to be careful not to overshoot its differentiated appeal by adding product features that raise costs but not perceived value in the minds of consumers. For example, any additional increase in screen resolution beyond Apple's retina display cannot be detected by the human eye at a normal viewing distance. Finally, a differentiator needs to be vigilant that its costs of providing uniqueness do not rise above the customer's willingness to pay.

COST-LEADERSHIP STRATEGY: BENEFITS AND RISKS

A cost-leadership strategy is defined by obtaining the lowest-cost position in the industry while offering acceptable value. The cost leader, therefore, is protected from other competitors because of having the lowest cost. If a price war ensues, the low-cost leader will be the last firm standing; all other firms will be driven out as margins evaporate. Since reaping economies of scale is critical to reaching a low-cost position, the cost leader is likely to have a large market share, which in turn reduces the threat of entry.

A cost leader is also fairly well isolated from threats of powerful suppliers to increase input prices, because it is more able to absorb price increases through accepting lower profit margins. Likewise, a cost leader can absorb price reductions more easily when demanded by powerful buyers. Should substitutes emerge, the low-cost leader can try to fend them off by further lowering its prices to reinstall relative value with the substitute. For example, Walmart tends to be fairly isolated from these threats. Walmart's cost structure combined with its large volume allows it to work with suppliers in keeping prices low, to the extent that suppliers are often the party that experiences a profit-margin squeeze.

Although a cost-leadership strategy provides some protection against the five forces, it also carries some risks. If a new entrant with relevant expertise enters the market, the low-cost leader's margins may erode due to loss in market share while it attempts to learn new capabilities. For example, Walmart faces challenges to its cost leadership. Dollar General stores, and other smaller low-cost retail chains, have drawn customers who prefer a smaller format than the big box of Walmart. The risk of replacement is particularly pertinent if a potent substitute emerges due to an innovation. Leveraging ecommerce, Amazon has become a potent substitute and thus a powerful threat to many brick-and-mortar retail outlets including Barnes & Noble, Best Buy, The Home Depot, and even Walmart. Powerful suppliers and buyers may be able to reduce margins so much that the low-cost leader could have difficulty covering the cost of capital and lose the potential for a competitive advantage.

The low-cost leader also needs to stay vigilant to keep its cost the lowest in the industry. Over time, competitors can beat the cost leader by implementing the same business strategy, but more effectively. Although keeping its cost the lowest in the industry is imperative, the cost leader must not forget that it needs to create an acceptable level of value. If continuously lowering costs leads to a value proposition that falls below an acceptable threshold, the low-cost leader's market share will evaporate. Finally, the low-cost leader faces significant difficulties when the focus of competition shifts from price to non-price attributes.

We have seen how useful the five forces model can be in industry analysis. None of the business-level strategies depicted in Exhibit 6.2 (cost leadership, differentiation, and focused variations thereof) is inherently superior. The success of each depends on context and relies on two factors:

- How well the strategy leverages the firm's internal strengths while mitigating its weaknesses.

- How well it helps the firm exploit external opportunities while avoiding external threats.

There is no single correct business strategy for a specific industry. The deciding factor is that the chosen business strategy provides a strong position that attempts to maximize economic value creation and is effectively implemented.

6.5 Blue Ocean Strategy: Combining Differentiation and Cost Leadership

So far we've seen that firms can create more economic value and the likelihood of gaining and sustaining competitive advantage in one of two ways—either increasing perceived consumer value (while containing costs) or lowering costs (while offering acceptable value). Should strategic leaders try to do both at the same time? In general the answer is *no*. To accomplish this, they would need to integrate two different strategic positions: differentiation *and* low cost.[37] Managers should not pursue this complex strategy because of the inherent trade-offs in different strategic positions, unless they are able to reconcile the conflicting requirements of each generic strategy.

To meet this challenge, strategy scholars Kim and Mauborgne advanced the notion of a **blue ocean strategy**, which is a business-level strategy that successfully combines differentiation and cost-leadership activities using value innovation to reconcile the inherent trade-offs in those two distinct strategic positions.[38] They use the metaphor of an ocean to denote market spaces. *Blue oceans* represent untapped market space, the creation of additional demand, and the resulting opportunities for highly profitable growth. In contrast, *red oceans* are the known market space of existing industries. In *red oceans* the rivalry among existing firms is cut-throat because the market space is crowded and competition is a zero-sum game. Products become commodities, and competition is focused mainly on price. Any market share gain comes at the expense of other competitors in the same industry, turning the oceans bloody red.

A blue ocean strategy allows a firm to offer a differentiated product or service at low cost. As one example of a blue ocean strategy, consider the grocery chain Trader Joe's. Trader Joe's had much lower costs than Whole Foods (prior to its 2017 acquisition by Amazon) for the same market of patrons desiring high value and health-conscious foods, and Trader Joe's scores exceptionally well in customer service and other areas. When a blue ocean strategy is successfully formulated and implemented, investments in differentiation and low cost are not substitutes but are

> **blue ocean strategy** Business-level strategy that successfully combines differentiation and cost-leadership activities using value innovation to reconcile the inherent trade-offs.

Strategic leaders may use value innovation to move to blue oceans, that is, to new and uncontested market spaces. Shown here is the famous "blue hole" just off Belize.
Mlenny/Getty Images

complements, providing important positive spill-over effects. A successfully implemented blue ocean strategy allows firms two pricing options: First, the firm can charge a higher price than the cost leader, reflecting its higher value creation and thus generating greater profit margins. Second, the firm can lower its price below that of the differentiator because of its lower-cost structure. If the firm offers lower prices than the differentiator, it can gain market share and make up the loss in margin through increased sales.

LO 6-5

Evaluate value and cost drivers that may allow a firm to pursue a blue ocean strategy.

VALUE INNOVATION

For a blue ocean strategy to succeed, managers must resolve trade-offs between the two generic strategic positions—low cost and differentiation.[39] This is done through **value innovation**, aligning innovation with total perceived consumer benefits, price, and cost (also see the discussion in Chapter 5 on *economic value creation*). Instead of attempting to out-compete rivals by offering better features or lower costs, successful value innovation makes competition irrelevant by providing a leap in value creation, thereby opening new and uncontested market spaces.

value innovation The simultaneous pursuit of differentiation and low cost in a way that creates a leap in value for both the firm and the consumers; considered a cornerstone of blue ocean strategy.

Successful value innovation requires that a firm's strategic moves lower its costs and also increase the perceived value for buyers (see Exhibit 6.9). Lowering a firm's costs is primarily achieved by eliminating and reducing the taken-for-granted factors that the firm's industry rivals compete on. Perceived buyer value is increased by raising existing key success factors and by creating new elements that the industry has not offered previously. To initiate a strategic move that allows a firm to open a new and uncontested market space through value innovation, strategic leaders must answer the four key questions below when formulating a blue ocean business strategy.[40] In terms of achieving successful value innovation, note that the first two questions focus on lowering costs, while the second two questions focus on increasing perceived consumer benefits.

Value Innovation—Lower Costs

1. *Eliminate.* Which of the factors that the industry takes for granted should be eliminated?
2. *Reduce.* Which of the factors should be reduced well below the industry's standard?

Value Innovation—Increase Perceived Consumer Benefits

1. *Raise.* Which of the factors should be raised well above the industry's standard?
2. *Create.* Which factors should be created that the industry has never offered?

The international furniture retailer IKEA, for example, has used value innovation based on the *eliminate-reduce-raise-create* framework to initiate its own blue ocean and to achieve a sustainable competitive advantage.[41]

ELIMINATE (TO LOWER COSTS). IKEA eliminated several taken-for-granted competitive elements: salespeople, expensive but small retail outlets in prime urban locations and

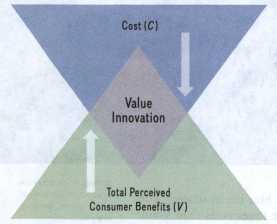

EXHIBIT 6.9   Value Innovation Accomplished through Simultaneously Pursuing Differentiation (V ↑) and Low Cost (C ↓)

Cost (C)

Value Innovation

Total Perceived Consumer Benefits (V)

Source: Adapted from C.W. Kim and R. Mauborgne (2005), *Blue Ocean Strategy: How to Create Uncontested Market Space and Make Competition Irrelevant* (Boston: Harvard Business School Publishing).

shopping malls, long wait after ordering furniture, after-sales service, and other factors. In contrast, IKEA displays its products in a warehouse-like setting, thus reducing inventory cost. Customers serve themselves and then transport the furniture to their homes in IKEA's signature flat-packs for assembly. IKEA also uses the big-box concept of locating supersized stores near major metropolitan areas (please refer to the discussion of "Taking Advantage of Certain Physical Properties" under "Economies of Scale" in Section 6.3).

Each IKEA store has a large self-service warehouse section, further driving down its cost.
Tooykrub/Shutterstock

REDUCE (TO LOWER COSTS). Because of its do-it-yourself business model regarding furniture selection, delivery, and assembly, IKEA drastically reduced the need for staff in its mega-stores. Strolling through an IKEA store, you encounter few employees. IKEA also reduced several other taken-for-granted competitive elements: 25-year warranties on high-end custom furniture, high degree of customization in selection of options such as different fabrics and patterns, and use of expensive materials such as leather or hardwoods, among other elements.

RAISE (TO INCREASE PERCEIVED CONSUMER BENEFITS). IKEA raised several competitive elements: It offers tens of thousands of home furnishing items in each of its big-box stores (some 300,000 square feet, roughly five football fields), versus a few hundred at best in traditional furniture stores; it also offers more than furniture, including a range of accessories such as place mats, laptop stands, and much more; each store has hundreds of rooms fully decorated with all sorts of IKEA items, each with a detailed tag explaining the item. Moreover, rather than sourcing its furniture from wholesalers or other furniture makers, IKEA manufactures all of its furniture at fully dedicated suppliers, thus tightly controlling the design, quality, functionality, and cost of each product.

IKEA also raised the customer experience by laying out its stores in such a way that customers see and can touch basically all of IKEA's products, including dishware, bedding, and furniture.

CREATE (TO INCREASE CONSUMER BENEFITS). IKEA created a new way for people to shop for furniture. Customers stroll along a predetermined path winding through the fully furnished showrooms. They can compare, test, and touch all the things in the showroom. The price tag on each item contains other important information: type of material, weight, and so on. Once an item is selected, the customer notes the item number (the store provides a pencil and paper). The tag also indicates the location in the warehouse where the customer can pick up the item in IKEA's signature flat-packs. After paying, the customer transports the products and assembles the furniture. The customer has 90 days to return items for a full refund.

In traditional furniture shopping, customers visit a small retail outlet where salespeople swarm them. After a purchase, the customer has to wait generally a few weeks before the furniture is shipped because many furniture makers do not produce items, such as expensive leather sofas, until they are paid for in advance. Finely crafted couches and chairs cost thousands of dollars (while IKEA's fabric couches retail for $399). When shopping at a traditional furniture store, the customer also pays for delivery of the furniture.

IKEA also created a new approach to pricing its products. Rather than using a "cost plus margin approach" like traditional furniture stores when pricing items, IKEA begins with the retail price first. For example, it sets the price for an office chair at $150, and IKEA's designers figure out how to meet this goal, which includes a profit margin. They need to consider the chair from start to finish, including not only design but also raw materials and the way the product will be displayed and transported. Only then will products go into production.

IKEA also created several other new competitive elements that allow it to offer more value to its customers: Stores provide on-site child care, house a cafeteria serving delicious food options including Swedish delicatessen such as smoked salmon at low prices, and offer convenient and ample parking, often in garages under the store, where escalators bring customers directly into the showrooms.

By implementing these key steps to achieving value innovation—eliminate, reduce, raise, and create—IKEA orchestrates different internal value chain activities to reconcile the tension between differentiation and cost leadership to create a unique market space. IKEA uses innovation in multiple dimensions—in furniture design, engineering, and store design—to solve the trade-offs between value creation and production cost. An IKEA executive highlights the difficulty of achieving value innovation as follows: "Designing beautiful-but-expensive products is easy. Designing beautiful products that are inexpensive and functional is a huge challenge."[42] IKEA leverages its deep design and engineering expertise to offer furniture that is stylish and functional and that can be easily assembled by the consumer. In this way, IKEA can pursue a blue ocean strategy based on value innovation to increase the perceived value of its products, while simultaneously lowering its cost and offering competitive prices. It opened a new market serving a younger demographic than traditional furniture stores. When young people the world over move into their own apartment or house, they frequently furnish it from IKEA.

LO 6-6

Assess the risks of a blue ocean strategy, and explain why it is difficult to succeed at value innovation.

BLUE OCEAN STRATEGY GONE BAD: "STUCK IN THE MIDDLE"

Although appealing in a theoretical sense, a blue ocean strategy can be quite difficult to translate into reality. Differentiation and cost leadership are distinct strategic positions that require important trade-offs.[43] A blue ocean strategy is difficult to implement because it requires the reconciliation of fundamentally different strategic positions—differentiation and low cost—which in turn require distinct internal value chain activities (see Chapter 4) so the firm can increase value *and* lower cost at the same time.

Exhibit 6.10 suggests how a successfully formulated blue ocean strategy based on *value innovation* combines both a differentiation and low-cost position. It also shows the consequence of a blue ocean strategy gone bad—the firm ends up being *stuck in the middle*, meaning the firm has neither a clear differentiation nor a clear cost-leadership profile. Being *stuck in the middle* leads to inferior performance and a resulting competitive disadvantage. Strategy Highlight 6.2 shows how Cirque du Soleil is searching for a new blue ocean to avoid being stuck in the middle.

EXHIBIT 6.10 Value Innovation vs. *Stuck in the Middle*

Strategy Highlight 6.2

Cirque du Soleil: Finding a New Blue Ocean?

Most of the 11 million people that bought tickets for a Cirque du Soleil show in 2018 were dazzled by its high-quality artistic performances. Founded in 1984 by two street performers, Guy Laliberté and Gilles Ste-Croix, in an inner-city area of Montreal, Canada, Cirque du Soleil today is the largest theatrical producer in the world. With its spectacularly sophisticated shows, Cirque's mission is to "evoke the imagination, invoke the senses, and provoke the emotions of people around the world."[44] Employing more than 5,000 people (with one-third of them performers) and with annual revenues of over $1 billion, Cirque is not only the largest live entertainment businesses in the world but also quite successful. How did Cirque become so successful while most circuses have either shut down or barely survived?

CIRQUE'S BLUE OCEAN STRATEGY AND VALUE INNOVATION Using a *blue ocean strategy* based on *value innovation,* Cirque du Soleil created a new and thus uncontested market space in the live entertainment industry. Let's take a closer look at how Cirque used the *eliminate-reduce-raise-create framework* to reinvent the circus and to create a blue ocean of uncontested market space where competition is less of a concern.

Eliminate. In redefining the circus, Cirque du Soleil eliminated several traditional circus elements. First, it did away with all animal shows, partly because of the public's growing concern in recent years about the humane treatment of animals, but also because their care, transportation, medical attention, insurance, and food consumption (a grown male lion can devour 90 pounds of meat a day) were the most expensive items to maintain. Second, Cirque did away with star performers, who were also expensive; name recognition of star performers in the circus industry is trivial compared to that of sports celebrities (e.g., LeBron James) or movie stars (e.g., Scarlett Johansson). Third, it abolished the standard three-ring stages. These were expensive to upkeep, but they also frequently created anxiety among audience members. Since different acts were being performed on all three stages at the same time, viewers felt forced to switch their attention rapidly from stage to stage. Finally, it did away with aisle concession sales. These annoyed most visitors not only because they frequently interrupted and interfered with the viewing experience, but also because audience members felt like they were being taken advantage of by the vendors' prices.

Cirque du Soleil, the largest live entertainment company globally, dazzles spectators with its high-quality artistic shows. Using a blue ocean strategy allowed Cirque to gain a competitive advantage by creating a new, uncontested market space. The question Cirque's strategic leaders now face is how to sustain its competitive advantage.
Xinhua/Alamy Stock Photo

Reduce. Cirque kept the clowns, but reduced their importance in the shows. It also reduced the amount of slapstick and low-brow clown humor, shifting instead to a more sophisticated and intellectually stimulating style.

Raise. Cirque significantly raised the quality of the live performance with its signature acrobatic and aerial acts featuring stunts never before seen. It also elevated the circus tent experience. While many other circuses replaced the extravagant circus tents of old with generic, low-cost and rented venues, Cirque, in contrast, revised the tent, turning it into a unique and magical venue. Its magnificent exteriors attracted the attention of the public, and its interiors provided luxurious seating and high-quality amenities. Given that Cirque's consumers were used to paying much higher ticket prices for live theater or ballet performances, Cirque decided to raise its ticket prices as well, starting at $75 up to $200. The fact that Cirque's audiences were primarily adults rather than children, made this possible because there were fewer adults attending shows with groups of children in tow.

Create. Cirque du Soleil created an entirely new entertainment experience: It combined in novel ways the fun and thrill of the traditional circus with the classical and cultivated storytelling of the ballet and musical theater—a sharp contrast to traditional circus productions that typically comprise a series of unrelated acts. All dance and musical performances are thoughtfully choreographed and skillfully orchestrated. Akin to Broadway shows, Cirque also offered multiple productions at all major venues across the world. With its productions generally in high demand and being performed in multiple venues around the globe, an increasing number of people were starting to attend the "circus" more frequently, even at high ticket prices.

A PERFECT STORM   Although the Cirque du Soleil experience remains high end and high brow, the company has fallen on hard times in recent years. A combination of external and internal factors led to a significant decline in performance. Cirque du Soleil was hit hard by the economic downturn resulting from the 2008–2010 global financial crisis. Its management worsened the situation through a series of poor strategic decisions, including offering too many shows that were too little differentiated (at least in the mind of the consumer). Consequently, Cirque lost its rarity appeal, its payroll and costs ballooned, and demand for its European shows declined by as much as 40 percent.

Misfortune continued to strike: Cirque du Soleil experienced its first fatality (in 2013) during its signature show Kà in Las Vegas, where one of its performers (a mother of two) fell 95 feet to her death. The U.S. Occupational Safety and Health Administration (OSHA) issued citations and fines, and conducted an in-depth investigation of safety practices that revealed a high injury rate. One investigation found that Kà alone resulted in 56 injuries per 100 workers, which is four times the injury rate for professional sports teams, according to the Bureau of Labor Statistics. Two more fatalities occurred during live shows in 2016 and 2018. Some Cirque performers claimed that the pressure to perform at high levels made it difficult to raise concerns about acrobat safety.

In 2015, Cirque du Soleil founder Guy Laliberté sold his controlling ownership stake to an investor group led by U.S. private-equity firm TPG. Other investors included Fosun, a Chinese investment firm, and a Canadian pension fund. This deal valued Cirque at $1.5 billion, down from a onetime $3 billion valuation. Once flying high, Cirque du Soleil's valuation had dropped by 50 percent.

In the search for a new blue ocean, Cirque is now pursuing a strategy of diversification. In 2017, it bought Blue Man Productions, the New York performance art company. In 2018, Cirque followed up its earlier acquisition by buying Vstar, a children's live entertainment touring group. Mitch Garber, chairman of Cirque du Soleil, who views the company's core competency as "live entertainment touring and logistics,"[45] argues that the two most recent acquisitions will allow Cirque to renew its core business, reach new audiences, and expand its repertoire of creative capabilities. To increase its appeal to high-growth markets outside North America, it is infusing Russian and Chinese influences as well as improv comedy.[46]

value curve   Horizontal connection of the points of each value on the strategy canvas that helps strategic leaders diagnose and determine courses of action.

strategy canvas   Graphical depiction of a company's relative performance vis-à-vis its competitors across the industry's key success factors.

THE STRATEGY CANVAS.   The **value curve** is the basic component of the **strategy canvas**. It graphically depicts a company's relative performance across its industry's factors of competition. A strong value curve has focus and divergence, and it can even provide a kind of tagline as to what strategy is being undertaken or should be undertaken.

Exhibit 6.11 plots the strategic profiles or value curves for three kinds of competitors in the U.S. airline industry. On the left-hand side, descending in underlying cost structure, are the legacy carriers (for example, Delta), JetBlue, and finally low-cost airlines such as Southwest Airlines (SWA). We also show the different strategic positions (differentiator, stuck in the middle, and low-cost leader) and trace the value curves as they rank high or low on a variety of parameters. JetBlue is stuck in the middle (as discussed in the ChapterCase). Low-cost airlines follow a cost-leadership strategy. The value curve, therefore, is simply a graphic representation of a firm's relative performance across different competitive factors in an industry.

Legacy carriers tend to score fairly high among most competitive elements in the airline industry, including different seating class choices (such as business class, economy comfort, basic economy, and so on); in-flight amenities such as Wi-Fi, personal video console to view movies or play games, complimentary drinks and meals; coast-to-coast coverage via

EXHIBIT 6.11　Strategy Canvas of JetBlue vs. Low-Cost Airlines and Legacy Carriers

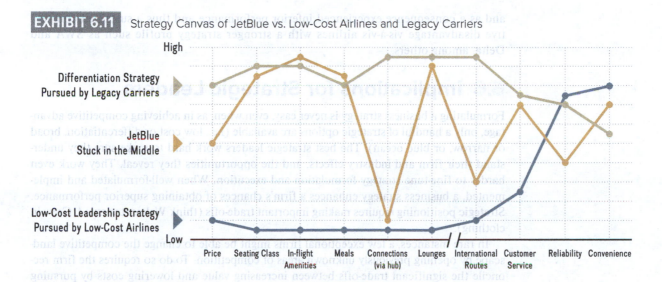

connecting hubs; plush airport lounges; international routes and global coverage; high customer service; and high reliability in terms of safety and on-time departures and arrivals. As is expected when pursuing a generic differentiation strategy, all these scores along the different competitive elements in an industry go along with a relative higher cost structure.

In contrast, the low-cost airlines tend to hover near the bottom of the strategy canvas, indicating low scores along a number of competitive factors in the industry, with no assigned seating, no in-flight amenities, no drinks or meals, no airport lounges, few if any international routes, low to intermediate level of customer service. A relatively lower cost structure goes along with a generic low-cost leadership strategy.

This strategy canvas also reveals key strategic insights. Look at the few competitive elements where the value curves of the differentiator and low-cost leader diverge. Interestingly, some cost leaders (e.g., SWA) score much higher than some differentiators (e.g., United Airlines) in terms of reliability and convenience, offering frequent point-to-point connections to conveniently located airports, often in or near city centers. This key divergence between the two strategies explains why generic cost leaders have frequently outperformed generic differentiators in the U.S. airline industry. Overall, both value curves show a consistent pattern representative of a more or less clear strategic profile as either differentiation or low-cost leader.

Now look at JetBlue's value curve. Rather than being consistent such as the differentiation or low-cost value curves, the JetBlue value curve follows a zigzag pattern. JetBlue attempts to achieve parity or even out-compete differentiators in the U.S. airline industry along the competitive factors such as different seating classes (e.g., the high-end Mint offering discussed in the ChapterCase), higher level of in-flight amenities, higher-quality beverages and meals, plush airport lounges, and a large number of international routes (mainly with global partner airlines). JetBlue, however, looks more like a low-cost leader in terms of the ability to provide only a few connections via hubs domestically, and it recently has had a poor record of customer service, mainly because of some high-profile missteps as documented in the ChapterCase. JetBlue's reliability is somewhat mediocre, but it does provide a larger number of convenient point-to-point flights than a differentiator such as Delta, but fewer than a low-cost leader such as SWA.

A value curve that zigzags across the strategy canvas indicates a lack of effectiveness in its strategic profile. The curve visually represents how JetBlue is *stuck in the middle* and as a consequence experienced inferior performance and thus a sustained competitive disadvantage vis-à-vis airlines with a stronger strategy profile such as SWA and Delta, among others.

6.6 Implications for Strategic Leaders

Formulating a business strategy is never easy, even when, as in achieving competitive advantage, only a handful of strategic options are available (i.e., low cost or differentiation, broad or narrow, or blue ocean). The best strategic leaders work hard to make sure they understand their firm and industry effects, and the opportunities they reveal. They work even harder to fine-tune strategy formulation and execution. When well-formulated and implemented, a business strategy enhances a firm's chances of obtaining superior performance. Strategic positioning requires making important trade-offs (think Walmart versus J. Crew in clothing).

In rare instances, a few exceptional firms might be able to change the competitive landscape by opening previously unknown areas of competition. To do so requires the firm reconcile the significant trade-offs between increasing value and lowering costs by pursuing both business strategies (differentiation and low cost) simultaneously. Such a blue ocean strategy tends to be successful only if a firm is able to rely on a value innovation that allows it to reconcile the trade-offs mentioned. Toyota, for example, initiated a new market space with its introduction of lean manufacturing, delivering cars of higher quality and value at lower cost. This value innovation allowed Toyota a competitive advantage for a decade or more, until this new process technology diffused widely. In a similar fashion, Cirque du Soleil also struggles to sustain competitive advantage based on an initially highly successful blue ocean strategy (see Strategy Highlight 6.2).

CHAPTER**CASE 6**   Part II

Carlosyudica/123RF

IN 2019, THE "BIG FOUR" airlines (American, Delta, SWA, and United) controlled about 70 percent of the U.S. domestic market, so the industry is fairly concentrated. JetBlue had 5.6 percent market share and close to $8 billion in annual revenues.

Early in its history JetBlue Airways achieved a competitive advantage based on *value innovation*. In particular, Jet-Blue was able to drive up perceived customer value while lowering costs. This allowed it to carve out a strong strategic position and move to a non-contested market space. This implies that no other competitors in the U.S. domestic airline industry were able to provide such value innovation at that point in time. Rather than directly competing with other airlines, JetBlue created a blue ocean.

Although JetBlue was able to create an initial competitive advantage, the airline was unable to sustain it. Because Jet-Blue failed to reconcile the strategic trade-offs inherent in combining differentiation and cost leadership, it was unable

to continue its blue ocean strategy, despite initial success. Between 2007 and 2019, JetBlue experienced a sustained competitive disadvantage, lagging the Dow Jones U.S. Airlines Index by more than 35 percentage points over the entire time period.

JetBlue's leadership team is attempting to reverse this trend; it made changes to improve the airline's flagging profitability. It is putting strategic initiatives in place to lower costs, while also trying to further increase its value offering. To lower operating costs, JetBlue decided to start charging $25 for the first checked bag and $35 for the second. It also removed the additional legroom JetBlue was famous for in the industry.

To drive up perceived customer value, JetBlue has added to its fleet more than 60 new airplanes (Airbus A-321), which significantly improve in-flight experience and thus customer satisfaction. Although JetBlue already flies internationally by serving destinations in Central and South America as well as the Caribbean, CEO Robin Hayes is considering adding selected flights to Europe. Flying non-stop to cities in Europe such as London is now possible with the new Airbus A-321. Flying longer, non-stop routes drives down costs. International routes, moreover, tend to be much more profitable than domestic routes because of less competition, for the time being.

Questions

1. Despite its initial success, why was JetBlue unable to sustain a blue ocean strategy?

2. JetBlue's chief commercial officer, Marty St. George, was asked by *The Wall Street Journal,* "What is the biggest marketing challenge JetBlue faces?" His response: "We are flying in a space where our competitors are moving toward commoditization. We have taken a position that air travel is not a commodity but a services business. We want to stand out, but it's hard to break through to customers with that message."[47]

a. Given St. George's statement, which strategic position is JetBlue trying to accomplish: differentiator, cost leader, or blue ocean strategy? Explain why.

b. Which strategic moves has the team around CEO Hayes put in place, and why? Explain whether they focus on value creation, operating costs, or both simultaneously. Do these moves correspond to St. George's understanding of JetBlue's strategic position? Why or why not? Explain.

3. Consider JetBlue's value curve in Exhibit 6.11. Why is JetBlue experiencing a competitive disadvantage? What recommendations would you offer to JetBlue to strengthen its strategic profile? Be specific.

4. JetBlue CEO Robin Hayes is contemplating adding international routes, connecting the U.S. East Coast to Europe. Would this additional international expansion put more pressure on JetBlue's current business strategy? Or would this international expansion require a shift in JetBlue's strategic profile? Why or why not? And if a strategic repositioning is needed, in which direction should JetBlue pivot? Explain.

mySTRATEGY

Low-Cost and Differentiated Workplaces

We have studied the differences in business-level strategies closely in this chapter, but how might these differences relate directly to you? As you've learned, firms using a differentiation strategy will focus on drivers such as product features and customer service, while firms using a cost-leadership strategy will prioritize cost of inputs and economies of scale. These strategic decisions can have an impact on an employee's experience with the firm's work environment and culture.

Hilton, Publix, and Wegmans Food Markets are companies that routinely end up on *Fortune's* list of "100 Best Places to Work." These companies use a differentiation business strategy. In contrast, Amazon and Walmart use the cost-

leadership strategy; and as low-cost leaders, they do not rate nearly as well. According to inputs from the employee review site Glassdoor.com, only 56 percent of the employees working at Walmart would recommend the firm to a friend. Compare this to the over 80 percent who would recommend both Hilton and Wegmans Food Markets.

As you seek options for starting or growing your career, carefully consider the strategy the firm takes in the marketplace. By no means should you avoid low-cost leaders in lieu of strong differentiators (nor should you deem all differentiators as great places to work). Fast-paced organizations that focus on driving tangible results for the organization offer much to learn. For example, Amazon has been a very successful company for the past decade, and many employees have had multiple opportunities to learn enormous amounts in a short period. Amazon employees are encouraged to criticize each other's ideas openly in meetings; they work long days and on weekends; and they strive to meet "unreasonably high" standards. "When you're shooting for the moon, the nature of the work is really challenging. For some people it doesn't work," says Susan Harker, a top recruiter for Amazon. The high standards and relentless pace are a draw for many employees who are motivated to push themselves to learn, grow, and create—perhaps beyond their perceived limits. Many former employees say the nimble and productive environment is great for learning and the Amazon experience has really helped their careers expand. Now consider the following questions.

1. Employees and consultants say the Amazon workplace is the epitome of a "do more for less cost" environment. We recognize this is a hallmark goal of a cost-leadership business strategy. But ask yourself this key question, *Is it the type of high-pressure work environment in which YOU would thrive?*

2. Amazon has surpassed 650,000 employees and is the second publicly traded company in the world to hit $1 trillion market capitalization (just after Apple). The company offers bold new ideas as a retailer and is under an intense pressure to deliver on its goals. The allure from this type of success is compelling and offers tremendous rewards to many employees, shareholders, and customers. What aspects of success are you seeking in your professional career?

3. Before you launch into a new project, job, or firm, or even before you make a change in industry in the effort to move forward in your career, always consider the trade-offs that you would and would not be willing to make.[48]

TAKE-AWAY CONCEPTS

This chapter discussed two generic business-level strategies: *differentiation* and *cost leadership*. Companies can use various tactics to drive one or the other of those strategies, either narrowly or broadly. A *blue ocean strategy* attempts to find a competitive advantage by creating a new competitive area, which it does (when successful) by value innovation, reconciling the trade-offs between the two generic business strategies discussed. These concepts are summarized by the following learning objectives and related take-away concepts.

LO 6-1 / Define business-level strategy and describe how it determines a firm's strategic position.

- Business-level strategy determines a firm's strategic position in its quest for competitive advantage when competing in a single industry or product market.

- Strategic positioning requires that managers address strategic trade-offs that arise between value and cost, because higher value tends to go along with higher cost.

- Differentiation and cost leadership are distinct strategic positions.

- Besides selecting an appropriate strategic position, managers must also define the scope of competition—whether to pursue a specific market niche or go after the broader market.

LO 6-2 / Examine the relationship between value drivers and differentiation strategy.

- The goal of a differentiation strategy is to increase the perceived value of goods and services so that customers will pay a higher price for additional features.

- In a differentiation strategy, the focus of competition is on value-enhancing attributes and features, while controlling costs.

- Some of the unique value drivers managers can manipulate are product features, customer service, customization, and complements.

- Value drivers contribute to competitive advantage only if their increase in value creation (ΔV) exceeds the increase in costs, that is: $(\Delta V) > (\Delta C)$.

LO 6-3 / Examine the relationship between cost drivers and cost-leadership strategy.

- The goal of a cost-leadership strategy is to reduce the firm's cost below that of its competitors.

- In a cost-leadership strategy, the focus of competition is achieving the lowest possible cost position, which allows the firm to offer a lower price than competitors while maintaining acceptable value.

- Some of the unique cost drivers that managers can manipulate are the cost of input factors, economies of scale, and learning- and experience-curve effects.

- No matter how low the price, if there is no acceptable value proposition, the product or service will not sell.

LO 6-4 / Assess the benefits and risks of differentiation and cost-leadership strategies vis-à-vis the five forces that shape competition.

- The five forces model helps managers use generic business strategies to protect themselves against the industry forces that drive down profitability.

- Differentiation and cost-leadership strategies allow firms to carve out strong strategic positions, not only to protect themselves against the five forces, but also to benefit from them in their quest for competitive advantage.

- Exhibit 6.8 details the benefits and risks of each business strategy.

LO 6-5 / Evaluate value and cost drivers that may allow a firm to pursue a blue ocean strategy.

- To address the trade-offs between differentiation and cost leadership at the business level, managers must employ value innovation, a process that will lead them to align the proposed business strategy with total perceived consumer benefits, price, and cost.

- Lowering a firm's costs is primarily achieved by eliminating and reducing the taken-for-granted factors on which the firm's industry rivals compete.

- Increasing perceived buyer value is primarily achieved by raising existing key success factors and by creating new elements that the industry has not yet offered.

- Strategic leaders track their opportunities and risks for lowering a firm's costs and increasing perceived value vis-à-vis their competitors by use of a strategy canvas, which plots industry factors among competitors (see Exhibit 6.11).

LO 6-6 / Assess the risks of a blue ocean strategy, and explain why it is difficult to succeed at value innovation.

- A successful blue ocean strategy requires that trade-offs between differentiation and low cost be reconciled.

- A blue ocean strategy often is difficult because the two distinct strategic positions require internal value chain activities that are fundamentally different from one another.

- When firms fail to resolve strategic trade-offs between differentiation and cost, they end up being "stuck in the middle." They then succeed at neither business strategy, leading to a competitive disadvantage.

KEY TERMS

Blue ocean strategy (*p. 215*)
Business-level strategy (*p. 195*)
Cost-leadership strategy (*p. 197*)
Differentiation strategy (*p. 196*)
Diseconomies of scale (*p. 206*)
Economies of scale (*p. 204*)

Economies of scope (*p. 200*)
Focused cost-leadership strategy (*p. 198*)
Focused differentiation strategy (*p. 198*)
Minimum efficient scale (MES) (*p. 206*)

Scope of competition (*p. 197*)
Strategic trade-offs (*p. 196*)
Strategy canvas (*p. 220*)
Value curve (*p. 220*)
Value innovation (*p. 216*)

DISCUSSION QUESTIONS

1. What are some drawbacks and risks to a broad generic business strategy? To a focused strategy?

2. In Chapter 4, we discussed the internal value chain activities a firm can perform (see Exhibit 4.8). The value chain priorities can be quite different for firms taking different business strategies. Create examples of value chains for three firms: one using cost leadership, another using differentiation, and a third using blue ocean strategy.

3. The chapter notes there are key differences between economies of scale and learning effects. Let us put that into practice with a brief example. A company such as Intel has a complex design and manufacturing process. For instance, one

fabrication line for semiconductors typically costs more than $1.5 billion to build. Yet the industry also has high human costs for research and development (R&D) departments. Semiconductor firms spend an average of 17 percent of revenues on R&D. For comparison the automobile industry spends under 4 percent of sales on R&D.[49] Thus Intel's management must be concerned with both scale of production and learning curves. When do you think managers should be more concerned with large-scale production runs, and when do you think they should be most concerned with practices that would foster or hinder the hiring, training, and retention of key employees?

ENDNOTES

1. This ChapterCase is based on: McCartney, S. (2019, Jan. 16), "The best and worst U.S. airlines of 2018," *The Wall Street Journal*; McCartney, S. (2018, Jan. 10), "The best and worst U.S. airlines of 2017," *The Wall Street Journal*; McCartney, S. (2017, Mar. 8), "Discount business class? Thank JetBlue," *The Wall Street Journal*; Carey, S. (2016, Dec. 16), "JetBlue unveils cost-cutting plan worth up to $300 million by 2020," *The Wall Street Journal*; Carey, S. (2016, Jul. 26), "JetBlue considers foray into Europe," *The Wall Street Journal*; Carey, S. (2016, Apr. 12), "JetBlue to expand its high-end service, dubbed Mint, to more routes," *The Wall Street Journal*; Nicas, J. (2015, Mar. 27), "Pilot sues JetBlue for allegedly letting him fly while mentally unfit," *The Wall Street Journal*; Mayerowitz, S. (2015, Feb. 16), "JetBlue's CEO vies to please passengers, stocks," *The Associated Press*; Vranica, S. (2015, Feb. 22), "JetBlue's plan to repair its brand," *The Wall Street Journal*; Harris, R.L. (2015, Feb. 11), "On JetBlue, passengers can use ApplePay," *The New York Times*; Rosenbloom, S. (2015, Jan. 22), "Flying deluxe domestic coast-to-coast for around $1,000," *The New York Times*; Nicas, J.

(2014, Nov. 19), "JetBlue to add bag fees, reduce legroom," *The Wall Street Journal*; Gardiner, S. (2010, Aug. 10), "Flight attendant grabs two beers, slides down the emergency chute," *The Wall Street Journal*; Miranda, C.A. (2007, Feb. 21), "Can JetBlue weather the storm?" *Time*; Bailey, J. (2007, Feb. 19), "JetBlue's C.E.O. is 'mortified' after fliers are stranded," *The New York Times*; Zeller, T. (2007, Feb. 16), "Held hostage on the tarmac: Time for a passenger bill of rights?" *The New York Times*; Bryce, D.J., and J.H. Dyer (2007, May), "Strategies to crack well-guarded markets," *Harvard Business Review*; Kim, C.W., and R. Mauborgne (2005), *Blue Ocean Strategy: How to Create Uncontested Market Space and Make Competition Irrelevant* (Boston: Harvard Business School Publishing); Friedman, T. (2005), *The World Is Flat: A Brief History of the Twenty-First Century* (New York: Farrar, Strauss and Giroux); and Neeleman, D. (2003, Apr. 30), "Entrepreneurial thought leaders lecture," *Stanford Technology Ventures Program*.

2. This discussion is based on: Porter, M.E. (2008, January), "The five competitive forces

that shape strategy," *Harvard Business Review*; Porter, M.E. (1996, November–December), "What is strategy?" *Harvard Business Review*; Porter, M.E. (1985), *Competitive Advantage: Creating and Sustaining Superior Performance* (New York: Free Press); and Porter, M.E. (1980), *Competitive Strategy: Techniques for Analyzing Industries and Competitors* (New York: Free Press).

3. These questions are based on: Priem, R. (2007), "A consumer perspective on value creation," *Academy of Management Review* 32: 219–235; Abell, D.F. (1980), *Defining the Business: The Starting Point of Strategic Planning* (Englewood Cliffs, NJ: PrenticeHall); and Porter, M.E. (1996, November–December), "What is strategy?" *Harvard Business Review*.

4. The discussion of generic business strategies is based on: Porter, M.E. (1980), *Competitive Strategy: Techniques for Analyzing Industries and Competitors* (New York: Free Press); Porter, M.E. (1985), *Competitive Advantage: Creating and Sustaining Superior Performance* (New York: Free Press); Porter, M.E. (1996, November–December), "What is

strategy?" *Harvard Business Review*; and Porter, M.E. (2008, January), "The five competitive forces that shape strategy," *Harvard Business Review*.

5. Porter, M.E. (1996, November–December), "What is strategy?" *Harvard Business Review*.

6. To decide if and how to divide the market, you can apply the market segmentation techniques you have acquired in your marketing and microeconomics classes.

7. This example is drawn from: "Companies are racing to add value to water," *The Economist* (2017, Mar. 25).

8. Christensen, C.M., and M.E. Raynor (2003), *The Innovator's Solution: Creating and Sustaining Successful Growth* (Boston: Harvard Business School Press).

9. The interested reader is referred to the strategy, marketing, and economics literatures. A good start in the strategy literature is the classic work of M.E. Porter: Porter, M.E. (1980), *Competitive Strategy: Techniques for Analyzing Industries and Competitors* (New York: Free Press); Porter, M.E. (1985), *Competitive Advantage: Creating* and *Sustaining Superior Performance* (New York: Free Press); and Porter, M.E. (2008, January), "The five competitive forces that shape strategy," *Harvard Business Review*.

10. www.oxo.com/about.jsp.

11. Hsieh, T. (2010), *Delivering Happiness: A Path to Profits, Passion, and Purpose* (New York: Business Plus).

12. "Amazon opens wallet, buys Zappos," *The Wall Street Journal* (2009, Jul. 23).

13. "Where in the Dickens can you find a Trader Joe's," store listing at www.traderjoes.com/pdf/locations/all-llocations.pdf; "Ten companies with excellent customer service," *Huffington Post* (2014, Aug. 15), www.huffingtonpost.com/2013/08/15/ best-customer-service_n_3720052.html.

14. Olivarez-Giles, N. (2015, Jul. 7), "Project Fi review: Google masters Wi-Fi calling, but needs better phones," *The Wall Street Journal*; Duran M. (2015, Jul. 7), "Google's Project Fi wireless service is crazy cheap. But should you switch?" *Wired*.

15. "Flights of hypocrisy," *The Economist* (2015, Apr. 25).

16. "Boeing 787: Orders and Deliveries (updated monthly)," *The Boeing Co.* (2019, February), www.boeing.com.

17. "Airbus: Orders and deliveries," www.airbus.com/aircraft/market/orders-deliveries.html (accessed March 21, 2019).

18. Microsoft Annual Report (various years).

19. "Nucor's new plant project still on hold," *The Associated Press* (2009, Jul. 23), www.nucor.com.

20. On strategy as simple rules, see: Sull, D., and K.M. Eisenhardt (2015), *Simple Rules: How to Thrive in a Complex World* (New York: Houghton Mifflin Harcourt).

21. Gladwell, Malcolm. *Tipping Point: How Little Things Can Make a Big Difference.* Turtleback Books, 2002, 301.

22. Wall, R. (2019, Feb. 14), "Airbus to retire the A380, the superjumbo that never quite took off," *The Wall Street Journal.*

23. Levitt, B., and J.G. March (1988), "Organizational learning," *Annual Review of Sociology* 14: 319–340.

24. For insightful reviews and syntheses on the learning-curve literature, see: Argote, L., and G. Todorova (2007), "Organizational learning: Review and future directions," *International Review of Industrial and Organizational Psychology* 22: 193–234; and Yelle, L.E. (1979), "The learning curve: Historical review and comprehensive survey," *Decision Sciences* 10: 302–308.

25. Wright, T.P. (1936), "Factors affecting the cost of airplanes," *Journal of Aeronautical Sciences* 3: 122–128.

26. The Tesla example draws on: Dyer, J., and H. Gregersen (2016, Aug. 24), "Tesla's innovations are transforming the auto industry," *Forbes*; Higgins T. (2017, Apr. 10), "How Tesla topped GM as most valuable U.S. automaker," *The Wall Street Journal Tech Talk*; "Tesla increases deliveries of electric cars," *The Economist* (2017, Apr. 6); Tesla Annual Report (various years); and GM Annual Report (various years).

27. Dyer, J., and H. Gregersen (2016, Aug. 24), "Tesla's innovations are transforming the auto industry," *Forbes*. The authors (in conjunction with David Kryscynski of Brigham Young University) estimate that the functional relationship between production volume and production cost for Tesla's Model S between 2012 and 2014 is

$$Y = 1726.5*(X^{-0.363})$$

Data underlying Exhibit 6.6:

Units	Per-Unit Cost ($)
100	$324,464
500	$180,901
1,000	$140,659
1,500	$121,407
2,000	$109,369
2,500	$100,859
3,000	$94,400
3,500	$89,263
4,000	$85,039
4,500	$81,480
5,000	$78,422
5,500	$75,756
6,000	$73,400
6,500	$71,298
7,000	$69,406
7,500	$67,689
8,000	$66,122
8,500	$64,683
9,000	$63,354
9,500	$62,123
10,000	$60,977
10,500	$59,907
11,000	$58,903
11,500	$57,961
12,000	$57,072

28. The exact data for learning curves depicted in Exhibit 6.7 are depicted below. A simplifying assumption is that the manufacturing of one aircraft costs $100 million, from there the two different learning curves set in. Noteworthy, that while making only one aircraft costs $100 million, when manufacturing over 4,000 aircraft the expected per-unit cost falls to only $28 million (assuming a 90 percent learning curve) and only $7 million (assuming an 80 percent learning curve).

Data underlying Exhibit 6.7

Learning Curves		
	Per-Unit Cost*	
Units	**90%**	**80%**
1	$100	$100
2	90	80
4	81	64
8	73	51
16	66	41
32	59	33
64	53	26
128	48	21
256	43	17
512	39	13
1,024	35	11
2,048	31	9
4,096	28	7

* Rounded to full dollar value in millions.

29. This discussion is based on: Gulati, R., D. Lavie, and H. Singh (2009), "The nature of partnering experience and the gain from alliances," *Strategic Management Journal* 30: 1213–1233; Thompson, P. (2001), "How much did the liberty shipbuilders learn? New evidence from an old case study," *Journal of Political Economy* 109: 103–137; Edmondson, A.C., R.M. Bohmer, and G.P. Pisano (2001), "Disrupted routines: Team learning and new technology implementation in hospitals," *Administrative Science Quarterly* 46: 685–716; Pisano, G.P., R.M. Bohmer, and A.C. Edmondson (2001), "Organizational differences in rates of learning: Evidence from the adoption of minimally invasive cardiac surgery," *Management Science* 47: 752–768; Rothaermel, F.T., and D.L. Deeds (2006), "Alliance type, alliance experience, and alliance management capability in high-technology ventures," *Journal of Business Venturing* 21: 429–460; Hoang, H., and F.T. Rothaermel (2005), "The effect of general and partner-specific alliance experience on joint R&D project performance," *Academy of Management Journal* 48: 332–345; Zollo, M., J.J. Reuer, and H. Singh (2002), "Interorganizational routines and performance in strategic alliances," *Organization Science* 13: 701–713; King, A.W., and A.L. Ranft (2001), "Capturing knowledge

and knowing through improvisation: What managers can learn from the thoracic surgery board certification process," *Journal of Management* 27: 255–277; and Darr, E.D., L. Argote, and D. Epple (1995), "The acquisition, transfer and depreciation of knowledge in service organizations: Productivity in franchises," *Management Science* 42: 1750–1762.

30. Ramanarayanan, S. (2008), "Does practice make perfect: An empirical analysis of learning-by-doing in cardiac surgery." Available at SSRN: http://ssrn.com/ abstract=1129350.

31. "Coronary artery bypass grafting," (2015), healthcarebluebook.com, doi:10.1016/B978-1-84569-800-3.50011-5; Gokhale, K. (2013, Jul. 29), "Heart surgery in India for $1,583 Costs $106,385 in U.S.," *Bloomberg Businessweek*; and Anand, G. (2009, Nov. 25), "The Henry Ford of heart surgery," *The Wall Street Journal*. See also: "Cardiac surgeon salary (United States)," *Payscale.com*, survey updated July 18, 2015; Pearl, R. (2014, Mar. 27), "Offshoring American he alth care: Higher quality at Lower costs?" *Forbes*.

32. Boston Consulting Group (1972), *Perspectives on Experience* (Boston: Boston Consulting Group).

33. See data presented in Endnote 28.

34. Anand, G. (2009, Nov. 25), "The Henry Ford of heart surgery," *The Wall Street Journal*.

35. This discussion is based on: Porter, M.E. (1979, March–April), "How competitive forces shape strategy," *Harvard Business Review*: 137–145; Porter, M.E. (1980), *Competitive Strategy: Techniques for Analyzing Industries and Competitors* (New York: Free Press); and Porter, M.E. (2008, January), "The five competitive forces that shape strategy," *Harvard Business Review*.

36. As of Q1 2019, the exact market share for Google's Android was 74.2 percent and for Apple's iOS was 23.3 percent, thus together they hold 97.5 percent of the entire mobile operating system market globally. Data drawn from http://gs.statcounter.com/os-market-share/mobile/worldwide (accessed March 22, 2019).

37. This discussion is based on: Kim, C.W., and R. Mauborgne (2017), *Blue Ocean Shift: Beyond Competing—Proven Steps to Inspire Confidence and Seize New Growth* (New York: Hachette); Kim, C.W., and R. Mauborgne (2005), *Blue Ocean Strategy: How to Create Uncontested Market Space and Make Competition Irrelevant* (Boston: Harvard Business School Publishing); Miller, A., and G.G. Dess (1993), "Assessing Porter's model

in terms of its generalizability, accuracy, and simplicity," *Journal of Management Studies* 30: 553–585; and Hill, C.W.L. (1988), "Differentiation versus low cost or differentiation and low cost: A contingency framework," *Academy of Management Review* 13: 401–412.

38. Kim, C.W., and R. Mauborgne (2005), *Blue Ocean Strategy: How to Create Uncontested Market Space and Make Competition Irrelevant* (Boston: Harvard Business School Publishing); Miller, A., and G.G. Dess (1993), "Assessing Porter's model in terms of its generalizability, accuracy, and simplicity," *Journal of Management Studies* 30: 553–585; and Hill, C.W.L. (1988), "Differentiation versus low cost or differentiation and low cost: A contingency framework," *Academy of Management Review* 13: 401–412

39. Kim, C.W., and R. Mauborgne (2005), *Blue Ocean Strategy: How to Create Uncontested Market Space and Make Competition Irrelevant* (Boston: Harvard Business School Publishing); Miller, A., and G.G. Dess (1993), "Assessing Porter's model in terms of its generalizability, accuracy, and simplicity," *Journal of Management Studies* 30: 553–585; and Hill, C.W.L. (1988), "Differentiation versus low cost or differentiation and low cost: A contingency framework," *Academy of Management Review* 13: 401–412.

40. Kim, C.W., and R. Mauborgne (2005), *Blue Ocean Strategy: How to Create Uncontested Market Space and Make Competition Irrelevant* (Boston: Harvard Business School Publishing); Miller, A., and G.G. Dess (1993), "Assessing Porter's model in terms of its generalizability, accuracy, and simplicity," *Journal of Management Studies* 30: 553–585; and Hill, C.W.L. (1988), "Differentiation versus low cost or differentiation and low cost: A contingency framework," *Academy of Management Review* 13: 401–412

41. The IKEA example is drawn from: "IKEA: How the Swedish retailer became a global cult brand," *Bloomberg Businessweek* (2005, Nov. 14); Edmonds, M. (2008, Jul. 8), "How IKEA works," http://money. howstuffworks.com/; and www.ikea.com.

42. "IKEA: How the Swedish retailer became a global cult brand," *Bloomberg Businessweek* (2005, Nov. 14).

43. This discussion is based on: Porter, M.E. (1980), *Competitive Strategy: Techniques for Analyzing Industries and Competitors* (New York: Free Press); and Porter, M.E. (1996, November–December), "What is strategy?" *Harvard Business Review*: 61–78.

44. Cirque du Soleil at a Glance, www. cirquedusoleil.com/en/home/about-us/at-a-glance.aspx.

45. Cirque du Soleil at a Glance, www. cirquedusoleil.com/en/home/about-us/at-a-glance.aspx.

46. Sources: Ambler, P. (2019, Mar. 21), "Voices of success: Cirque du Soleil chairman's biggest 'ah ha' moment in business," *Forbes* video, www.forbes.com/video/6016335943001/#4371b2425fe6; Picker, L. (2017, Jul. 6), "Private equity-backed Cirque du Soleil inks deal for Blue Man Group as it looks to expand beyond circus," *CNBC*; "Son of a Cirque du Soleil founder killed on set," *The Wall Street Journal* / Associated Press (2016, Nov. 30); Berzon, A., and M. Maremont (2015, Apr. 24), "The perils of workers' comp for injured Cirque du Soleil performers," *The Wall Street Journal*; WSJ video on Cirque du Soleil, www.wsj.com/articles/ injuries-put-safety-in-spotlight-at-cirque-du-soleil-1429723558; Berzon, A., and M. Maremont (2015, Apr. 22), "Injuries put safety in spotlight at Cirque du Soleil," *The Wall Street Journal*; King, C. (2015, Apr. 20), "Cirque du Soleil being sold to private-equity group," *The Wall Street Journal*; Berzon, A. (2014, Dec. 1), "Cirque du Soleil's next act: Rebalancing the business," *The Wall Street Journal*; Sylt, C. (2015, Feb. 22), "Cirque du Soleil tour revenue tumbles to £40m," *The Telegraph*; and Kim, W.C., and Mauborgne, R. (2005), *Blue Ocean Strategy: How to Create Uncontested Market Space and Make the Competition Irrelevant* (Boston: Harvard Business Review Press).

47. Vranica S. (2015, Feb. 22), "JetBlue's plan to repair its brand," *The Wall Street Journal*.

48. Sources for this myStrategy include: Kantor, J., and D. Streitfeld (2015, Aug. 15), "Inside Amazon: Wrestling big ideas in a bruising workplace," *The New York Times*; "100 best companies to work for," *Fortune*, 2014, 2015; and www.glassdoor.com.

49. "McKinsey on semiconductors," McKinsey & Co. (2011, Autumn).

chapter

7

Group Influences on Consumer Behavior

Source: lululemon

LEARNING OBJECTIVES

LO1 Explain reference groups and the criteria used to classify them.

LO2 Discuss consumption subcultures, including brand and online communities and their importance for marketing.

LO3 Summarize the types and degree of reference group influence.

LO4 Discuss within-group communications and the importance of word-of-mouth communications to marketers.

LO5 Understand opinion leaders (both online and offline) and their importance to marketers.

LO6 Discuss innovation diffusion and use an innovation analysis to develop marketing strategy.

For most products and brands, the basic purchase motivation relates to the ability of the product or service itself to meet a need of the consumer. Other purchases are fundamentally different in that consumers buy membership into a group as well. A prime example is the lululemon brand.[1] This athletic apparel retailer opened its first yoga-inspired store in Canada in 2000 and has since grown to over 400 stores worldwide. The company competes in the "athleisure" market, which sells casual comfortable clothing that can be worn both inside and outside a gym. This athletic wear is attractive to Millennials/Generation Yers, yet some competitors struggle in this market. But not lululemon. The company continues to grow, recording sales of more than $2.3 billion in 2017. It is not just the product that attracts the Millennials, but the sense of community created by the brand. Community is at the center of lululemon's vision and company manifesto, and building healthy communities is a priority. With a focus on healthy living, lululemon sells not only clothes but a lifestyle. A former executive stated: "And so when you think about lululemon and its history, it's an investment in people, giving them their best life, personal development and creating incredible product that allows them to live their life." Thus, lululemon centers on the customer, or "guest," by creating a community to which these guests want to belong. According to a top executive,

"We have a very loyal and passionate guest and we're hyper-focused on whom we're speaking to. We're not afraid to say things that are typically on people's tongues, or maybe talk about the things that others aren't comfortable talking about and realize that actually, people really appreciate that. It's a level of authenticity. When you're focused on your muse and what you're doing, you get a following regardless of what group you're going after. We just try to be as consistent as possible to that guest and really serve him or her."

The strength of the brand can be attributed to lululemon's ability to bond with its customers and the community.

- **Company connects with its customers—** lululemon guests are immediately welcomed into the lululemon community at their first purchase. The company provides guests the opportunity to offer feedback on products while shopping by writing their suggestions on chalkboards near the fitting rooms.

- **Customers are loyal—**Although their product offerings may be seen as expensive (yoga pants can cost over $100), almost half of the company's customers would continue to shop at lululemon even if prices were to increase 5 to 10 percent. Blogs, such as www.luluaddict.com, highlight guests' passion for the brand. As one guest exclaimed, "Once you go lululemon, you never go back."

- **Shopping is an event—**Guests can shop and get a workout while at lululemon. The retailer offers free yoga and fitness classes in the store, and online for those not near a store. Interestingly, most sales are made in conjunction with these classes.

- **Brand builds community**—Community is not only built physically through the in-store classes, but also emotionally by wearing the brand's clothes. Also, in each store, a community board provides information on local yoga studios and running clubs. The store employees, or "educators," can post personal goals and aspirations on store walls for all to see.
- **Brand ambassadors expand the community**—Brand community is reinforced through the company's *brand ambassador* program. A **brand ambassador** is a person who is paid or given free products by a company in exchange for wearing or using its products and trying to encourage others to do so. lululemon's ambassador program includes "driven athletes and inspirational people who harness their passion

to elevate their communities." The company enlists over 1,600 ambassadors worldwide, and they comprise local influencers, elite athletes, and outstanding yoga instructors who provide feedback on the company's product and create community. In exchange for teaching free classes, the ambassadors are given free clothing and other lululemon merchandise.

The lululemon brand has been fostering this community since the first store opened. Its members tend to be passionate, active, and devoted. They are connected to the lululemon brand, the lululemon community, and the lifestyle it represents in a very deep way that permeates their lives and helps define who they are.

As demonstrated in the opening example, even in an individualistic society like America, group memberships and identity are very important to all of us. And while we don't like to think of ourselves as conformists, most of us conform to group expectations most of the time. For example, when you decided what to wear to the last party you attended, you probably based your decision in part on the anticipated responses of the other individuals at the party. This represents a response to group influence and expectations.

TYPES OF GROUPS

LO1 The terms *group* and *reference group* need to be distinguished. A **group** is defined as *two or more individuals who share a set of norms, values, or beliefs and have certain implicitly or explicitly defined relationships to one another such that their behaviors are interdependent.* A **reference group** is *a group whose presumed perspectives or values are being used by an individual as the basis for his or her current behavior.* Thus, a reference group is simply a group that an individual uses as a guide for behavior in a specific situation.

Most of us belong to a number of different groups and perhaps would like to belong to several others. When we are actively involved with a particular group, it generally functions as a reference group. As the situation changes, we may base our behavior on an entirely different group, which then becomes our reference group. We may belong to many groups simultaneously, but we generally use only one group as our primary point of reference in any given situation. This tendency is illustrated in Figure 7–1.

Groups may be classified according to a number of variables. Four criteria are particularly useful: (1) membership, (2) strength of social tie, (3) type of contact, and (4) attraction.

The *membership* criterion is dichotomous: Either one is a member of a particular group or one is not a member of that group. Of course, some members are more secure in their membership than others are; that is, some members feel they really belong to a group, while others lack this confidence.

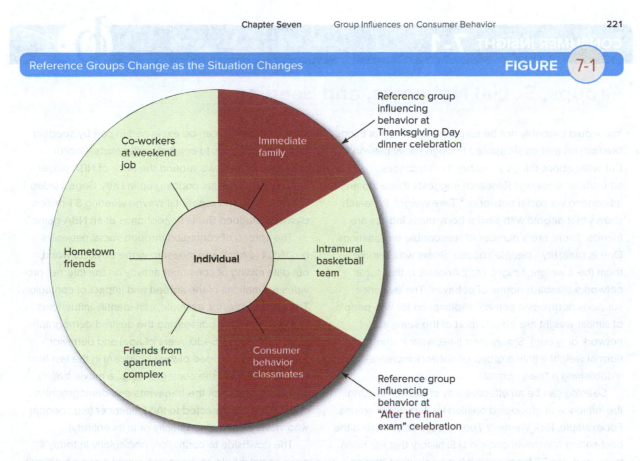

Reference Groups Change as the Situation Changes   **FIGURE** 7-1

Strength of social tie refers to the closeness and intimacy of the group linkages. **Primary groups,** such as family and friends, involve strong ties and frequent interaction. Primary groups often wield considerable influence. **Secondary groups,** such as professional and neighborhood associations, involve weaker ties and less-frequent interaction.

Type of contact refers to whether the interaction is direct or indirect. Direct contact involves face-to-face interaction; indirect contact does not. The Internet, in particular, has increased the importance of indirect reference groups in the form of *online communities,* which are discussed in more detail later in the chapter.

Attraction refers to the desirability that membership in a given group has for the individual. This can range from negative to positive. Groups with negative desirability—**dissociative reference groups**—can influence behavior just as those with positive desirability do.[2] For example, teenagers tend to avoid clothing styles associated with older consumers. Nonmembership groups with a positive attraction—**aspiration reference groups**—also exert a strong influence. Individuals frequently purchase products thought to be used by a desired group in order to achieve actual or symbolic membership in the group.

Consumer Insight 7-1 shows the power of groups and social networks to influence attitudes and behaviors.

Consumption Subcultures

A **consumption subculture** is a distinctive subgroup of society that self-selects on the basis of a shared commitment to a particular product class, brand, or consumption activity. These groups have (1) an identifiable, hierarchical social structure; (2) a set of shared beliefs or values; and (3) unique jargon, rituals, and modes of symbolic expression.[3] Thus, they are reference groups for their members as well as those who aspire to join or avoid them.

LO2

CONSUMER INSIGHT 7-1

Groups, Social Networks, and Seeding

You would probably not be surprised to learn that things like fashion and music spread through social networks. But what about things like obesity, happiness, altruism, or smoking? Research suggests these too are influenced via social networks.[4] Take weight. Research shows that people with similar body mass indices are friends. There are a number of reasonable explanations. One is similarity—people choose others who are like them (be it weight, height, etc.). Another is that social networks establish norms of behavior. The evidence supports norms as a primary explanation for why people of similar weight are friends (part of the same social network or group). Slowly over time, what is considered normal weight within a group or network increases, establishing a "new normal."

Seeding can be an effective way of marketing using the influence of group and opinion leaders within groups. For example, Rick Warren's *The Purpose Driven Life* is the best-selling hardcover book in U.S. history that has been translated into 85 languages. It is a book with Christian topics, relevant to individuals of that faith, but not so much for others who don't share that faith. It is a niche book that spread rapidly and in record numbers to evangelicals for whom the book was relevant but remained relatively unknown to people outside of this social network. *The Purpose Driven Life* was launched using "seeding," whereby free samples are given away to influential members of existing social networks. Rick Warren nurtured a group of some 1,200 pastors, provided them a free copy of the book, and encouraged them to lead their congregations through the 40-day program.

The phenomenal ability of Beats headphones to grow fivefold and reach $1 billion between 2010 and 2012, despite negative press reviews that suggested Beats headphones were overpriced and underperforming, can be explained in part by seeding Beats headphones to celebrity influentials—locker room photos of Beats around the neck of NBA player LeBron James, Beats popping up in Lady Gaga's video "Poker Face," and rapper Lil Wayne wearing $1 million diamond-studded Beats headphones at an NBA game.

The spread of contagion through social networks is difficult to track and measure in the physical world, but data mining of consumer activity on the Internet provides estimations of the spread and impact of contagion. The firm Lotame, for example, can identify influencers in social networks possessing the desired demographics (e.g., women 25–30 years of age) and behavior (e.g., uploaded a video of their child(ren) in the last four hours), send them the contagion (e.g., a movie trailer), and count and track the behaviors and demographics of the people connected to the influencer (e.g., people who viewed the trailer partially or in its entirety).

The downside to contagion, particularly in today's open social media environment, is that it can be difficult to control what is "put out there" and linked to a specific brand and company. Employees who engage in such negative behaviors (e.g., prank and negatively toned videos involving a restaurant's products and/or facilities) can be dismissed, but correcting the damage done can be much more difficult and time-consuming.

Critical Thinking Questions

1. What is seeding, and how is it an effective tool for marketers?

2. Use group structure to explain why *The Purpose Driven Life* had little awareness outside a specific social network.

3. In what ways has the Internet enhanced marketers' ability to draw on social networks for marketing purposes?

A number of such subcultures, ranging from hip-hop to gardening to skydiving, have been examined. Each has a set of self-selecting members. They have hierarchies at the local and national levels. And they also have shared beliefs and unique jargon and rituals. Most hobbies and participation sports have consumption-based group subcultures built around them. Consumption need not be shared physically to be a shared ritual that creates and sustains a group.[5]

Note that not all, or even most, product owners or participants in an activity become members of the consumption subculture associated with it. For example, one can enjoy the *Star Trek* TV shows without becoming a member of the associated subculture. Self-selecting into a consumption subculture requires commitment, acquisition of the group's beliefs and values, participation in its activities, and use of its jargon and rituals. Consider the following excerpt regarding the consumption subculture revolving around high-end, limited-edition sneakers, where the most devoted members are called "sneakerheads":

> By 9:35 on a recent Friday night, Dominique Thomas had been camped outside the Niketown store in South Miami for two full days. Thomas, who goes by the street name DK the Line Pimp, had flown in from Denver and was the first in line to buy the $100 Cowboy Air Max 180s, which were scheduled to go on sale at 10 that night. Just 140 pairs of these limited-edition sneakers . . . were manufactured and they would be sold only at the Miami store and only that night. . . . Thomas, 21, reflected on how much getting the shoes meant to him. "Shoes run my life," he said. "Without shoes, I don't exist."[6]

As with other types of groups, members of consumption subcultures vary in their commitment to and interpretation of the group's values and norms. Consider the following quotes from sneakerheads regarding whether or not the sneakers should actually be worn:

> It's just like owning a Porsche. Every time you ride by, everyone looks at you. Well, if you have a rare, sought-after sneaker and you wear it down the street, everyone looks at you. . . . Most collectors, you can't tell they're sneakerheads. They usually wear really run-of-the-mill sneakers. Real collectors don't want to get their shoes dirty or dusty or worn. . . .[7]

Marketing and Consumption Subcultures   Consumption subcultures based on activities obviously are markets for the requirements of the activity itself, such as golf clubs for golfers. However, these groups develop rituals and modes of symbolic communication that often involve other products or services. Golf is renowned for the "uniform" that many of its adherents wear. Clothes, hats, and other items designed for golfers are based as much on providing symbolic meaning as they are for functional benefits.

While these subcultures adopt consumption patterns in large part to affirm their unique identity, the larger market often appropriates all or parts of their symbols, at least for a time. Thus, clothing initially worn by a consumption subculture, such as snowboarders or surfers, for functional or symbolic reasons may emerge as a style for a much larger group. The sneaker culture discussed earlier has given rise to a global market that puts a premium on new and cool styles. Companies like Sneakerhead and StockX provide platforms for customers to get these exclusive products. Also, the name of British shoemaker Boxfresh is a reference to hip-hop slang meaning sneakers fresh from the box, as shown in Illustration 7–1. It is attempting to appeal to this broader sneaker culture, if not directly at sneakerheads themselves.

Marketers can and should attempt to use the most respected members of a consumption subculture as a means for identifying trends and influencing consumers in the mass market. Again, the sneaker culture is instructive, as indicated by the director of Adidas's Sports Style Division:

> We have seen the sneaker culture increase over the past several years to the point where, today, bloggers [typically sneakerheads] are integral partners in helping spread the word about coming products. We're putting a lot of effort into this type of consumer, and we're spending a lot of time on them.[8]

ILLUSTRATION 7-1

Brands such as Boxfresh may appropriate the slang and symbols of a consumption subculture to appeal to a broader audience.

Source: Boxfresh

Brand Communities

Consumption subcultures focus on the interactions of individuals around an activity, product category, or occasionally a brand. A **brand community** is *a nongeographically bound community, based on a structured set of social relationships among owners of a brand and the psychological relationship they have with the brand itself, the product in use, and the firm.*[9] A **community** is *characterized by consciousness of kind, shared rituals and traditions, and a sense of moral responsibility.*[10]

Athleisure apparel company lululemon has effectively created a brand community, as described at the beginning of this chapter. Brand communities are also prevalent in the auto and motorcycle industry among various manufacturers and their owner-enthusiasts, including Tesla, Jeep, Harley-Davidson, and MG (a British sports car). The following examples illustrate the nature of brand communities.[11]

Consciousness of Kind
There are several new classes of riders fouling the wind with the misapprehension that merely owning a Harley [Davidson] will transform them into a biker. This is the same type of dangerous ignorance that suggests that giving a dog an artichoke turns him into a gourmet.

Rituals and Traditions
For the past 7 years, we have sponsored a fall trip. [W]e always go the first weekend in October. [W]e . . . get on the Blue Ridge Parkway [which was] made for MGs, you know—high mountain roads, curves, and hills. We spend Friday and Saturday night in the mountains and then come back. The 1st year we had seven or eight people, last year we had 23 cars.

Moral Responsibility
A Tesla owner and enthusiast indicates a sense of dedication to help other Tesla enthusiasts. One such owner made a point of helping a terminally-ill man fulfill his dying wish of owning his own Tesla Model 3. The man was in a queue to receive delivery of the limited production car, but not likely in time, given his prognosis. The Tesla owner not only was able to get him a test drive of the car, but she also sent out a plea to Tesla to see if the man could receive his car sooner than later. He shortly did. She later posted online about the man's experience at Tesla, "private factory tour, intros around, everyone grinning to be part of this."

Marketing and Brand Communities   Brand communities can add value to the owner-ship of the product and build intense loyalty. A "mere" Jeep owner derives the functional and symbolic benefits associated with owning a Jeep. A member of the Jeep community derives these benefits plus increases in self-esteem from gaining skill in the off-road operation of a Jeep, the ability and confidence to use the Jeep in a wider range of situations, new friendships and social interactions, a feeling of belongingness, a positive association with FCA US LLC, and a deeper relationship with his or her Jeep.

As the Jeep example suggests, brand communities create value through sets of activities or "practices" that create brand engagement. Four categories of activities and an example of each relating to the Mini Cooper brand are shown in Table 7–1.

From the firm's perspective, building a brand community involves establishing relationships with the owner and helping owners establish relationships with each other. In addition, Table 7–1 suggests a host of activities that can be encouraged and facilitated by both the brand and brand owners to enhance brand value and loyalty. For example, Mini allows individuals to customize their cars during ordering (brand use enhancement via customization) and then track the production and delivery of their vehicle as part of the "birthing" ritual (community engagement via milestoning). The Mini website also features a Mini Owners' Lounge, which is an owners-only area where members share information about upcoming events and so on (social networking via welcoming). One such event is the Mini Getaway Tour. Brand-related events often are termed "brand fests," which are *gatherings of owners and others for the purposes of interacting with one another in the context of learning about and using the brand.*

Value Creation Activities in the Mini Brand Community	TABLE 7-1

Social Networking—Creating, enhancing, and sustaining ties among members by welcoming, empathizing, and governing.

- **Empathizing**—Lending emotional or other support to members
- **Example** (relating to members "birthing" rituals for their Mini's): Good job, Birdman! I'm like you. I watched cameras, checked tracking. . . . You'll treasure having these for your "scrap book" or should I say Minibirds's "baby book"? Jack [the car] was not on a WW ship so there were a lot less options for catching glimpses of the journey. Hang in there. Minibird is almost home!

Community Engagement—Reinforce members' escalating engagement with community by documenting, badging, milestoning, and staking.

- **Milestoning**—Noting significant events in brand ownership and consumption
- **Example** (relating to length of relationship with Mini): The odometer hit 100k miles and I loved my Mini more than ever.

Brand Use—Improving or enhancing the use of the focal brand by customizing, grooming, and commoditizing.

- **Grooming**—Caring for the brand
- **Example** (relating to washing the Mini appropriately): I try to wash at least once a week with a quick detail spray during the middle of the week to keep my Zaino shining. Newt [thread initiator] prepare yourself for an onslaught of posts suggesting that you should keep your car away from those car washes.

Impression Management—Creating positive view of brand community to nonmembers by evangelizing and justifying.

- **Evangelizing**—Sharing about the brand and inspiring others to use the brand
- **Example** (relating to the safety of the Mini): In another MINI forum that I used to visit a lot, there were a few people who had major accidents in their MINIs and I was shocked at just how tough and safe these little cars are. [T]hey weigh more than most small cars and are amazingly rigid and protective from what I've seen.

Source: Adapted from H. J. Schau, A. Muniz Jr., and E. J. Arnould, "How Brand Community Practices Create Value," *Journal of Consumer Research,* September 2009, pp. 30–51.

Online Communities and Social Networks

An **online community** is *a community that interacts over time around a topic of interest on the Internet.*[12] These interactions can take place in various forms, including online message boards and discussion groups, blogs, as well as corporate and nonprofit websites. Research indicates that online communities exist for many participants and that there is often a sense of community online, which moves beyond mere interactions to include an affective or emotional attachment to the online group. Studies have found ongoing communications among subsets of these interest groups. In addition, the patterns of communication indicate a group structure, with the more experienced members serving as experts and leaders and the newer members seeking advice and information. These groups develop unique vocabularies, netiquette, and means for dealing with behaviors deemed inappropriate.

Extent of connection can vary dramatically across members. Many members observe the group discussions without participating. Others participate but only at a limited level. Others manage and create content for the group.[13]

The ongoing evolution relating to online communities involves online social network sites. An **online social network site** is *a web-based service that allows individuals to (1) construct a public or semipublic profile within a bounded system, (2) articulate a list of other users with whom they share a connection, and (3) view and traverse their list of connections and those made by others within the system.*[14] Online social network sites take many forms, including friendship (Facebook and Instagram), media sharing (Vimeo and YouTube), corporate or brand (LEGO Ideas), business networking (LinkedIn), and micro-blogging (Twitter).

Illustration 7–2 shows how Care2, "the world's largest community for good," uses various avenues including a website and Facebook to foster an online community and further solidify brand loyalty.

Marketing and Online Communities and Social Networks   Online communities and social networks are attractive to marketers, who are spending over $15 billion on U.S. advertising on social network sites alone, which is nearly 10 percent of all online advertising.[15]

ILLUSTRATION 7-2

Online social network sites such as Care2, shown here, are increasingly popular for both consumers and brands as a way to foster and be connected to a community with similar lifestyles, values, and interests.

Source: Care2.com, inc.

Options range from relative standard banner and pop-up ads to more tailored approaches that maximize the specific characteristics of the venue such as sponsored Tweets, branded YouTube channels, or branded fan pages on Facebook.

Online communities and social networks are attractive for a number of reasons, including

- Consumer use is high and rising, with more than two-thirds of online adults and three-quarters of online teens saying they use social networking sites.[16]
- A majority of consumers who use social network sites use them to share information, including information about brands and products.[17]
- Customer acquisition potential seems high, with 51 percent of firms on Twitter and 68 percent of firms on Facebook indicating they have acquired a customer through these channels.[18]
- Roughly two-thirds of consumers who interact with a brand via social media are more likely to recall the brand, share information about the brand with others, feel connected to the brand, and purchase the brand.[19]

However, consumers don't just want entertainment or marketing; they want content that is relevant and useful to them. Research found that more than three-fourths of those polled prefer social media to provide incentives such as free products and coupons, and close to half want social media to provide information or solutions to their problems.[20]

While marketers are still learning about how to most effectively utilize social media, a few general guiding principles have emerged.[21] The first guiding principle is to be *transparent*. In online communities, it is critical that companies identify themselves and any posted content as such. Marketers who fail to do so risk being found out and subject to massive criticism from the community. Consider the case of Sony's PSP "Flog," or fake blog, as reported on *The Consumerist* blog:

[T]he forces of the internet outed a marketing company working for Sony for creating fake PSP blog. The ps3do site says it's written by "Charlie" who wants to get the parents of his friend, "Jeremy," to buy "Jeremy" a PSP for Christmas. The domain name is registered to the *Zipatoni* marketing company.[22]

Indeed, not only are consumers concerned about transparency, so is the FTC, the government body tasked with regulating false and misleading advertising. When Ann Taylor offered a special gift to bloggers who posted coverage about their upcoming line, the FTC investigated. The FTC has issued new guidelines for bloggers requiring them to "clearly disclose any 'material connection' to an advertiser including payments for an endorsement or free product."[23] Consequently, transparency is important when companies interact with online groups.

The second principle is to *be a part of the community*. Online communities often expect that the company will be part of the community and not just market to it. Consider the following excerpt:

[M]anagers tend to view social media first as a marketing tool, and indeed it is. But consumers are looking for more help, not [marketing] pitches. About two-thirds of U.S. consumers believe that companies should ramp up social media usage to "identify service/support issues and contact consumers to resolve [them]."[24]

Search Twitter for a company of interest and gauge the ratio of promotion to customer service. You are likely to find it skewed to promotion, although the better companies also will engage in product and service-failure recovery efforts. Companies such as Target and KLM Royal Dutch Airlines are reacting to customer complaints and issues delivered via Twitter and are reacting to them in real time.

The third principle is to *take advantage of the unique capabilities of each venue.* Many of the social network sites have special areas for corporate advertising and activities that extend beyond traditional banner and pop-up ads. For example, companies can have their own channel on YouTube, which they manage, monitor, and facilitate, as Jeep does. An additional example is the "like" component of Facebook. Oreo, for instance, has accumulated over 43 million likes of the cookie company's Facebook page due to its specialized, creative, and high-quality content. The company recently ran a "playwithoreo" promotion, inspiring consumers to post pictures or videos of their favorite way to eat an Oreo.[25] Caution should be heeded, though. Companies need to be aware of the limitations of Facebook and social media in altering a consumer's behavior. Recent research has shown that liking a company's Facebook page does not lead to increased purchasing:[26]

> Merely liking a page did not change behavior. Put another way, liking a company that offers flu shots does not translate into getting a flu shot.

Nevertheless, many companies like Oreo have managed Facebook in such a way that it is meaningful and engaging to customers and thus creates real value, in the form of new product ideas, for the firm.

REFERENCE GROUP INFLUENCES ON THE CONSUMPTION PROCESS

LO3

We all conform in a variety of ways to numerous groups. Sometimes we are aware of this influence, but many times we are not. Before examining the marketing implications of reference groups, we need to examine the nature of reference group influence more closely.

The Nature of Reference Group Influence

Reference group influence can take three forms: *informational, normative,* and *identification.* It is important to distinguish these types because marketing strategies depend on the type of influence involved.

Informational influence *occurs when an individual uses the behaviors and opinions of reference group members as potentially useful bits of information.* This influence is based on either the similarity of the group's members to the individual or the expertise of the influencing group member.[27] Thus, a person may notice that runners on the track team use a specific brand of nutrition bar. He or she then may decide to try that brand because these healthy and active runners use it. Use by the track team members thus provides information about the brand. The Built with Chocolate Milk ad in Illustration 7–3 shows another form of informational influence whereby a positive nonmember expert referent group endorses or recommends the brand.

Normative influence, sometimes referred to as *utilitarian* influence, *occurs when an individual fulfills group expectations to gain a direct reward or to avoid a sanction.*[28] You may purchase a particular brand of wine to win approval from a colleague. Or you may refrain

Source: MilkPEP

from wearing the latest fashion for fear of being teased by friends or to fit in with or be accepted by them. As you might expect, normative influence is strongest when individuals have strong ties to the group and the product involved is socially conspicuous.[29] Ads that promise social acceptance or approval if a product is used are relying on normative influence. Likewise, ads that suggest group disapproval if a product is not used, such as a mouthwash or deodorant, are based on normative influence.

Identification influence, also called *value-expressive* influence, *occurs when individuals have internalized the group's values and norms.* These then guide the individuals' behaviors without any thought of reference group sanctions or rewards. The individual has accepted the group's values as his or her own. The individual behaves in a manner consistent with the group's values because his or her values and the group's values are the same.

Figure 7-2 illustrates a series of consumption situations and the type of reference group influence that is operating in each case.

Degree of Reference Group Influence

Reference groups may have no influence in a given situation, or they may influence usage of the product category, the type of product used, or the brand used. Table 7-2 shows how two consumption situation characteristics—necessity/nonnecessity and visible/private consumption—combine to affect the degree of reference group influence likely to operate in a specific situation.

FIGURE 7-2   Consumption Situations and Reference Group Influence

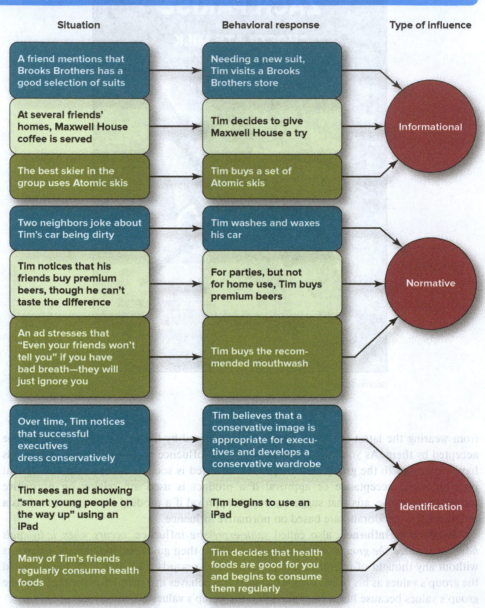

Based on Table 7–2, the following two determinants of reference group influence emerge:

- Group influence is strongest *when the use of product or brand is visible to the group.* Products such as running shoes are highly visible. Products such as vitamins are generally not. Reference group influence typically affects only those aspects (e.g., category or brand) that are visible to the group.[30]
- Reference group influence is higher *the less of a necessity an item is.* Thus, reference groups have strong influence on the ownership of products such as designer clothes but much less influence on necessities such as a washing machine.

Two Consumption Situation Characteristics and Product/Brand Choice		TABLE 7-2
	Degree Needed	
	Necessity	**Nonnecessity**
Consumption	Weak reference group influence on product	Strong reference group influence on product

Visible
 Strong reference group influence on brand
	Public Necessities
	 Influence: Weak product and strong brand
	 Examples:
	   Shoes
	   Automobiles
		Public Luxuries
		 Influence: Strong product and brand
		 Examples:
		   Jewelry
		   Health club

Private
 Weak reference group influence on brand
	Private Necessities
	 Influence: Weak product and brand
	 Examples:
	   Refrigerator
	   Insurance
		Private Luxuries
		 Influence: Strong product and weak brand
		 Examples:
		   Hot tub
		   Home theater system

Three additional determinants of reference group influence include

- In general, *the more commitment an individual feels to a group, the more the individual will conform to the group norms.*
- *The more relevant a particular activity is to the group's functioning, the stronger the pressure to conform to the group norms concerning that activity.* Thus, style of dress may be important to a social group that frequently eats dinner together at nice restaurants and unimportant to a group that meets for basketball on Thursday nights.
- The final factor that affects the degree of reference group influence is *the individual's confidence in the purchase situation.* This can happen even if the product is not visible or important to group functioning as a result of the importance of the decision and a lack of personal decision confidence. Individual personality traits can influence confidence and thus be susceptible to reference group influence.[31]

Figure 7–3 summarizes these determinants, which marketers can use to assess the degree of group influence on their product category and brand.

MARKETING STRATEGIES BASED ON REFERENCE GROUP INFLUENCES

Marketers first must determine the degree and nature of the reference group influence that exists, *or can be created,* for the product in question. Figure 7–3 provides the starting point for this analysis.

Personal Sales Strategies

The power of groups was initially demonstrated in a classic series of studies. Eight subjects are shown four straight lines on a board—three unequal lines are grouped close together, and another appears some distance from them. The subjects are asked to determine which one of the three unequal lines is closest to the length of the fourth line shown some distance away.

FIGURE **7-3** Consumption Situation Determinants of Reference Group Influence

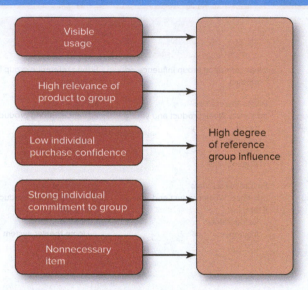

The subjects are to announce their judgments publicly. Seven of the subjects are working for the experimenter, and they announce incorrect matches. The order of announcement is arranged so that the naive subject responds last. The naive subject almost always agrees with the incorrect judgment of the others. This is known as the **Asch phenomenon.** Imagine how much stronger the pressures to conform are among friends or when the task is less well defined, such as preferring one brand or style to another.

Consider this direct application of the Asch phenomenon in personal selling. A group of potential customers is brought together for a sales presentation. As each design is presented, the salesperson scans the expressions of the people in the group, looking for the one who shows approval (e.g., head nodding) of the design. The salesperson then asks that person for an opinion because the opinion is certain to be favorable. The person is asked to elaborate. Meanwhile, the salesperson scans the faces of the other people, looking for more support, and then asks for an opinion of the person now showing the most approval. The salesperson continues until the person who initially showed the most disapproval is reached. In this way, by using the first person as a model, and by social group pressure on the last person, the salesperson gets all or most of the people in the group to make a positive public statement about the design. *Do you see any ethical issues in using group influences in this way?*

Advertising Strategies

Marketers often position products as appropriate for group activities. French wines gained an image of being somewhat expensive and snobbish. Many consumers viewed them as appropriate only for very special occasions. Illustration 7–4 shows an ad for DC Cool that positions itself toward a specific group activity.

Marketers use all three types of reference group influence when developing advertisements. Informational influence in advertising was shown earlier in Illustration 7–3. This type of ad uses an expert reference group (e.g., dentists, doctors, and teachers) as the information agent. Another approach is showing members of a group using a product.

The message, generally unstated, is that "these types of people find this brand to be the best; if you are like them, you will too."

Normative group influence is not portrayed in ads as much as it once was. It involves the explicit or implicit suggestion that using, or not using, the brand will result in having members of a group you belong to or wish to join rewarding or punishing you. One reason for the reduced use of this technique is the ethical questions raised by implying that a person's friends would base their reactions to the individual according to his or her purchases. Ads showing a person's friends saying negative things about the person behind his or her back because that person's coffee was not great (yes, there was such an ad campaign) were criticized for playing on people's insecurities and fears.

Identification influence is based on the fact that the individual has internalized the group's values and attitudes. The advertising task is to demonstrate that the product is consistent with the group's—and therefore the individual's—beliefs. This often involves showing the brand being used by a particular type of group, such as socially active young singles or parents of young children.

©Destination DC

ILLUSTRATION 7-4

Marketers often position products as appropriate for group activities, as shown in this DC Cool ad.

COMMUNICATIONS WITHIN GROUPS AND OPINION LEADERSHIP

LO4

We learn about new products, services, and brands, as well as retail and information outlets, from our friends and other reference groups in two basic ways. First is by observing or participating with them as they use products and services. Second is by seeking or receiving advice and information from them in the form of **word-of-mouth (WOM) communications.** WOM involves *individuals sharing information with other individuals in a verbal form, including face-to-face, on the phone, and over the Internet.* As indicated in Consumer Insight 7–2, social media and the Internet continue to transform interpersonal communications and WOM.

Consumers generally trust the opinions of people (family, friends, acquaintances) more than marketing communications because, unlike marketing communications, these personal sources have no reason not to express their true opinions and feelings. As a consequence, WOM can have a critical influence on consumer decisions and business success. It is estimated that 82 percent of consumer purchases are influenced by WOM.[32] This WOM can be more effective the more explicit it is. Recent research shows that purchase intentions increase when a person recommends, as opposed to likes, the product.[33] Consumers put their faith in WOM versus advertising across a number of products and services. The information following shows the percentage of adults who put people (WOM from friends, family, or other people), as compared with advertising, at the top of their list of best sources for information.

CONSUMER INSIGHT 7-2

Consumer-Generated Content: A Brand's Best Friend or Worst Enemy

The social media revolution has allowed users not only to form, join, and communicate with groups and individuals online, but also to create and distribute original content in ways not possible in the past. Such *consumer-generated content* is changing the marketing landscape, and brands are joining this online conversation with customers. Consumer-generated content (CGC), or user-generated content, is a highly effective and cost-efficient way for brands to engage with consumers, raise awareness, and increase sales. CGC encompasses all sorts of content relating to a brand, such as reviews, pictures, videos, brief comments, stories, emotional outbursts, and hashtags.[34]

Numerous studies show several extremely positive outcomes of CGC. For example, when consumers interact with CGC, revenue increased on average by 116 percent on retail sites and 101 percent on brand sites. Also, rate at which consumers perform a desired action on the brand's web page (e.g., sign up to receive e-mails), known as conversions, increased on average by 106 percent and 97 percent respectively. In a study of Facebook, CGC drove 6.9 times the level of brand engagement as brand-generated content.

Consumers invest the time and effort to create these types of content usually out of a desire to help, inform, protect, entertain, or inspire confidence in other consumers. Consumers develop an affinity to brands associated with CGC because they believe it to be quite authentic. Authenticity is considered to be of paramount importance by 87 percent of consumers, and 60 percent of consumers perceive CGC to be the most authentic form of all content (as compared to 23 percent for celebrity endorsements).

There are many examples of CGC campaigns that worked beautifully, including

- Aerie, a women's clothing company, launched a social media campaign asking consumers to post natural pictures of themselves in the company's clothing with the hashtag #AerieREAL. The goal was to bring awareness to photo retouching in the fashion industry and the impact it has on women's self-esteem. For every use of #AerieREAL, Aerie donated $1 to the National Eating Disorders Association. The company also pledged to stop retouching swimsuit photos.

	People	Advertising
Restaurants	83%	35%
Places	71	33
Prescription drugs	71	21
Hotels	63	27
Health tips	61	19
Movies	61	67
Best brands	60	33
Retirement planning	58	9
Automobiles	58	36
Clothes	50	59
Computer equipment	40	18
Websites to visit	37	12
Combined purchases: restaurant, TV, and movies	43	43

Source: Adapted from *The Influentials: One American in Ten Tells the Other Nine How to Vote, Where to Eat, and What to Buy,* by Edward Keller and Jonathan Berry. Published in 2003 by Roper ASW, LLC. CivicScience Insight Report, October 16, 2014.

- Starbucks' annual red cup CGC campaign garnered over 40,000 posts of customers' pictures of their Starbucks red holiday cups in various contexts with #RedCupsContest. The contest gave consumers the chance to express their creativity and win a large Starbucks gift card. This campaign also stimulated sales because consumers first had to make a purchase to obtain a red cup for their pictures.

However, not every CGC campaign is so successful. Here are some examples:

- McDonalds' CGC campaign that encouraged consumers to use the hashtag #McDStories was a flop. The fast-food retailer had hoped that this CGC campaign would produce positive and heartwarming posts. Instead, many consumers used this hashtag to express dissatisfaction with the brand. For example, some select tweets included "Ate McFish and vomited 1 hour later . . . The last time I got McDonalds was seriously 18 years ago in college" and "My father used to bring us to McDonalds as a reward when we were kids. Now he's horribly obese and has diabetes. Lesson learned."
- Quiznos restaurants hosted a CGC campaign in which they asked consumers to submit videos that would illustrate why Quiznos sandwiches were better than Subway sandwiches. This campaign resulted in a lawsuit from Subway that argued that

Quiznos had encouraged consumers to make false negative claims about Subway sandwiches.

CGC also can involve specific requests by firms for consumer input into product design decisions. The Budweiser ad shown in Illustration 7–5 is a great example.

Consumers who generate content online are, in essence, the opinion leaders, which we discuss shortly, whose influence cannot be underestimated. Marketers are embracing these consumer conversations to help, and hopefully not hurt, their brands.

Critical Thinking Questions:

1. As mentioned, the Internet abounds with examples of CGC campaigns. Browse a social media site and find a CGC campaign. Write a brief paragraph describing your findings.

2. Reflect on and describe ways that you personally have participated in CGC. Have you created any content yourself? Do you consume CGC when shopping and/or browsing online? Please elaborate.

3. How authentic do you perceive CGC campaigns to be? What aspects of CGC campaigns would increase or decrease perceptions of authenticity?

4. Based on the examples you read in this consumer insight and your own experience with CGC, what advice would you give to a marketer who is embarking on his or her first CGC campaign?

As this information suggests, the importance of WOM is generally high, and its importance relative to advertising varies somewhat across product types. In addition, traditional mass-media advertising still plays a role, particularly at the earlier stages of the decision process, including building brand awareness.

Negative experiences are powerful motivators of WOM, a factor that must be considered by marketers because negative WOM can strongly influence recipients' attitudes and behaviors.[35] Negative experiences, which are highly emotional and memorable, motivate consumers to talk. While the number varies by situation and product, it is not at all uncommon to find that dissatisfied consumers tell twice as many people about their experience than do satisfied consumers.[36] While merely satisfying consumers (delivering what they expected) may not always motivate WOM, going beyond satisfaction to deliver more than was expected also appears to have the potential to generate substantial WOM. Thus, companies may consider strategies for "delighting" consumers or otherwise creating positive emotional experiences that consumers are motivated to pass along in the form of positive WOM (see Chapter 18).[37] Obviously, it is imperative for companies to provide both

Firms such as Budweiser are increasingly using social media to request consumer input into product, service design, and marketing decisions.

Source: Anheuser-Busch Companies, LLC

consistent product and service quality and quick, positive responses to consumer complaints.

Moreover, it is important to note that not all personal sources are equal in value. Some folks are known in their circles as the "go-to person" for specific types of information. These individuals actively filter, interpret, or provide product- and brand-relevant information to their family, friends, and colleagues. An individual who does this is known as an **opinion leader.** The process of one person's receiving information from the mass media or other sources and passing it on to others is known as the **two-step flow of communication.** The two-step flow explains some aspects of communication within groups, but it is too simplistic to account for most communication flows. What usually happens is a multistep flow of communication. Figure 7–4 contrasts the direct flow of information from a firm to customers with the more realistic multistep flow of mass communications.

The **multistep flow of communication** involves opinion leaders for a particular product area who actively seek relevant information from the mass media as well as other sources. These opinion leaders process this information and transmit their interpretations of it to some members of their groups. These group members also receive information from the mass media as well as from group members who are not opinion leaders. Figure 7–4 also indicates that these non–opinion leaders often initiate requests for information and supply feedback to the opinion leaders. Likewise, opinion leaders receive information from their followers as well as from other opinion leaders. Note how social media facilitates this multistep flow process online.

FIGURE 7-4   Mass Communication Information Flows

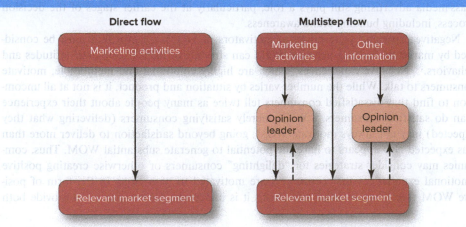

Situations in Which WOM and Opinion Leadership Occur

The exchange of advice and information between group members can occur *directly* in the form of WOM when (1) one individual seeks information from another or (2) one individual volunteers information. It also can occur *indirectly* through observation as a by-product of normal group interaction.

LO5

Imagine that you are about to make a purchase in a product category with which you are not very familiar. Further imagine that the purchase is important to you—perhaps a new sound system, skis, or a bicycle. How would you go about deciding what type and brand to buy? Chances are you would, among other things, ask someone you know who you believe is knowledgeable about the product category. This person would be an opinion leader for you. Notice that we have described a *high-involvement* purchase situation in which the purchaser has limited product knowledge about an important decision. Figure 7–5 illustrates how these factors lead to varying levels of opinion leadership.[38]

In addition to *explicitly* seeking or volunteering information, group members provide information to each other through observable behaviors. Consider Clarisonic, a sonic-wave skin care device:

> One of Seattle's hottest tech startups has everything to do with making more than 2 million women so far—Lady Gaga and Oprah among them—look good and feel good about themselves. The company started on its current path by introducing the Clarisonic to highly influential skin professionals—dermatologists and spas—then branched out into luxury retail stores. Without writing checks, Oprah, Cameron Diaz, Tyra Banks, and Justin Timberlake all said publicly they were fans of Clarisonic. "Once people use it, they are our best advocates. Word of mouth is our best friend," the company president said. The product made $1.7 million in its first year and surpassed $100 million in sales five years later.[39]

The Clarisonic has succeeded mainly through observation. To illustrate, initial spa users experienced cleaner and healthier skin for others to see. Then more customers and their healthier skin were observed by others. Finally, celebrities shared their personal experiences and success with the product on social media.

Likelihood of Seeking an Opinion Leader   **FIGURE 7-5**

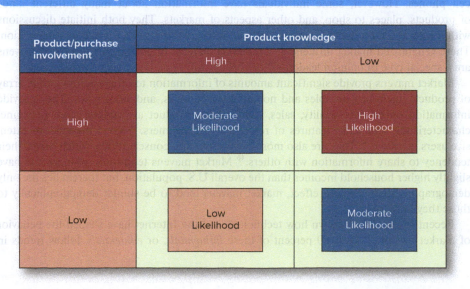

Obviously, observation and direct WOM often operate together. For example, you might be in the market for a digital camera and notice that a friend uses an Olympus. This might jump-start a conversation about digital cameras, the Olympus brand, and where to find the best deals. And while Clarisonic's success depended on observation, WOM also was involved as friends told other friends.

Characteristics of Opinion Leaders

The most salient characteristic of opinion leaders is greater long-term involvement with the product category than the non-opinion leaders in the group. This is referred to as **enduring involvement,** and it leads to enhanced knowledge about and experience with the product category or activity.[40] This knowledge and experience make opinion leadership possible.[41] Thus, an individual tends to be an opinion leader only for a specific product or activity clusters.

Opinion leadership functions primarily through interpersonal communications and observation. These activities occur most frequently among individuals with similar demographic characteristics. Thus, it is not surprising that opinion leaders are found within all demographic segments of the population and seldom differ significantly on demographic variables from the people they influence. Opinion leaders tend to be more gregarious than others are, which may explain their tendency to provide information to others. They also have higher levels of exposure to relevant media than do non-opinion leaders. And opinion leaders around the world appear to possess similar traits.[42]

Identifying and targeting opinion leaders is important. Offline, opinion leaders can be targeted through specialized media sources. For example, Adidas could assume that many subscribers to *Runner's World* serve as opinion leaders for jogging and running shoes.[43] Online, opinion leaders often can be identified in terms of their activity and influence in a given arena.[44] Matt Halfill, a sneakerhead-turned-blogger (his blog is NiceKicks), is seen as an opinion leader in the sneaker culture and companies like Adidas advertise on his blog.

Market Mavens   Opinion leaders are specialists. Their knowledge and involvement tend to be product or activity specific. Therefore, while a person might be an opinion leader for motorcycles, she or he is likely to be an opinion seeker for other products, such as cell phones. However, some individuals have information about many different kinds of products, places to shop, and other aspects of markets. They both initiate discussions with others about products and shopping, and respond to requests for market information. These generalized market influencers are **market mavens.** In essence, then, market mavens are a special type of opinion leader.

Market mavens provide significant amounts of information to others across a wide array of products, including durables and nondurables, services, and store types. They provide information on product quality, sales, usual prices, product availability, store personnel characteristics, and other features of relevance to consumers. Market mavens are extensive users of media.[45] They are also more extroverted and conscientious, which drives their tendency to share information with others.[46] Market mavens tend to be younger and have slightly higher household incomes than the overall U.S. population, but therein lies the only demographic distinction. In effect, market mavens tend to be similar demographically to those they influence.

Recent research has shown how technology and the Internet have shaped the behavior of market mavens.[47] Over 80 percent of these *influentials,* or *e-fluentials,* follow trends in technology and electronics. Also, they are more likely than the rest of the population to engage in the following behaviors:

- Seek out and write online reviews.
- Compare prices.
- Shop online.
- Purchase products that allow them to try new things.
- Exhibit brand loyalty because of product quality.
- Use multiple media devices at the same time.

Their interests and influence extend beyond technology. More than half follow trends in health and fitness, and almost half monitor trends in food and cooking, as well as music. A market maven's reach cannot be ignored by marketers, as these influencers can help a company attract new customers.

Marketing Strategy, WOM, and Opinion Leadership

Marketers are increasingly relying on WOM and influential consumers as part of their marketing strategies. Driving factors include fragmented markets that are more difficult to reach through traditional mass media, greater consumer skepticism toward advertising, and a realization that opinion leaders and online creators and critics can provide invaluable insights in the research and development process.

This is not to say that marketers have given up on traditional advertising and mass media approaches. Instead, they realize that in many cases they could make their traditional media spending go a lot further if they could tap into these influential consumers who will spread the word either indirectly through observation or directly through WOM. We examine some marketing strategies designed to generate WOM and encourage opinion leadership next.

Advertising Advertising can stimulate and simulate WOM and opinion leadership. *Stimulation* can involve themes designed to encourage current owners to talk about (tell a friend about) the brand or prospective owners to ask current owners (ask someone who owns one) for their impressions.[48] Ads can attempt to stimulate WOM by generating interest and excitement. Dove generated interest using a combination of advertising and so-called pass-it-on tools to stimulate WOM. They ran an ad offering two free bars of Dove to anyone who would recommend three friends, who also got a free bar of soap that was gift-wrapped with the name of the initiating friend on the outside. So instead of a sample from a giant company, it felt like a gift from a friend.[49]

Simulating opinion leadership involves having an acknowledged opinion leader—such as Phil Mickelson for golf equipment—endorse a brand. Illustration 7–6 is an example of this approach. Or it can involve having an apparent opinion leader recommend the product in a "slice of life" commercial. These commercials involve an "overheard" conversation between two individuals in which one person provides brand advice to the other. Finally, advertising can present the results of surveys showing that a high percentage of either knowledgeable individuals ("9 out of 10 dentists surveyed recommend . . .") or typical users recommend the brand.[50]

Product Sampling *Sampling,* sometimes called "seeding," involves getting a sample of a product into the hands of a group of potential consumers. Sampling can be a particularly potent WOM tool when it involves individuals likely to be opinion leaders. They, in turn, can serve as brand ambassadors, as in the case of lululemon described in the chapter's opener.

Consumers often use personal sources as primary opinion leaders. However, experts whom they don't know personally also can fill this role, as can survey results indicating that the brand is recommended by experts or typical users.

©Finnbarr Webster Editorial/Alamy

In an attempt to increase the preference for Dockers among the key 24-to-35-year-old urban market, Levi Strauss created the position of "urban networker" in key cities. The networkers identified emerging trendsetters in their cities and tied them to Dockers. This could involve noticing a new band that was beginning to catch on and providing Dockers to the members. The objective was to be associated with emerging urban "happenings" and young influentials as they evolved.[51]

BzzAgent (www.BzzAgent.com) recruits everyday people to actively spread WOM about products they like. BzzAgent is adamant that its "agents" acknowledge their association with BzzAgent and provide honest opinions. Most of the WOM occurs offline in normal conversations. Agents receive a free product sample to use and are coached on various WOM approaches. Agents report back to BzzAgent about each WOM episode and redeemable points are rewarded. Importantly, the motive of most is not the points because many don't redeem them. BzzAgent's client list is long and growing and includes Kraft Foods, Goodyear, and Wharton School Publishing. Companies hire BzzAgent to create and field a WOM campaign. Costs vary, but a 12-week campaign involving 1,000 agents can cost $100,000 or more.[52]

Retailing/Personal Selling   Numerous opportunities exist for retailers and sales personnel to use opinion leadership. Clothing stores can create "fashion advisory boards" composed of likely style leaders from their target market. An example would be a young woman in a sorority for a store like Lilly Pulitzer, trying to attract the college-aged and older Millennial.

Retailers and sales personnel can encourage their current customers to pass along information to potential new customers. When those consumers are given rewards such as discounts, it is called a referral reward program. For example, an automobile salesperson, or the dealership, might provide a free car wash or oil change to current customers who send friends in to look at a new car. Such programs are growing in popularity and companies such as United Airlines, and RE/MAX are using them. Research demonstrates that the programs are effective, particularly for encouraging positive WOM to those with whom consumers have weak rather than strong ties.[53]

Creating Buzz   **Buzz** can be defined as *the exponential expansion of WOM.* It happens when "word spreads like wildfire" with no or limited mass media advertising supporting it. Buzz drove demand for Clarisonic, as described earlier. It also made massive successes of Pokémon, Beanie Babies, the original *Blair Witch Project,* the Harry Potter books, and *Toy Story 3.*[54] Marketers create buzz by providing opinion leaders advance information and product samples, having celebrities use the product, placing the product in movies, sponsoring "in" events tied to the product, restricting supply, courting publicity, and otherwise generating excitement and mystique about the brand.

Buzz generally is not supported by large advertising budgets, but it is often created by marketing activities. In fact, creating buzz is a key aspect of *guerrilla marketing*—marketing with a limited budget using nonconventional communications strategies. Guerrilla marketing is about making an "intense connection with individuals and speed[ing] up the natural word-of-mouth process."[55] Examples of guerrilla techniques include

- Sony Ericsson hired attractive actors to pose as tourists in various metro areas. They would then hand their cell phone/digital camera to locals and ask them to take a picture in an attempt to get the camera in their hands and get them talking about it.
- Bounty, the paper towel company, installed giant "messes"—such as a spilled cup of coffee or melting ice cream—on the streets of New York City and Los Angeles. People could not help but stop to see these life-size creations and nearby signage that said "Bounty—Makes small work of BIG spills."[56]

Buzz is not just guerrilla marketing, and guerrilla tactics must be used with care. Consumer advocates are increasingly concerned about certain guerrilla tactics. There are (a) consumer, (b) ethical, and (c) legal issues with stealth or covert marketing efforts. Consider the following example:

Gillette sponsored an unbranded website called NoScruf.org. NoScruf stands for the National Organization of Social Crusaders Repulsed by Unshaven Faces. The site was created by Porter Novelli for PR reasons on Gillette's behalf and the .org designation was to further obfuscate Gillette's role.

From a consumer standpoint, research shows that when consumers become aware of such covert marketing efforts, consumer trust, commitment, and purchase intentions are damaged. From an ethical standpoint, hiding a brand's participation in a marketing effort puts consumers at a disadvantage because, when they know, they tend to be more wary of the influence attempt. From a legal standpoint, there is movement in the direction of more stringent guidelines against such covert marketing, with one example being the FTC's new guidelines regarding bloggers and their link to marketers.[57] *Can you see additional ethical concerns surrounding "covert" or "guerrilla" marketing? How is BzzAgent's approach different from Sony Ericsson's?*

Creating buzz is often part of a larger strategy that includes significant mass media advertising. Clairol attempted to create WOM for its True Intense Color line via an online sampling program. It also launched a sweepstakes, "Be the Attraction," with a

Online Buzz, WOM, and Astroturfing

As we've seen, the Internet continues to change the nature of interpersonal communications. New avenues are rapidly evolving, and the rewards can be huge for companies that can harness the speed and ease of interconnectivity that the Internet allows. Here are a few examples:[58]

- **Viral marketing** is an online "pass-it-along" strategy. It "uses electronic communications to trigger brand messages throughout a widespread network of buyers." Viral marketing comes in many forms but often involves social media. Worldwide Breast Cancer started a Facebook campaign to create awareness of the signs and risk factors of breast cancer as well as to raise funds for the organization. The "Know Your Lemons" campaign gained over 7 million impressions on Facebook. The viral aspect kicked in when the ad was shared over 40,000 times. In addition, the campaign also raised more than $160 million for breast cancer research and awareness. Nonprofits are not the only organizations using viral techniques. Companies like Nike, Adidas, and Heineken also have enjoyed successful viral campaigns recently.

- *Snapchat* is a platform that allows users to message others privately by sending pictures or short videos that uniquely disappear a few seconds upon viewing the message. Snapchat Stories are clips that can be viewed by all of the user's Snapchat friends. These news-like feeds stay posted for 24 hours before disappearing. Snapchat is popular among Millennials, with 60 percent of users under the age of 24. Brands, especially those targeting a younger demographic, are creatively using Snapchat and its "stories" feature to connect with their customers. For example, the candy brand Sour Patch Kids attracted over 100,000 new followers with its recent "Blue Kid" Snapchat story campaign. Amazon also has used Snapchat to offer exclusive promotional deals on Black Friday.

- *Twitter* is a micro-blogging tool that allows users to communicate with others through short messages. It limits posts to 280 (formerly 140) characters. It has evolved quickly into one of the largest and fastest-growing social media outlets. For marketers there are a number of uses for Twitter. First, as we saw earlier, consumers can post complaints or information requests to

grand prize of an all-expenses-paid trip for four to the premiere of *Legally Blonde* to fuel the buzz. However, these efforts were soon supplemented with a major mass media advertising campaign.[59]

Buzz and WOM are not confined to traditional offline strategies. As discussed in Consumer Insight 7–3, marketers are leveraging increasing numbers of online strategies as well.

DIFFUSION OF INNOVATIONS

An **innovation** is *an idea, practice, or product perceived to be new by the relevant individual or group.* Whether or not a given product *is* an innovation is determined by the perceptions of the potential market, not by an objective measure of technological change. The manner by which a new product is accepted or spreads through a market is basically a group phenomenon. In this section, we will examine this process in some detail.[60]

a brand's Twitter account, to which companies can respond. Second, companies can utilize a Twitter feature called Promoted Tweets. The promotion indicator (like an advertisement) shows up on the Tweet and then the Tweet itself comes up on the search results, even of those who aren't the brand's followers on Twitter. Finally, companies like Sponsored Tweets and Opendorse are connecting brands with influential tweeters. These tweeters, often celebrities or athletes like LeBron James and Kim Kardashian who have millions of followers, get paid for tweeting about specific brands. James was recently paid $140,000 for a 140-character tweet, which amounted to $1,000 per character! For a brand to be effective on this platform, full disclosure is important.

- **Customer reviews** and review functionality on a website can be a critical marketing tool. Amazon and others allow consumers to easily post reviews of products on their sites. Given the power of WOM, this online version of WOM is a powerful decision influencer. For example, restaurant revenues have been found to increase between 5 and 9 percent if they increase their ranking on Yelp by one star. However, there are at least two factors that marketers must be concerned with regarding online reviews. First, because existing reviews are "public information," they tend to "sway" future reviews in that direction. So, if reviews trend down, that likely feeds more downward bias than if reviews were done independent of knowledge of prior reviews. Marketers can find themselves in a battle against a misguided trend, and consumers likely are not getting the best, most accurate advice. A second concern is fake reviews, where it is estimated that one in seven reviews is fake. Astroturfing is the practice whereby companies buy positive reviews of themselves and negative reviews for their competitors. The "buying" of fake reviews by one company for another is akin to false advertising. Samsung was recently fined for hiring people to criticize HTC (a competitor) products.

Clearly marketers are learning how to leverage the WOM potential of the Internet. It will be interesting to see what the future brings!

Critical Thinking Questions

1. What other Internet alternatives exist for interpersonal communication?

2. Do you trust online sources to provide accurate information? What can marketers do to increase consumer trust in online sources?

3. What do you think are typical characteristics of those who are heavy Snapchat or Twitter users?

Categories of Innovations

Try to recall new products that you have encountered in the past two or three years. As you reflect on these, it may occur to you that there are degrees of innovation. For example, wireless speakers such as Amazon's Echo are more of an innovation than is a new fat-free snack. The changes required in one's behavior, including attitudes and beliefs, or lifestyle if a person adopts the new product or service determine the degree of innovation, not the technical or functional changes in the product.

We can place any new product somewhere on a continuum ranging from no change to radical change, depending on the target market's perception of the item. This continuum is often divided into three categories or types of innovations.

Continuous Innovation Adoption of this type of innovation requires relatively minor changes in behavior or changes in behaviors that are unimportant to the consumer.

ILLUSTRATION 7-7

Crest 3DWhite Whitening Therapy toothpaste would be considered a continuous innovation by most.

Source: The Procter & Gamble Company

Examples include Crest 3DWhite Whitening Therapy toothpaste, Wheaties Energy Crunch cereal, and Purex 3-in-1 laundry sheets. Note that some continuous innovations require complex technological breakthroughs. However, their use requires little change in the owner's behavior or attitude. Crest 3DWhite Whitening Therapy toothpaste, shown in Illustration 7–7, is another example of a continuous innovation.

Dynamically Continuous Innovation Adoption of this type of innovation requires a moderate change in an important behavior or a major change in a behavior of low or moderate importance to the individual. Examples include digital cameras, personal navigators, mobile apps, and Bella and Birch textured paints that are applied like wallpaper but without glue, using a special applicator. The Shout Color Catcher ad in Illustration 7–8 is a good example of a product that is a dynamically continuous innovation for most consumer groups.

ILLUSTRATION 7-8

Using Shout Color Catcher would require a major change in an area of moderate importance for most individuals. For these individuals, it would be a dynamically continuous innovation.

Source: S.C. Johnson & Son, Inc.

Source: Tesla

ILLUSTRATION 7-9

Most consumers will react to the Tesla car as a discontinuous innovation.

Discontinuous Innovation Adoption of this type of innovation requires major changes in behavior of significant importance to the individual or group. Examples would include the Norplant contraceptive, becoming a vegetarian, and the Tesla electric car (see Illustration 7–9).

Most of the new products or alterations introduced each year tend toward the no-change end of the continuum. Much of the theoretical and empirical research, however, has been based on discontinuous innovations. For example, individual consumers presumably go through a series of distinct steps or stages known as the **adoption process** when purchasing an innovation. These stages are shown in Figure 7–6.

Adoption Process and Extended Decision Making   FIGURE   7-6

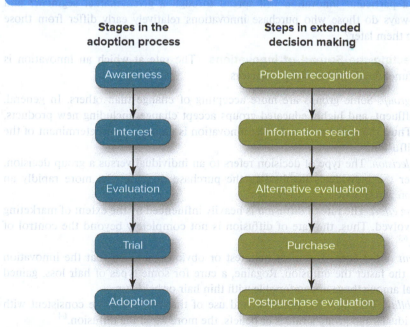

Stages in the adoption process	Steps in extended decision making
Awareness	Problem recognition
Interest	Information search
Evaluation	Alternative evaluation
Trial	Purchase
Adoption	Postpurchase evaluation

Figure 7–6 also shows the steps in extended decision making, described in Chapter 1. As can be seen, the *adoption process* is basically a term used to describe extended decision making when a new product is involved. As we will discuss in detail in Chapter 14, extended decision making occurs when the consumer is *highly involved* in the purchase. High purchase involvement is likely for discontinuous innovations such as the decision to purchase a hybrid or electric car, and most studies of innovations of this nature have found that consumers use extended decision making.

However, it would be a mistake to assume that all innovations are evaluated using extended decision making (the adoption process). In fact, most continuous innovations probably trigger limited decision making. As consumers, we generally don't put a great deal of effort into deciding to purchase innovations such as Diet Coke's Ginger Lime–flavored drink or Glad microwave steaming bags.

Diffusion Process

The **diffusion process** is *the manner in which innovations spread throughout a market.* The term *spread* refers to purchase behavior in which the product is purchased with some degree of regularity.[61] The market can range from virtually the entire society (for a new soft drink, perhaps) to the students at a particular high school (for an automated fast-food and snack outlet).

For most innovations, the diffusion process appears to follow a similar pattern over time: a period of relatively slow growth, followed by a period of rapid growth, followed by a final period of slower growth. This pattern is shown in Figure 7–7. However, there are exceptions to this pattern. In particular, it appears that for continuous innovations such as new ready-to-eat cereals, the initial slow-growth stage may be skipped.

An overview of innovation studies reveals that the time involved from introduction until a given market segment is saturated (i.e., sales growth has slowed or stopped) varies from a few days or weeks to years. This leads to two interesting questions: (1) What determines how rapidly a particular innovation will spread through a given market segment? and (2) In what ways do those who purchase innovations relatively early differ from those who purchase them later?

Factors Affecting the Spread of Innovations   The rate at which an innovation is diffused is a function of the following 10 factors.

1. *Type of group.* Some groups are more accepting of change than others. In general, young, affluent, and highly educated groups accept change, including new products, readily. Thus, the target market for the innovation is an important determinant of the rate of diffusion.[62]

2. *Type of decision.* The type of decision refers to an individual versus a group decision. The fewer the individuals involved in the purchase decision, the more rapidly an innovation will spread.

3. *Marketing effort.* The rate of diffusion is heavily influenced by the extent of marketing effort involved. Thus, the rate of diffusion is not completely beyond the control of the firm.[63]

4. *Fulfillment of felt need.* The more manifest or obvious the need that the innovation satisfies, the faster the diffusion. Rogaine, a cure for some types of hair loss, gained rapid trial among those uncomfortable with thin hair or baldness.

5. *Compatibility.* The more the purchase and use of the innovation are consistent with the individual's and group's values or beliefs, the more rapid the diffusion.[64]

Diffusion Rate of an Innovation over Time   FIGURE 7-7

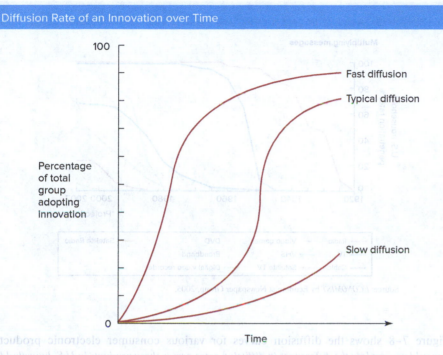

6. *Relative advantage.* The better the innovation is perceived to meet the relevant need compared with existing methods, the more rapid the diffusion. Both the performance and the cost of the product are included in relative advantage. The digital audio tape (DAT) had neither advantage compared with CDs and DVDs and thus never took off.

7. *Complexity.* The more difficult the innovation is to understand and use, the slower the diffusion. The key to this dimension is ease of use, *not* complexity of product. Specialized blogging software is making an otherwise complex task easy and fun.[65]

8. *Observability.* The more easily consumers can observe the positive effects of adopting an innovation, the more rapid its diffusion will be. Smartphones are relatively visible. Laser eye surgery, while less visible, may be a frequent topic of conversation. On the other hand, new headache remedies are less obvious and generally less likely to be discussed.

9. *Trialability.* The easier it is to have a low-cost or low-risk trial of the innovation, the more rapid is its diffusion. The diffusion of products like laser eye surgery has been hampered by the difficulty of trying out the product in a realistic manner. This is much less of a problem with low-cost items such as headache remedies, or such items as smartphones, which can be borrowed or tried at a retail outlet.

10. *Perceived risk.* The more risk associated with trying an innovation, the slower the diffusion. Risk can be financial, physical, or social. Perceived risk is a function of three dimensions: (1) *the probability that the innovation will not perform as desired;* (2) *the consequences of its not performing as desired;* and (3) *the ability (and cost) to reverse any negative consequences.*[66] Thus, many consumers may feel a need for the benefits offered by laser eye surgery and view the probability of its working successfully as being quite high. However, they perceive the consequences of failure as being extreme and irreversible and therefore do not adopt this innovation.

248   Part Two   External Influences

269

FIGURE ⬤ **7-8**   Diffusion Rates for Consumer Electronics

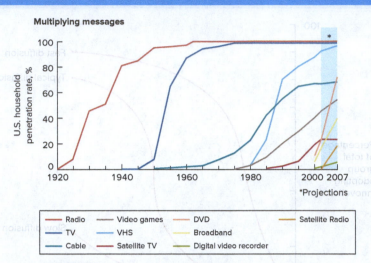

Source: *ECONOMIST* by Economist Newspaper Group, 2005.

Figure 7–8 shows the diffusion curves for various consumer electronic products. *How would you explain the differences in diffusion rates across these products in U.S. households?*

Characteristics of Individuals Who Adopt an Innovation at Varying Points in Time

The curves shown in Figures 7–7 and 7–8 are cumulative curves that illustrate the increase in the percentage of adopters over time. If we change those curves from a cumulative format to one that shows the percentage of a market that adopts the innovation at any given point in time, we will have the familiar bell-shaped curves shown in Figure 7–9.

Figure 7–9 reemphasizes the fact that a few individuals adopt an innovation very quickly, another limited group is reluctant to adopt the innovation, and the majority of the group adopts at some time in between the two extremes. Researchers have found it useful to divide the adopters of any given innovation into five groups based on the relative time at which they adopt. These groups, called **adopter categories,** are shown in Figure 7–9 and defined below:

Innovators: The first 2.5 percent to adopt an innovation.

Early adopters: The next 13.5 percent to adopt.

Early majority: The next 34 percent to adopt.

Late majority: The next 34 percent to adopt.

Laggards: The final 16 percent to adopt.

How do these groups differ? The following descriptions, though general, provide a good starting point. Clearly, however, research by product category would be necessary in fully understanding specific marketing situations.

Innovators are venturesome risk takers. They are capable of absorbing the financial and social costs of adopting an unsuccessful product. They are cosmopolitan in outlook and use other innovators rather than local peers as a reference group. They tend to be

Adoptions of an Innovation over Time   **FIGURE** 7-9

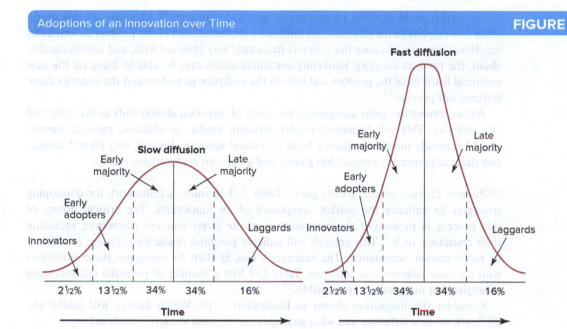

younger, better educated, and more socially mobile than their peers. Innovators make extensive use of commercial media, sales personnel, and professional sources in learning of new products.

Early adopters tend to be opinion leaders, like market mavens, in local reference groups. They are successful, well educated, and somewhat younger than their peers. They are willing to take a calculated risk on an innovation but are concerned with failure. Early adopters also use commercial, professional, and interpersonal information sources, and they provide information to others.

Early majority consumers tend to be cautious about innovations. They adopt sooner than most of their social group but also after the innovation has proved successful with others. They are socially active but seldom leaders. They tend to be somewhat older, less well educated, and less socially mobile than the early adopters. The early majority rely heavily on interpersonal sources of information.

Late majority members are skeptical about innovations. They often adopt more in response to social pressures or a decreased availability of the previous product than because of a positive evaluation of the innovation. They tend to be older and have less social status and mobility than those who adopt earlier.

Laggards are locally oriented and engage in limited social interaction. They tend to be relatively dogmatic and oriented toward the past. Laggards adopt innovations only with reluctance.

Marketing Strategies and the Diffusion Process

Market Segmentation   Because earlier purchasers of an innovation differ from later purchasers, firms should consider a "moving target market" approach. That is, after selecting a general target market, the firm initially should focus on those individuals within the target market most likely to be innovators and early adopters.[67] Messages to this group often can emphasize the newness and innovative characteristics of the product as well as its functional features. Because this group is frequently very involved with, and knowledgeable about, the product category, marketing communications may be able to focus on the new technical features of the product and rely on the audience to understand the benefits these features will provide.[68]

As the innovation gains acceptance, the focus of attention should shift to the early and late majority. This will frequently require different media. In addition, message themes should generally move away from a focus on radical newness. Instead, they should emphasize the acceptance the product has gained and its proven performance record.

Diffusion Enhancement Strategies   Table 7–3 provides a framework for developing strategies to enhance the market acceptance of an innovation. The critical aspect of this process is to analyze the innovation *from the target markets' perspective,* including their resistance to it.[69] This analysis will indicate potential obstacles—*diffusion inhibitors*—to rapid market acceptance. The manager's task is then to overcome these inhibitors with *diffusion enhancement strategies.* Table 7–3 lists a number of potential enhancement strategies, but many others are possible.

Consider the innovation shown in Illustration 7–10. Which factors will inhibit the dji Spark drone's diffusion, and what strategies can be used to overcome them?

TABLE 7-3   Innovation Analysis and Diffusion Enhancement Strategies

Diffusion Determinant	Diffusion Inhibitor	Diffusion Enhancement Strategies
1. Nature of group	Conservative	Search for other markets Target innovators within group
2. Type of decision	Group	Choose media to reach all deciders Provide conflict reduction themes
3. Marketing effort	Limited	Target innovators within group Use regional rollout Leverage buzz
4. Felt need	Weak	Extensive advertising showing importance of benefits
5. Compatibility	Conflict	Stress attributes consistent with normative values
6. Relative advantage	Low	Lower price Redesign product
7. Complexity	High	Distribute through high-service outlets Use skilled sales force Use product demonstrations Extensive marketing efforts
8. Observability	Low	Use extensive advertising Target visible events when appropriate
9. Trialability	Difficult	Use free samples to early adopter types Offer special prices to rental agencies Use high-service outlets
10. Perceived risk	High	Success documentation Endorsement by credible sources Guarantees

ILLUSTRATION 7-10

Ten factors determine the success of innovations. How do you think the DJI Spark drone innovation will fare based on these 10 factors?

Source: DJI

SUMMARY

LO1: Explain reference groups and the criteria used to classify them.

A *reference group* is a group whose presumed perspectives or values are being used by an individual as the basis for his or her current behavior. Thus, a reference group is simply a group that an individual uses as a guide for behavior in a specific situation. Reference groups, as with groups in general, may be classified according to a number of variables including membership, strength of social tie, type of contact, and attraction.

LO2: Discuss consumption subcultures, including brand and online communities and their importance for marketing.

A *consumption subculture* is a group that self-selects on the basis of a shared commitment to a particular product or consumption activity. These subcultures also have (1) an identifiable, hierarchical social structure; (2) a set of shared beliefs or values; and (3) unique jargon, rituals, and modes of symbolic expression. A *brand community* is a nongeographically bound community, based on a structured set of social relationships among owners of a brand and the psychological relationship they have with the brand itself, the product in use, and the firm. Brand communities can add value to the ownership of the product and build intense loyalty.

An *online community* is a community that interacts over time around a topic of interest on the Internet. Online communities have evolved over time to include *online social network sites,* which are web-based services that allow individuals to (1) construct a public or semipublic profile within a bounded system, (2) articulate a list of other users with whom they share a connection, and (3) view and traverse their list of connections and those made by others within the system.

LO3: Summarize the types and degree of reference group influence.

Informational influence occurs when an individual uses the behaviors and opinions of reference group members as potentially useful bits of information. *Normative influence,* sometimes referred to as utilitarian influence, occurs when an individual fulfills group expectations to gain a direct reward or to avoid a sanction. *Identification influence,* also called value-expressive influence, occurs when individuals have internalized the group's values and norms.

The degree of *conformity* to a group is a function of (1) the visibility of the usage situation, (2) the level of commitment the individual feels to the group, (3) the relevance of the behavior to the functioning of the group, (4) the individual's confidence in his or her own judgment in the area, and (5) the level of necessity reflected by the nature of the product.

LO4: Discuss within-group communications and the importance of word-of-mouth communications to marketers.

Communication within groups is a major source of information about certain products. Information is communicated within groups either directly through *word-of-mouth (WOM)* communication or indirectly through observation. WOM via personal sources such as family and friends is trusted more than marketer-based messages and therefore can have a critical influence on consumer decisions and business success. Two-thirds of all consumer product decisions are thought to be influenced by WOM. Negative experiences are a strong driver of negative WOM for all consumers.

LO5: Understand opinion leaders (both online and offline) and their importance to marketers.

Opinion leaders are highly knowledgeable about specific products or activities and are seen as the "go-to person" for specific types of information. These individuals actively filter, interpret, or provide product- and brand-relevant information to their family, friends, and colleagues. A defining characteristic of opinion leaders is their enduring involvement with the product category, which leads to their expertise and the trust people have in their opinions.

A special type of opinion leader is *market mavens*. These are individuals who are general market influencers. They have information about many different kinds of products, places to shop, and other aspects of markets. These influencers can share information both offline (*influentials*) and online (*e-fluentials*).

Marketers attempt to identify opinion leaders primarily through their media habits and social activities. Identified opinion leaders then can be used in marketing research, product sampling, retailing/personal selling, advertising, and buzz creation. Various offline and online strategies exist for stimulating WOM, opinion leadership, and buzz. Online strategies include viral marketing, Snapchat, and Twitter.

LO6: Discuss innovation diffusion and use an innovation analysis to develop marketing strategy.

Groups greatly affect the diffusion of innovations. *Innovations* vary in degree of behavioral change required and the rate at which they are diffused. The first purchasers of an innovative product or service are termed *innovators;* those who follow over time are known as *early adopters, early majority, late majority,* and *laggards.* Each of these groups differs in personality, age, education, and reference group membership. These characteristics help marketers identify and appeal to different classes of adopters at different stages of an innovation's diffusion.

The time it takes for an innovation to spread from innovators to laggards is affected by several factors: (1) nature of the group involved, (2) type of innovation decision required, (3) extent of marketing effort, (4) strength of felt need, (5) compatibility of the innovation with existing values, (6) relative advantage, (7) complexity of the innovation, (8) ease in observing usage of the innovation, (9) ease in trying the innovation, and (10) perceived risk in trying the innovation.

KEY TERMS

REVIEW QUESTIONS

1. How does a *group* differ from a *reference group?*
2. What criteria are used by marketers to classify groups?
3. What is a *dissociative reference group?* In what way can dissociative reference groups influence consumer behavior?
4. What is an *aspiration reference group?* How can an aspiration reference group influence behavior?
5. What is a *consumption-based group* or a *consumption subculture?* How can marketers develop strategy based on consumption subcultures?
6. What is a *brand community?* What are the characteristics of such a group?
7. How can a marketer foster a brand community?
8. What is an *online social network site?* What are the guidelines for marketers operating in online communities and social networking sites?
9. What types of group influence exist? Why must a marketing manager be aware of these separate types of group influence?
10. What five factors determine the strength of reference group influence in a situation?
11. What is the *Asch phenomenon* and how do marketers utilize it?
12. How can a marketer use knowledge of reference group influences to develop advertising strategies?

13. What is an *opinion leader?* How does an opinion leader relate to the *multistep flow of communication?*
14. What characterizes an opinion leader?
15. What determines the likelihood that a consumer will seek information from an opinion leader?
16. How does a *market maven* differ from an *opinion leader?*
17. Explain the role of *enduring involvement* in driving opinion leadership.
18. How can marketing managers identify opinion leaders?
19. How can marketers utilize opinion leaders?
20. What is *buzz?* How can marketers create it?
21. Compare and contrast *Twitter* and *Snapchat.*
22. What is an *innovation?* Who determines whether a given product is an innovation?
23. What are the various categories of innovations? How do they differ?
24. What is the *diffusion process?* What pattern does the diffusion process appear to follow over time?
25. Describe the factors that affect the diffusion rate for an innovation. How can these factors be utilized in developing marketing strategy?
26. What are *adopter* categories? Describe each of the adopter categories.
27. How can a marketer use knowledge of adopter categories to develop marketing strategy?

DISCUSSION QUESTIONS

28. Respond to the questions in Consumer Insight 7–1.
29. Using college students as the market segment, describe the most relevant reference group(s) and indicate the probable degree of influence on decisions for each of the following:
    a. Brand of toothpaste
    b. Purchase of an electric car
    c. Purchase of breakfast cereal
    d. Becoming a vegetarian
    e. Choice of a wireless speaker such as the Amazon Echo

Answer Questions 30 to 33 using (a) shoes, (b) barbeque grill, (c) car, (d) toaster, (e) iPad, and (f) adopting a pet from a shelter.

30. How important are reference groups to the purchase of the above-mentioned products or activities? Would their influence also affect the brand or model? Would their influence be informational, normative, or identification? Justify your answers.
31. What reference groups would be relevant to the decision to purchase the product or activity (based on students on your campus)?
32. What are the norms of the social groups of which you are a member concerning the product or activity?
33. Respond to the questions in Consumer Insight 7–2.

34. Describe two groups that serve as aspiration reference groups for you. In what ways, if any, have they influenced your consumption patterns?

35. Describe two groups to which you belong. For each, give two examples of instances when the group has exerted (*a*) informational, (*b*) normative, and (*c*) identification influence on you.

36. Develop two approaches using reference group theory to reduce drug, alcohol, or cigarette consumption among teenagers.

37. What ethical concerns arise in using reference group theory to sell products?

38. Describe a consumption subculture to which you belong. How does it affect your consumption behavior? How do marketers attempt to influence your behavior with respect to this subculture?

39. Do you belong to a brand community? If so, describe the benefits you derive from this group and how it affects your consumption.

40. Do you belong to an online community or social network site? If so, describe the benefits you derive from this group and how it affects your consumption.

41. Answer the following questions for (*i*) Dyson bladeless fan, (*ii*) space flight, (*iii*) cell phone–based GPS.
    a. Is the product an innovation? Justify your answer.
    b. Using the student body on your campus as a market segment, evaluate the perceived attributes of the product.

c. Who on your campus would serve as opinion leaders for the product?
d. Will the early adopters of the product use the adoption process (extended decision making), or is a simpler decision process likely?

42. Describe two situations in which you have served as or sought information from an opinion leader. Are these situations consistent with the discussion in the text?

43. Are you aware of market mavens on your campus? Describe their characteristics, behaviors, and motivation.

44. Have you used Twitter recently? Why? How did it work? What marketing implications does this suggest?

45. Identify a recent (*a*) continuous innovation, (*b*) dynamically continuous innovation, and (*c*) discontinuous innovation. Justify your selections.

46. Analyze the Roomba (robotic vacuum cleaner) in terms of the determinants in Table 7–3 and suggest appropriate marketing strategies.

47. Conduct a diffusion analysis and recommend appropriate strategies for the innovation shown in Illustration 7–10.

48. Assume that you are a consultant to firms with new products. You have members of the appropriate market segments rate innovations on the 10 characteristics described in Table 7–3. Based on these ratings, you develop marketing strategies. Assume that a rating of 9 is extremely favorable (e.g., strong relative advantage or a lack of complexity) and 1 is extremely unfavorable. Suggest appropriate strategies for each of the following consumer electronic products (see table).

Attribute	Product								
	A	B	C	D	E	F	G	H	I
Fulfillment of felt need	9	7	3	8	8	5	7	8	9
Compatibility	8	8	8	8	9	2	8	9	8
Relative advantage	9	2	8	9	7	8	9	8	8
Complexity	9	9	9	9	9	3	8	8	7
Observability	8	8	9	1	9	4	8	8	8
Trialability	8	8	8	9	9	2	9	2	9
Nature of group	3	8	7	8	9	9	7	7	8
Type of decision	3	7	8	8	6	7	7	3	7
Marketing effort	6	7	8	7	8	6	3	8	7
Perceived risk	3	8	7	7	3	8	8	8	5

APPLICATION ACTIVITIES

49. Find two advertisements that use reference groups in an attempt to gain patronage. Describe the advertisement, the type of reference group being used, and the type of influence being used.

50. Develop an advertisement for (*i*) teeth whitening strips, (*ii*) an energy drink, (*iii*) an upscale club, (*iv*) Red Cross, (*v*) scooters, or (*vi*) vitamins using the following:
    a. An informational reference group influence
    b. A normative reference group influence
    c. An identification reference group influence

51. Interview two individuals who are strongly involved in a consumption subculture. Determine how it affects their consumption patterns and what actions marketers take toward them.

52. Interview an individual who is involved in a brand community. Describe the role the firm plays in maintaining the community, the benefits the person gets from the community, and how it affects his or her consumption behavior.

53. Identify and interview several opinion leaders on your campus for the following. To what extent do they match the profile of an opinion leader as described in the text?
    a. Local restaurants
    b. Sports equipment
    c. Music
    d. Computer equipment

54. Interview two salespersons for the following products. Determine the role that opinion leaders play in the purchase of their product and how they adjust their sales process in light of these influences.
    a. Smartphones
    b. Golf equipment
    c. Computers
    d. Art
    e. Jewelry
    f. Sunglasses

55. Follow a brand on Twitter for a week. What types of marketing strategies are they engaged in and how are they utilizing Twitter to facilitate brand awareness and solve customer problems.

REFERENCES

1. The Chapter 7 opener is based on J. H. McAlexander, J. W. Schouten, and H. F. Koenig, "Building Brand Community," *Journal of Marketing,* January 2002, pp. 38–54; H. Malcom, "Lululemon Lovers Buy into Healthy Lifestyle," *USA Today,* March 19, 2013, www.usatoday.com, accessed March 19, 2018; A. Lutz, "Lululemon's Effective Technique for Hooking Customers," *Business Insider,* May 21, 2015, www.businessinsider.com, accessed March 19, 2018; M. Newlands, "How Lululemon Made Their Brand Iconic: An Interview with SVP of Brand Programs Eric Petersen," *Forbes,* February 21, 2016, www.forbes.com, accessed March 19, 2018; M. Schlossberg, "One Sentence Sums Up Why Millennials Are Flocking to Nike, Under Armour and Lululemon," *Business Insider,* July 6, 2016, www.businessinsider.com, accessed March 19, 2018; J. Fromm, "The Lululemon Lifestyle: Millennials Seek More Than Just Comfort from Athleisure Wear," *Forbes,* July 6, 2016, www.forbes.com, accessed March 19, 2018; B. Pearson, "The Hidden Value of Thanks: 3 Ways Apple, Lululemon and Others Do It," *Forbes,* September 7, 2016, www.forbes.com, accessed March 19, 2018; C. Fernandez, "Inside Lululemon's Unconventional Influencer Network," *Fashionista,* November 2, 2016, www.fashionista.com, accessed March 19, 2018; A. Foote, "#SquadGoals: 21 Outstanding Brand Communities to Emulate," *L and T Co.,* January 12, 2017, www.landt.co,

accessed March 19, 2018; E. Bary, "Lululemon Has a Big New Fan Base," *Barron's,* March 16, 2017, www.barrons.com, accessed March 19, 2018; as well as information from various websites, including www.lululemon.com, accessed March 19, 2018; www.luluaddict.com, accessed March 19, 2018; and www.reuters.com, accessed March 19, 2018.

2. K. White and D. W. Dahl, "To Be or *Not* Be?," *Journal of Consumer Psychology* 16, no. 4 (2006), pp. 404–14.

3. J. W. Schouten and J. H. McAlexander, "Subcultures of Consumption," *Journal of Consumer Research,* June 1995, p. 43.

4. N. Christakis and J. Fowler, *CONNECTED* (New York: Little, Brown & Company, 2009); S. Clifford, "Video Prank at Domino's Taints Brand," *New York Times,* April 15, 2009, www.nytimes.com/2009/04/16/business/media/16dominos.html?_r50, accessed September 1, 2014; E. Rosen, *The Anatomy of Buzz Revisited: Real-Life Lessons in Word-of-Mouth Marketing* (New York: Random House, 2009); J. Sanburn, "How Dr. Dre Made $300 Headphones a Must-Have Accessory," *Time,* January 16, 2013, business.time.com/2013/01/16/how-dr-dre-made-300-headphones-a-must-have-accessory/, accessed September 1, 2014; D. Gilgoff, "Short Takes: Gauging the Impact of 'Purpose Driven Life,' 10 Years on," *Belief blog,* November 29, 2012, http://religion.

256   Part Two   External Influences

blogs.cnn.com/2012/11/29/short-takes-gauging-the-impact-of-purpose-driven-life-10-years-on/, accessed September 1, 2014.

5. B. Gainer, "Ritual and Relationships," *Journal of Business Research,* March 1995, pp. 253–60. See also E. J. Arnould and P. L. Price, "River Magic," *Journal of Consumer Research,* June 1993, pp. 24–45.

6. A. Hamilton and J. DeQuine, "Freaking for Sneakers," *Time,* March 13, 2006.

7. Excerpts from L. Beward, "Sneakerheads Share a Passion for Rare Soles," *McClatchy-Tribune Business News,* July 10, 2009.

8. T. Wasserman, "Sneakerheads Rule," *Adweek,* October 19, 2009, pp. 10–14.

9. Based on McAlexander, Schouten, and Koenig, "Building Brand Community."

10. A. M. Muniz Jr. and T. C. O'Guinn, "Brand Community," *Journal of Consumer Research,* March 2001, p. 413. See also R. P. Bagozzi, "On the Concept of Intentional Social Action in Consumer Behavior," *Journal of Consumer Research,* December 2000, pp. 388–96; A. M. Muniz Jr. and H. J. Schau, "Religiosity in the Abandoned Apple Newton Brand Community," *Journal of Consumer Research,* March 2005, pp. 737–47.

11. Harley-Davidson example from Schouten and McAlexander, "Subcultures of Consumption." MG example from T. W. Leigh, C. Peters, and J. Shelton, "The Consumer Quest for Authenticity: The Multiplicity of Meanings within the MG Subculture of Consumption," *Journal of the Academy of Marketing Science* 34, no. 4 (2006), pp. 481–93. Tesla example from F. Lambert, "Tesla Fulfils Bucket List of Dying Man by Delivering His Model 3 Early," *Electrek,* December 13, 2017, https://electrek.co/2017/12/13/tesla-model-3-bucket-list-dying-man/, accessed March 26, 2018; and other Tesla websites found at www.forums.tesla.com, accessed March 26, 2018; and www.teslamotorgroup.com, accessed March 26, 2018.

12. Q. Jones, "Virtual Communities, Virtual Settlements, and CyberArchaeology," *Journal of Computer-Mediated Communication* 3, no. 3 (1997), www.ascusc.org/jcmc/vol3/issue3/jones.html, accessed March 26, 2018; C. Okleshen and S. Grossbart, "Usenet Groups, Virtual Community and Consumer Behaviors," and S. Dann and S. Dann, "Cybercommuning," both in *Advances in Consumer Research,* vol. 25, ed. J. W. Alba and J. W. Hutchinson (Provo, UT: Association for Consumer Research, 1998), pp. 276–82 and 379–85, respectively; C. L. Beau, "Cracking the Niche," *American Demographics,* June 2000, pp. 38–40; P. Maclaran and M. Catterall, "Researching the Social Web," *Marketing Intelligence and Planning* 20, no. 6 (2002), pp. 319–26.

13. A. L. Blanchard and M. L. Markus, "The Experienced 'Sense' of a Virtual Community," *Database for Advances in Information Systems,* Winter 2004, pp. 65–79.

14. D. M. Boyd and N. B. Ellison, "Social Network Sites," *Journal of Computer-Mediated Communication* 13, no. 1 (2007), http://jcmc.indiana.edu, accessed June 17, 2008.

15. Statistics are estimates for 2016 from eMarketer.com.

16. A. Lenhart et al., *Teens, Social Media & Technology Overview 2015* (Washington, DC: Pew Research Center, April 9, 2015); A. Smith and M. Anderson, *Social Media Use in 2018* (Washington, DC: Pew Research Center, March 1, 2018).

17. B. Thompson, *How to Use Social Media to Improve Customer Service and Cut Costs* (Burlingame, CA: Customer Think, March 2010).

18. *State of Inbound Marketing Report* (Cambridge, MA: HubSpot, 2010).

19. *2010 Cone Consumer New Media Study Fact Sheet* (Boston, MA: Cone LLC, 2010).

20. Ibid.

21. For additional information and expertise, visit *Site Logic Marketing* at www.sitelogicmarketing.com and the online marketing blog "Marketing Logic," written by Matt Bailey, Site Logic's president.

22. Excerpt from http://consumerist.com/consumer/blogs/sonys-pspblog-flog-revealed-221384.php.

23. N. Zmuda, "Ann Taylor Investigation Shows FTC Keeping Close Eye on Blogging," *Advertising Age,* April 28, 2010.

24. B. Thompson, *Voice of Customer 2.0* (Burlingame, CA: Customer Think, March 2010).

25. J. Comm, "How Oreos Got 40 Million Likes on Facebook," *Inc.,* January 6, 2016, www.inc.com, accessed April 4, 2018; Oreo website, www.facebook.com/oreo/, accessed April 4, 2018.

26. L. K. John, D. Mochon, O. Emrich and J. Schwartz, "What's the Value of a Like?," *Harvard Business Review,* March–April 2017, pp. 108–15.

27. See T. F. Mangleburg and T. Bristol, "Socialization and Adolescents' Skepticism toward Advertising," *Journal of Advertising,* Fall 1998, pp. 11–20. See also T. F. Mangleburg, P. M. Doney, and T. Bristol, "Shopping with Friends and Teens' Susceptibility to Peer Influence," *Journal of Retailing* 80 (2004), pp. 101–16.

28. See R. J. Fisher and D. Ackerman, "The Effects of Recognition and Group Need on Volunteerism," *Journal of Consumer Research,* December 1998, pp. 262–77.

29. See K. R. Lord, M.-S. Lee, and P. Choong, "Differences in Normative and Informational Social Influence," in *Advances in Consumer Research,* vol. 28, ed. M. C. Gilly and J. Meyers-Levy (Provo, UT: Association for Consumer Research, 2001), pp. 280–85.

30. See W. Amaldoss and S. Jain, "Pricing and Conspicuous Goods," *Journal of Marketing Research,* February 2005, pp. 30–42.

31. See, e.g., M. Mourali, M. Laroche, and F. Pons, "Individualistic Orientation and Consumer Susceptibility to Interpersonal Influence," *Journal of Services Marketing* 19, no. 3 (2005), pp. 164–73.

32. T. Patton, "How Are Consumers Influenced by Referral Marketing?," *Ambassador,* March 9, 2016, www.getambassador.com, accessed April 7, 2018.

33. G. Packard and J. Berger, "How Language Shapes Word of Mouth's Impact," *Journal of Marketing Research* 54 (August 2017), pp. 572–88.

34. Insight is based on S. Bernazzani, "The 10 Best User-Generated Content Campaigns on Instagram," https://blog.hubspot.com/marketing/best-user-generated-content-campaigns, accessed March 18, 2018; D. Kirkpatrick, "Study: User-Generated Content Drives Higher Facebook Engagement Than Ads," *Marketing Dive,* February 14, 2017, www.marketingdive.com/news/study-user-generated-content-drives-higher-facebook-engagement-than-ads/436139/, accessed March 18, 2018; K. Morrison, "How Consumer-Generated Content Drives Brand Value (Report)," *Adweek,* April 25, 2016, www.adweek.com/digital/how-consumer-generated-content-drives-brand-value-report/, accessed March 18, 2018; E. Siu, "10 User Generated Content

Campaigns That Actually Worked," https://blog.hubspot.com/marketing/examples-of-user-generated-content, accessed March 18, 2018; "The 2017 Consumer Content Report: Influence in the Digital Age 2017," https://stackla.com/go/2017-consumer-content-report-influence-in-digital-age/, accessed March 18, 2018; T. Weinberg, "When User-Generated Content Goes Bad," *TNW*, June 17, 2016, https://thenextweb.com/insider/2016/06/17/user-generated-content-goes-bad/, accessed March 18, 2018; "Why Your User-Generated Content Campaign Failed," www.sitereportcard.com/1656/user-generated-content-campaign-failed/, accessed March 18, 2018; "Worst UGC Fails," https://duel.tech/worst-ugc-fails/, accessed March 18, 2018.

35. See, e.g., R. N. Laczniak, T. E. DeCarlo, and S. N. Ramaswami, "Consumers' Responses to Negative Word-of-Mouth Communication," *Journal of Consumer Psychology* 11, no. 1 (2001), pp. 57–73; A. Wilson, M. Giebelhausen, and M. Brady, "Negative Word of Mouth Can Be a Positive for Consumers Connected to the Brand," *Journal of the Academy of Marketing Science* 45 (2017), pp. 534–47.

36. E. Rosen, *The Anatomy of Buzz* (New York: Doubleday, 2000); see also D. S. Sundaram, K. Mitra, and C. Webster, "Word-of-Mouth Communications," in *Advances in Consumer Research*, vol. 25, ed. Alba and Hutchinson, pp. 527–31; A. A. Bailey, "The Interplay of Social Influence and Nature of Fulfillment," *Psychology & Marketing*, April 2004, pp. 263–78.

37. M. Johnson, G. M. Zinkhan, and G. S. Ayala, "The Impact of Outcome, Competency, and Affect on Service Referral," *Journal of Services Marketing* 5 (1998), pp. 397–415.

38. For a thorough discussion, see D. F. Duhan, S. D. Johnson, J. B. Wilcox, and G. D. Harrell, "Influences on Consumer Use of Word-of-Mouth Recommendation Sources," *Journal of the Academy of Marketing Science*, Fall 1997, pp. 283–95; C. Pornpitakpan, "Factors Associated with Opinion Seeking," *Journal of Global Marketing* 17, no. 2/3 (2004), pp. 91–113.

39. L. Timmerman, "Clarisonic Cracks Big-Time with $100M Sales, Riding Rave Reviews from Lady Gaga, Oprah," *Xconomy*, March 30, 2011, www.xconomy.com, accessed April 7, 2018; "Unpaid Celebrity Endorsements," *Celebrity Cred*, March 4, 2016, www.celebritycred.com, accessed April 7, 2018.

40. G. M. Rose, L. R. Kahle, and A. Shoham, "The Influence of Employment-Status and Personal Values on Time-Related Food Consumption Behavior and Opinion Leadership," in *Advances in Consumer Research*, vol. 22, ed. F. R. Kardes and M. Sujan (Provo, UT: Association for Consumer Research, 1995), pp. 367–72; U. M. Dholakia, "Involvement-Response Models of Joint Effects," in *Advances in Consumer Research*, vol. 25, ed. Alba and Hutchinson, pp. 499–506.

41. See M. C. Gilly, J. L. Graham, M. F. Wolfinbarger, and L. J. Yale, "A Dyadic Study of Interpersonal Information Search," *Journal of the Academy of Marketing Science*, Spring 1998, pp. 83–100.

42. R. Marshall and I. Gitosudarmo, "Variation in the Characteristics of Opinion Leaders across Borders," *Journal of International Consumer Marketing* 8, no. 1 (1995), pp. 5–22.

43. See I. M. Chaney, "Opinion Leaders as a Segment for Marketing Communications," *Marketing Intelligence and Planning* 19, no. 5 (2001), pp. 302–308.

44. Methods for understanding network influences online are still being developed. For one approach, see M. Trusov, A. V. Bodapati, and R. E. Bucklin, "Determining Influential Users in Internet Social Networks," *Journal of Marketing Research*, August 2010, pp. 643–58.

45. L. F. Feick and L. L. Price, "The Market Maven," *Journal of Marketing*, January 1987, pp. 83–97. See also R. A. Higie, L. F. Feick, and L. L. Price, "Types and Amount of Word-of-Mouth Communications about Retailers," *Journal of Retailing*, Fall 1987, pp. 260–78; K. C. Schneider and W. C. Rodgers, "Generalized Marketplace Influencers' Attitudes toward Direct Mail as a Source of Information," *Journal of Direct Marketing*, Autumn 1993, pp. 20–28; J. E. Urbany, P. R. Dickson, and R. Kalapurakal, "Price Search in the Retail Grocery Market," *Journal of Marketing*, April 1996, pp. 91–104.

46. T. A. Mooradian, "The Five Factor Model and Market Mavenism," in *Advances in Consumer Research*, vol. 23, ed. K. P. Corfman and J. G. Lynch (Provo, UT: Association for Consumer Research, 1996), pp. 260–63. For additional motivations driving mavens, see G. Walsh, K. P. Gwinner, and S. R. Swanson, "What Makes Mavens Tick?," *Journal of Consumer Marketing* 21, no. 2 (2004), pp. 109–22; "An In-Depth Look at the Market Maven Persona," *Civic Science*, February 25, 2016, https://civicscience.com, accessed April 8, 2018.

47. E. Keller and J. Berry, *The Influentials* (New York: Free Press, 2003). See also D. Godes and D. Mayzlin, "Firm-Created Word-of-Mouth Communication," *Harvard Business School Marketing Research Papers*, no. 04-03 (July 2004); I. Cakim, "E-Fluentials Expand Viral Marketing," *iMedia Connection*, October 28, 2002, www.imediaconnection.com; see also information on Burson-Marsteller's website at www.bm.com; "An In-Depth Look at the Market Maven Persona."

48. See E. Keller and B. Fay, "The Role of Advertising in Word of Mouth," *Journal of Advertising Research*, June 2009, pp. 154–58.

49. Rosen, *The Anatomy of Buzz*.

50. See C. S. Areni, M. E. Ferrell, and J. B. Wilcox, "The Persuasive Impact of Reported Group Opinions on Individuals Low vs. High in Need for Cognition," *Psychology & Marketing*, October 2000, pp. 855–75.

51. A. Z. Cuneo, "Dockers Strives for Urban Credibility," *Advertising Age*, May 25, 1998, p. 6.

52. See R. Walker, "The Hidden (in Plain Sight) Persuaders," *New York Times Magazine*, December 5, 2004; materials on BzzAgent's website at www.BzzAgent.com.

53. See E. Biyalogorsky, E. Gerstner, and B. Libai, "Customer Referral Management," *Marketing Science*, Winter 2001, pp. 82–95; G. Ryu and L. Feick, "A Penny for Your Thoughts," *Journal of Marketing*, January 2007, pp. 84–94.

54. R. Dye, "The Buzz on Buzz," *Harvard Business Review*, November 2000, p. 140; J. Lehrer, "Head Case: The Buzz on Buzz," *Wall Street Journal*, October 16, 2010, p. C12.

55. T. F. Lindeman, "More Firms Use Unique 'Guerrilla Marketing' Techniques to Garner Attention," *Knight Ridder Tribune Business News*, January 18, 2004, p. 1.

56. Ibid.; A. Zantal-Wiener, "What Is Guerrilla Marketing? 7 Examples to Inspire Your Brand," *HubSpot*, July 28, 2017, https://blog.hubspot.com/marketing/guerilla-marketing-examples, accessed April 8, 2018.

57. C. Ashley and H. A. Leonard, "Betrayed by the Buzz?," *Journal of Public Policy and Marketing*, Fall 2009, pp. 212–20.

58. A. Dobele, D. Toleman, and M. Beverland, "Controlled Infection!," *Business Horizons* 48 (2005), pp. 143–49; "7 Best

258   Part Two   External Influences

Viral Campaigns—2017," *National Positions,* January 8, 2018, https://nationalpositions.com/7-best-viral-campaigns-2017/, accessed March 24, 2018; S. Patel, "7 Brands That Are Killing It on Snapchat," *Entrepreneur,* February 6, 2017, www.entrepreneur.com, accessed March 28, 2018; J. Wertz, "Which Social Media Platforms Are Right for Your Business?," *Forbes,* February 18, 2017, www.forbes.com, accessed March 28, 2018; E. Moreau, "What Is Snapchat? An Intro to the Popular Ephemeral App," *Lifewire,* February 11, 2018, www.lifewire.com, accessed March 28, 2018; *Who Tweets?* (Washington, DC: Pew Internet, 2009); J. Van Grove, "Sponsored Tweets Launches," *Mashable,* August 3, 2009, www.mashable.com, accessed May 23, 2011; "Americans Spend 2 Hours, 12 Minutes per Month on Twitter," *Search Engine Watch,* January 26, 2011, http://blog.searchenginewatch.com, accessed March 17, 2011; "How Charlie Sheen and Other Stars Get Paid to Tweet," *Wall Street Journal Blog,* March 6, 2011, https://blogs.wsj.com, accessed May 25, 2011; "How Does Twitter Make Money?," www.buzzle.com, accessed May 23, 2011; D. Rovell, "LeBron James-sponsored Tweets Valued at $140K or $1K per character," *ESPN,* August 20, 2015, www.espn.com/nba/story/_/id/13470682/lebron-james-sponsored-tweets-232-million-followers-cost-140k, accessed March 26, 2018; D. Pogue, "Critical Mass," *Scientific American,* May 17, 2011, www.scientificamerican.com/article/critical-mass/, accessed September 1, 2014; D. Streitfeld, "In a Race to Out-Rave, 5-Star Web Reviews Go for $5," *New York Times,* August 19, 2011, www.nytimes.com/2011/08/20/technology/finding-fake-reviews-online.html, accessed September 1, 2014; D. Streitfeld, "Give Yourself 5 Stars? Online, It Might Cost You," *New York Times,* September 22, 2013, www.nytimes.com/2013/09/23/technology/give-yourself-4-stars-online-it-might-cost-you.html?_r=0, accessed September 1, 2014; C. Conner, "Online Reputation," *Forbes,* October 30, 2013, www.forbes.com/sites/cherylsnappconner/2013/10/30/online-reputation-new-methods-emerge-for-quashing-fake-defamatory-reviews/, accessed September 1, 2014.

59. K. Fitzgerald, "Bristol-Meyers Builds Buzz," *Advertising Age,* April 23, 2001, p. 18.

60. See also V. Mahajan, E. Muller, and F. M. Bass, "New Product Diffusion Models in Marketing," *Journal of Marketing,* January

1990, pp. 1–26; E. M. Rogers, *Diffusion of Innovations,* 4th ed. (New York: Free Press, 1995). For an alternative to the traditional adoption diffusion model, see C.-F. Shih and A. Venkatesh, "Beyond Adoption," *Journal of Marketing,* January 2004, pp. 59–72.

61. See M. I. Nabith, S. G. Bloem, and T. B. C. Poiesz, "Conceptual Issues in the Study of Innovation Adoption Behavior," in *Advances in Consumer Research,* vol. 24, ed. M. Bruck and D. J. MacInnis (Provo, UT: Association for Consumer Research, 1997), pp. 190–96.

62. See, e.g., S. L. Wood and J. Swait, "Psychological Indicators of Innovation Adoption," *Journal of Consumer Psychology* 12, no. 1 (2002), pp. 1–13.

63. See, e.g., E.-J. Lee, J. Lee, and D. W. Schumann, "The Influence of Communication Source and Mode on Consumer Adoption of Technological Innovations," *Journal of Consumer Affairs,* Summer 2002, pp. 1–27.

64. See N. Y.-M. Siu and M. M.-S. Cheng, "A Study of the Expected Adoption of Online Shopping," *Journal of International Consumer Marketing* 13, no. 3 (2001), pp. 87–106.

65. For a discussion of how type of innovation and consumer expertise interact, see C. P. Moreau, D. R. Lehmann, and A. B. Markman, "Entrenched Knowledge Structures and Consumer Response to New Products," *Journal of Marketing Research,* February 2001, pp. 14–29.

66. For a more complete analysis, see U. M. Dholakia, "An Investigation of the Relationship between Perceived Risk and Product Involvement," in *Advances in Consumer Research,* vol. 24, ed. Bruck and MacInnis, pp. 159–67; M. Herzenstein, S. S. Posavac, and J. J. Brakus, "Adoption of New and Really New Products," *Journal of Marketing Research,* May 2007, pp. 251–60.

67. For a discussion of when this is not appropriate, see V. Mahajan and E. Muller, "When Is It Worthwhile Targeting the Majority Instead of the Innovators in a New Product Launch?," *Journal of Marketing Research,* November 1998, pp. 488–95.

68. See, e.g., Chaney, "Opinion Leaders as a Segment for Marketing Communications."

69. M. Claudy, R. Garcia and A. O'Driscoll, "Consumer Resistance to Innovation—A Behavioral Reasoning Perspective," *Journal of the Academy of Marketing Science* 43 (2015), pp. 528–44.

CHAPTER 8

Creativity and Product Development

There is pleasure in the pathless woods.
Confucius

How can an organization establish an environment that fosters bringing new products and services to market on a consistent and timely basis?

Over the past 20 years, product life cycles have gotten shorter and shorter—in large part due to faster technological breakthroughs. To keep pace with this environment of rapid change, companies must establish a creative culture that strongly encourages spending time on new ideas, concepts, and solutions. The creative enterprise is based on six resources, which are outlined in Table 8.1. Creative ideas, concepts, and solutions are turned into products and services through the product design and development process. This process is concerned with the concrete details that embody a new product or service. Prototypes are models of a product or service and can help a new technology venture to learn about the right form of the product for the customer. Scenarios are used to create a mental model of a possible sequence of future events or outcomes. Good product development relies on the five practices listed in Table 8.5. ■

TABLE 8.1 Six resources for a creative enterprise.

- Knowledge in the required domain and fields and knowing what is new

- Capability to recognize connections, redefine problems, and envision and analyze possible practical ideas and solutions

- Inventive thinking about the problem in novel ways

- Motivation toward action

- Opportunity-oriented culture and openness to change

- Contextual understanding that supports creativity and mitigates risks

8.1 Creativity and Invention

Creativity is the ability to use the imagination to develop new ideas, strategies, business models, or solutions. Creative thinking is a core competency of most new ventures, and entrepreneurs strive to have creative people on their team. Creative ideas often arise when creative people look at established solutions, practices, or products and think of something new or different. These creative ideas enable invention and innovation. Thus, firms committed to innovation must fundamentally strive to encourage and support creativity. This section examines several outstanding ways of understanding creativity.

The creative enterprise is based on six resources as shown in Table 8.1 [Sternberg et al., 1997]. To create something new, one needs knowledge of the field and of the domain of knowledge required. Domains are areas such as science, engineering, or marketing. Fields within a domain might be circuit design or market research.

Creativity requires the ability to see linkages between opportunities, redefine problems, and envision and analyze possible practical solutions. Creative people use inventive thinking that reflects in novel ways on a problem. A creative thinker is motivated to make something happen and is open to change. Finally, the creative person understands the context of the problem and is willing to take a reasonable risk. The person who has most of these skills is often called *intuitive*; that is, he or she has an instinctive ability to perceive or understand relationships, ideas, and solutions.

One process of creative thinking is shown in Figure 8.1. The entrepreneur begins by seeking to describe the problem, taking time to validate his or her understanding through an incubation period of observation and study. Then, brainstorming is used to generate tangible ideas and insights that can be evaluated and tested. Finally, a prototype is built and shown to the potential customer. This process may lead the entrepreneur to revise the question or problem and to begin a second cycle through the process. This continues until the entrepreneur is confident that the resulting prototype is capable of addressing the user's core needs.

Creativity often involves associational thinking. Associational thinking is the ability to connect seemingly unrelated information or ideas and to create

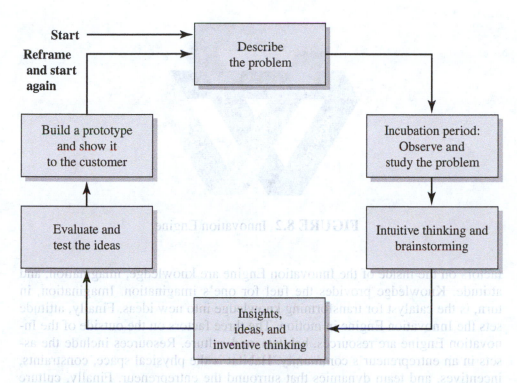

FIGURE 8.1 Creativity process.

value out of the novel combination. Four key actions can trigger associational thinking: Questioning, observing, networking with diverse others, and experimenting [Furr and Dyer, 2014].

Although daunting to a small entrepreneurial team seeking innovation, it is useful to view promoting creativity as akin to assembling multiple personas. Each persona has its own skills and points of view. The first three personas occupy learning roles: the *anthropologist* observes behaviors and develops a deep understanding of how people interact with products, services, and each other; the *experimenter* prototypes new ideas continuously; and the *cross-pollinator* explores other industries and settings and borrows relevant ideas from them. The next three personas occupy organizing roles: the *hurdler* develops a knack for overcoming and outsmarting potential obstacles; the *collaborator* helps to bring diverse groups together; and the *director* gathers and inspires the team. The last four personas occupy building roles: the *experience architect* designs compelling experiences that go beyond mere functionality; the *set designer* transforms physical environments to facilitate the work of innovative team members; the *caregiver* anticipates and attends to customer needs; and the *storyteller* conveys a compelling narrative about the project [Kelley and Littman, 2005].

Figure 8.2 illustrates the "Innovation Engine," which shows how different internal and external factors can work together to enhance creativity. The three

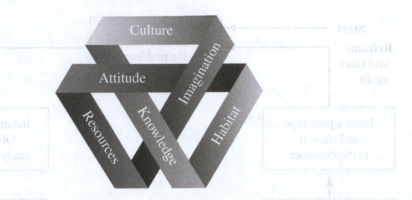

FIGURE 8.2 Innovation Engine.

factors on the inside of the Innovation Engine are knowledge, imagination, and attitude. Knowledge provides the fuel for one's imagination. Imagination, in turn, is the catalyst for transforming knowledge into new ideas. Finally, attitude sets the Innovation Engine in motion. The three factors on the outside of the Innovation Engine are resources, habitats, and culture. Resources include the assets in an entrepreneur's community. Habitat is the physical space, constraints, incentives, and team dynamics that surround the entrepreneur. Finally, culture refers to collective beliefs, values, and behaviors in the entrepreneur's community [Seelig, 2012].

An entrepreneur can improve all six factors to increase innovation. Imagination can be enhanced by reframing problems, connecting ideas, and challenging assumptions [Seelig, 2012]. For example, in 1954, Kay Zufall was looking for new things for children to do. She did not like the modeling clay sold for children because it was too stiff. However, her brother-in-law made a doughy mixture for cleaning wallpaper. Zufall tried it as a modeling medium and discovered it was soft and easy to mold and cut up. She and her brother-in-law reformulated it as a safe and colorful product for children, and they came up with the name: PlayDoh [Sutton, 2002].

A powerful method for enhancing the imagination is brainstorming. In a brainstorming session, diverse people come together to generate new ideas through conversation and interaction. Creative solutions emerge as team members integrate different perspectives [Harvey, 2016]. Brainstorming sessions typically require significant planning, setup, and follow-through. Table 8.2 lists eight guidelines for effective brainstorming sessions.

The mindset of the brainstorming group is particularly important. To be effective, teams should follow certain brainstorming "rules," as listed in Table 8.3. Entrepreneurs can be naturally inclined to judge ideas immediately, leading them to filter the ideas that they discuss and record in a brainstorming session. The point of a brainstorming session, however, is to stir the imagination in order to generate new ideas. Some firms, like the product-design firm IDEO, post

TABLE 8.2 Guidelines for effective brainstorming sessions.

Right people	A brainstorming group should be diverse, relatively small, and free of internal politics.
Right challenge	A brainstorming group should focus on a clearly stated challenge.
Right mindset	A brainstorming group should adopt a creative and generative mindset, saving idea evaluation for the end of the session.
Right empathy	A brainstorming group should focus on understanding the people who are affected by the challenge.
Right stimulus	A brainstorming group should use questions that question assumptions, consider extreme cases, employ analogies, and explore technology scenarios and trends.
Right facilitation	A brainstorming group should ensure that everyone participates, while keeping the conversation fresh and energetic.
Right follow-up	A brainstorming group should have some way to ensure that ideas can later be considered and, where appropriate, implemented.

Source: Liedtka, J., & Ogilvie, T. (2011). *Designing for Growth.* Columbia Business School Publishing.

TABLE 8.3 Brainstorming "rules."

Defer judgment	Don't confuse idea generation, where brainstorming excels, with idea evaluation
Capture all ideas	Even ideas that seem irrelevant or "bad" can be the basis of other ideas
Encourage wild ideas	Wild ideas can lead to insights
Hold one conversation at a time	Listen to other people in the group
Build on other people's ideas	Consider how you might modify or extend an idea into a new idea
Be visual	Use pictures and diagrams, not just words, to capture ideas
Go for volume	Emphasize quantity over quality

Source: Seelig, Tina. *inGenius: A Crash Course on Creativity.* New York: HarperCollins Publishers, 2012.

printouts of the brainstorming rules in Table 8.3 in their work environments to remind team members of this goal.

Entrepreneurs also can act to enhance parts of the Innovation Engine beyond imagination. For example, an entrepreneur can enhance her knowledge of a market by engaging deeply with potential customers through conversations and observations. Entrepreneurs also can work to apply their knowledge across different domains. For example, Tina Seelig completed her Ph.D. in neuroscience at the Stanford University School of Medicine. Soon after she completed her degree, she decided that she wanted to enter the world of business. Though neuroscience and business may seem very different, Seelig realized that her ability to do scientific research was directly applicable to the kinds of problems that she would face in the business world; even though Seelig did not have a degree in business, she did have highly relevant knowledge. Research shows that teams that include problem solvers from disparate but analogous markets outperform teams in which members all have expertise in the target market [Franke et al., 2013].

An important part of attitude lies in maintaining a willingness to experiment and the drive to push through challenges to solve problems. Research shows that the human mind is malleable and that people who maintain a positive and learning-oriented attitude have different brain activity than people who do not.

Finally, habitat plays an important role in facilitating creativity. Part of habitat is the physical environment itself. Many startups feature brightly colored and open spaces with easily movable furniture, whiteboards, and even games. These physical environments support creativity by encouraging informal interactions and by providing an easy way to capture and share key insights and ideas.

Habitat also includes incentives and team dynamics. All firms need a culture that promotes a creative process that enables team members to engage and interact with new solutions. The leaders of a new venture can play a particularly important role in establishing this culture; firms with leaders who empower employees experience greater creativity [Zhang and Bartol, 2010]. Leaders also should work to establish a collaborative culture around creativity. Collaborative teams are more likely to achieve creative breakthroughs, since they can draw upon multiple perspectives, and they are less likely to have very poor outcomes, since groups typically have a more rigorous selection process [Singh and Fleming, 2010].

Entrepreneurial leaders influence the culture by putting in place rules, rewards, and incentives that can foster innovation. Even those employees who are not in a leadership role that has direct control over the corporate culture can indirectly influence the culture by reinforcing other parts of the Innovation Engine. For example, by increasing their use of imagination, they might recognize opportunities that can ultimately affect the entire organizational culture.

Table 8.4 conveys several ideas for managing and leading in a creative work environment. These ideas can clash, however, with conventional management practices [Sutton, 2002]. A natural conflict exists between managing for creativity or exploration on one hand and implementation or exploitation on the other hand: New ideas and inventions depend upon creativity; bringing these inventions to market, however, may require routine processes [Freeman and Engel, 2007]. A small, emerging firm can accommodate both tendencies within it. As a firm grows, it needs to build a culture that reinforces the best qualities of creativity as well as efficient execution of its business processes [Brown and Duguid, 2001].

TABLE 8.4 Conventional versus creative management practices.

Conventional practice	Creative practice
Hire people who are "fast learners" of the organizational code.	Hire people who are "slow learners" of the organizational code.
Hire people whom you like and feel comfortable with.	Hire those you may dislike, and who make you feel uncomfortable.
Hire people you need.	Hire people you probably don't need.
Recruit and screen new employees using job interviews.	Get new ideas through interviewing people.
Stress importance of paying attention to and obeying bosses and peers.	Stress importance of ignoring and defying bosses and peers.
Locate happy people and make sure they don't fight.	Locate happy people and encourage them to fight.
Reward success and penalize failure and idleness.	Reward success and failure and penalize idleness.
Plan something that will most likely succeed, and convince everyone success is guaranteed.	Plan something that will most likely fail, then convince everyone success is guaranteed.
Consider logical or practical ideas, and plan to do them.	Consider unrealistic ideas, and plan to do them.
Cater to people who will analyze and support the work.	Stay away from, divert, or bore anyone who just wants to discuss money.
Take advantage of the knowledge of people who have faced the same problems you face.	Ignore the advice of people who say they have faced the same problems you face.
Duplicate the previous successes of your company.	Forget about any past success by your company.

Courtesy of Sutton, Robert. *Weird Ideas That Work*. 2002. Simon and Schuster, New York City.

8.2 Product Design and Development

One of the early tasks of a venture is the design and development of the new product. The entrepreneurial team wants to develop a new product or service that can establish a leadership position. One of the strengths of a new enterprise is that the leadership of the venture plays a central role in all stages of the development effort. Furthermore, the small firm could move quickly to gather the specialized capabilities necessary for product development [Burgelman, 2002].

In recent years, product complexity has dramatically increased. As products acquire more functions, the difficulty of forecasting product requirements rises exponentially. Furthermore, the rate of change in most markets is also increasing, thereby reducing the effectiveness of traditional approaches to forecasting future product requirements. As a result, entrepreneurs need to redefine the problem from one of improving forecasting to one of eliminating the need for accurate long-term forecasts. Thus, many product designers try to keep the product characteristics flexible as the development proceeds. A design and development project can be said to be flexible to the extent that the cost of any change is low. Project leaders can then make product design choices that allow the product to accommodate changes in the team's understanding of user needs [Thompke and Reinertsen, 1998]. For example, a designer might determine a base hardware platform and then make continual improvements to the product via software updates.

Uncertainty is an inevitable aspect of all design and development projects, and most entrepreneurs have difficulty controlling it. The challenge is to find the right balance between planning and learning. Planning provides discipline, and learning provides flexibility and adaptation. Openness to learning is necessary for most new ventures that are finding their way into the market [DeMeyer et al., 2002].

Design of a product leads to the arrangement of concrete details that embodies a new product idea or concept. A product's visible design attributes, such as color, shape, and texture, enable a firm to excite users and thus drive sales; they also enable the firm to explain what a product does and how best to use it [Eisenman, 2013]. More generally, the design process is the organization and management of people, concepts, and information utilized in the development of the form and function of a product.

The role of design is, in part, to mediate between the novel concept and established institutional needs. For example, Thomas Edison designed and described the electric light in terms of the established institutions and culture, making this new innovation appear and function in a familiar way that fit the existing infrastructure. As a result, he succeeded in developing an electric lighting system that gained rapid acceptance as an alternative to the gas lamp [Hargadon and Douglas, 2001]. As new products are designed, the challenge ultimately lies in providing familiar cues that locate and describe new ideas without binding users too closely to the old ways of doing things. Entrepreneurs must find the balance between novelty and familiarity, between impact and acceptance [Anthony et al., 2016].

Tony Fadell: Thermostat Breakthrough

Tony Fadell is a prototypical breakthrough thinker. While at Apple, he thought of the concept of a small portable digital music player, which later became the iPod. He then went on to be a key player in the development of the iPhone, which catapulted Apple to its current position as one of the world's highest valued firms. Tony looks at products and then re-envisions how these products might be made easier to use or more accessible. Fadell followed up his work at Apple by creating the Nest Learning Thermostat. The idea for a smart thermostat came to him while shopping for thermostats for an energy-efficient home he was building. At the time, Fadell realized that the state of at-home and office thermostats seemed to be caught in a time warp. These devices had few features and limited intelligence. With this knowledge, he reimagined an easy-to-use thermostat that could be controlled both manually and over the Internet. His invention is upending what had been a stagnant market for decades. Nest is now vying to replace hundreds of millions of thermostats in homes and businesses, and its product line has expanded to include security cameras and smoke detectors. In 2014, Google acquired Nest for $3.2 billion.

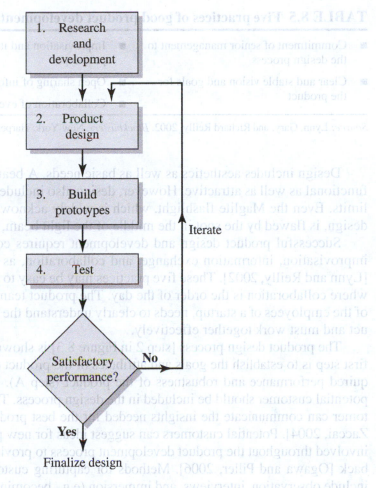

FIGURE 8.3 Overall development process.

Good, effective products or services are the outcome of a methodology based on solid, proven design principles [Brown, 2008]. Innovation is powered by a thorough understanding of how people want products made, packaged, marketed, sold, and supported. The overall development process is shown in Figure 8.3 [Thompke and Von Hippel, 2002]. This process includes design of the product and its architecture, its physical design, and testing. The iPad and the Tesla Roadster sports car are examples of the outcome of a creative, artistic process of design. Part of the user experience is the look and feel of a product. A good product is attractive to look at and easy to use and understand. Furthermore, customers want a product that does a few things really well. Fortunately, customers can participate fruitfully in the product design process when the innovations are incremental [Nambisan, 2002]. Good designers think about the qualities of a product as well as its soft benefits such as warmth, status, and community.

TABLE 8.5 Five practices of good product development.

■ Commitment of senior management to the design process	■ Improvisation and iteration to develop a prototype
■ Clear and stable vision and goals for the product	■ Open sharing of information
	■ Collaboration of everyone on the team

Source: Lynn, Gary, and Richard Reilly. 2002. *Blockbusters*. New York: Harper Collins.

Design includes aesthetics as well as basic needs. A beautiful glass must be functional as well as attractive. However, design also includes compromises and limits. Even the Maglite flashlight, which is widely acknowledged for its good design, is flawed by the spot in the middle of the light beam.

Successful product design and development requires commitment, vision, improvisation, information exchange, and collaboration, as listed in Table 8.5 [Lynn and Reilly, 2002]. These five practices may be easy to achieve in a startup where collaboration is the order of the day. The product team, which may be all of the employees of a startup, needs to clearly understand the vision for the product and must work together effectively.

The product design process [step 2 in Figure 8.3] is shown in Figure 8.4. The first step is to establish the goals and attributes of the product expressed as the required performance and robustness of the product (step A). When possible, the potential customer should be included in the design process. The voice of the customer can communicate the insights needed for the best products [Lojacono and Zaccai, 2004]. Potential customers can suggest ideas for new products and can be involved throughout the product development process to provide continuous feedback [Ogawa and Piller, 2006]. Methods for capturing customers' perspectives include observation, interviews, and immersion (e.g., becoming the user).

In step B of Figure 8.4, the components and parameters available for adjustment are identified, and specifications for the product are agreed upon. Specifications are the precise description of what the product has to do. In addition, the set of physical and social constraints should be determined. Next, the product configuration is established, and the components of the product are recorded. Finally, the parameters of the product are optimized to achieve the best performance and robustness at a reasonable cost [Ullman, 2003]. A robust product is one that is relatively insensitive to aging, deterioration, small variations in components, and environmental conditions. For example, Wikipedia is constantly subject to attempted degradation by hackers. Yet Wikipedia's design enables it to continually improve over time [Dixon, 2011].

Usability is a measure of the quality of a user's experience when interacting with a product. Usability is a combination of the five factors listed in Table 8.6. Examples of a common product with poor usability are most DVR and DVD players. New products should pass the five-minute test, which requires that the product be simple enough to use after quickly reading the instructions and then

From research and development—step 1

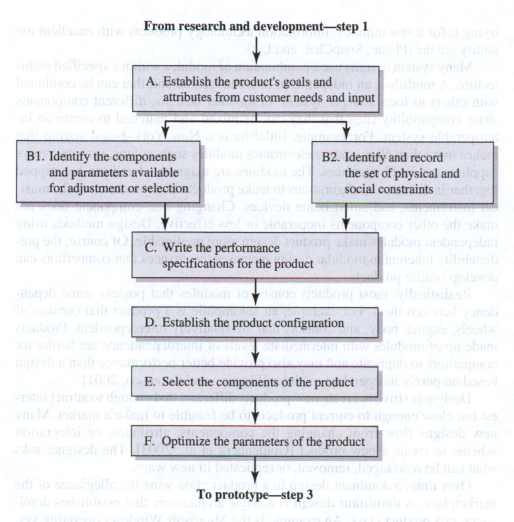

A. Establish the product's goals and attributes from customer needs and input

B1. Identify the components and parameters available for adjustment or selection

B2. Identify and record the set of physical and social constraints

C. Write the performance specifications for the product

D. Establish the product configuration

E. Select the components of the product

F. Optimize the parameters of the product

To prototype—step 3

FIGURE 8.4 Product design process (step 2 of Figure 8.3).

TABLE 8.6 Five factors of usability.

1.	**Ease of learning:**	How long does it take to learn the product's operation?
2.	**Efficiency of use:**	Once experienced, how fast can the user complete the necessary steps?
3.	**Memorability:**	Can the user remember how to use the product?
4.	**Error frequency and severity:**	How often do users make errors, and how serious are these errors?
5.	**Satisfaction:**	Does the user like operating the product?

trying it for a few minutes. Information technology products with excellent usability are the iPhone, SnapChat, and Lyft.

Many system designs use a combination of modules within a specified architecture. A **module** is an independent, interchangeable unit that can be combined with others to form a larger system. In modular designs, different components share compatibility such that they can be mixed and matched to create an interoperable system. For example, littleBits is a New York–based startup that makes more than 60 miniature electronics modules such as fans, sensors, power supplies, and WiFi interfaces. The modules are magnetized and can be snapped together in different configurations to make products like remote controls, musical instruments, and smart-home devices. Changing one component does not make the other components inoperable or less effective. Design methods using independent modules make product design more predictable. Of course, the predictability inherent in modular design increases the chances that competitors can develop similar products.

Realistically, most products consist of modules that possess some dependency between them. For example, an automobile is a product that consists of wheels, engine, body, and controls that are relatively interdependent. Products made up of modules with intermediate levels of interdependence are harder for competitors to duplicate and may also provide better performance than a design based on purely independent modules [Fleming and Sorenson, 2001].

Designers strive to create new products differentiated enough to attract interest but close enough to current products to be feasible to make a market. Many new designs flow from changing the components, attributes, or integration scheme to create a new product [Goldenberg et al., 2003]. The designer asks what can be rearranged, removed, or replicated in new ways.

Over time, a dominant design in a product class wins the allegiance of the marketplace. A **dominant design** is a single architecture that establishes dominance in a product class. An example is the Microsoft Windows operating system, used in the vast majority of personal computers. Eventually, a dominant design becomes embedded in linkages to other systems. For example, the use of Windows shapes hardware interfaces and the other software programs that computers can run.

A **product platform** is a set of modules and interfaces that forms a common architecture from which a stream of derivative products can be efficiently developed and produced. For example, Google's Android and Apple's iPhone seek to be the leading platform for smartphone applications. Firms target new platforms to meet the needs of a core group of customers but design them for ready modification into derivative products through the addition, substitution, or removal of features. Well-designed platforms also provide a smooth migration path between generations so neither the customer nor the distribution channel is disrupted. A good example of a platform is Hewlett-Packard's electronics and software used for its printers; although Hewlett-Packard offers a wide range of printers, these products draw upon relatively similar electronics and software.

8.3 Product Prototypes

Whenever possible, new business ventures should create a prototype of their product. A **prototype** is a rough model of a proposed product or service that conveys the essential features but remains open to modification. Prototypes can be pictures, sketches, mock-ups, or diagrams that can be collaboratively studied. They also can be physical, digital, pictorial, or some combination of media.

Prototypes can be used to identify and test requirements for the product by eliciting comments from designers, users, and others. New ventures can use prototypes to redefine not only their product but also their business models and strategies. For example, Twitter began as an internal messaging service for employees at the company where the company's founders originally met. By learning how it was used in practice, they greatly improved the product before its public release.

Instagram: Insights from Prototypes

Kevin Systrom and Michael Krieger did not have a photo-sharing platform in mind when they set out to start a company. Their first product was Burbn, an app that allowed users to broadcast their current locations, with an option to attach a photo. The app did not get much traction, but the founders noticed that the photo-posting feature was more popular than they anticipated. This observation was the inspiration for Instagram, which was sold to Facebook for $1 billion in 2012.

In the creation of a movie or play, many innovators use sketches, storyboards, and videos to describe the product. The designers of a movie or play want to see how it works and engage in a collaborative redesign. The iterative procedure for prototype development is shown in Figure 8.5. Multiple iterations of the process are necessary to arrive at a satisfactory prototype.

New technologies such as computer simulations can make the creation of a prototype fast and cheap. **Rapid prototyping** is the fast development of a useful prototype that can be used for collaborative review and modification. An initial prototype can be rough since it enables the team to view the product and improve it. The ability to see and manipulate high-quality computer images helps create innovative designs. For example, BMW uses computers to help engineers visualize automobile design and the results of crash tests [Leonardi, 2012]. Maker spaces or hackerspaces are community facilities that provide shared equipment such as computers, 3D printers, and machine tools to enable members to develop and share prototypes.

Product-development firm IDEO believes that prototypes should be "rough, ready, right." While working with Gyrus ENT to develop a better sinus-surgery tool, IDEO employees demonstrated the value of having a prototype to show customers. During one discussion, 10 surgeons struggled to explain the

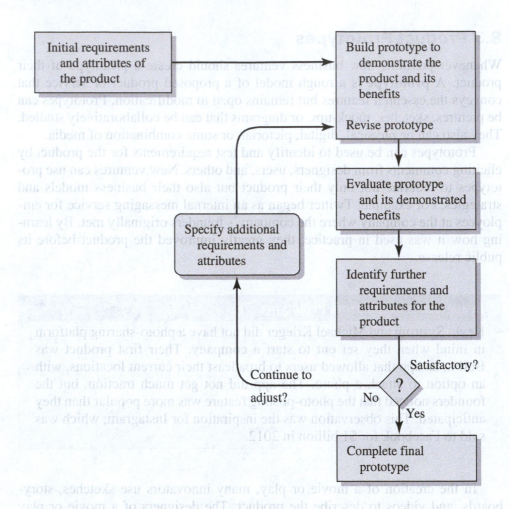

FIGURE 8.5 Prototype development process.

discomfort involved in using the existing tool. An IDEO manager picked up a film canister, a white-board marker, and a clothespin and taped them together as a prototype. The physical prototype helped to move the conversation along, allowing the surgeons to hold and adjust it. The rough prototype was just that—rough and unfinished—encouraging the surgeons to modify and tinker with it. Creating a rough prototype allowed customers to engage in the development of the product, and to enthusiastically adopt it in surgery. Eventually, IDEO and Gyrus produced a tool that is used in over 300,000 procedures in the United States every year.

Firms often use rapid prototyping to develop a **minimum viable product (MVP)**, which you may recall from Section 2.2 is a product having the minimal feature set required to solve the problem or address the need and obtain customer feedback. After developing an MVP, the next step is to develop what might be termed a minimum awesome product—one that becomes irresistible to customers because of its function, design, and social or emotional connection [Furr and Dyer, 2014].

It is often best to carry multiple product concepts into the prototyping phase and to select the best of those designs later in the process [Dahan and Srinivasan, 2000]. Keeping multiple product concept options open and freezing the concept late in the development process affords the flexibility to respond to market and technology shifts.

It is possible to create static and dynamic virtual prototypes that are displayed at a website for review and testing by suppliers, customers, and designers. Virtual prototypes cost considerably less to build and test than their physical counterparts, so design teams using Internet-based product research can afford to explore a much larger number of concepts. Furthermore, Internet-based prototypes can help to reduce the uncertainty in a new product introduction by allowing more ideas to be tested in parallel. At the same time, however, designers should recognize that certain aspects of products and services are more easily tested virtually than others. For example, it is possible to test a wide range of colors for a potential toothbrush virtually, but it is difficult to determine how it feels in the user's mouth.

For the innovator, a prototype is a mechanism for teaching the market about the technology and for learning from the market how valuable that technology is in that application arena. Uses for robots in situations too dangerous for people have long been imagined. Many robotics companies tried and failed to create robots that could successfully enter and explore disaster zones and other dangerous environments. For example, iRobot first demonstrated a prototype of the Urbie robot in 1997. This was the first commercially available robot that was able to climb stairs. This prototype showed the market that iRobot's products had overcome many of the fundamental limitations of other contemporary robots. By 2016, iRobot's revenue was over $630 million, and its products were available worldwide in over 55 major retail chains. Robots like the Urbie were used to explore the rubble of the World Trade Center, and they have been used by the military to explore situations that would be extremely dangerous for troops. Over three million units of the Roomba, the consumer version of the Urbie, have been sold. The Roomba uses similar technology to that of the Urbie to sweep and vacuum floors.

Many firms have developed their products by entering potential markets with early versions of the products, learning from the tests, and probing again. These firms ran a series of market experiments, which introduced prototypes into a variety of market segments. The initial product design was not the culmination of the development process but rather the first step, and the first step in the development process was in and of itself less important than the learning and the subsequent, better-informed steps that followed. Software products lend themselves to rapid prototyping and early tests by using A/B testing methods with potential customers.

178

8.4 Scenarios

Any new enterprise can benefit from creating a set of scenarios to address complex, uncertain challenges as it develops its strategy. A **scenario** is an imagined sequence of possible events or outcomes, sometimes called a mental model. A few realistic scenarios based on the industry context and a few associated possible sequences of events help an entrepreneur to plan for the future. Each scenario tells a story of how the various elements might interact under a variety of assumptions. It paints a vivid narrative of the future. The goal of scenario planning is not to forecast what is going to happen but to encourage an openness of mind, a flexibility of response, and a habit of questioning conventional wisdom.

Scenarios lead to learning in a two-step process: constructing a scenario and using the content of the scenario to learn [Fahey and Randall, 1998]. The key elements of a scenario are shown in Figure 8.6. A scenario tries to answer key questions and is based on a statement of the driving forces and the rationale for the story. For example, entrepreneurs often weigh whether a new technology will be radical or nonlinear and have a profound impact on the marketplace. A scenario can help define the impact and time frame for a new technology. Creating four or five scenarios will help portray the range of potential outcomes to core questions facing any organization.

An example of the outline of a scenario for the growth of electric auto sales is shown in Figure 8.7. The structure of the story for electric vehicles can be used to build several possible scenarios that can be used to learn about the opportunities in this market.

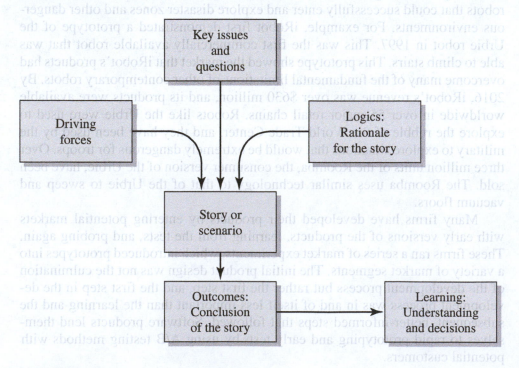

FIGURE 8.6 Elements of a scenario.

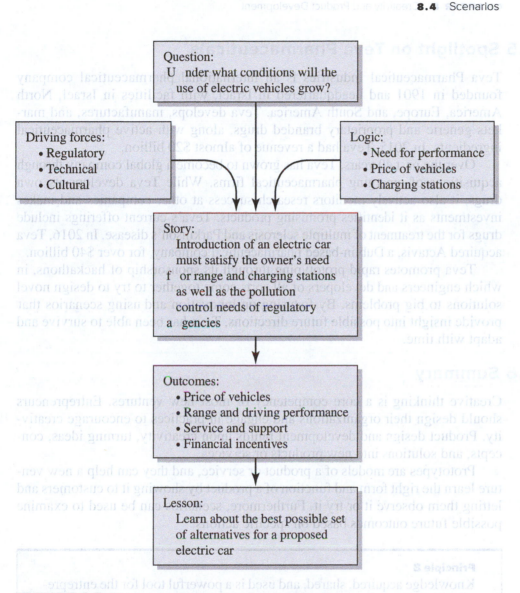

FIGURE 8.7 Elements of scenarios for electric cars.

Entrepreneurs should ensure that the scenarios they craft are realistic and not too optimistic. Otherwise, there is a danger that a scenario can become a mirage. For example, by 2001, many futurists had created a scenario for the future of telecommunications that was overblown and ill-timed. This rosy, nirvana-like scenario missed the regulatory issues and the concept of excess capacity, leading to overinvestment in the sector and a painful downturn [Malik, 2003].

To avoid this fate, entrepreneurs are well-served by crafting multiple scenarios that consider different situations. For example, in the scenario outlined in Figure 8.7, they might consider situations in which vehicle manufacturing capabilities scale slowly versus quickly, or in which the regulatory environment is skeptical versus supportive.

180   **CHAPTER 8** Creativity and Product Development

8.5 Spotlight on Teva Pharmaceuticals

Teva Pharmaceutical Industries is an international pharmaceutical company founded in 1901 and headquartered in Israel, with facilities in Israel, North America, Europe, and South America. Teva develops, manufactures, and markets generic and proprietary branded drugs, along with active pharmaceutical ingredients. In 2015, Teva had a revenue of almost $20 billion.

Over the past 40 years, Teva has grown to become a global company through acquisitions of emerging pharmaceutical firms. While Teva develops its own drugs, it also actively monitors research success at other companies and makes investments as it identifies promising products. Teva's current offerings include drugs for the treatment of multiple sclerosis and Parkinson's disease. In 2016, Teva acquired Actavis, a Dublin-based pharmaceutical company, for over $40 billion.

Teva promotes rapid prototyping through its sponsorship of hackathons, in which engineers and developers of all sorts come together to try to design novel solutions to big problems. By focusing on innovation and using scenarios that provide insight into possible future directions, Teva has been able to survive and adapt with time.

8.6 Summary

Creative thinking is a core competency of most new ventures. Entrepreneurs should design their organizations and engage in practices to encourage creativity. Product design and development builds upon creativity, turning ideas, concepts, and solutions into new products or services.

Prototypes are models of a product or service, and they can help a new venture learn the right form and function of a product by showing it to customers and letting them observe it or try it. Furthermore, scenarios can be used to examine possible future outcomes based on specific actions.

> **Principle 8**
> Knowledge acquired, shared, and used is a powerful tool for the entrepreneur to build a learning organization that can design innovative products and grow effectively.

Video Resources

Visit http://techventures.stanford.edu to view experts discussing content from this chapter.

Unlock Creativity with Motivation and Experimentation	Tina Seelig	Stanford
Ideas Come from Everywhere	Marissa Mayer	Yahoo!
Product Development Process: Observation	David Kelley	IDEO

8.7 Exercises

8.1 How might you influence innovation in a company using each of the six parts of the Innovation Engine from Figure 8.2?

8.2 What role should the "end customer" have in the product design and development process? Do customers always know what they want?

8.3 Capstone Turbine is a developer, assembler, and supplier of microturbine technology. Its primary customers are in the on-site power production and hybrid-electric car markets (www.capstoneturbine.com). Using the format of Figure 8.6, describe a scenario for the growth of Capstone over the next five years.

8.4 The advantages of the Web as a distribution platform delivering services and content are well known. Describe a few examples of its impact on product prototyping and product design and development.

8.5 A number of software development methodologies exist to encourage rapid design and implementation (e.g., agile software development, extreme programming, etc.). Select two of these methodologies and compare and contrast the specific product design and development processes each is attempting to address and improve.

8.6 A *Scientific American* magazine article in November 2014 (https://www.scientificamerican.com/article/pogue-5-most-embarrassing-software-bugs-in-history/) featured some of the largest software failures ever. Examine the list and select your favorite. Describe why failure of knowledge management and the lack of behaving as a learning organization led to this result.

VENTURE CHALLENGE

1. Examine your creative strengths and areas of improvement and share them with your team.

2. Discuss the robustness and usability of your product.

3. Discuss your plans for developing a prototype of your product.

9

THE ORGANIZATIONAL PLAN

1

To understand the importance of the management team in launching a new venture.

2

To understand the advantages and disadvantages of the alternative legal forms for organizing a new venture.

3

To explain and compare the S corporation and limited liability company as alternative forms of incorporation.

4

To understand the implications of the new tax laws on various organization forms.

5

To learn the importance of both the formal and the informal organization.

6

To illustrate how the board of directors or board of advisors can be used to support the management of a new venture.

7

To understand what difficulties may arise when owners are reluctant to delegate or give up responsibility.

OPENING PROFILE

SARA BLAKELY

Not too many entrepreneurs have had the success of Sara Blakely. She has turned her company Spanx Shapewear into a company with a net worth of about $1.3 billion. She did this with little or no knowledge of business or the design of women's clothing.

Sara Blakely was born in February 1971 in Clearwater, Florida. Her father, a trial attorney, was very instrumental in her motivation as he would often ask her "What did you fail at today?" In her family and growing up, failure was a good thing. What he taught her was that you should always be willing to try new things regardless of the outcome and fear of failure. This attitude was important to her in building an organization that has made her into one of the top 100 most powerful women in the world.

www.spanx.com

At a young age, Sara thought that she might like to become an attorney like her father but that option was nullified when she failed the entrance exam into law school. After graduating from Florida State University, she accepted a job at Walt Disney World in Florida where she worked for three months dressed up in a chipmunk costume. After this short period, she took a job selling fax machines and by the age of 25 proved herself to be an excellent salesperson, such that the company promoted her to sales trainer. It was while a salesperson that she first got the idea for her first product. Her uniform as a salesperson necessitated for her to wear pantyhose which she disliked because of the hot Florida climate as well as her dislike for the look of the seamed foot when wearing open-toed shoes. So to eliminate this problem, she decided to cut off the feet of the pantyhose while also wearing them under a new pair of slacks. The pantyhose consistently rolled up her legs but she did feel more comfortable as well as achieved the desired look she wanted. She thought at this point that the idea might have some value.

At the age of 27, she moved to Atlanta while still working for the company selling fax machines. During this time, she continued to develop her idea of making a comfortable and good fitting undergarment out of hosiery material. Realizing that she needed a patent, she inquired about the cost of a patent attorney but quickly decided that she would not spend the money but would instead write her own patent using a textbook she purchased as a guide. The only expense she incurred was for the patent search and application fee. With patent in hand, she then started visiting hosiery mills and manufacturers only to be met with rejection every time. Finally, she found a manufacturer who decided to help her because his two daughters thought that it was a great idea. She spent a lot of time at the factory asking questions and observing the manufacturing process. She noted that products were typically sized on plastic forms and that they used the same waistband on all sizes of products. This was not what she wanted and instead had real women test her prototypes as well as waistbands that correlated with the size of the product.

Sara managed to schedule a meeting with a buyer from Neiman Marcus Group. After changing into her product in the ladies room, she was able to show the buyer the benefits of the product. At this point, the buyer offered to sell the product in seven of their stores. Spanx was now on its way as Bloomingdales, Saks, and Bergdorf Goodman followed suit. Blakely also sent a basket of her products to the office of Oprah Winfrey with a card explaining the product and why she had developed it. Oprah then named Spanx one of her favorite products which immediately caused a boom in sales. In its first year, Spanx reached $4 million in sales and $10 million by the end of year two. With the development of many different undergarments using hosiery material that also mastered the comfort and fit aspect, the company began to grow quickly. New products, including shoes, jeans, and other undergarments, have been added over the years such that by 2017 the company reached a net worth of about $1.3 billion making her one of the wealthiest women in the world. In addition to innovating lots of new products, the company has also opened its own retail stores.

In spite of all her success, Sara claims that one of her most difficult decisions was stepping back and giving up some of the decision making in the organization. In the early years, the company grew so fast that she found herself having to add to the management team on a regular basis. Often she had to hire people that did not necessarily have the right experience but were willing to try new things without the fear of failure. Her belief was that if people did it 80 percent of how she would do it than that would be acceptable. Even to this day she feels this is the most effective hiring approach and so far her decisions have surpassed her expectations.

Her recent biggest challenge came when she had to hire a new CEO. According to Sara, the first thing she looked for when making this hiring decision was to find someone who had passion and could provide leadership. She felt that 70 percent of the decision to hire this person should be based on her feeling about him or her and 30 percent should be based on knowledge and ability to handle the position. Her 70 percent reaction is based on the fact that this person is smart, quick, and scrappy who sees the glass half full. Sara feels that you can tell a lot about a person by the questions they ask or do not ask.

Rapid growth such as seen in Spanx can lead to many organizational issues as to communication, responsibility, and accountability. This chapter focuses on organization both from a legal structure and to building a quality effective team.[1]

DEVELOPING THE MANAGEMENT TEAM

We can see from the Sara Blakely and her company Spanx example the importance of employees and their loyalty and commitment to the organization. Also significant to potential investors is the management team and its ability and commitment to the new venture.

Investors will usually demand that the management team not attempt to operate the business as a sideline or part-time venture while employed full time elsewhere. It is assumed that the management team is prepared to operate the business full time and at a modest salary. It is unacceptable for the entrepreneurs to try to draw a large salary out of the new venture, and investors may perceive any attempt to do so as a lack of psychological commitment to the business. Later in this chapter, the roles of various team members are discussed, particularly as the firm evolves into a legitimate ongoing concern. In addition, the entrepreneur should consider the role of the board of directors and/or a board of advisors in supporting the management of the new venture. At this point, however, the entrepreneur needs to consider the alternatives regarding the legal form of the organization. Each of these forms has important implications for taxes, liability, continuity, and financing the new venture.

LEGAL FORMS OF BUSINESS

C corporation Most common form of corporation, regulated by statute and treated as a separate legal entity for liability and tax purposes

There are three basic legal forms of business formation with some variations available depending on the entrepreneurs' needs. The three basic legal forms are (1) proprietorship, (2) partnership, and (3) corporation, with variations particularly in partnerships and corporations. Another form of business is the limited liability company (LLC), which is now possible in all 50 states and the District of Columbia. The typical corporation form is known as a *C corporation*. Table 9.1 describes the legal factors involved in each of these forms with the differences in the limited liability partnership (LLP) and S corporation noted where appropriate. These three basic legal forms are compared with regard to ownership, liability, startup costs, continuity, transferability of interest, capital requirements, management control, distribution of profits, and attractiveness for raising capital. Later in the chapter, the S corporation and the LLC are compared and discussed as alternative forms of business, especially for the new venture.

It is very important that the entrepreneur carefully evaluate the pros and cons of the various legal forms of organizing the new venture. This decision should be made before the submission of a business plan and request for venture capital.

The evaluation process requires the entrepreneur to determine the priority of each of the factors mentioned in Table 9.1, as well as tax factors discussed later in this chapter. These factors will vary in importance, depending on the type of new business. Also keep in mind that a family business can elect any of the legal forms of business.

The variations of organizational structure as well as the advantages and disadvantages are numerous and can be quite confusing to the entrepreneur. In the next section of this chapter, some of these differences are clarified to assist the entrepreneur in making the best decision regarding organizational structure.

Ownership

proprietorship Form of business with single owner who has unlimited liability, controls all decisions, and receives all profits

partnership Two or more individuals having unlimited liability who have pooled resources to own a business

corporation Separate legal entity that is run by stockholders having limited liability

In the *proprietorship*, the owner is the individual who starts the business. He or she has full responsibility for the operations. In a *partnership*, there may be some general partnership owners and some limited partnership owners. There are also limited liability partnerships (LLPs) in which the partnership is treated as a legal entity. In the *corporation*, ownership is reflected by ownership of shares of stock. Unlike the S corporation, where the maximum number of shareholders is 100, there is no limit as to the number of shareholders who may own stock in a corporation.

AS SEEN IN *BUSINESS NEWS*

FAMILY BUSINESS CONFLICT AND SECRETS FOR SUCCESS

Family businesses have unique organizational and management issues that are not often discussed as part of an entrepreneurship course or program. Research has begun to separate the family business and the unique challenges they face particularly in their management, governance, and transition strategy. It is most difficult in a family business to separate decision-making activities between work and family and between home and the office. Conflicts arise when these activities become entangled. These entanglements are often the result of one or a combination of the following:

1. Owners who are parents forget their role as a boss of their children that are involved in the business.

2. Children on the other hand will not always stand up to their parents or elders for the good of the company.

3. Nonfamily members can feel uncomfortable because they do not see any opportunity to get ahead in the company.

4. Company meetings are more like family gatherings and important business decisions are not made or avoided.

There are however some good rules of thumb that family entrepreneurs can follow in order to avoid conflict and enhance the long-term success of the business.

1. Do not segregate family from nonfamily employees. Everyone should be treated equally.

2. Family members not working at the company should not be placed on the payroll.

3. Communication to all employees is very important particularly regarding important business decisions.

4. Husband and wife businesses should have clear lines of responsibility. Business and home decisions should not be intertwined.

5. Have a clear succession strategy. (See Chapter 15.)

6. Establish a good independent board with nonfamily members whose advice is always considered seriously.

Family businesses play an important role in the global economy. In the United States, they account for about 60 percent of workers and create more than 75 percent of the new jobs. Very often we perceive family businesses as mom and pop operations which is far from reality as more than 30 percent of the S&P are family operated businesses.

Sources: Carolyn Brown, "7 Rules for Avoiding Conflicts of Interest in a Family Business," www.inc.com/guides/201102; Denise H. Kenyon-Rouvinez, "Secrets of Success in Long-Lasting Family Firms," www.imd.org/research/perspective-for-managers (June 2017); Josh Baron and Rob Lachenauer, "How to Thrive While Leading a Family Business," *Harvard Business Review* (February 20, 2015) pp. 2–4; Davis Wright Tremaine LLP, "Five Good Reasons to Have Independent Board Members," www.jdsupra.com (April 17, 2017).

Liability of Owners

Liability is one of the most critical reasons for establishing a corporation rather than any other form of business. The proprietor and general partners are liable for all aspects of the business. Since the corporation is an entity or legal "person," which is taxable and absorbs liability, the owners are liable only for the amount of their investment unless there is negligence or fraud involved. In the case of a proprietorship or regular partnership, no distinction is made between the business entity and the owner(s). Then, to satisfy any outstanding debts of the business, creditors may seize any assets the owners have outside the business.

In a partnership, the general partners usually share the amount of personal liability equally, regardless of their capital contributions, unless there is a specific agreement to the contrary. The only protection for the partners is insurance against liability suits and each partner putting his or her assets in someone else's name. The government may disallow the latter action if it feels this was done to defraud creditors.

In a general partnership, there also may be limited partners. These limited partners are liable for only what they contribute to the partnership. This amount, by law, must be registered

TABLE 9.1   Factors in Three Forms of Business Formation

Factors	Proprietorship	Partnership	Corporation
Ownership	Individual.	No limitation on number of partners.	No limitation on number of stock-holders.
Liability of owners	Individual liable for business liabilities.	In general partnership, all individuals liable for business liabilities. Limited partners are liable for amount of capital contribution. In limited liability partnership (LLP), there is no liability except when negligence exists.	Amount of capital contribution is limit of shareholder liability.
Costs of starting business	None, other than filing fees for trade name.	Partnership agreement, legal costs, and minor filing fees for trade name.	Created only by statute. Articles of incorporation, filing fees, taxes, and fees for states in which corporation registers to do business.
Continuity of business	Death dissolves the business.	Death or withdrawal of one partner terminates partnership unless partnership agreement stipulates otherwise. Death or withdrawal of one of limited partners has no effect on continuity.	Greatest form of continuity. Death or withdrawal of owner(s) will not affect legal existence of business.
Transferability of interest	Complete freedom to sell or transfer any part of business.	General partner can transfer his/her interest only with consent of all other general partners. Limited partner can sell interest without consent of general partners. No transfer of interest in an LLP.	Most flexible. Stockholders can sell or buy stock at will. Some stock transfers may be restricted by agreement. In S corporation, stock may be transferred only to an individual.
Capital requirements	Capital raised only by loan or increased contribution by proprietor.	Loans or new contributions by partners require a change in partnership agreement. In LLP partnership, entity raises money.	New capital raised by sale of stock or bonds or by borrowing (debt) in name of corporation. In S corporation, only one class of stock and limited to 100 shareholders.
Management control	Proprietor makes all decisions and can act immediately.	All general partners have equal control, and majority rules. Limited partners have limited control. Can vary in an LLP.	Majority stockholder(s) have most control from legal point of view. Day-to-day control in hands of management, who may or may not be major stockholders.
Distribution of profits and losses	Proprietor responsible and receives all profits and losses.	Depends on partnership agreement and investment by partners.	Shareholders can share in profits by receipt of dividends.
Attractiveness for raising capital	Depends on capability of proprietor and success of business.	Depends on capability of partners and success of business.	With limited liability for owners, more attractive as an investment opportunity.

at a local courthouse, thus making this information public. The LLP has become very popular among larger law firms and accounting CPA firms. It is actually a form of limited liability company (LLC), where the firm elects this status when filing its entity classification with the IRS on Form 8832. Thus, the advantages of the LLP are the same as the LLC, allowing the partners to protect their personal assets from liability risk. The LLP will be distinguished from the general partnership as appropriate in our comparison of the various forms of organization that follows.[2]

Costs of Starting a Business

The more complex the organization, the more expensive it is to start. The least expensive is the proprietorship, where the only costs incurred may be for filing for a business or trade name. In a partnership, in addition to filing a trade name, a partnership agreement is needed. This agreement requires legal advice and should explicitly convey all the responsibilities, rights, and duties of the parties involved. A limited partnership may be somewhat more complex than a general partnership because it must comply strictly with statutory requirements.

The corporation can be created only by statute. This generally means that before the corporation may be legally formed, the owners are required to (1) register the name and articles of incorporation and (2) meet the state statutory requirements (some states are more lenient than others). In complying with these requirements, the corporation will likely incur filing fees, an organization tax, and fees for doing business in each state. Legal advice is necessary to meet all the statutory requirements.

Continuity of Business

One of the main concerns of a new venture is what happens if one of the entrepreneurs (or the only entrepreneur) dies or withdraws from the business. Continuity differs significantly for each of the forms of business. In a sole proprietorship, the death of the owner results in the termination of the business. Sole proprietorships are thus not perpetual, and there is no time limit on how long they may exist.

The partnership varies, depending on whether it is a general partnership or a limited liability partnership (LLP). In a general partnership, the death or withdrawal of one of the partners results in termination of the partnership unless the partnership agreement stipulates otherwise. Thus, the partnership agreement may contain stipulations that allow for a buyout of the deceased or withdrawn partner's share, based on some mechanism or predetermined value. It also may be possible to have a member of the deceased partner's family take over as a partner and share in the profits accordingly. Life insurance owned by the partnership can be valuable protection for the partnership, often providing the funds necessary to buy out the deceased partner's share.

If there are limited liability partners in a general partnership, their death or withdrawal has no effect on the continuity of the business. A limited partner also may be replaced depending on the partnership agreement.

In a LLP, the death or withdrawal of a partner has no effect on the partnership. The deceased or withdrawn partner may be replaced much like any employee of a corporation.

The corporation has the most continuity of all the forms of business. Death or withdrawal has no impact on the continuation of the business. Only in a closely held corporation, where a few people hold all the shares, may there be some problems trying to find a market for the shares. Usually, the corporate charter requires that the corporation or the remaining shareholders purchase the shares. In a public corporation this, of course, would not be an issue.

Transferability of Interest

There can be mixed feelings as to whether the transfer of interest in a business is desirable. In some cases, the entrepreneur(s) may prefer to evaluate and assess any new owners before giving them a share of the business. On the other hand, it is also desirable to be able to sell one's interest whenever one wishes. This may be of particular significance when there is the need to consider a succession plan or strategy. This is discussed in more detail in Chapter 15. Each form of business offers different advantages as to the transferability of interest.

In the sole proprietorship, the entrepreneur has the right to sell or transfer any assets in the business. Limited partners, if existing in a general partnership organization, have more flexibility and may typically sell their interest at any time without consent of the general partners. The new limited partner's rights will remain the same as those of the prior partner. However, this may vary depending on the partnership agreement. General partners usually cannot sell their interest without first refusal from the remaining general partners, even if the partnership agreement allows for the transfer of interest.

In an LLP, the transfer of interest of one limited partner is typically not allowable. As stated previously, the LLP has become popular among law and CPA firms. Limited partners also may vary in distinction (e.g., there may be associate partners or junior partners), in which case they also may not share the same profit percentages as full partners. Full partners in law or CPA firms may elect to sell the business, but such a decision usually requires the approval of all or a majority.

The corporation has the most freedom in terms of selling one's interest in the business. Shareholders may transfer their shares at any time without consent from the other shareholders. The disadvantage of the right is that it can affect the ownership control of a corporation through election of a board of directors. Shareholders' agreements may provide some limitations on the ease of transferring interest, usually by giving the existing shareholders or corporation the option of purchasing the stock at a specific price or at the agreed-on price. Thus, they sometimes can have the right of first refusal. In the S corporation, the transfer of interest can occur only as long as the buyer is an individual.

Capital Requirements

The need for capital during the early months of the new venture can become one of the most critical factors in keeping a new venture alive. The opportunities and ability of the new venture to raise capital will vary, depending on the form of business.

For a proprietorship, any new capital can come only from loans by any number of sources or by additional personal contributions by the entrepreneur. In borrowing money from a bank, the entrepreneur in this form of business may need collateral to support the loan. Often, an entrepreneur will take a second mortgage on his or her home as a source of capital. Any borrowing from an outside investor may require giving up some of the equity in the proprietorship. Whatever the source, the responsibility for payment is in the hands of the entrepreneur, and failure to make payments can result in foreclosure and liquidation of the business. However, even with these risks, the proprietorship is not likely to need large sums of money, as might be the case for a partnership or corporation.

In the partnership, loans may be obtained from banks but will likely require a change in the partnership agreement. Additional funds contributed by each of the partners will also require a new partnership agreement. As in the proprietorship, the entrepreneurs are liable for payment of any new bank loans.

In the corporation, new capital can be raised in a number of ways. The alternatives are greater than in any of the other legal forms of business. Stock may be sold as either voting or nonvoting. Nonvoting stock will of course protect the power of the existing major stockholders. Bonds also may be sold by the corporation. This alternative would be more difficult for the new venture since a high bond rating will likely occur only after the business has been successful over time. Money also may be borrowed in the name of the corporation. As stated earlier, this protects the personal liability of the entrepreneur(s).

Management Control

In any new venture, the entrepreneur(s) will want to retain as much control as possible over the business. Each of the forms of business offers different opportunities and problems as to control and responsibility for making business decisions.

In the proprietorship, the entrepreneur has the most control and flexibility in making business decisions. Since the entrepreneur is the single owner of the venture, he or she will be responsible for and have sole authority over all business decisions.

The partnership can present problems over control of business decisions if the partnership agreement is not concise regarding this issue. Usually, in a partnership, the majority rules unless the partnership agreement states otherwise. It is quite important that the partners be friendly toward one another and that delicate or sensitive decision areas of the business be spelled out in the partnership agreement. These issues are very important in a family business. (See business news box earlier in this chapter.)

The existence of limited partners in a general partnership offers a compromise between the partnership and the corporation. In this type of organization, we can see some of the separation of ownership and control. The limited partners in the venture have no control over business decisions. As soon as the limited partner is given some control over business decisions, he or she then assumes personal liability and can no longer be considered a limited partner. In the LLP, the rights of all partners are clearly defined in the partnership agreement. As mentioned earlier, these types of organizations use titles such as junior partner, associate partner, and so on as a means of designating management responsibilities.

Control of day-to-day business in a corporation is in the hands of management, who may or may not be major stockholders. Control over major long-term decisions, however, may require a vote of the major stockholders. Thus, control is separated based on the types of business decisions. In a new venture, there is a strong likelihood that the entrepreneurs who are major stockholders will be managing the day-to-day activities of the business. As the corporation increases in size, the separation of management and control becomes more probable.

Stockholders in the corporation can indirectly affect the operation of the business by electing someone to the board of directors who reflects their personal business philosophies. These board members, through appointment of top management, then affect the operation and control of the day-to-day management of the business.

Distribution of Profits and Losses

Proprietors receive all distributions of profits from the business. As discussed earlier, they are also personally responsible for all losses. Some of the profits may be used to pay back the entrepreneur for any personal capital contributions that are made to keep the business operating.

In the partnership, the distribution of profits and losses depends on the partnership agreement. It is likely that the sharing of profits and losses will be a function of the partners' investments. However, this can vary depending on the agreement. As in the proprietorship, the partners may assume liability. Limited partners in a general partnership, or the formation of an LLP, are alternatives that protect those limited partners against personal liability but that may also reduce their share in any profits.

Corporations distribute profits through dividends to stockholders. These distributions are not likely to absorb all the profits that may be retained by the corporation for future investment or capital needs of the business. Losses by the corporation will often result in no dividends. These losses will then be covered by retained earnings or through other financial means discussed earlier.

Attractiveness for Raising Capital

In both the proprietorship and the partnership, the ability of the entrepreneurs to raise capital depends on the success of the business and the personal capability of the entrepreneur. These two forms are the least attractive for raising capital, primarily because of the problem of personal liability. Any large amounts of capital needed in these forms of business should be given serious consideration.

The corporation, because of its advantages regarding personal liability, is the most attractive form of business for raising capital. Shares of stock, bonds, and/or debt are all opportunities for raising capital with limited liability. The more attractive the corporation, the easier it will be to raise capital.

TAX RATES FOR VARIOUS FORMS OF BUSINESS

The tax advantages and disadvantages of each of the forms of business differ significantly particularly with the new tax laws passed at the end of 2017. A few of the major differences are discussed next. There are many minor differences that, in total, can be important to the entrepreneur. If the entrepreneur has any doubt about these advantages, he or she should get outside advice. Some of the major changes to the tax laws are discussed in the following paragraphs. Note that there are many additional issues that cannot be discussed here so it is always wise for the entrepreneur to seek advice on any doubtful tax issues.

All C Corporations will receive a tax cut from 35 percent to 21 percent. This is a permanent rate change. Pass through businesses such as proprietorships, S-Corps, LLC'c, and partnerships where the income generated from the business previously passed through to the individual owner or members (S Corp) will be taxed differently. Thus, instead of all of the business income being taxed at the individual owner's tax rate these types of organizations received 20 percent reduction of their business income. So a small pass through business that earned $200,000 in income would only have $160,000 of it passed on to the owner or member to be taxed at the individual's tax rate. The changes for these pass through businesses however are not permanent and expire at the end of 2025.

It should also be noted that there are some exceptions to the above tax rates particularly for these pass through business organizations. For example in the case of service-based businesses such as attorneys, doctors, realtors, engineers, and accountants to name a few the 20 percent deduction is only applicable to income after salary with a threshold of $315,000 for married couples filing jointly and an $157,000 for single taxpayers.[3]

For other employee-driven businesses such as restaurants and manufacturers, that are passed through organizations, the tax deduction of 20 percent is limited to 50 percent of the company's payroll. There is likely to be much confusion regarding taxes, particularly for pass through organizations, thus necessitating the hiring of a tax consultant.

THE LIMITED LIABILITY COMPANY VERSUS THE S CORPORATION

Although the perception among entrepreneurs is that the C corporation is the entity desired by investors, the actual entity desired by venture capitalists is the limited liability company (LLC), which is similar to the S corporation. The emergence of the LLC as a more popular alternative has resulted from a change in regulation. Regulations now allow an LLC to be automatically taxed as a partnership, unless the entrepreneur actively makes another choice (taxed as a corporation). This easing of election is one important factor that has enhanced the LLC's popularity.

The S corporation (the S refers to Subchapter S of the Internal Revenue Code) had been the most popular choice of organization structure by new ventures and small businesses. However, the growth rate of the formation of S corporations has actually declined in the last few years primarily because of acceptance of the LLC in all states and amendments in several states making the LLC more attractive. However, with the new tax law and with the complicated exceptions there may be a change in how these organizations are viewed.[4]

S CORPORATION

S corporation Special type of corporation where profits are distributed to stockholders and taxed as personal income

The *S corporation* combines the tax advantages of the partnership and the corporation. It is designed so that venture income is declared as personal income on a pro rata basis by the shareholders. In fact, the shareholders benefit from all the income and the deductions of the business. Before the passing of the Small Business Job Protection Act of 1996, the rules governing the S corporation were considered too rigid. The passage of the 1996 law loosened some of the restrictions that existed in regard to number of shareholders, ownership of stock of another corporation, role of trusts as stockholders, classes of stock, and a number of other changes. In 2004, Congress again responded to some of the criticisms of the restrictions on S corporations as compared to LLCs. As a result, a number of changes were made, such as an increase in the number of shareholders to 100, allowing family members to be treated as one stockholder, allowing IRAs to own shares in banks that are declared S corporations, as well as some modifications regarding the transfer of stock in a divorce. The intent was to make the S corporation as advantageous as the LLC since it is difficult to change status once a firm has declared itself an S corporation. There have been a few changes made by Congress (Small Business Job Acts) that have had some minor impact on the S corporation. It is important for the entrepreneur to be aware of such changes especially regarding new tax implications.[5]

One of the issues with the S corporation is that its status must be carefully monitored and maintained. For example, its tax status as a pass-through entity (with its income taxed as personal income of shareholders) still requires an affirmative election of shareholders. If the S corporation status is ever lost, it usually cannot be reelected for five years and with some costs. As stated earlier, the differences between the S corporation and the LLC are generally minimal but should be evaluated on a case-by-case basis because of the existing company and shareholder circumstances.

Advantages of an S Corporation

The S corporation offers the entrepreneur some distinct advantages over the typical corporation, or C corporation. However, there are also disadvantages.[6] In those instances when the disadvantages are great, the entrepreneur should elect the C corporation form. Some of the advantages of the S corporation are as follows:

- Capital gains or losses from the corporation are treated as personal income or losses by the shareholders on a pro rata basis (determined by number of shares of stock held). The corporation is thus not taxed.
- Shareholders retain the same limited liability protection as the C corporation.
- The S corporation is not subject to a minimum tax, as is the C corporation.
- Stock may be transferred to low-income-bracket family members (children must be 14 years or older).
- Stock may be voting or nonvoting.

 ETHICS

WHAT ETHICAL RESPONSIBILITIES DOES A PARTNER HAVE WHEN THERE IS A CONFLICT OF INTEREST?

There are many different ways that a conflict of interest in a partnership can occur. Some examples are cited below as they all reflect ethical issues with regard to the behavior of one of the partners. Resolution is often difficult because the conflicts are not always carefully documented in the partnership agreement. What do you think should be the resolution of each of the following examples?

EXAMPLE 1

In a law office of four law partners, one of the partners decides to leave for another law firm and wants to take some of her or his clients with her or him. The other partners are in disagreement with her or him and feel that it is unethical for her or him to take clients from the firm that provided them to her or him in the first place. She or he argued that the clients were all new clients and were brought into the firm by her or him and that she or he has an obligation to continue supporting their legal needs. The partnership agreement does not stipulate how to resolve this conflict since it does not involve clients that existed when she or he joined the firm. How would you resolve this conflict? Does the lawyer have an ethical responsibility to the firm that hired her or him in the first place?

EXAMPLE 2

Joan started a small online unique jewelry business that grew quickly. She then decided she needed a partner and brought in a friend who also made her own jewelry but only sold to friends and at crafts fairs. The business flourished until the two had many disagreements on how to sell the jewelry. The friend then left the partnership and started her own online jewelry business that competed directly with Joan. Does Joan have any recourse against her friend? What factors might be important in determining whether any ethical or legal agreements were broken? What might resolve this conflict?

EXAMPLE 3

One of the partners of a software consulting company has independently taken on a family friend as a client without knowledge of his or her partners. The partners upon learning of this arrangement then demanded that the client be part of their business. The partners pointed out that the partnership agreement prohibits any partner from servicing a client outside the realm of the business. The partner argues that this is a family friend and because of this would not be obligated to consider the friend as a client of the company. Do you agree with this argument? What factors might be important in the resolution of this conflict? Even if this is not clear in the partnership agreement, is there an ethical issue here?

- This form of business may use the cash method of accounting.
- Corporate long-term capital gains and losses are deductible directly by the shareholders to offset other personal capital gains or losses.

Disadvantages of an S Corporation

Although the advantages appear to be favorable for the entrepreneur, this form of business is not appropriate for everyone. The disadvantages of the S corporation are as follows:

- There are still some restrictions regarding qualification for this form of business. More recent Small Business Job Acts passed in 2010 and 2011 have also had some impact on the S corporation and should be consulted when considering this form of organization.
- Depending on the actual amount of the net income, there may be a tax advantage to the C corporation. (See earlier discussion on tax implications of various forms of organization.) This will depend on the company payout ratio, the corporate tax rate, the capital gains tax rate for the investor, and the personal income tax rate of the investor.

- The S corporation may not deduct most fringe benefits for shareholders.
- The S corporation must adopt a calendar year for tax purposes.
- Only one class of stock (common stock) is permitted for this form of business.
- The net loss of the S corporation is limited to the shareholder's stock plus loans to the business.
- S corporations cannot have more than 100 shareholders.

THE LIMITED LIABILITY COMPANY

As stated earlier, the new flexibility offered by LLC status has enhanced its choice by entrepreneurs. The tax rules for an LLC fall under Subchapter K, and this business form is considered a partnership-corporation hybrid with the following characteristics:

- Whereas the corporation has shareholders and partnerships have partners, the LLC has members.
- No shares of stock are issued, and each member owns an interest in the business as designated by the articles of organization, which is similar to the articles of incorporation or certificates of partnership.
- Liability does not extend beyond the member's capital contribution to the business. Thus, there is no unlimited liability, which can be detrimental in a proprietorship or general partnership.
- Members may transfer their interest only with the unanimous written consent of the remaining members.
- The Internal Revenue Service now automatically treats LLCs as partnerships for tax purposes, unless another option is elected. Thus, as mentioned earlier in this chapter, members may elect to designate the firm as a partnership or a corporation.
- The standard acceptable term of an LLC is 30 years. Dissolution is also likely when one of the members dies, the business goes bankrupt, or all members choose to dissolve the business. Some states allow continuity with majority or unanimous consent of the members. One of the important characteristics of the LLC is that the laws governing its formation may differ from state to state. Thus, a firm that is operating in more than one state may be subject to different treatment. An analysis of these differences should be considered before choosing this form of organization.

Advantages of an LLC

A number of advantages of an LLC over an S corporation are described here.[7]

- In a highly leveraged enterprise, the LLC offers the partnership a distinct advantage over an S corporation in that the partners can add their proportionate shares of the LLC liabilities to their partnership interests.
- States vary on the requirements of taxation but the LLC may have tax advantages depending on the state in which the business operates.
- One or more (without limit) individuals, corporations, partnerships, trusts, or other entities can join to organize or form an LLC. This is not feasible in an S corporation.
- Members are allowed to share income, profit, expense, deduction, loss and credit, and equity of the LLC among themselves. This is the only form of organization that offers all these features.

The one major concern with the LLC is in international business, where the context of unlimited liability is still unclear. Otherwise the LLC offers all the distinct advantages of a C corporation but with a pass-through tax to the members. Owners of an LLC can neither be paid as employees nor participate in certain employee benefits. Instead, they are paid in the form of guaranteed payments with no federal or state withholding involved. Thus, members are responsible for filing estimated taxes on a regular basis. The LLC appears to be the favorite choice for venture capitalists since it offers more flexibility based on the advantages already discussed. However, entrepreneurs should compare all the alternative forms of organization before election. This should be done with the advice of a tax attorney, since once a decision is made, it may be difficult to change without some penalty.

Earlier in this chapter in one of the business news boxes, we discussed some of the issues faced by family businesses. It is important to understand that the family business startup has the same organizational options as any new venture. However, there may be different reasons for the final choice of organization given the possible need to consider succession of the business to another family member. This topic is discussed in more detail in Chapter 15.

DESIGNING THE ORGANIZATION

Generally, the design of the initial organization will be simple. In fact, the entrepreneur may find that he or she performs all the functions of the organization alone. This is a common problem and a significant reason for many failures. The entrepreneur sometimes thinks that he or she can do everything and is unwilling to give up responsibility to others or even include others in the management team. In most cases when this occurs, the entrepreneur will have difficulty making the transition from a startup to a growing, well-managed business that maintains its success over a long period of time. Regardless of whether one or more individuals are involved in the startup, as the workload increases, the organizational structure will need to expand to include additional employees with defined roles in the organization. Effective interviewing and hiring procedures will need to be implemented to ensure that new employees will effectively grow and mature with the new venture. All the design decisions involving personnel and their roles and responsibilities reflect the formal structure of the organization. In addition to this formal structure, there is an informal structure or organization culture that evolves over time that also needs to be addressed by the entrepreneur. Although we are speaking of an organization culture rather than an organization design, the entrepreneur can have some control over how it evolves. Since issues related to this culture can be just as critical as the formal design of the organization for ensuring a successful and profitable enterprise, they will be discussed in more detail in the next section of this chapter.

For many new ventures, predominantly part-time employees may be hired, raising important issues of commitment and loyalty. However, regardless of the number of actual personnel involved in running the venture, the organization must identify the major activities required to operate it effectively.

The design of the organization will be the entrepreneur's formal and explicit indication to the members of the organization as to what is expected of them. Typically, these expectations can be grouped into the following five areas:[8]

- *Organization structure.* This defines members' jobs and the communication and relationship these jobs have with each other. These relationships are depicted in an organization chart.
- *Planning, measurement, and evaluation schemes.* All organization activities should reflect the goals and objectives that underlie the venture's existence. The entrepreneur must spell out how these goals will be achieved (plans), how they will be measured, and how they will be evaluated.

- *Rewards.* Members of an organization will require rewards in the form of promotions, bonuses, praise, and so on. The entrepreneur or other key managers will need to be responsible for these rewards.
- *Selection criteria.* The entrepreneur will need to determine a set of guidelines for selecting individuals for each position.
- *Training.* Training, on or off the job, must be specified. This training may be in the form of formal education or learning skills.

The organization's design can be very simple—that is, one in which the entrepreneur performs all the tasks (usually indicative of a startup)—or more complex, in which other employees are hired to perform specific tasks. As the organization becomes larger and more complex, the preceding areas of expectation become more relevant and necessary.

As the organization evolves, the manager or entrepreneur's decision roles also become critical for an effective organization. As an entrepreneur, the manager's primary concern is to adapt to changes in the environment and seek new ideas. When a new idea is found, the entrepreneur will need to initiate development either under his or her own supervision or by delegating the responsibility to someone else in the organization. Delegation may be the most difficult to achieve in a family business. In addition to the role of adaptor, the manager will also need to respond to pressures such as an unsatisfied customer, a supplier reneging on a contract, or a key employee threatening to quit. Much of the entrepreneur's time in the startup will be spent "putting out fires."

Another role for the entrepreneur is that of allocator of resources. The manager must decide who gets what. This involves the delegation of budgets and responsibilities. The allocation of resources can be a very complex and difficult process for the entrepreneur since one decision can significantly affect other decisions. The final decision role is that of negotiator. Negotiations of contracts, salaries, prices of raw materials, and so on are an integral part of the manager's job, and since he or she can be the only person with the appropriate authority, it is a necessary area of decision making.

BUILDING THE MANAGEMENT TEAM AND A SUCCESSFUL ORGANIZATION CULTURE

In conjunction with the design of the organization, the entrepreneur will need to assemble the right mix of people to assume the responsibilities outlined in the organization structure. Some of the issues identified in the organization design will be revisited here since they are not only critical to the building of the team but are just as important in establishing a positive and successful organization culture. This strategy must be maintained through the stages of startup and growth of the enterprise. There are some important issues to address before assembling and building the management team. In essence, the team must be able to accomplish three functions:

- Execute the business plan.
- Identify fundamental changes in the business as they occur.
- Make adjustments to the plan based on changes in the environment and market that will maintain profitability.

Although these functions may seem simple and easy to achieve, the people engaged and the culture promoted by the entrepreneur are critical in accomplishing these functions. As we discussed in the organization design section previously, the entrepreneur will first need to assume the responsibility of determining what skills and abilities are needed to meet the goals in the business plan. Not only are the skills and abilities important, but the entrepreneur also will need to consider the personality and character of each individual to create a viable organization culture. The organization culture will be a blend of attitudes, behaviors, dress, and communication styles that make one business different from another. There is no specific technique for accomplishing this since every organization will be different. These differences are significant if the venture involves marketing in multiple markets or more than one location. In these instances, it may be important to have more than one management team with appropriate leadership. One thing that is important is that the entrepreneur(s) need to be able to delegate responsibility in order to create a vibrant organizational culture. We will explore some of the important considerations and strategies in recruiting and assembling an effective team and hence in creating an effective and positive organization culture.

First, the entrepreneur's desired culture must match the business strategy outlined in the business plan. Tony Hsieh, CEO of Zappos, believes in a hands off approach with his employees. His plan involves providing an organizational culture, he refers to as "holacracy," where employees are allowed to move around in the organization to get involved in what they are passionate about. Thus, he has created a self-organized governance approach where meetings are held on a regular basis allowing employees to contribute to the structure of the organization.[9]

Second, the leader of the organization must create a workplace where employees are motivated and rewarded for good work. Paul English, the co-founder of Kayak (sold to Priceline) and more recently the founder of Lola is a strong believer in the team concept. Lola is a mobile app that allows users to text with human travel agents to get assistance booking flights and hotels as well as getting recommendations for restaurants. In hiring for his company, he looks for two important characteristics: first can the person get things done and secondly are they someone whom people enjoy being around? He sees his leadership role as one of a coach of the team so he constantly observes interactions and finds solutions where needed to insure that employees or team members have the same goals in mind.[10]

Third, the entrepreneur should be flexible enough to try different things. This is not always possible in a very small organization but has been the successful strategy in the growth of Google. The leadership of this company has an abundance of talent, and the attitude of management is that this talent needs to be given enough flexibility to make decisions, as long as they do so within the model established by the company. Founders Larry Page and Sergey Brin encourage all their employees to use 20 percent of their time pursuing any interesting projects that are not part of their regular duties. They are also encouraged to post any ideas they have on an interactive in-house message board. In addition to free food, pool tables, and beanbag chairs and other perks, the company hosts an all-employee meeting on Mondays where anyone can challenge any decisions made by the organization.[11]

Fourth, it is necessary to spend extra time in the hiring process. There is sometimes a tendency to want to hurry the process of finding the appropriate skills to fill the organization's needs. As stated earlier, there is more to a person than his or her skills. Character is also an important factor in building an effective organization culture. Recall in the opening profile that Sara Blakely personally made may of the early management hiring decisions. She based her hiring decisions, not on whether the person had the right experience but more so whether the individual was willing to try new things without the fear of failure. She still feels this is an effective approach to any company hiring decisions.

Next, the entrepreneur needs to understand the significance of leadership in the organization. Leadership should help establish core values and provide the appropriate tools so

AS SEEN IN *BUSINESS NEWS*

ELEVATOR PITCH FOR UNIQUE TRAVEL STARTUP

A friend of yours that likes to travel but dislikes typical tours saw a write-up on a new unique travel company that offers tours from local experts that are unusual and interesting. This friend inquired and discovered that this startup is looking for capital to expand to additional cities and destinations and has approached you to ask if you might be interested in investing in this company. Would you be willing to invest in this startup? How can this new venture deal with the possibility that there may not be enough sellers of activities for tours in any of the expansion cities? What issues might they face with competition?

Vayable's mission is to promote cultural understanding and to provide customers with a new and unique way to explore the world. Launched by Jamie Wong and Shelly Roche, both travel lovers, they decided that in the $27 billion travel industry no one was offering activities for travelers that are unique. Instead of the standard city

bus tour why not go on a street art tour led by a graffiti artist in San Francisco, feast on ethnic foods in New York City's neighborhoods, or go on a wine tasting tour in Paris, all tours guided by local artists and experts. In 2014, with an additional $2 million in funding, the company has expanded to 850 destinations including all major European cities. Also, recently added is a phone or tablet app that allows customers to purchase tours at a moment's notice.

Any local person who wants to offer a unique tour is interviewed by the co-founders either in person or on Skype. All the tours that are submitted by the local persons are reviewed before they are permitted to appear on the website or in any marketing material.

Sources: See www.vayable.com; Wilson Peng, "Vayable Is the Ultimate Travel Experience Startup," www.entrepreneursky.com, February 1, 2014; and David Zax, "With Vayable's New Travel App, Everyone's Local," www.fastcompany.com/3032816, July 10, 2014.

that employees can effectively complete their jobs. An approach such as, "We're all in this together, no one is bigger than anyone else, and here are the rules we live by," can lead to greater challenges and job satisfaction. A reward system can play an important role in providing consistent and positive behavior patterns.

Finding the most effective team and creating a positive organization culture is a challenge for the entrepreneur but is just as critical as having an innovative, marketable product. It is an important ingredient in an organization's success.

THE ROLE OF A BOARD OF DIRECTORS

An entrepreneur may find it necessary in his or her organization plan to establish a board of directors or board of advisors. The board of advisors is discussed in the next section. The board of directors may serve a number of functions: (1) reviewing operating and capital budgets, (2) developing longer-term strategic plans for growth and expansion, (3) supporting day-to-day activities, (4) resolving conflicts among owners or shareholders, (5) ensuring the proper use of assets, or (6) developing a network of information sources for the entrepreneurs. These functions may be a formal part of the organization, with responsibilities assigned to the directors depending on the needs of the new venture.

Most important in establishing these responsibilities is the consideration of the impact of the Sarbanes-Oxley Act passed in 2002. Passage of this act resulted because of accounting irregularities, fraud, bankruptcy, insider trading, excessive management compensation, and other illegal or unethical actions that have become newsworthy in the years leading up to 2002 (see Chapter 6 for more discussion of the Sarbanes-Oxley Act). Although there is still some concern about the effectiveness of the new law, its intent is to establish a more independent functioning board. This is particularly relevant in public companies where the board members must represent all shareholders and are responsible for "blowing the whistle" on any discrepancies that may be suspected. In spite of its intent, this act has come under criticism in light of the economic crisis that led to the demise of a number of large financial services companies. However, many feel that it is not the law that is the problem but more the issues of having the right mix of board members. There is also a possibility that Congress may decide to revise the law which some believe has resulted in compliance costs that are excessive.[12]

Many startup ventures do not plan to have a formal board of directors. However, if there are equity investors, they will usually insist on the formation of a board and at least one board seat. Carl Dorvil, who had a strong passion for education, started a tutoring and mentoring company in 2004 called Group Excellence. With a $20,000 grant from Texas Instruments, he was able to grow the company to over $40 million in sales, create over 2,000 jobs and tutor over 30,000 students across the state of Texas. The company was sold to a private equity group in 2011 but Carl continued to manage and grow his other entrepreneurial investments. In 2016 he took one of his portfolio companies, GEX Management public and became the youngest African American to do so. During his success as an entrepreneur Carl insisted that every entrepreneur should have a personal board of directors. You should make sure that the board is diverse, be an odd number, meet regularly, and you should always be looking for new members that can assist in the growth of the venture. He also makes it clear that you do not have to be a large corporation to have a board of directors.[13]

After launching her company Better Batter Gluten Free Flour, Naomi Poe realized that she needed an infusion of capital and some advice from a board of directors. She did not realize that board members needed to be vested in the company. However, she asked a number of business acquaintances if they would serve on her board and those that accepted also agreed to provide seed capital for her startup. With the added capital in small sums ranging from $1,200 to $2,000 and one large sum of $20,000, she was able to launch her company. Today Naomi still tries to maintain the business as a family operation. She has also valued the advice of her board and from this experience has been able to add many new products.[14]

As we can see from the preceding examples, the purpose of the board of directors is to provide important leadership and direction for the new venture, and it should be carefully chosen to meet the requirements of the Sarbanes-Oxley Act and also the following criteria:[15]

- Select individuals who have specific skills needed for your business, have experience in your industry, and are committed to the venture's mission.
- Select candidates who are willing to spend some time to be informed directors who can assist the company in making important decisions.
- Select candidates who are willing to exchange ideas, using their experience, in making board decisions.

Candidates should be identified using referrals of business associates or from any of the external advisors such as banks, investors, lawyers, accountants, or consultants. Ideally, the board should consist of 3, 5, 7, or some odd number of members to avoid deadlock and with limited terms to allow for continuous infusion of new ideas from different people.

Board of director performance needs to be regularly evaluated by the entrepreneurs. It is the chair's responsibility to provide an appraisal of each board member. To provide this appraisal, the chairperson (and/or founders) should have a written description of the responsibilities and expectations of each member.

Compensation for board members can be shares of stock, stock options, or dollar payment. Often the new venture will tie compensation to the performance of the new venture. Compensation is important since it reinforces the obligation of board members. If board members were only volunteers, they would tend to take the role lightly and not provide any value to the entrepreneur.

THE BOARD OF ADVISORS

Compared to a board of directors, a board of advisors would be more loosely tied to the organization and would serve the venture only in an advisory capacity for some of the functions or activities mentioned before. It has no legal status, unlike the board of directors, and hence is not subject to the regulations stipulated in the Sarbanes-Oxley Act. These boards are likely to meet less frequently or depending on the need to discuss important venture decisions. A board of advisors is very useful in a family business where the board of directors may consist entirely of family members.

The selection process for advisors can be similar to the process for selecting a board of directors, including determining desired skills and interviewing potential candidates. Advisors may be compensated on a permeeting basis or with stock or stock options. Just as in the case of the board of directors, the members should be evaluated as to their contribution to meeting the mission of the new venture.

Boards of advisors can provide an important reality check for the entrepreneur or owner of any noncorporate type of business. John Teevan, the founder of SoshItech, believes that one of the most important traits of an entrepreneur is the ability to know what he or she does not know. He has employed this wisdom by building his company with a strong board of advisors. He chose individuals for his board based on how well they complemented his personal weaknesses as an entrepreneur.[16]

Haroon Mokhtarzada gave up an opportunity to work with a prestigious law firm while a law student at Harvard Law School in order to start a business venture. He and his two brothers had been experimenting with a Web design business that would allow anyone including their nontechnical mother to build a website. As students, he and his brothers launched the business and within a few short years had 50 million registered users. After their huge startup success, the brothers sold webs.com to Vistaprint for $117.5 million. What gave him the impetus to grow this company was an advisor who recommended that Mokhtarzada try to raise capital and grow this business into something substantial. Mokhtarzada's model for creating a board of advisors is based on three recommendations:[17]

1. Identify potential members who share your vision so that they will look out for your best interests.
2. Offer the members a quarter to a half point of equity so that they will not only offer their expertise but will provide valuable contacts to grow the business.
3. Timing is important when you add or bring in advisors. Use them at critical points in business decision making such as raising capital, entering new markets, or hiring high-level managers.

Project World School, a producer of international learning retreats for homeschooled teens, decided that it needed a board of advisors. The school's cofounder Lainie Liberti indicated that the individuals selected for the board have decades of wisdom and insight regarding alternative education. Early on the school hosted learning communities in the United States, Canada, Australia, and Brazil. With its wealth of experience, the board of advisors has played a significant role guiding the company into new programs (retreats) across numerous new countries.[18]

As we can see from these diverse examples, the board of advisors represents an alternative or complementary option for the entrepreneur and to organizations of all sizes in providing expertise and direction in critical areas. Even large corporations will often assemble an advisory board to assist them in specific areas of the business. The flexibility in size, background requirements, number of meetings, and compensation makes these boards a very desirable alternative to the more formal boards of directors.

THE ORGANIZATION AND USE OF ADVISORS

The entrepreneur will usually use outside advisors such as accountants, bankers, lawyers, advertising agencies, and market researchers on an as-needed basis. These advisors, who are separate from the more formal board of advisors, can also become an important part of the organization and thus will need to be managed just like any other permanent part of the new venture.

The relationship of the entrepreneur and outside advisors can be enhanced by seeking out the best advisors and involving them thoroughly and at an early stage. Advisors should be assessed or interviewed just as if they were being hired for a permanent position. References should be checked and questions asked to ascertain the quality of service as well as compatibility with the management team.

Hiring and managing outside experts can be effectively accomplished by considering these advisors as advice suppliers. Just as no manager would buy raw materials or supplies without knowledge of their cost and quality, the same approval can apply for advisors. Entrepreneurs should ask these advisors about fees, credentials, references, and so on, before hiring them.

Even after the advisors have been hired, the entrepreneur should question their advice. Why is the advice being given? Make sure you understand the decision and its potential implications. There are many good sources of advisors, such as the Small Business Administration, other small businesses, chambers of commerce, universities, friends, and relatives. Careful evaluation of the entrepreneur's needs and the competency of the advisor can make advisors a valuable asset to the organization of a new venture.

IN REVIEW

SUMMARY

One of the most important decisions the entrepreneur(s) must make in the business plan is the legal form of business. The three major legal forms of business are the proprietorship, partnership, and corporation. Each differs significantly particularly given the new tax laws voted in by Congress and should be evaluated carefully before a decision is made. This chapter provides considerable insight and comparisons regarding these forms of business to assist the entrepreneur in this decision.

The S corporation and the limited liability company are alternative forms of business that are gaining popularity. Each of these allows the entrepreneur to retain the protection from personal liability provided by a corporation as well as the tax advantages provided by a partnership. There are important advantages as well as disadvantages to these forms of business, and entrepreneurs should carefully weigh both before deciding.

The organization plan for the entrepreneur also requires some major decisions that could affect long-term effectiveness and profitability. It is important to begin the new venture with a strong management team that is committed to the goals of the new venture. The management team must be able to work together effectively toward these ends.

History indicates that many entrepreneurs try to perform too many tasks in the new venture, often spreading themselves too thin and thus negatively affecting all their tasks. Assigning and delegating tasks is part of being a good leader and in the long run will enhance the confidence and motivation of all employees and contribute to a strong management team.

The design of the organization requires the entrepreneur to specify the types of skills needed and the roles that must be filled. These would be considered part of the formal organization. In addition to the formal organization, the entrepreneur must consider the informal organization or culture that is desired to match the strategy stipulated in the business plan. This organization culture represents the attitudes, behaviors, dress, and communication styles that can differentiate one company from another. Both of these are important in establishing an effective and profitable organization.

A board of directors or board of advisors can provide important management support for an entrepreneur starting and managing a new venture. Boards of directors are now governed by the Sarbanes-Oxley Act, which was passed because of a rash of illegal and unethical behaviors that were newsworthy. The intent of this new law is to make the board of directors more independent and to make its members accountable to the shareholders. The law is particularly relevant to public companies and has less impact on privately held companies. The board of advisors is a good alternative to a board of directors when the stock is held privately or in a family business.

In spite of the new regulations, a board of directors or advisors can still provide excellent support for an organization. Either one can be formed in the initial business planning phase or after the business has been formed and financed. In either case, the selection of board members should be made carefully, so that members will take their roles seriously and will be committed to their roles and responsibilities.

Advisors will also be necessary in the new venture. Outside advisors should be evaluated as if they were being hired as permanent members of the organization. Information on their fees and referrals can help determine the best choices.

RESEARCH TASKS

1. In this country, what proportion of all businesses are (a) proprietorships, (b) partnerships, (c) private companies, and (d) public companies? Provide an example of an industry that has a large share of proprietorships. Why is this the case? Provide an example of an industry that has a large share of partnerships. Why is this the case? Provide an example of an industry that has a large share of private companies. Why is this the case? Provide an example of an industry that has a large share of public companies. Why is this the case?

2. Review current business magazines and identify one large public corporation and one startup that have a board of advisors. How will these boards be used differently or similarly? How would you expect a board of advisors to interact with a board of directors?

3. Study the local newspaper and choose three good examples and three poor examples of job advertisements. Be prepared to explain your choices.

4. Interview two entrepreneurs and ask them how they delegate responsibility in their organization. Ask them how they feel about delegating responsibility or involving an employee when a critical decision that could impact the financial stability of their company is necessary.

CLASS DISCUSSION

1. Why would entrepreneurs open themselves up to personal financial losses by choosing a proprietorship rather than a company form of organization?

2. Why do suppliers sometimes ask entrepreneurs of small companies to provide personal guarantees for a line of business credit? If an entrepreneur is asked (forced) to provide personal guarantees, then what personal protection does a company as a legal form really provide?

3. Does the old saying "You get what you pay for" apply to a board of directors or a board of advisors?

4. Identify three corporations that are different in their legal form of organization (e.g., an S corporation, an LLC, and a C corporation). How are these companies different? How are they similar? What advantages and disadvantages does each company achieve by maintaining their legal form or organization?

SELECTED READINGS

Banerjee, Gaurango; and Halil D. Kaya. (2017). Short-Term and Long-Term Impact of Sarbanes-Oxley Act on Director Commitment and Composition of Corporate Board Members. *Journal of Financial Management & Analysis*, vol. 41, no. 5, pp. 743–71.

This study looks at a number of issues related to the Sarbanes-Oxley Act and their effect on board members. The study focuses on variables such as director commitment and governance changes resulting from this law. Questions considered are: how the board structure changed and have boards focused on different functions after passage of the law?

Capelle, Ronald G. (2017). Improving Organization Performance by Optimizing Organization Design. *People and Strategy*, vol. 40, no. 2, pp. 26–39.

This article is a summary from the author's book on optimizing organizational design. Based on years of research the author suggests that organization design if based on the alignment of five factors: positions, accountability, people, deliverables, and tasks. Each of these factors is discussed in the article providing a basis for effective organization design.

Carr, Jon; and Keith M. Hmieleski. (2015). Differences in the Outcomes of Work and Family Conflict Between Family and Non-Family Businesses: An Examination of Business Founders. *Entrepreneurship Theory and Practice*, vol. 39, no. 6, pp. 1413–32.

This study examines the effects of work and family conflict on work tension for founders of family versus nonfamily businesses. Results indicated that founders of family businesses experienced significantly greater work tension from family work conflict than for founders of nonfamily businesses. In addition, they found that work family conflict exerted more negative effects on founders on nonfamily businesses than for those running family businesses.

Codemo, Roberta. (2016). Difference between LLC and LLP. *www.legalzoom.com.*

There is often confusion as to the differences between an LLC and an LLP. This article provides a basic understanding of the differences. It is important to note the differences because choosing one of these organization options can have long-term repercussions for any new enterprise.

Frankenberg, Ellen. (2015). Ten excuses for not establishing a board of advisors. *Directors & Boards*, pp. 27–29.

This author argues that one of the most significant factors in determining the survival and success of a small business is the presence of a board of advisors. Too often the entrepreneur makes excuses for organization a board. Examples of excuses are: don't have enough issues to discuss, no one will want to serve on my board, don't want outsiders to know my business, and don't want to give up control to name a few. Ten excuses are identified and discussed in the article.

Hopson, James F; and Patricia D. Hopson. (2014). Making the Right Choice of Business Entity. *CPA Journal*, vol. 84, no. 10, pp. 42–47.

This article discusses the business entity options for a sole proprietor. The main issues are personal liability risks and tax issues to protect personal property. For a sole proprietor, the limited liability was recognized as the best option.

268 PART 3 FROM THE OPPORTUNITY TO THE BUSINESS PLAN

Keller, Scott; and Mary Meaney. (2017). High Performing Teams: A Timeless Leadership Topic. *McKinsey Quarterly*, no. 3, pp. 81–87.

This article focuses on how to build high performing teams. Discussion centers on team composition, size, and dynamics. In addition, the authors discuss decision making, attracting talent, and managing time as a basis for high performance teams.

Kramer, Marc. Ten Criteria for Selecting Board Members. *www.bizjournals.com.*

This article provides some important criteria that an entrepreneur should consider in selection of the board of directors. The author suggests that some important considerations are: select people who are problem solvers, select individuals who will challenge others, make sure that the individuals are effective strategic thinkers, and lastly the entrepreneur should consider diversity in board selection.

Sheridan, Daniel. (2017). S Corporation or Limited Liability Companies: Pick Your Paradigm. *Business Law Today*, pp. 1–6.

Limited Liability companies and other entities not organized as a corporation are allowed to elect to be classified for federal tax purposes as a corporation or as an S Corporation. This article explores some of the rationale for choosing the S Corporation tax regime.

Stamper, Connie. (2010). Hiring Tips for Small Business Leaders. *CMA Management*, vol. 84, no. 4, pp. 11–13.

The article stresses the importance of making great hiring decisions even though there is no in-house human resource department because of the size of the firm.

Wagner, Stephan. (2015). Partner Problems. *Entrepreneur*, vol. 43, no. 3, pp. 60–61.

This article discusses several issues related to a business partnership. According to the author, it is necessary to install checks and balances when each partner may oversee different aspects of the business. Any issues involving finances should be clarified before entering a partnership.

END NOTES

1. See Teresa Novellino, "Billionaire Spanx Founder Sara Blakely Has Stacks of Advice for Teens," www.upstart.bizjournals.com (26 March 2015); Jermaine Harris, "Why Sara Blakely Is so Successful," www.addicted2success.com/entrepreneur-profile (18 February 2015); Roger Vozar, "Sara Blakely Reshapes the Undergarment Business with Spanx," www.sbnonline.com (4 November 2014); Robert Frank, "Billionaire Sara Blakely Says Secret to Success Is Failure," www.cnbc.com (16 October 2013); and www.spinx.com.

2. Nellie Akalp, "Legal Structure: The Difference Between LLC's and LLP's," www.smallbiztrends.com.

3. See: Pete Woodring, "Small business Owners Win Big In New Tax Law With 20% Off Deal." www.kiplingeer.com (December 26, 2017); Kelly Phillips, "What Tax Reform Means for Small Businesses & Pass-Through Entities," www.forbes.com (December 22, 2017); and Brittany DeLea, "What Tax Reform Really Means for Small Businesses," www.foxbusiness.com (December 28, 2017).

4. J.B. Maverick, "S Corp vs LLC: Which Should I Choose," www.investopedia.com/articles/personal-finance/011216 (November 8, 2017).

5. Laura M. MacDonough, Sarah A. McGregor, Samuel P. Starr, and Robert W. Jamison Jr. "Current Developments In S Corporations," *Tax Advisor* (December 2017) pp. 5–8.

6. Georgia McIntyre, "S Corp vs C Corp: How They Differ and How To Decide," www.fundera.com/blog (December 21, 2017).

7. Christina Dixon, "Why Start an LLC? Limited Liability Company Advantages and Disadvantages," www.rocketlawyer.com.

8. J. W. Lorsch, "Organization Design: A Situational Perspective," in J. R. Hackman, E. E. Lawler III, and W. Porter (eds.), Perspectives on Behavior in Organizations, 2nd ed. (New York: McGraw-Hill, 1983), pp. 439–47.

9. Tony Hsieh, Aaron De Smet, and Chris Gagnon, " Safe Enough to Try: An Interview With Zappos CEO Tony Hsieh," *McKinley Quarterly* (Fall 2017) issue 4, pp. 112–122.

10. Ashlea Halpern, "Building a Billion Dollar Team," *Entrepreneur* (March 2017) pp. 13–15.

11. Casey Wright, "Google's Awesome Culture," www.huffingtonpost.com (May 2, 2017)

12. Jeanette M. Franzel, "A Decade After Sarbanes-Oxley: The Need for Ongoing Vigilance, Monitoring, and Research," Accounting Horizons (December 2014), vol 28, no. 4, pp. 917–30.

13. Carolyn Brown, "Why Every Entrepreneur Needs a Personal Board of Directors," www.blackenterprise.com (17 April 2015).

14. See: www.betterbatter.org and Gwen Moran, "Pocket Money," Entrepreneur (February 2011), p. 66.

15. David K. Aaker, "Tips For Creating A Strong Board of Directors," www.institute.uschamber.com (April 6, 2016) and Bo Ilsoe, "Eeight Steps to Building a Strong Board of Directors," www.venturebeat.com (July 2, 2017).

16. John Teevan, "Startup Wisdom: Knowing What You Don't Know," www.crunchbase.com (23 December 2013).

17. See Joel Holland, "It Passes the Mom Test," Entrepreneur (January 2011), p. 63; and Faisal Masooda and Sabiha Ansari, "Haroom Mokhtarzada Sells Webs.Com for $117.5 Million," www.muslimobserver.com (August 27, 2015).

18. See "Project World School Announces the Launch of its Board of Advisors," www.releasewire.com (17 December 2014); and www.projectworldschool.com.

Conclusion:

Throughout the ages, a tension, and at times utter dismissiveness, exists amongst people and practices over right or wrong discourse, much to do with perspective and practice between the humanities and science, even a pecking order within disciplines for superiority. Polyneering accepts no uncertain truths and posits not in the absolute but rather delights in the inexplicable. The human quest to put everything into a formula, all consuming, remains a chase for an end. Polyneering seeks new beginnings over finality, options instead of one choice. The many gives way to abundance in which a single reduction is staid, rote, remedial.

A curricular ethos and ethnosphere of entrepreneurship fervor create innovative modes of instruction. Entrepreneurial values enhance not just academic institutions but entire communities. Polyneering is an animated force to make entrepreneurship and compendium subjects an umbrella for increasing and improving humanity. A polyneering society establishes a basis of understanding as a result of education, not as a byproduct. Under this environment, academic guilds and accrediting agencies go beyond departmental or school agendas; learning outcomes must be measured on of-the-moment actions and not post hoc on foregone conclusions. Polyneering, then, is mainstream and not tangential to disciplines. Polyneering requires innovation and implementation; it mandates enterprise thinking and veritable execution. Contemporary life without transformation, without polyneering, is ineffective, since tapping into what may seem mysterious requires intelligibility and adaptability. Thoroughgoing improvements to the fabric of any ecosystem through new paths, new ways, and new answers to old or recent questions goes on.

A polyneer does not see an either/or world around phenomena, only ways to advocate new tools, systems, pathways, intelligences, methods, models, and even theories to distinguish and make distinctive science from non-sense or non-science. Where Karl Popper once sought truth in falsifying science and Thomas Kuhn sought what is to be observed and scrutinized relative to structures, the value judgement of the polyneer lies in coming full circle to the essence of science. Scientia, means knowledge, and as Caltech Professor and Theoretical Physicist Sean Carroll quips:

"Science is nothing more nor less than the most reliable way of gaining knowledge about anything, whether it be the human spirit, the role of great figures in history, or the structure of DNA."

And yet, the 'humanitas' is ever a part of the whole to inform 'factions' of fact and fiction. Johann von Wowern defined polymathy in 1603 as "knowledge of various matters, from all kinds of studies, through fields of disciplines, as far as the human mind, with unwearied Industry" to pursue inventive imagination. The modern polyneer synthesizes different subject areas of complex knowledge to solve specific problems.

Synthesizing requires the ability to challenge assumptions and accept chaos as a positive challenge. The meritocracy of polyneering is ability-based, achievement-oriented, and effort-centric; otherwise mediocrity's ordinariness, commonness, and insufficiency emit academic marginality. Polyneering is the epitome of a potential, universal education grounded in an ascendancy towards polymetric mastery through boundless ways. As you look to the future as a polyneer, you are required to travel to inner space and outer space by challenging "Spacetime" (space and time domains). You will interact with virtual think tanks and explore virtual field trips. The reward and recognition structure for a polyneer is the natural blending of both intrinsic and extrinsic applications, composed like an orchestra in which the conductor uses all of the instruments at the perfect time.

Systems thinking is composed of theoretical black holes which all polyneers will ultimately journey to and explore inside futuristic organizations. Polyneers are sometimes seen by others as shape shifters with the capacity to help move organizations forward in a positive direction.

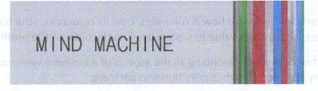

GLOSSARY:

ACQUI-HIRE: An act or instance of buying out a company primarily for the skills and expertise of its staff, rather than for the products or services it supplies.

ANGEL INVESTOR: An investor who provides financial backing for email startups or entrepreneurs. Investors are usually found among an entrepreneur's family and friends. The capital they provide can be a one-time injection of seed money or ongoing support to carry the company through difficult times.

BLITZSCALING: Pursuit of rapid growth by prioritizing speed over efficiency in an environment of uncertainty (Reid Hoffman and Chris Yeah).

BLUE OCEAN STRATEGY: Business-level strategy that successfully combines differentiation and cost-leadership activities using value innovation to reconcile the inherent trade-offs (Frank Rothaermel).

BOOTSTRAPPING: Using creativity, ingenuity, or any means possible to obtain resources other than borrowing money or raising capital from traditional sources.

BREAKEVEN ANALYSIS: A break-even analysis is a calculation of the point at which revenues equal expenses.

BRICOLAGE: To make do by applying combinations of the resources at hand to new problems and opportunities (Claude Levi-Strauss).

BUSINESS MODEL: A company's plan for how it competes, uses its resources, structures its relationships, interfaces with customers, and creates value to sustain itself on the basis of the profits it generates.

BUSINESS PLAN: A written document describing all the aspects of a business venture, which is usually necessary to raise money and attract high-quality business partners.

C-CORPORATION: Refers to any corporation that, under United States federal income tax law, is taxed separately from its owners.

COMMUNITY: Characterized by consciousness of kind, shared rituals and traditions, and a sense of moral responsibility.

COMPETITIOR ANALYSIS: A detailed evaluation of a firm's direct, indirect, and future competitors.

COST LEADERSHIP STRATEGY: Generic strategy in which firms strive to have the lowest costs in the industry relative to competitors' costs and typically attract customers on the basis of price.

CROWD FUNDING: The use of small amounts of capital from a large number of individuals to finance a new business venture. Makes use of easy accessibility of vast networks of friends, family, and colleagues through social media websites.

CULTURAL INTELLIGENCE (CQ): The capability to relate and work effectively across cultures (P. Christopher Earley, 2002).

DESIGN-THINKING: The cognitive, strategic, and practical processes by which design concepts are developed.

DIFFERENTIATION STRATEGY: A strategy that firms use to provide unique or different products to customers. Firms using this strategy typically compete on the basis of quality, service, timeliness, or some other dimension that creates a unique value for customers.

DIFFUSION PROCESS: The manner in which innovations spread throughout a market.

DIRECT COMPETITORS: Businesses offering identical or similar products/services.

DYNABOOK: A conceptual portable educational device for children; A precursor to the tablet or laptop devices (Alan Kay,1968).

EDUTAINMENT: A portmanteau of the term's education and entertainment, instruction through engagement, especially video.

EFFECTUATION: A process that starts with what one has (who they are, what they know, and whom they know) and selects among possible outcomes (Saras Sarasvathy).

ENTREPRENEURSHIP: The process by which individuals pursue opportunities without regard to resources they currently control.

ETHNOSPHERE: The sum total of all thoughts and intuitions, myths, and beliefs, ideas and inspirations brought into being by the human imagination since the dawn of consciousness (Wade Davis, 2005).

FEASIBILITY ANALYSIS: A preliminary evaluation of a business idea to determine if it is worth pursuing.

FIVE FORCES MODEL: Identifies five key competitive forces that strategic leaders need to consider when analyzing the industry environment and formulating competitive strategy to include: Threat of entry, Power of suppliers, Power of buyers, Threat of substitutes, and Rivalry among existing competitors plus an additional sixth force as the Power of compliments (Michael Porter).

FIXED COSTS: The costs that a company incurs in operating a business whether it generates sales or not.

FRANCHISING: A form of business organization in which a firm that already has a successful product or service (franchisor) licenses its trademark and method of doing business to other businesses (franchisees) in exchange for fee and royalty payments.

FUTURE COMPETITORS: Businesses that are not yet direct or indirect competitors but could be at any time.

GROUP: Two or more individuals who share a set of norm, values, or beliefs (David Mothersbaugh).

HOOP: A person that marches to a different beat; a character; one who is colorful (Billy Herbert, 1950).

INDUSTRY: A group of firms producing a similar product or service, such as airlines, fitness drinks or video games.

INDUSTRY ANALYSIS: Business research that focuses on the potential of an industry.

INITIAL PUBLIC OFFERING (IPO): The first sale of a company's stock to the public and an important milestone for a firm for four reasons: it is a way to raise equity capital; it raises a firm's public profile; it is a liquidity event; and it creates another form of currency (company stock) that can be used to grow the company.

INNOVATION: A thinking change (physical, procedural, mental) for doing something sustainably different (Deardorff, 2000).

INNOVATION ENGINEER: Different internal and external factors working together to enhance creativity including knowledge, imagination, attitude, resources, habitats, and culture (Tina Seelig).

INNOVATIONARY: An innovative dictionary through hypertext where the information is non-linear, not stepwise, and inspirational for startup and dynamic communities. Example: yuiwe.com.

LEADERSHIP: The ability to create change or transform organizations.

LIFELONG LEARNING: A form of self-initiated thoroughgoing education focused on personal development.

LIFESTYLE COMPANY: Businesses that provide their owners the opportunity to pursue a particular lifestyle and earn a living while doing so (e.g. ski instructors, golf pros, tour guides).

LIMITED LIABILITY COMPANY (LLC): A form of business organization that combines the limited liability advantage of the corporation with the tax advantages of a partnership.

LIMITED LIABILITY PARTNERSHIP (LLP): Similar business structure as partnership but with three exceptions: (1) Limited partner is only liable up to the amount of invested capital, (2) Limited partner cannot have direct control, (3) Limited partner can transfer ownership and continue based on agreement and continue beyond removal of that partner.

MARGIN: Difference between the cost price and selling price of a product or service.

MARKET ANALYSIS: An analysis that breaks down the industry into segments and zeros in on the specific segment (or target market) to which the firm will try to appeal.

MARKET RESEARCH: The process of gathering, analyzing and interpreting information about a market, about a product or service to be offered for sale in that market, and about the past, present, and potential customers for the product or service; research into the characteristics, spending habits, location and needs of your business's target market, the industry as a whole, and the particular competitors you face.

MARKETING: A set of activities with the objective of securing, serving, and retaining customers for the firm's product offerings.

MARKETING STRATEGY: A firm's overall approach for marketing its products and services.

MINIMAL VIABLE PRODUCT (MVP): A product having the minimal feature set required to solve the problem or address the need and obtain customer feedback.

NAICS CODES: Government applied industry codes based on products/services offered and primary business activity (in revenues).

NOVATE: Process of design thinking logic containing 6 steps with an interconnected flow that allows you to think forward, think backward, and then continue to think forward again.

OPERATING LEVERAGE: Extent to which a firm commits itself to high levels of fixed operating costs (which vary with time, such as insurance, rent, salaries but not interest) as compared with the levels of variable costs (which vary with volume, such as for energy, labor, material).

OPPORTUNITY: A favorable set of circumstances that creates a need for a new product, service or business.

OPPORTUNITY COST: The benefit foregone.

OPPORTUNITY RECOGNITION: The process of perceiving the possibility of a profitable new business or a new product or service.

PARTNERSHIP: A business organization in which two or more individuals manage and operate the business. Both owners are equally and personally liable for the debts of the business.

PARTNERSHIP AGREEMENT: A document that entails the responsibility and the ownership shares of the partners involved in the organization.

PATENT: A grant from the federal government conferring the rights to exclude others.

PESTEL: Factor in the firm's general environment into six segments as an acronym: political, economic, sociocultural, technological, ecological, legal.

POLYTROPES: Science: 1. self-gravitating gaseous spheres that were, and still are, very useful as crude approximation to more realistic stellar models, or in Literature: 2. a figurative or metaphorical use of a word or expression, or 3. **tropes** that are widespread such as irony, metaphor, juxtaposition, and hyperbole, or themes such as 'the noble savage' or 'the reluctant hero' (Paul Friedrichs, 1999).

PRACADEMIC: A person that thinks, tinkers, practices with purpose by drawing on practical experience and academic principles; a portmanteau of the terms practical and academic.

PRICE: The amount of money consumers pay to buy a product or service.

PRIMARY MARKET RESEARCH: Research that is original and collected firsthand by the entrepreneur by, for example, talking to potential customers and key industry participants.

PRIVATE PLACEMENT: A variation of the IPO in which there is a direct sale of an issue of securities to a large institutional investor.

PROJECT MANAGEMENT: Overseeing a one-time effort limited by time, budget, and resources specifically designed to meet customer or stakeholder needs and/or demands.

PROTOSTORMING: Technique where you stretch your creative and design thinking problem solving skills to create functional models, prototypes, and conceptual representation of ideas very rapidly to learn where they will either succeed or fail.

RAPID PROTOTYPING: The fast development of a useful prototype that can be used for collaborative review and modification.

REVENUE: The income generated from sale of goods or services, or any other use of capital or assets, associated with the main operations of an organization before any costs or expenses are deducted.

S-CORPORATION: A regular corporation that has between 1 and 100 shareholders and that passes through net income or losses to shareholders under in accordance with Internal Revenue Code.

SECONDARY MARKET RESEARCH: Data collected previously by someone else for a different purpose that can be applied to an entrepreneur's market analysis.

SEGMENTATION STRATEGY: Approaches to subdivision of a market or population into segments with defined similar characteristics. Five major segmentation strategies are   (1) behavior segmentation, (2) benefit segmentation, (3) demographic segmentation, (4) geographic segmentation, and (5) psychographic segmentation.

SOLE PROPRIETORSHIP (D/B/A): The simplest business form under which one can operate a business. The sole proprietorship is not a legal entity; it simply refers to a person who owns the business and is personally responsible for its debts.

TARGET MARKET: The limited group of individuals or businesses that a firm goes after or tries to appeal to at a certain point in time.

TECHNOLOGY: Includes devices, artifacts, processes, tools, methods, and materials that can be applied to industrial and commercial purposes (Thomas Byers).

THINKINAUT: A cognitive astronaut who specializes in imagination.

TINKERER: (in crafts) A travelling mender of pots and pans.

TRANSSPECIES: The field of psychology that states that humans and nonhuman animals share commonalities in cognition (thinking) and emotions (feelings).

VALUE PROPOSITION: A concise statement that summarizes why a consumer should buy a product or use a service. Should convince a potential customer that one particular product or service will add more value or better solve a problem than other similar offerings.

VARIABLE COSTS: The costs that are not fixed that a company incurs as it generates sales.

VENTURE CAPITAL: The money that is invested by venture capital firms in start-ups and small business with exceptional growth potential.

VOLUME: The number of units of product or service a firm sells or provides.

WORD-OF-MOUTH (WOM): Involves individuals sharing information with other individuals in a verbal form, including face-to-face (F2F), on the phone, and over the internet.

WORK BREAKDOWN STRUCTURE (WBS): A hierarchical process and method for collecting information in an outline of phases to measure performance against the strategic plan of an organization (Gary Larson).

YUIWE: A term of cryptic pronouns that sounds like 'Yahweh' with references to university-industry and the nature of I, we, you as a way to come together of terms, ideas, and dreams.

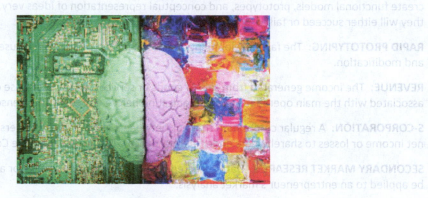

EXERCISES:

Exercise One: The "Ikigai" PassionVenn Template

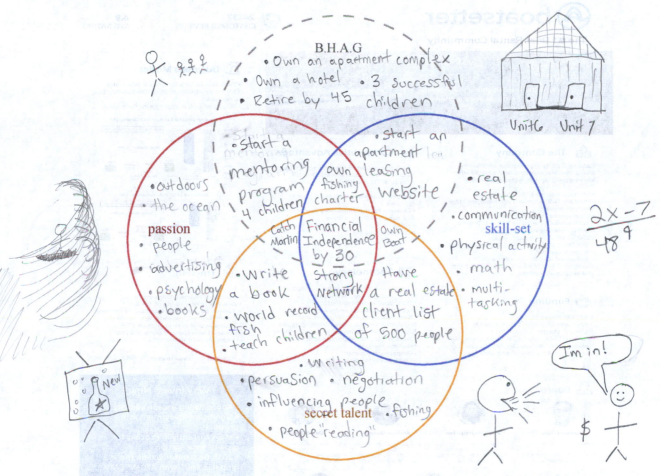

B.H.A.G
- Own an apartment complex
- Own a hotel • 3 successful
- Retire by 45   children

- Start a mentoring program 4 children
- outdoors
- the ocean
- **passion**
- people
- advertising
- psychology
- books

- Start an apartment leasing website
- own fishing charter
- **real estate**
- communication
- **skill-set**
- physical activity
- math
- multi-tasking

Catch Marlin Financial Independence by 30 Own Boat
Strong Network Have a real estate client list of 500 people

- Write a book
- world record fish
- teach children

- writing
- persuasion • negotiation
- influencing people
- **secret talent** • fishing
- people "reading"

Unit 6   Unit 7

$$\frac{2x - 7}{48\ 9}$$

I'm in!

Your individual purpose statement: I am a person who hates small talk. I talk about deep subjects, with real purpose, and real passion. This translates to my professional goals in that I don't like to flirt with ideas or dance around them half-hazardly. I am creative, yet seriously pragmatic and logistical. My carreer goal is to lead already successful companies down a path of exponential sucess with top notch advertising and then invest in real estate.

*Ikigai — your live for, passion-driven roadmap

Exercise Two: The Ikara One-pager - A Business Canvass Example and Template

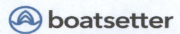 boatsetter

The #1 Boat Rental Community

 24837 CUSTOMER REVIEWS   4.9 AVG RATING

Vision

To become the leading global marketplace, providing great on-the-water experiences for anyone, anywhere.

The Company

Leading 3 party marketplace connecting boats, owners, captains, and anyone who seeks a great on-the-water experience.

- Global presence in 600 locations, including: U.S, Mexico, Caribbean, and the Mediterranean
- Clear market leader in the U.S.
- 12M recreational boats in the U.S get used an average of 14 days/year
- $50B TAM - Citi Group
- 40 people with HQ in Fort Lauderdale and offices in Ibiza SP.
- Seasoned leadership team with experience in Marine industry, Technology and scaling operations

Funding

- $21+ M raised to date
- Key investors: Airbnb, Valor Equity Partners, Weston Capital, Brunswick, Stanford University Daper Fund, Endeavor Catalyst, The Venture City, Nordic Eye, Global Founders Capital and others.

Competitive Advantage

- Exclusive access to the leading P2P boat insurance with Geico Marine/BoatUS
- Up to $27M in coverage for a single incident
- Largest database of US coast guard captains
- Channel Partnerships - Key demand and supply global partners
- Exclusive agreements with leading marinas across US

Technology

- World class CTO with in-house product team, web and app. developers
- Significant investment into product/technology underway.
- New consumer App (engaged with MetaLab, have assisted in creating apps for Uber, Slack, Coinbase, and many more)
- SaaS product for supply adoption and real-time booking
- Global marketplace
- Channel partnership tools

Business Model

- Take rate of 35% for private boats and 15% for professional, plus 10% booking fee to renters
- Strongest unit economics in the market:

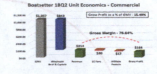

Traction

- 5x growth 17'-18'
- +20K transactions completed
- Average review rating of 4.9/5
- Chanel Partnerships with Luxury Retreats, Airbnb, Beyond, Inspirato, Brunswick etc.
- Exclusive access to insurance, P2P insurance with Geico Marine and tech. integration with underwriting & claims

Why Invest Now?

- Approaching escape velocity
- Significant investment into product
- M&A currently in process for growth acceleration
- 2019 Boatsetter will be the global leader, with $70+M GMV
- Opening a new market: successfully accessing younger demographics: 79% under age of 45 and 54% under age 35

Board

Laurence Tosi
- Former CFO of Airbnb and Blackstone
- Managing Director of Weston Capital Management

Jaclyn Baumgarten
- Former founding partner and COO of AH Global
- Former Director of Strategy at Davita Rx

Andrew Sturner
- Founder of Collaborative Boating
- Former President of Corp. & BD at Sportsline.com

David Siminoff
- Silicon Valley luminary
- Over 1,100 IPOs
- Has invested with funds such as Sequoia, Benchmark, Accel

Greg Ennis
- Managing Director of Peninsula Ventures
- Director and former President of the Stanford DAPER fund.
- 20+ years of VC experience

Alex Warner
- Founder of Gulfstream Boat Club, serving thousands of clients

Peter Warnoe
- Managing partner of NordicEye
- Technology sector investor

www.boatsetter.com

*Ikara – is an aboriginal word defined as a meeting place or throwing stick.

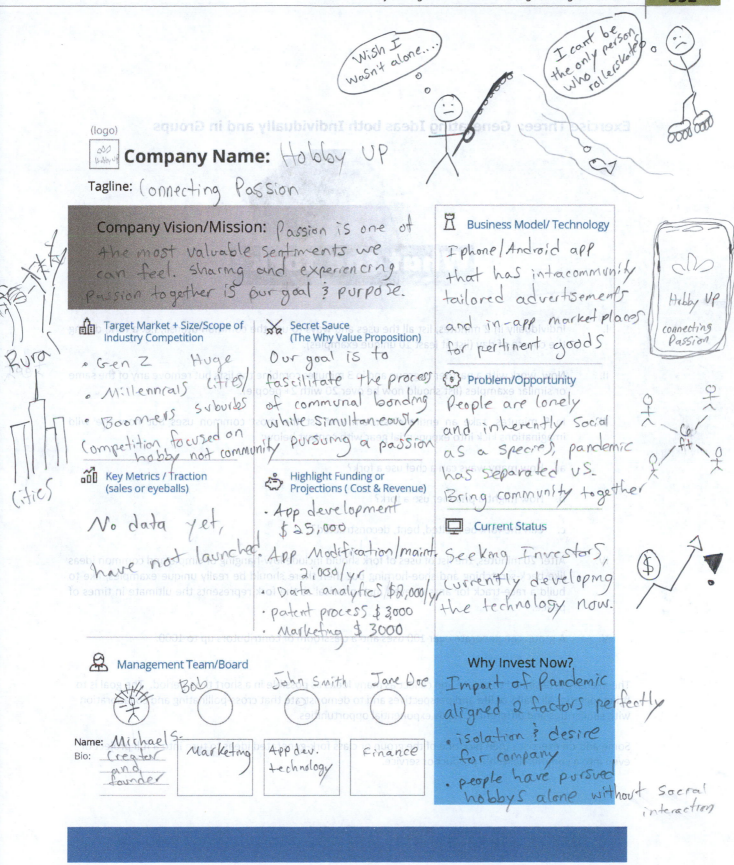

(logo)

Company Name: Hobby UP

Tagline: Connecting Passion

Company Vision/Mission: Passion is one of the most valuable sentiments we can feel. Sharing and experiencing passion together is our goal & purpose.

Business Model/ Technology

Iphone/Android app that has intracommunity tailored advertisements and in-app market places for pertinent goods

Target Market + Size/Scope of Industry Competition

- Gen Z   Huge
- Millennials (cities/
- Boomers   svburbs

Competition focused on hobby not community

Secret Sauce (The Why Value Proposition)

Our goal is to fascilitate the process of communal bonding while simultaneously pursuing a passion

Problem/Opportunity

People are lonely and inherently social as a species, pandemic has separated us. Bring community together

Key Metrics / Traction (sales or eyeballs)

No data yet, have not launched

Highlight Funding or Projections (Cost & Revenue)

- App development $25,000
- App Modification/maint. 2,000/yr
- Data analytics $2,000/yr
- patent process $3,000
- Marketing $3000

Current Status

Seeking Investors, currently developing the technology now.

Management Team/Board

Bob   John Smith   Jane Doe

Name: Michael S.
Bio: Creator and founder

| Marketing | App dev. technology | Finance |

Why Invest Now?

Impact of Pandemic aligned 2 factors perfectly
- isolation & desire for company
- people have pursued hobbys alone without social interaction

Rural cities

Hobby UP connecting Passion

Exercise Three: Generating Ideas both Individually and in Groups

I. Individually in 2 minutes, list all the uses and ways to use the common utensil, i.e. a fork, during the course of day (list at least 10 unique examples).

II. Now, work with a partner or group and in 3 minutes combine the lists but remove any of the same or similar examples (list should now be over 20 with 2+ people).

III. In 5 minutes, take an entire classroom and list the most common uses but now the wild imaginations kick into exponential gear with context below:

    a. How many ways can a chef use a fork?

    b. How might a prisoner use a fork?

    c. Can the fork be melted, bent, deconstructed?

IV. After 20 minutes, the list of uses of fork should include low-hanging or simple and common ideas like back-scratching and shoe-horning but then there should be really unique examples, like to build a race-track for ants or even metaphorical as the fork represents the ultimate in times of peace.

V. A group can generate over 100 uses and a classroom of contributors up to 1000.

The exercise is designed to create and collect as many ideas as possible in a short time period. The goal is to bring together all walks of life and perspectives and to demonstrate that cross-pollinating and collaboration with similarities and differences yields exponential opportunities.

Some add-on exercises then pick one of the group or class fork-generated ideas to turn into a full project or even into a commercializable product or service.

Exercise Four: Wild Imaginations

Scenario:

You have been selected to be part of the Ideation Team at Ben and Jerry's to create new ideas for an ice cream product, process, service or unique application to explore Wild Imaginations.

There are five (5) unique Wild Imaginations strategy styles as described in the Polyneering workbook:

- Abstract Imagination
- Replication Imagination
- Surrogate Imagination
- Prophesy Imagination
- Ingenious Imagination

The descriptions for each style will help you and/or your team understand the concepts to use with the specific imagination technique. Each imagination style is different and can generate different ideas based upon that style.

Step - 1

In this step, you will complete three different 15-minute imagination sessions. Within your team, identify new ideas for three different Ben & Jerry's areas:

- Product area – A new flavor or style of ice cream or ice cream product.
- Process area – An improvement to the process or manufacturing of ice cream.
- Service/Application area – A new service, use, or application of ice cream or any Ben & Jerry's philosophy for sustainability.

You will need to use a trigger statement for each area to start using the imagination process – use the statement "New Ideas for a Ben & Jerry's" and then add the word Product, Process or Service Application. Next, read the statement descriptions for one of the imagination styles you want to use. There would be a total of fifteen (15) possible statement combinations that could be used. Provided below are three as an example:

- '***Abstract Imagination*** description creating ideas for new ice cream ***products***'
- '***Replication Imagination*** description creating ideas for new ice cream ***processes***'
- '***Ingenious Imagination*** description creating ideas for a new ice cream ***services or applications***'

Once you have made these selections you can start Step – 2.

Step - 2

Now it's time to create new ideas for each imagination statement. Write any ideas that come into your or your team's minds.

The hard part is to remember that there is no such thing as a bad idea at this point – don't look for perfect solutions, look for possibilities!

Write each idea down on a post-it note and capture as many as possible – don't filter the ideas at this point. You can use any virtual post-it note application to document the ideas. There is a free application available from Microsoft available identified below:

Free post-it note application - https://www.post-it.com/3M/en_US/post-it/ideas/app/

A reminder that the new ideas you're creating can be "Wild", "Wooly" and "Crazy" or they can be complex, structured and conceptually detailed. You can also create ideas on top of other ideas (Have fun and be silly and serendipitous).

Step – 3

The final stage for your Ben & Jerry's Wild Imagination session exercise is to create a presentation of the best ideas your team developed for each of the focal areas (Product, Process, Service or Application). As a team, you will need to review all of the ideas for each focal section and select one idea that you think would fit the requirements of being unique and novel.

This means you will have (3) three team ideas which you will describe and elaborate into a presentation. It can include any words and details, idea pictures, or idea sketches you want to use. You can use any media format you want to present to an "imaginary" Board of Directors at the Ben & Jerry's company.

The outbrief presentation can be a power point presentation, 2-minute elevator pitch, PREZI, Haikudeck.com, a series of web pages, animated or recorded video. Use any media you think will ultimately impress and capture the attention of the Ben & Jerry's company.

Exercise Five: Generating a Blue Ocean Strategy

Scenario:

You are a member of a leadership and management team for the Ben and Jerry's company. You have been assigned to help create a Blue Ocean Strategy for the company to generate a clear presentation using a Porter's "Five Forces" diagram after you develop research for the tool.

"Blue ocean strategy is the simultaneous pursuit of differentiation and low cost to open up a new market space and create new demand. It is about creating and capturing an uncontested market space, thereby making the competition irrelevant. It is also based on the view that market boundaries and the industry structure are not a given and can be reconstructed by the actions and beliefs of industry players" (Kim, Mauborgne, 2004).

Review your workbook text, outside references and internet web links to help identify the current and future position of the Ben & Jerry's company. Additionally, you should identify rival competitors and any strategy information available on ice cream companies and manufacturers.

Step - 1

Break your team into 5 separate research areas based on the Porter's "Five Forces" instrument. You should have 1-2 people work on each one of these focal areas.

- New Market Entrants
- Supplier Power
- Competition, Rivalry
- Buyer Power
- Product and Technology Development

It is also recommended that you use the template illustrated below as a format to capture and provide your research information.

Once you have completed this extensive research on Ben & Jerry's and their competition, you are ready to move to Step - 2.

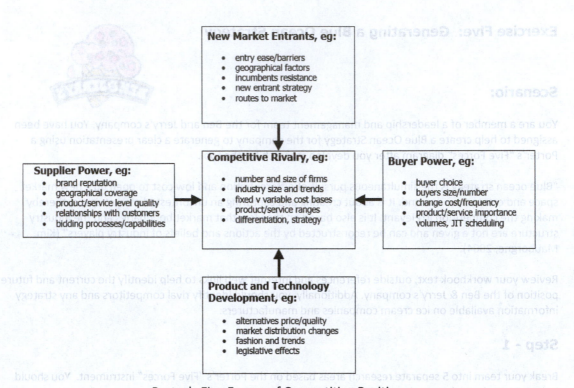

Porter's Five Forces of Competitive Position

Step - 2

Now that you have completed a very comprehensive illustration of the Ben & Jerry's company and the competition, continue to explore the Blue Ocean Strategy development by brainstorming the 6 obvious and hidden factors below:

Ask "How can we" …

- Create an uncontested market space?
- Make the competition irrelevant?
- Create and capture new demand?
- Break the value-cost trade-off?
- Align the whole system of Ben & Jerry's in pursuit of differentiation and low cost?
- Identify Value Innovation = innovation value

Start with the first focal area and identify any strategic ideas, strategy statements or strategic target goals and objectives and capture them into a Four Actions Framework as shown below:

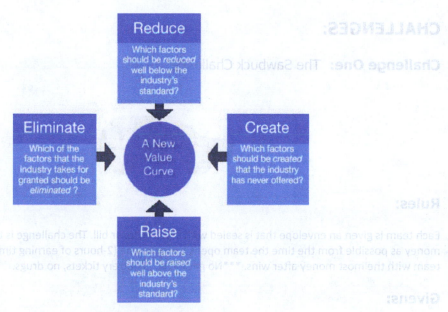

Four Actions Framework

Step – 3

The final stage for your Ben & Jerry's Blue Ocean Strategy exercise is to create a presentation of the information, ideas, and research data you have created. You can use any media format for your presentation to an "imaginary" board of directors at Ben & Jerry's.

It can be a power point presentation, PREZI, Haikudeck.com, a series of web pages, animated or recorded video. Use any media you think will ultimately impress and capture the attention of the Ben & Jerry's company.

CHALLENGES:

Challenge One: The Sawbuck Challenge

Rules:

Each team is given an envelope that is sealed with a $5.00-dollar bill. The challenge is to make as much money as possible from the time the team opens the envelope (2-hours of earning time) to perform. The team with the most money after wins. ***No gambling, no lottery tickets, no drugs.

Givens:

I.   The $5.00-dollar investment can be matched with participant money to total $10.00
II.   A 5-minute presentation slot in the classroom or boardroom.

The team must figure out ways to amortize and leverage their group skills and where to operate, and what to sell or feature. The exercise looks for ways the team challenges assumptions, avoids pit-falls, leverages resources, designs up-front strategies, and coordinates or designates out-of-the-envelope imagination to yield the best results.

Challenge Two: The Pineapple Pracademic Challenge: (Poets, Physicists, Practitioners)

A pop-up Workshop: Engineering, Entrepreneurship, & Edutainment Toolsets/Handsets: Fostering collaboration and design for the 21st Century global citizen.

Overture:

The participants will design, iterate, collaborate, and present demonstrable projects to promote engineering or emerging business disciplines demanding leadership, followership, efficiency, affordability, and sustainable concepts.

The pop-up workshop draws on the use of Kaplan's iconic symbols to engage in an emerging, disruptive, way to design while still being inclusive yet far and out-of-the- ordinary classroom context. It is a space and place that is out of time, as in liminal, where random participants come together to build trust, to forge a make-shift ritual, and to create a long-term enduring understanding of meaning. The objective is to touch the head, the hand, and the heart (Sullivan, 2005) by very different learners. Affective and adaptive expertise is the linchpin to lifelong learning.

Pineapple Project Challenge: (Poets, Physicists, Practitioners, Pracademics)

Rules: 30 minutes to earn 30 points using core steps: Selection / Saliency / Salability

(10 minutes to Select; 18 minutes for Saliency; 2 minutes for Salability)

1. Build the most beautiful **Presentation** based on the following criteria (10 points):
   a. Taste – is the pineapple sweet, juicy, delicious?
   b. Mood - *how* did you accentuate your offering?
   c. Display – what peripherals if any were used to enhance or effect?

2. Use the pineapple by incorporating the following **Processes** (10 points):
   a. Zero waste (using <u>everything</u> of the fruit)?
   b. The least number of counted / calculated cuts (efficiency)?
   c. Sanitation and Safety matter, *which* factors did you consider?

3. Ensure everyone participates and applies their **Passion** and expression (10 points):
   a. Explain in 2 minutes or less your team's theme using words, symbols, or other available tools.
   b. What secret skillsets did you use from your team?
   c. Reflect on the '*why*' the pineapple exercise matters to you and others?

Course Tools:
Cutlery
Fruit
Non-perishable objects
Software

Challenge Three: The USF Survival on the Moon Challenge

Scenario:

You are a member of the United Space Forces (USF) space crew originally scheduled to rendezvous with a mother ship on the lighted surface of the moon. Due to mechanical difficulties, your space ship was forced to land at a spot some 200 miles from the targeted point. During reentry and landing much of the equipment aboard was damaged and, since you and your team's survival depends on reaching the mother ship, the most critical items available must be chosen for the 200-mile trip. Listed below are the fifteen (15) items left intact and undamaged after landing. Your task is to individually rank in order of importance for your crew to make the destination point. Place the number **1** by the most important item, and so on through number **15**.

Your Ranking

14	Box of wood matches +1
3	Food concentrate + 1
11	50 feet of Kevlar rope +5
12	20 yards of Parachute silk +4
6	Portable heating unit +7
13	Two .9mm caliber pistols with bullets +2
10	One case of dehydrated milk +2
1	Two 100 lb. tanks of oxygen +0
5	Stellar map +2
15	Self-inflating life raft +6
7	Magnetic compass +7
2	20 liters of water +0
8	Nuclear flashlight +2
9	First aid kit, including injection needle +2
4	Solar-powered FM receiver-transmitter +1

42

Step - 2

Once you have completed your individual ranking for all of the objects, you should get together with your team and discuss your collective results. Explain why you selected the ranking for each object to the other members of your team. You must then create a collaborative ranked team listing of the objects where everyone agrees through consensus.

Team Ranking		United Space Forces Ranking
14	Box of wood matches +1	15
3	Food concentrate +1	4
8	50 feet of Kevlar rope +2	6
11	20 yards of Parachute silk +3	8
6	Portable heating unit +7	13
13	Two .9 mm caliber pistols with bullets +2	11
7	One case of dehydrated milk +5	12
1	Two 100 lb. tanks of oxygen. +0	1
5	Stellar map +2	3
12	Self-inflating life raft +3	9
15	Magnetic compass +1	14
2	20 liters of water +0	2
9	Nuclear flashlight +1	10
10	First aid kit, including injection needle +3	7
4	Solar-powered FM receiver-transmitter +1	5

32

*USF Moon Answer Key in the Appendix section below

Step - 3

Answers the 3 questions below to create a comparison for your individual and your team rankings. In your team, you should discuss the written results with everyone:

Q1 – *Was your individual score higher or lower than the team ranked score?*

My individual score was 10 points higher than the team ranked score. Clearly, as a team we were more accurate than we were by ourselves.

Q2 – *What was the hardest part of working together with other people on your team?*

The hardest part was reaching a consensus about which number to give each item. We had a few "disagreements" but reached a group decision eventually.

Q3 – *When you worked in a collaborative effort as a Polyneer, what are the most important skills and why?*

The most important skills when collaborating are listening, communicating, and productively debating with each other. Listening is critical because everyone must be able to participate and have their opinion acknowledged. Communicating is essential for effective discussion, and productively debating is important so that the group is not narrow minded and challenges each other

APPENDIX: USF Moon Exercise Answer Key

Item	Ranking	Reasoning
Box of wood matches	15	Virtually worthless -- there's no oxygen on the moon to sustain combustion
Food concentrate	4	Efficient means of supplying energy requirements
50 feet of Kevlar rope	6	Useful in scaling cliffs and tying injured together
20 yards of Parachute silk	8	Protection from the sun's rays
Portable heating unit	13	Not needed unless on the dark side
Two .9 mm caliber pistols with bullets	11	Possible means of self-propulsion
One case of dehydrated milk	12	Bulkier duplication of food concentrate
Two 100 lb. tanks of oxygen	1	Most pressing survival need (weight is not a factor since gravity is one-sixth of the Earth's -- each tank would weigh only about 17 lbs. on the moon)
Stellar map	3	Primary means of navigation - star patterns appear essentially identical on the moon as on Earth
Self-inflating life raft	9	CO_2 bottle in military raft may be used for propulsion
Magnetic compass	14	The magnetic field on the moon is not polarized, so it's worthless for navigation
20 liters of water	2	Needed for replacement of tremendous liquid loss on the light side
Nuclear Flashlight	10	Use as distress signal when the mother ship is sighted
First aid kit, including injection needle	7	Needles connected to vials of vitamins, medicines, etc. will fit special aperture in space suit
Solar-powered FM receiver-transmitter	5	For communication with mother ship (but FM requires line-of-sight transmission and can only be used over short ranges)

Scoring:

For each item, mark the number of points that your score differs from the United Space Force's ranking, then add up all the points. Disregard plus or minus differences. The <u>lower</u> the total, the better your individual and team score.

0 - 25 excellent Polyneering logic

26 - 32 good Polyneering logic

33 - 45 average logic

46 - 55 fair logic

56 - 70 poor -- suggests use of Earth-bound logic

71 - 112 very poor – you're one of the casualties of the United Space Forces program!

(Adapted from the July 1999 issue of the NightTimes)

<u>NOTES</u>

Credits